Business Continuity from Preparedness to Recovery

Business Continuity from Preparedness to Recovery
A Standards-Based Approach

Eugene Tucker

ELSEVIER

AMSTERDAM • BOSTON • HEIDELBERG • LONDON
NEW YORK • OXFORD • PARIS • SAN DIEGO
SAN FRANCISCO • SINGAPORE • SYDNEY • TOKYO

Butterworth-Heinemann is an imprint of Elsevier

Acquiring Editor: *Sara Scott*
Editorial Project Manager: *Marisa LaFleur*
Project Manager: *Punithavathy Govindaradjane*
Designer: *Mark Rogers*

Butterworth-Heinemann is an imprint of Elsevier
The Boulevard, Langford Lane, Kidlington, Oxford OX5 1 GB, UK
225 Wyman Street, Waltham, MA 02451, USA

ISBN: 978-0-12-420063-0

British Library Cataloguing-in-Publication Data
A catalogue record for this book is available from the British Library

Library of Congress Cataloging-in-Publication Data
A catalogue record for this book is available from the Library of Congress

For information on all Butterworth-Heinemann publications
visit our website at http://store.elsevier.com/

Working together
to grow libraries in
developing countries

www.elsevier.com • www.bookaid.org

Contents

Preface

I remember as a child in Kindergarten climbing up the stairs to the slide in the playground when a 3.75 magnitude earthquake struck very close to the area of my school in Daly City, CA. Daly City was the closest town to the epicenter of the 1906 San Francisco earthquake. The teachers in the playground were yelling "What was that, what was that?" I do not know why at that age I knew it was an earthquake, but thought the teachers were pretty dumb for not recognizing the cause of the ground moving beneath their feet. An earthquake of that size, depending on the type and soil conditions, is noticeable, especially if close to the epicenter, but not enough to start pulling out your cache of emergency provisions.

In the days prior to the earthquake, my mother would walk with me to and from school, but on that day she started a new job and I was to make the trek solo. Just two blocks from home after Kindergarten let out for the day, the strongest earthquake to hit the Bay Area since 1906 registered 5.3 on the Richter scale. I was all alone. I could see the street turn into rolling waves coming toward me. I tried to run but remember going nowhere. I could not stand and fell down. Above the noise generated by the earth movement, my grandmother at home could hear me screaming a city block away. I was so traumatized, I did not return to school for the remainder of the term. I can honestly say that I flunked Kindergarten.

My interest in natural phenomena is likely an outgrowth of my early years. Educating and protecting people from the harm they can cause and helping organizations become resilient in the face of disasters so the economies that support the workers remain intact seems like the right thing to do.

As the former librarian for a major business continuity professional organization, I was amazed that the great majority of the books I reviewed did not give the reader a road map to put together an effective holistic business continuity program. My interests in emergency management, emergency response, data systems, and business management gave me, I believe, a unique perspective that was missed by most authors. When I was asked to write a book solely dedicated to business continuity, I struggled with the dilemma of what I could do that was different from my first book and different from the hundreds of other books on the same subject. The competing standards have value to the profession, but there are few publications on the market that adequately explain what is required in a manner that does not cause a great deal of confusion. I hope this publication cuts through the confusion and leads the Business Continuity Manager to a path that produces an effective management system that will hold up to the standards. Bear in mind that my intent is NOT to say "Here is how you get certified under the standards." If you are looking for certification, buy a copy of the standards. My intent is to show how to develop a program (management system) built under the standards that will help ensure resilience when a disaster happens.

The standards are intended to tell you "what" you need for an auditable program but not "how" to develop and manage the program. The purpose of this publication is to allow the reader to design and implement an effective Business Continuity Management System according to the ISO 22301 Societal security—Business continuity management systems standard, the ASIS SPC.1-2009 Organizational Resilience: Security, Preparedness, and Continuity Management Systems standard, and to the NFPA 1600:2010 and 2013 Standard on Disaster/Emergency Management and Business Continuity Programs. It draws on many of the related ISO standards that include The Risk Management Standard and the Internal Auditing Guidance. While I have included information on all three standards, I have emphasized the ISO standard. When I refer to a standard in the text without qualification (i.e., ASIS or NFPA), I am referring to ISO 22301.

For my own use, and in preparation for this publication, I have attended a number of presentations, classes, and webinars and have sifted through piles of literature on the implementation of the standards. I have seen and heard a lot of confusion and misinformation about what to do with the Plan, Do, Check, Act of the Deming Cycle. At almost every class or webinar I attend, I make it a point to ask how business continuity managers are to incorporate PDCA into their planning and into their plans. I ask this in part to gauge the presenter's knowledge of the standards. The answers I got were all over the spectrum — "It is not needed at all" to "Forget everything before Clause 4" to "The plan must be organized along the lines of PDCA and of the clauses in the standard." This reminds me of a number of years ago when the focus was on planning according to the Incident Command System (ICS). It seemed that none of the seminar presenters knew much about ICS or how to apply it to business continuity. Similarly, the presenters on the standards know a lot about business continuity (most seem to be sales people though) but fewer understand the standards or management systems in general.

Like James F. Broder and I did in *Risk Analysis and the Security Survey*, now in its fourth edition, where we listed specific procedures the reader could use when responding to a variety of emergency situations, I have included in this publication lists of Business Impact Analysis questions for the common functional areas of an organization. I have listed common business continuity strategies for these functions as well. Although we have placed them in the Appendix, I ask that they are reviewed in total to give the reader a better understanding of how to design Business Impact Questions and continuity strategies but mostly because important requirements under all of the standards are contained in the questions and strategies.

As I was finishing this manuscript, a 6.0 earthquake struck the lower Napa Valley of California at around 3:30 in the morning. This was the largest earthquake to hit the San Francisco Bay Area in the 25 years since the Loma Prieta Earthquake. Had the earthquake occurred later in the day, too many lives would have been lost. There were no immediate fatalities but a high degree of damage, including the loss of a major percentage of the inventory at some smaller wineries. The earthquake helped to remind me of the value of the standards, especially with their requirement for preparedness, mitigation, and response.

I did, however, go back to work the next day.

Acknowledgments

Acknowledgments on some levels are easy to give. Many start by making a point to thank their families and in particular their spouse for their support and understanding while writing the manuscript. I now know why. All of the beautiful summer weekends spent at home while I stared at a computer screen instead of sitting on the beach sharing a great sandwich and glass of wine was a sacrifice my family was willing to make. Thank you, Marci.

Gratitude is almost always given to the publishers. They really are a big help and in my case a source of motivation, encouragement, and good advice. Their suggestions were always on target and positive. They are true professionals and simply good people. Pam Chester of Elsevier, who roped me into this project and who I worked with as a co-author to *Risk Analysis and the Security Survey*, is the type of person whom you cannot thank enough. But I will keep trying. Pam has moved on to other endeavors, and Sara Scott and Marisa LaFleur have stepped up to lead the charge. Why should the reader care about the publishers? I suspect they do not get the recognition they are due and they truly are contributors to the value these publications bring to the profession. Thank you so much, ladies.

Thank you Joe Couch of the Texas A&M Engineering Extension Service (TEEX), a great instructor, for your help with permissions and to Dave Morgan, longtime President of the Business Recovery Managers Association, one of the respected and true Business Continuity Professionals. I should also thank Barry Cordoza, whose advice on the standards I should have sought with more regularity.

But the most difficult part of this book and with this acknowledgment, more so than the endless hours of research, last minute revisions due to newly published standards, typing until midnight, and trying to make sense of what was left after my laptop deleted entire paragraphs from the manuscript is how to thank someone who has enabled so many opportunities in my professional life. James F. Broder, one of the heavyweights in the Security and Investigations Profession, whom I have worked with and known for so many years, asked me many years ago to contribute a few chapters to the second edition of his book mentioned above. It was, as I recall, Butterworth–Heinemann's top security publication that is now in its 4th edition and just translated into Chinese. Without that, I would not be writing this book. Broder is one of the kindest people, insightful beyond belief, and full of the type of experiences that one would find in a novel. To try to describe his positive attributes would take many pages. I am humbled in his presence. For this association, I am truly indebted. While I have always strived to attain his professional level and knowledge, the day that he called me "friend" will always be treasured. A good deal of his knowledge and influence is reflected in this publication.

Digital Assets

Thank you for selecting Butterworth Heinemann's *Business Continuity*. To complement the learning experience, we have provided a number of online tools for instructors to accompany this edition.

Please consult your local sales representative with any additional questions.

FOR THE INSTRUCTOR

Qualified adopters and instructors need to register at the this link for access: http://textbooks.elsevier.com/web/manuals.aspx?isbn=978012400630.

- *Test bank*: Compose, customize, and deliver exams using an online assessment package in a free Windows-based authoring tool that makes it easy to build tests using the unique multiple choice and true or false questions created for *Business Continuity*. What is more, this authoring tool allows you to export customized exams directly to Blackboard, WebCT, eCollege, Angel, and other leading systems. All test bank files are also conveniently offered in Word format.
- *PowerPoint lecture slides*: Reinforce key topics with focused PowerPoints slides, which provide a perfect visual outline with which to augment your lecture. Each individual book chapter has its own dedicated slideshow.
- *Instructor's manual*: Design your course around customized learning objectives, instructor's notes, discussion questions, and research topics.

Introduction

Ask one experienced Business Continuity Manager what is the best thing in the last 10 years that has happened to improve the profession and he or she might reply "a set of management standards." Ask another experienced Business Continuity Manager what is the worst thing in the last 10 years that has happened to his or her profession and the answer might be "a set of management standards."

The requirements and organization of the standards can be confusing. The necessary elements to build a Business Continuity Management System are difficult to understand because of new terminology and the sequence in which instructions are found in the standards documents. For example, many business continuity professionals understand the term "incident response" to mean that when there is a fire, one should grab a fire extinguisher and put out the flames, but under the standards it also means the actions of a business continuity or disaster recovery team to execute the instructions listed in their plans (an incident is defined in ISO 22301 as "a situation that might be, or could lead to, a disruption, loss, emergency or crisis"). ISO 22301 and ASIS SPC.1-2009 say that the order in which the organization conducts the Risk Assessment and Business Impact Analysis is dependent on the method of analysis used, but it mentions completing the Business Impact Analysis first. This is how we presented these concepts in this publication, although many would argue that the ordering should be the opposite, completing the Risk Assessment first. Others would say that the order is not significantly important since the two are generally combined into a single effort and combined report.

The standards, as far as business continuity practices are concerned, do not introduce anything that is really new to a mature, well-managed Business Continuity program. But since the standards are so closely related to the world of Quality Management, they speak in terms of process and management systems. The introduction to ISO 22301 says that "like any other management system a Business Continuity Management System is comprised of policy, responsibility, management processes that include management review and continuous improvement." It provides the requirements it believes are necessary to set up and manage such a system. What may be new to most managers, and a task that most believe is onerous, is the degree of auditable documentation required for its compliance with its provisions.

For the seasoned professional manager, the standards do not require too many tasks that he or she would normally do to set up and manage a business continuity program. They may embrace or reject the requirement for a steering committee or the demand for a higher level of documentation, but the greatest difference they may find with the implementation of the standards is one of a different mindset. The standards are set up to provide audit evidence that is used to compare against audit criteria for certification. Unless experienced in certification to a set of standards, the expectations of auditors may be quite foreign to the manager. Auditors will not only want to see that every "I" is dotted and every "T" is crossed as the saying goes, but they will also want to know where they are dotted and crossed, who crossed them, and how management has enabled a culture that supports the dotting and crossing. While I might be proud that I dotted and crossed everything, and of the belief that I have met my audit mandate, along will come an auditor who will want to also discuss the concept of dotting and crossing before my management system is certified.

In addition to the emphasis on continual improvement, the standards take us away from the old and still active notion that the emphasis is to have a plan in place instead of a dynamic management system.

The standards place a high emphasis, and rightfully so, on Enterprise Risk Management, not only in the identification of risk to the prioritized business functions, but on the processes themselves. The level of Top Management support required by the standards may be considered by some business continuity professionals as fantasy, but organizations are increasingly recognizing the value of their active participation and the integration of business continuity into all facets of their strategic and operational planning. Business continuity is increasingly driven by customer requirements. This is a strong motivator for their involvement.

BUSINESS CONTINUITY PROGRAM DEVELOPMENT

My first boss in my first full-time job dedicated to business continuity was fond of saying "Business continuity is not rocket science." In many respects, he is correct. At a higher level, business continuity consists of a strategy to continue the operation of data functions if the original capability is diminished or destroyed and finding alternate workspace for people to connect to the data if their normal workspace is not available. In fact, the DRI International's (DRII) Professional Practices lists 10 major steps (subject areas) necessary to develop a Business Continuity Management System:

- Program Initiation and Management Support
- Risk Evaluation and Control
- Business Impact Analysis
- Business Continuity Strategies
- Emergency Response and Operations
- Business Continuity Plans
- Awareness and Training Programs
- Business Continuity Plan Exercise, Audit, and Maintenance
- Crisis Communications
- Coordination with External Agencies

The reality is that these 10 subject areas contain many subordinate steps that combine to create a Business Continuity Program resulting in an organization that is resilient to the effects of catastrophic risk. Well, almost.

Program Initiation and Management Support begins with the justification of the program assuming that it is not mandated by and supported by upper management. When the idea for the program is conceived by a lower level manager, it could become Sisyphean labor to get management to devote the necessary resources to establish a Business Continuity Management System. Justifications for the program often include:

- Cost of downtime can be tremendous to certain types of organizations
- Loss of competitive advantage
- Minimize devaluation of the organization
- Fulfill requirements by financial auditors or by potential customers
- Capitalize on the lack of planning by competitors
- Uphold fiscal responsibility
- Avoid stockholder liability

- Fulfill regulatory and contractual requirements
- Retain key employees (who may leave the company if furloughed)
- Prevent the loss of key research
- Help ensure the safety of employees
- Preserve customer confidence and prevent the loss of customers
- Assist in the economic recovery of the community in the case of a regional disaster
- Pressure on cash flow and the need to borrow funds
- Prevent brand name damage

While these reasons may seem compelling, they should be supported with risk and impact data. This is most effectively provided by the results of the Risk Assessment and Business Impact Analysis. These are usually not completed until the program is approved, so many managers will ask for funding to conduct the Risk Assessment and Business Impact Analysis outside of the program. This is why it is often suggested that a Top-Management (i.e., executive-level) sponsor is recruited to help shepherd the commitment for the program. Once the program is approved and funded, a person to lead the program is selected and policy and procedure is developed. The structure and methodologies of the business continuity function are established.

A Risk Assessment (used to be a Risk Analysis) is conducted to identify hazards that can affect the mission of the organization. The risks are evaluated and appropriate cost-effective controls are put in place to eliminate or mitigate their effects. Coupled with the Business Impact Analysis, the organization will develop a picture of which of its functions are the most critical and will understand how resources and strategies are best applied to continue their operation during and after a catastrophic event, or during and after an incident of lesser magnitude that may have an impact on the financial, operational, or regulatory requirements of the organization.

Emergency situations that include fires, floods, the effects of earthquakes and other natural and man-made hazards must be prepared for, stabilized, and controlled before they become a crisis or disaster. The organization must develop a capability to respond to emergencies during a time when the dependence on normal emergency response agencies may be severely limited if not nonexistent.

The implementation of the business continuity and recovery strategies developed though the Risk Assessment and Business Impact Analysis processes are written into plans for teams of employees and others to execute at the time of a disaster. The resources necessary to support the strategies are included in the plans. The structure of the business continuity organization, how communication is enabled internally and externally to the organization, and where the functions are to relocate and connect to any relocated Information Technology resources are explained.

Those employees with responsibilities under the plans are trained in the expectations of the program and in what their tasks may require when the plans are activated ("invoked" in the terminology of the standards). Ideally, this training will include awareness of the steps they should take to be prepared for disasters at home and in the workplace. From the safety, operational efficiency, and liability potential, emergency responders are trained in the protocols they will need to use to control foreseeable emergencies.

Although related, Business Continuity Plan Exercise, Audit, and Maintenance are processes of such importance that they should be considered as separate steps. The plans (and as we will discuss, the program) are exercised and tested at increasing levels of complexity to validate that they will meet the objectives of the Business Continuity Management System. Exercises carry a component of training and continual improvement through the identification of corrective actions. Outdated information in the plans is useless if not detrimental to its implementation so the plans must be maintained and updated on a regular basis. An audit process is a new convention created by the standards and adds to the component of continuous improvement.

Crisis Communications combines responsibilities of the Public Relations function, Marketing Communications, and other functions that need to communicate continuity information to the outside world in a manner that prevents misconception and controls damage to the organization's reputation.

The Coordination with External Agencies involves the interface with responding agencies in an emergency (understanding the Incident Command System (ICS), inviting the fire department to tour the site), complying with regulations, and full-scale exercises. It touches on the concept of "Public–Private Partnerships."

Planning according to the standards will take these steps to a higher level.

PLANNING ACCORDING TO THE STANDARDS

So why, in the face of added difficulty, would an organization wish to set up their Business Continuity Program according to the standards? An obvious reason is PS-Prep certification or third-party certification to the standards. Certification sends a powerful message to customers and regulators that the business continuity program has stood the test of an independent assessment of the organization's ability to survive a disastrous situation. Consider that planning according to the standards has the following advantages to the organization:

- Certification by a third party or at a minimum by internal first-party audit of a standards-based management system (including NFPA 1600, which is not a management system standard) is a marketing tool that will say to a customer that the organization has minimized risk and can continue to deliver products or services even in the face of a disaster.
- Roughly 80% of standards are purchased by lawyers, according to a source in the Health and Safety profession. Standards are used in litigation as a benchmark for organizations to compare themselves to, or to be compared against. A program built according to the standards may help indemnify the organization against stockholder or other third-party liability.
- Third-party certification, and to some extent first-party (internal) audit certification, will likely reduce the number of requests for an audit of your program by customers.
- The standards force a more holistic approach to business continuity by incorporating risk management, the elements of Emergency Management, and continuous improvement.
- Will add credibility to the program and better motivate internal interest and participation.
- Guides an inexperienced Business Continuity Manager toward developing an effective program.

CERTIFICATION PROCESS

The standards provide a process that is auditable for certification by a third party. The organization must understand the requirements of the standard it wishes to be certified against, including any related standards and guidance, decide what portion of the organization will be included in the certification (i.e., scope), and ensure it is as ready for audit.

For the ISO standards, certification is a three-year process that includes an optional preaudit that identifies gaps in documentation or conformance with the standard. The preaudit has the advantage of preparing those involved with the audit process. It begins with a "Stage-1" audit that reviews the active commitment of Top Management to the program, requirements necessary for a management system, the Business Impact Analysis, and other documentation. It determines the organization's readiness for the "Stage-2" audit.

The Stage-2 audit, the "real audit," examines the entire management system and looks at compliance with all of the standard's requirements. It will also evaluate the effectiveness of the management system. Based on the results and seriousness of the nonconformities found, it will determine if certification is recommended. The Stage-2 audit is typically conducted at least 30 but no more than 90 days after the Stage-1 audit.

All identified nonconformities must be corrected before certification is granted. There are two levels of nonconformities: major and minor. Both levels must include the identification and documentation of the cause of the nonconformity, and corrective actions to fix the issue, but a major nonconformity will require a root cause analysis. A deadline for the implementation of any corrective actions is agreed to by the organization and the auditor and verified upon completion.

Certification is good for a three-year period, during which the organization's management system will be reviewed (the term they use is "Surveillance") 12 months after the completion of the Stage-2 audit and again 12 months later. Recertification is required after the three years but the recertification process that generally requires less time than the original must be completed before its expiration.

CHOOSING THE CORRECT STANDARD

These three standards currently qualify for certification under PS-Prep (see Chapter 1). The one best suited for use depends on many factors that include the type of organization and the background of the person who will manage the program — someone coming out of the Information Technology world may best choose ISO 22301, someone from the Emergency Management world may choose NFPA 1600. The standards seem to be coming closer together in their requirements, but they still retain their own flavor.

ISO 22301 is an international standard and probably the best standard to use if the organization conducts overseas operations or has critical suppliers located in different countries. The ISO standards are better recognized in the business world and are known as quality standards, especially in the high-technology arena. It is the most widely used business continuity standard worldwide for nongovernmental organizations. It may also be the easiest for an organization to certify against. Both ISO 22301 and ASIS SPC.1-2009 are management standards, NFPA is not. This allows for easier integration with other ISO or ANSI standards in use within the organization.

Although both standards have a strong focus on risk management, the ASIS standard frames its requirements more from the integration of risk into its processes. Its Organizational Resilience title and greater emphasis on security may appeal to an organization that deals with critical infrastructure and asset protection if not required to use NFPA. The ASIS standard is a bit more straightforward in its implementation and comes with a very good set of reference guidance. Its Risk Assessment scheme is more aligned with the methods used by the United States Department of Homeland Security and also looks at the impacts of the organization's operations on the environment, including endangered species.

NFPA 1600 is not the most business friendly of the standards, partly because it emphasizes the use of the ICS (the 2013 version does not directly mention the ICS but does discuss the use of an Incident Action Plan and Management by Objectives, both components of ICS. Its requirements for resource usage are very ICS-esque). It more directly mandates the use of the elements of emergency management and an all hazards planning approach (a good thing) but unless the organization already operates under the ICS, the manager may have difficulty adapting it to a nongovernmental agency. It also emphasizes controls for financial issues that will make the response and recovery to an incident more effective and it also requires a resource needs assessment. The 2013 version still requires the organization to develop a strategy to affect legislation and industry practices. Legislation is, however, increasingly mandating its use for certain organizations, including public hospitals. The 2013 version also requires the organization to develop a strategy for employee assistance and support for the temporary or long-term housing, feeding, and care of those displaced by an incident. According to its guidance, employee assistance should also apply to family and significant others.

THE HOW AND WHAT OF THE STANDARDS

Many business continuity professionals say that the requirements of the standards are too high-level, leaving little direction on "how" to accomplish "what" that the standards require. This was done by the designers of the standards so that they can apply to large or small organizations in a number of different environments. While we cannot predict exactly what an auditor will look for (as we mentioned above, some auditors view the requirements very literally and some focus on a more broad-based, conceptual application of the standards—or both), we hope to show how to establish a comprehensive Business Continuity Management System that will position your organization to survive a catastrophic event.

REFERENCES

International Standard ISO 22301:2012 Societal security—business continuity management systems—Requirements.

NFPA 1600 Standard on Disaster/Emergency Management and Business Continuity Programs, 2013 edition.

Organizational Resilience: Security, preparedness, and continuity management systems—requirements with guidance for Use, ASIS SPC.1–2009 American National Standard, (ASIS International).

BUSINESS CONTINUITY— A DEFINITION AND A BRIEF HISTORY

CHAPTER SUMMARY

Business continuity is the management of a sustainable process that identifies the critical functions of an organization and develops strategies to continue these functions without interruption or to minimize the effects of an outage or loss of service provided by these functions. The history of business continuity management brings with it the perspectives and skills of each of the disciplines that contributed to its present-day form. The two major perspectives, one from the militaristic, emergency management side of the house with strict adherence to the dogmas of disaster management, and the other from the data center, which focused solely on the internal recovery of information technology, combined to bring business continuity planning to its present state. This chapter will help the reader to understand these perspectives and allow the business continuity manager to evaluate new ideas as truly representing progress and more effectively move programs forward when working with those who hold these different outlooks. Today, with the help of the new standards, the profession has matured into a management process that helps ensure the resilience of all essential business functions.

KEY TERMS

ASIS SPC.1-2009; Certification; Emergency management; ISO 22301; NFPA 1600; PS-Prep; Regulations; Risk management; Social science; Standards.

KEY POINTS

*   Backgrounds and the point of view from varied professions influenced the development of business continuity management
*   Business continuity planning evolved from a project focus to a sustainable management process
*   Competing standards define programs
*   Emergency management and business continuity planning defined
*   Understand how the term "business continuity" is used today

1.1 INTRODUCTION

The concept of formal business continuity planning (BCP) is a relatively recent invention that owes its development to the increased dependency of business and government (actually, virtually everything and everyone) on the explosion of technology. The impact on business is well documented when data systems or production is disrupted, causing losses to stockholders, employees, and the community. The social dependencies of technology are illustrated by the computer outages of three major air carriers in 2012–2013 that resulted in the cancellation of close to 2250 flights. Apart from the financial losses to the carriers and their dependent partners (hotels, car rentals, etc.), many travelers were at the very least inconvenienced by delayed or cancelled vacations, missed appointments and meetings, or an uncomfortable night sleeping at the airport. The outage of a social network for more than a few hours becomes an international headline. These are just a few examples of why the continuity or recovery of information technology (IT) is a vital part of business continuity management.

Despite its youth, an understanding of the evolution of business continuity management and the influences that have brought it to its present state is important for developing a perspective that moves the profession forward and allows planners to best manage their programs. These influences emerge from the doctrines brought by those entering the profession from information technology, the fire service and emergency management, security and law enforcement, risk and insurance management, and post-September 11 political appointees. Business continuity management has embraced many of their ideas, but some professionals believe their practices, including a number found in the standards, could take the profession backward.

This chapter will not chronicle events and disasters from the past except where results produced relevant effects on business continuity management. For example, it is useful to know that after the San Fernando California earthquake of 1971, seismic safety building codes were greatly improved (as they and other lessons learned are refined after each new disaster). One lesson learned, however, is that the building standards and practices do not always meet the requirements of the codes. Shortcuts, poor construction practices, and the use of substandard materials were responsible for the collapse of many structures in Greece after a moderate earthquake—a country with strict modern building codes. Even in the United States (US), major damage to a warehouse in the Silicon Valley after the Loma Prieta earthquake was traced to substandard construction.

The formal definition of business continuity has metamorphosed over time with no agreement within the industry on a single meaning, although the contents of the business continuity Glossary published by the *Disaster Recovery Journal* were accepted by many professionals as the most appropriate definition. Each of the standards (International Organization for Standardization (ISO), American Society for Industrial Security (ASIS), and National Fire Protection Association (NFPA)) describe it in similar but somewhat significantly different ways.

1.2 HISTORY
1.2.1 EMERGENCY MANAGEMENT

A history of business continuity management is not complete without a basic understanding of the evolution of emergency management. Emergency managers entering the field of business continuity management have needed to enable businesses to position their functions for resilience and sustainability by heavily influencing planning methodologies in both positive ways such as the focus on mitigation and negative ways such as continuity planning under an incident command system (ICS) structure. ICS is a field tactical response concept that many planners had difficulty adapting to business continuity management in an effective and meaningful manner, apart from the response phase that we will describe in another chapter.

Emergency management is the managerial function charged with creating the framework within which communities reduce vulnerability to hazards and cope with disasters (Dr B. Wayne Blanchard, CEM, FEMA Emergency Management Institute). It is also defined as an interdisciplinary field dealing with the strategic organizational management processes used to protect critical assets of an organization from hazard risks that can cause events such as disasters or catastrophes and to ensure the resiliency of the organization within their planned lifetime (Haddow and Bullock, 2003).

Emergency management, from the governmental perspective of planning and responding to disasters on a macro level (i.e., regional and not focused on an individual business), deals with situations such as earthquakes, hurricanes, and floods that cause business outages. It is a process in which qualified persons plan and prepare for identified hazards and risks to the community, and coordinate the response and recovery once they occur.

Just over 25 years after the signing of the US Constitution, legislation was passed to provide federal funding for disaster relief. Today, separate legislation is no longer necessary thanks to the Robert T. Stafford Disaster Relief and Assistance of 1974 (Stafford Act), which combined similar prior acts (such as the Disaster Relief Act of 1950) that gave the federal government the authority to provide assistance without going to Congress after each disaster. Of the many significant achievements of the Stafford Act, it also addressed the funding for preparedness and civil defense warning systems.

Also in 1950, the Civil Defense Act and its amendments established government's role in disaster preparedness but its focus was the preparation and defense from nuclear attack. Later, Civil Defense would be replaced by the Federal Emergency Management Agency (FEMA) eventually becoming the lead agency for disaster relief and preparedness, switching its attention from nuclear attack to the more common incidents encountered throughout the nation.

In 1978, the National Governors' Association study of emergency management practices in the US introduced the concept of comprehensive emergency management. With its four components—preparedness, response, recovery, and mitigation—it emphasized an all-hazards approach to planning, further steering away from the nuclear defense mindset (Figure 1.1). It is significant because it provides a framework for a complete planning and management process that avoids the tendency to plan for only one element of an emergency. In 1997, FEMA placed emphasis on mitigation and sustainability with its Project Impact programs, an initiative that worked to create disaster-resistant communities that relied on public–private partnerships and on comprehensive emergency management.

FIGURE 1.1

Comprehensive emergency management.

After September 11, 2001, FEMA lost its cabinet position within the US government and political appointees, in part, shifted its emphasis away from disaster planning, causing seasoned emergency managers to leave and take positions in the private sector. Many of those who left the agency for private business brought with them their military civil defense focus on emergency management and business continuity.

Closely related to and part of emergency management is the influence of the Fire Service. Tried and true response protocols that worked exceptionally well on the fire ground under trying and dangerous conditions flavored the approach of firefighters once they migrated into the business world. Their often dogmatic, structured response orientation and evangelical support for the use of the ICS in BCP is a prime example.

Many of the acts, agencies, and protocols mentioned above spawned planning structures that were used in governmental response to disaster that have relevance to BCP structures used today. Multi-hazard functional planning is an example.

1.2.2 COMMUNITY DISASTER SERVICES

The American Red Cross, although not a government agency, was chartered by the US Congress in 1900 to provide services to members of the armed forces and relief to disaster victims at home. Providing food, water, and shelter to victims of disasters, their role in disaster preparedness, blood services, and first aid training is a huge resource to organizations in preparing workers to be self-resilient at home. They are a good source of preparedness and prevention information for workers and program managers alike. Today, they are expanding this preparedness training to include technological disasters caused by toxic chemicals and weapons of mass destruction. The Red Cross was one of the first agencies to expand its services to include disaster planning guidelines for businesses.

1.2.3 SOCIAL SCIENCE

Around the early 1950s, spurred on by the Cold War, social science became more involved in research to understand how society would react during times of crisis. Established at Ohio State University in 1963, the Disaster Research Center was the first social science research institution devoted to the study of human behavior in disasters. Fortunately, this research continues today with the efforts of Thomas E. Drabek, Enrico L Quarantelli, Kathleen Tierney, and many others. In addition to social science, a number of other institutions conduct research on other characteristics of disasters such as the Natural Hazards Center at the University of Colorado at Boulder and the Center for Natural Hazards Research at East Carolina University.

Although their emphasis is directed at the societal level, this research brings valuable information to business continuity management. In the past, planning was often performed in a vacuum, inconsiderate of the social realities that affect those tasked with the recovery of business processes and data systems. "Recently, hazard researchers studying disasters have moved slightly from what might be considered an 'agent centered' approach to a greater focus on vulnerability." David Alexander (1993, p. 4) pointed out that natural disasters can be thought of as quick-onset events with significant impacts on the "natural environment upon the socio-economic system." In later writings, he elaborated on this by saying that disasters are not defined by fixed events "but by social constructs and these are liable to change" (Alexander, 2005, p. 29). The concern expressed by Alexander is that disasters are not just the events, but also the social consequences (which are ever-changing) of the event. Dennis Mileti (1999, p. 3) also emphasized that disasters flow from overlaps of the physical, built, and social environments, but that they are "social in nature" (Rodríguez et al., 2007). The researchers also pointed out that we create our own disasters by building or rebuilding in areas that are prone to the effects of natural hazards. FEMA's Project Impact program is partially the result of their work.

Effective business continuity managers must become students of social science research because they are expected to be subject matter experts in the understanding of human behavior during an emergency, especially when developing emergency response plans. For example, many if not most emergency plans instruct people to "avoid panic" or "don't panic." Worst yet, some plans instruct their response personnel to "control panic" without providing procedures or training on how this is accomplished. Simply, research shows that people rarely panic in an emergency, and in fact often do just the opposite by failing to take rapid and effective action. Disaster myths persist despite 50 years of social science research. The myths suggest that disasters produce social breakdown, whereas experience consistently points to the resilience of human societies. For years, researchers have argued that the most effective response to disaster is one that is decentralized, flexible, and based on realistic assumptions of human behavior under stress. Yet, as Dynes (1993) pointed out, many public officials subscribe to a "command and control" ideology that promotes the centralization of authority, implements rigid structures, and makes inaccurate assumptions about how people respond to disasters. Tierney (2003) argued that the perpetuation of disaster myths benefits certain powerful groups in society. These myths have led to significant changes at the federal level, with FEMA becoming a part of the Department of Homeland Security (DHS). Clearly, disaster myths, an aspect of the popular culture of disaster, matter (Rodríguez et al., 2007).

1.2.4 DATA CENTER

Business continuity grew out of the data center, with early planners creating backup copies of important data. Mainframe computers required centralized processing that usually were located in a single room, except for the tape vault where primary and backup data was stored. Although there were some redundancies built into the systems, the loss of this room or its equipment meant long delays for rebuilding and recreating its environmental needs (air conditioning, raised floors, power requirements, and fire suppression systems), and the cost of replacement of the mainframe would have a significant impact on the enterprise.

The responsibility to proceduralize the backup process and develop instructions to recover the operations of the data center after a disaster was usually assigned to a technician within the IT department (then called electronic data processing) by the data center manager. These early planners had little business knowledge or focus outside their department. Their efforts were only for the data center and not the business as a whole. The skill set required to develop these plans required a technical knowledge of the equipment, data, and software, and the environment required to make it all work. This task was often viewed as a project, not as an ongoing process. When the plans, i.e., the project, were completed, they often sat on a bookshelf, as modern planners lament, collecting dust. Because the systems operated 24/7 and were large and expensive, and redundant systems were often impractical, testing of the plans usually did not occur unless there was an actual recovery situation.

Hence the term "disaster recovery," but as businesses realized there are direct interdependencies between the availability of data and the people and processes who use the data, planning was expanded to include all aspects of business operations, strategic management notwithstanding. A large percentage of business continuity programs today are managed by the IT department.

Managers recognized the growing dependence of their organization's need for access to data and in the mid 1970s, disaster recovery services such as hot site vendors began to appear. A commercial hot site, as we will describe later, is a location with computer systems and workspace standing in ready for the client to occupy in the event of the loss of their data center.

Primarily as a cost savings strategy, the goal was to restore systems and processes to a minimally acceptable level. Many years ago, the author stood in front of the board of directors and confidently told them that this is exactly what we would offer them. One member of the board responded sarcastically that it was not their intention to operate through the disaster at less than predisaster levels, but to use the disaster and their survivable position to take advantage of their competitors, who were located in geographically close proximity, and use the disaster strategically to gain market share. As we describe below, the term "business continuity" implies there is no interruption to critical processes and functions, especially for organizations in which the loss of processing is calculated in millions of dollars per minute. Although most professionals moved beyond the concept of minimally acceptable restoration and into continuity or resiliency, the planning standards mention what many believe to be an outdated concept. But I suppose "minimally acceptable" could mean 99.999% up-time of systems, critical functions, and processes.

Early data center recovery plans and planning resources suggested that the plans should be based on individual hazards, disasters, or emergencies. Experts at the time advised that "responses geared to a specific set of emergencies must be established" (Lord, 1981). Loosely referred to as scenario planning, the development of plans for individual types of emergencies is effective for emergency response plans but not for continuity plans. Examination of these plans found that generally 80% of the tasks required for recovery after events with different causes are the same. Developing a plan for each contingency can produce shelves of documents. Today, the listing of scenarios and plans for each outage scenario is a significant step backward, but seems to be required by some of the recent standards (analysis of the scenarios that can cause a loss is important for understanding the conditions, constraints, and planning needs and resource requirements, including preparedness and mitigation).

1.2.5 **REGULATIONS**

The literature often tells us that up to 70% of businesses fail within 3 years after a disaster, primarily owing to the loss of business records: in particular, accounts receivable. This figure has also been represented as 60% and as two out of five businesses (40% from a 1992 industry group study), but few seem to know where these figures originated or to what level of rigor data collection and analysis was reviewed. Most of these failures were likely small business enterprises. The regulation of the financial industry is responsible for beginning the path toward the maturity of business continuity management, with many of its orders and circulars requiring these institutions to protect their records. As early as October 30, 1969, Executive Order 11490 directed financial institutions to prepare "emergency plans and procedures" that assigned responsibility to a specific individual, developed a program for safeguarding and duplicating records, and required succession planning for senior officers.

The Foreign Corrupt Practices Act, amended in 1977, also required publically held companies to keep accurate records and protect assets that the courts later defined to include computer systems and their data, but it went further to mandate that companies create records. This was generally regarded as an indirect mandate for disaster recovery plans because it would have been difficult to accomplish without the use of the computer system.

The Comptroller of the Currency (the administrator of the National Banking System) in 1983 issued Banking Circular 177. Its amendment in 1987 was significant because it required the expansion of disaster planning to include major operational areas of the bank beyond the data center. Later the Comptroller, in conjunction with the Federal Financial Institutions Examination Council (FFIEC), would issue additional circulars that expanded the scope of the planning efforts. The Federal Home Loan Bank Board also issued requirements related to disaster planning. Today the FFIEC publishes a comprehensive set of business continuity management guidelines in their 12 handbooks. Before the American National Standards Institute (ANSI) and ISO standards, they were the most stringent from a compliance standpoint, but applied only to financial institutions.

Several recent regulations are thought to require the development of business continuity plans. These include the Sarbanes–Oxley Act of 2002 and the Health Insurance Portability and Accountability Act (HIPPA). The Sarbanes–Oxley Act states that all business records of publically traded companies (greater than $75 million in assets), including electronic records and electronic messages, must be saved for "not less than 5 years." They must be able to prove that their internal controls and audit trails are capable of producing correct and certifiable data. The consequences for noncompliance are large fines, imprisonment of senior executives, or both. Although the Public Company Accounting Oversight Board said that a business continuity plan is not required, compliance may be helped by the presence of a business continuity management process.

HIPPA appears to be more direct when it comes to requirements for business continuity in the health care industry. Section 142.308(3), the Security Standard of HIPPA, states: *A contingency plan, a routinely updated plan for responding to a system emergency that includes performing backups, preparing critical facilities that can be used to facilitate continuity of operations in the event of an emergency, and recovering from a disaster.* It goes on to require elements found in the business continuity process that include risk analysis and the testing of plans.

The Occupational Safety and Health Act was signed by President Richard Nixon on December 29, 1970, and created the Occupational Safety and Health Administration under the US Department of Labor. In 1980, along with other federal regulations pertaining to hazardous materials, they required emergency response plans for all business operations. The complexity of these plans varies according to type of hazards present and their level of risk. An emergency response capability is an element of comprehensive emergency management and of the new standards.

1.2.6 INSURANCE AND RISK MANAGEMENT

The insurance industry has long recognized the effects of disasters on their reserves and takes steps to both force and assist their customers in mitigating risk. This is especially true in light of the fact that a good portion of their insured risk is the built environment located in harm's way. Discounts in premiums for the installation of automatic fire suppression systems, requirements for industrial fire brigades, and the availability of professional loss control consultants are tactics insurance companies have used to indirectly position client organizations to recover or continue critical operations after a disaster. Recent years have seen these loss control consultants specialize in BCP. Because insurance is most often a function of the finance or risk manager within an organization, business continuity management frequently reports to this function. Business continuity management is properly defined under the umbrella of risk management.

1.2.7 SPECIFIC DISASTERS

The 1923 Great Kantō Japan earthquake resulted in 142,800 deaths and such economic hardship that many believe it is partly the reason for the attack on the US in World War II. The Fukushima nuclear power plant disaster that occurred after Japan's most powerful earthquake on record (March 11, 2011), and among the five strongest in the world, demonstrated that even the best prepared nation is susceptible to technological, political, and sociological failures. Hurricane Katrina is known for its political fallout, not to mention the personal and economic suffering. The list of worldwide disasters and the reaction to them, or the failure to react by taking the appropriate measures to prevent their effects in future disasters, is extensive, but some are more relevant to the development of business continuity management.

The destruction of the Olive View and the Veterans Administration Hospital, the collapse of freeway overpasses, and damage to the Lower Van Norman Dam during the 1971 6.6 magnitude San Fernando, California earthquake resulted in the strengthening of building codes and implementation of the State of California Alquist Priolo Special Studies Zone Act, passed in 1972. The purpose of this act is to prohibit the building of structures for human occupancy across active fault traces.

Specific localized disasters such as the Thanksgiving Day fire of 1982 at Norwest Financial in Minneapolis, the First Interstate Fire in Los Angeles, the Department of Defense Processing Center Fire in Oklahoma City, and the Hinsdale Phone Switch fire demonstrated the value of a plan or showed the consequences of ineffective planning, directing attention to the advantages of BCP. The costs of these and natural disaster in the 1990s totaled billions of dollars in losses. The aftermath of the *1993* Twin Tower bombing in New York also saw a renewed effort in BCP. The Great Hanshin earthquake, or Kobe earthquake of January 17, 1995, measured MM6.8, reinforced the attention to supply chain risk.

1.2.8 MILLENNIUM BUG (Y2K)

The practice of computer programmers to represent dates with two, not four, numbers caused worldwide fear that when the date changed from 1999 to the year 2000, computers, including programming embedded in many electronic devices, would either stop working or return incorrect information, destroying financial systems and shutting down utilities including nuclear power plants and transportation systems, and all manner of bad things. Even before the New Year, there was also the fear that the same might happen on September 9, 1999, because in some programming languages, 9999 represented the code for "end of file" and the programs would stop running.

Although the potential problem was identified in the mid 1980s, the years just before the turn of the century saw programmers scrambling to fix potential date errors, businesses audited their suppliers and equipment, and many put rudimentary Y2K continuity plans in place. In the end, the actual number of problems created was minor, but it did create an increased awareness not only of our dependency on data systems and embedded devices, but also on our need for alternate processes.

1.2.9 BUSINESS CONTINUITY ORGANIZATIONS AND CERTIFICATION

In 1988, DRI International (originally the Disaster Recovery Institute) was established as one of the first business continuity professional organizations to advance the knowledge and training of its members. With its adoption of a code of ethics and the introduction of a Common Body of Knowledge

(Professional Practices), it established a benchmark for a standard planning methodology. Other organizations followed in the early 1990s, including the Business Continuity Institute (BCI), the Association of Contingency Planners (1983), and the Business Recovery Managers Association.

Based on their Professional Practices and/or the requirements of the new standards, DIR International and the BCI (among others) administer the testing and certification of business continuity practitioners. A combination of experience, education, examination, and professional reference/verification is required. Certifications include:

- Certified Business Continuity Professional (CBCP)
- Master Business Continuity Professional (MBCP)
- Certified Business Continuity Auditor (CBCA)
- Certified by the Business Continuity Institute (CBCI)
- Certified Emergency Manager (CEM, issued by the International Association of Emergency Managers. This is more of a governmental emergency management certification than that of business continuity).

Professional certification demonstrates that the recipient has achieved a level of professional knowledge and competence. Certification helps to ensure qualified individuals gain employment; it is often a required element in new-hire job descriptions. It provides peer recognition and personal satisfaction in its achievement, and offers both increased career advancement opportunities and some degree of protection in litigation. It also forces maintenance of competence in the field by requiring continuing education as a recertification requirement.

1.2.10 EFFECT OF SEPTEMBER 11, 2001

As a result of the loss of over 3000 people killed during the attacks in New York City and Washington, DC, including more than 400 police officers and firefighters, an estimated $40.2 billion in insurance payments, and the stated intent of the terrorists to destroy our economy (when the New York Stock Exchange reopened, the Dow Jones industrial average had dropped 685 points), the Homeland Security Act of 2002 was signed into law. The 17 Titles under the Act created the Department of Homeland Security (DHS) (Title V relates to emergency preparedness and response). FEMA was absorbed into the DHS, initially changing much of FEMA's focus away from disaster planning to terrorism response. These agencies developed the National Response and the National Disaster Recovery Framework.

The National Response Framework of 2008 outlines an all-hazards approach to domestic incident response in the US by identifying the major roles, structures, and response methods to be used by the federal government to work in conjunction with state and local governments and with the private sector when responding to regional disasters or terrorist events.

Developed as a companion document to the National Response Framework, the National Disaster Recovery Framework was drafted in 2010 and was intended for the use of government executives, private and nongovernmental leaders, and disaster recovery management practitioners. According to the document, it "establishes a scalable system that coordinates and manages disaster recovery operations to more effectively deliver recovery assistance to severely impacted communities." Although focused on governmental recovery, business continuity managers should be not only aware of its contents, but work closely with local jurisdictions to integrate their continuity efforts with these state and local agencies where appropriate.

In the days subsequent to the September 11 attack, many emergency and business continuity managers and even security professionals believed that the event was not predictable and that many lessons were learned. A simple study of the unclassified literature shows that the method of attract was entirely predictable and the only lesson learned was that we did not learn our lessons. Increased attention to the human impact of disasters on resilience (one firm in the Twin Towers, Cantor Fitzgerald, lost 658 employees), restricted access issues, and the geographical separation of backup facilities are but a few examples of these lessons.

1.2.11 STANDARDS

A standard is a formal set of rules or specifications that establishes a norm that can be used as a basis for comparison such as an audit by internal or external organizations. It attempts to codify existing and minimal practices, if not best practices, and to ensure the viability, quality, and reliability of programs. It forces commonality and consistency and helps ensure programs are in place.

It can carry the weight of law or establish a level of care that organizations can be civilly responsible to follow. Programs developed under a particular standard or set of standards may be required by third parties, i.e., clients, and could therefore represent a competitive advantage. Business continuity managers or those within an organization who have recognized the need for a business continuity program but who have had difficulty convincing management to commit to the establishment of a program look at these standards as a hammer to force the development of a sustainable program. Those just entering the field may find the standards a useful roadmap to develop their program; however, experienced business continuity managers may find them restricting and difficult to implement, a hindrance, or simply a bureaucratic nuisance. Audits of numerous plans and programs reveal deficient processes, the absence of a managerial framework or command structure, and the inexperienced understanding, mostly by outside consultants and planning service contractors, of how business continuity is integrated with the goals of the organization. Careful attention to the standards can prevent or solve most of these issues.

1.2.11.1 NFPA 1600

In 1991, work began on the establishment of standards for emergency management that were later published as the NFPA Standard on Disaster/Emergency Management and Business Continuity Programs (NFPA 1600). First issued as a recommended practice and then as an ANSI standard, it was adopted as a National Preparedness Standard in 2004 under the National Intelligence Reform Act (the Intelligence Reform and Terrorism Prevention Act of 2004). Originally focused on the emergency management and response community, it included guidelines for business and emphasized use of the ICS. Because the National Commission on Terrorist Attacks Upon the United States (also known as the 9/11 Commission) believes that "the private sector controls 85 percent of the critical infrastructure in the nation," and "the 'first' first responders will almost certainly be civilians," later versions of the standard have focused more on BCP.

1.2.11.2 British standards 25999

The British Standards (BS) Institution and Business Continuity Institute in 2003 developed an informal standard, Publicly Available Specification 56 (PAS 56). Originally published as a guide, it was later replaced in 2006 by BS 25999. Both PAS and BS 25999-1/BS 25999-2 (the audit and guidance document) contained elements that focused on the management of a business continuity program, not simply the steps necessary to build a plan. BS 25999-2 became the basis for future standards that include the ANSI/ASIS SPC.1-2009 Organizational Resilience standard and ISO 22301 Societal Security-Business Continuity Management Systems standard that replaced BS 25999.

1.2.11.3 ASIS SPC.1-2009

In an effort to create a new standard acceptable to global standards organizations, ASIS International in 2009 used BS 25999 as the basis of their Organizational Resilience: Security, Preparedness and Continuity Management Systems—Requirements with Guidance for Use standard. Recognized as an ANSI standard, ASIS SPC.1-2009 is designed to integrate with ISO standards on quality and risk management systems. According to the standard, it adopts a process approach to building an organizational resilience management system. "An organization needs to identify and manage many activities in order to function effectively. Any activity using resources and managed to enable the transformation of inputs into outputs can be considered to be a process. Often the output from one process directly forms the input to the next process. The application of a system of processes within an organization, together with the identification and iterations of these processes and their management, can be referred to as a process approach" (ASIS SPC.1-2009).

1.2.11.4 ISO 22301

Released in 2012, the ISO Standard 22301 Societal Security—Business Continuity Management Systems—Requirements specifies its directions for developing and managing a program that it calls a Business Continuity Management System. A companion guidance document, ISO 22313 provides information on how best to implement the requirements of ISO 22301. According to the ISO Web page (http://www.iso.org/), ISO 22301 specifies requirements to plan, establish, implement, operate, monitor, review, maintain, and continually improve a documented management system to prepare for, respond to, and recover from disruptive events when they arise. The requirements specified in ISO 22301 are generic and are intended to be applicable to all organizations (or parts thereof), regardless of type, size, and nature of the organization. The extent of application of these requirements depends on the organization's operating environment and complexity.

Other standards in the Societal Security series include:

- ISO 22323: Societal Security—Organizational resilience management system
- ISO 22397: Societal Security—Guidelines to set up a public private partnership
- ISO 22398: Societal Security—Guidelines for exercises and testing
- ISO 22320: Societal Security—Emergency management—Requirements for incident response

1.2.11.5 Other standards

The Australian Business Continuity Standard AS/NZS 5050:2010, one of the first to integrate with risk management principles, and the Singapore Standard for Business Continuity are other recognized standards in use today.

The standards aligned with ISO management systems allow for integration into other business systems and standards, and impose a process management framework using Dr J. Edwards Deming's Shewhart Cycle of Plan, Do, Check, Act (PDCA). Deming later changed "PDCA" to "Plan, Do, Study, Act" because he believed that "Check" emphasized inspection over analysis. ISO 22301 and ASIS SPC.1-2009 translate "plan" into "establish (policy, objectives, targets, controls, processes, and procedures)," "do" into "implement and operate," and "check" into "monitor and review (measure and report performance)," and "act" is described as "maintain and improve" (implement corrective actions based on management review and audits).

Many of the standards (ASIS and NFPA in particular) contain appendices that help implement their requirements and in most cases can be used to form the basis of a business continuity program.

1.2.12 ACCREDITATION

To help mitigate the risk from the failure of the supply chain and sole source suppliers, business continuity managers require these suppliers either through verbiage in purchase orders or through contractual agreements to maintain tested BCPs and make the plans available for review and evaluation. But because BCPs contain proprietary information, many suppliers are reluctant to release them for review. This task could become burdensome to a company if required to release many copies of its plan, and time-consuming for businesses with numerous supply chains to review. A simple inspection of the plan usually does not fully reveal the depth of the planning effort (i.e., mitigation, preparedness) and a letter attesting to the maturity of a business continuity program provides little to audit. Certification by a third party that the organization's program meets the requirements of one of the standards solves all of these issues.

1.2.13 PRIVATE SECTOR PREPAREDNESS ACCREDITATION AND CERTIFICATION PROGRAM

In an effort to accredit and certify an organization's efforts that enable preparedness, disaster and emergency management, and business continuity using standards adopted by the US Department of Homeland Security, in response to Title IX of the Implementing Recommendations of the 9/11 Commission Act of 2007, a voluntary certification program for private organizations was developed, referred to as the private sector preparedness accreditation and certification program (PS-Prep). The DHS has adopted the ASIS, NFPA 1600:2013, and ISO 22301 standards. It has dropped NFPA 1600:2010 and BS 25999 from its accreditation list. Certification is established by an accredited third-party organization.

1.2.14 EMERGENCY MANAGEMENT ACCREDITATION PROGRAM

The Emergency Management Accreditation Program (EMAP) began using NFPA 1600 as criteria for accreditation of public sector emergency management programs. With its 1997 origins in the National Emergency Management Association, EMAP is a voluntary, national accreditation process for public emergency management programs at the state, territorial, and local level. EMAP now uses its own Emergency Management Standard.

1.2.15 FUTURE

The future of BCP is in the continued and successful push by professionals, standards, and senior management to incorporate business continuity management concepts into all areas of the organization as a strategic and operational managerial function. In far too many organizations today, senior management is aware of the existence of the business continuity effort but clueless about the details of the program or of their responsibilities in the direction and control of a response to a disruptive event. If the program is managed properly, senior management is intimately involved in the progress of the program, its strategies and goals, and the status of risks that affect the continuity of its operations. Most senior managers occupy their positions because they possess a take-charge personality and in the absence of the awareness or acceptance of their roles at the time of a disaster will proceed to follow their own course of action that may be counter to the goals of the business continuity manager's efforts. Standalone planning efforts are increasingly acknowledged to be of less value.

Successful business continuity managers must stay up to date on the latest technological changes (cloud computing, for example) and changes in their organization's risk environment, and develop the skills to become a true organizational manager.

1.2.15.1 Social media

The increasing use of social media in business continuity management is less of a paradigm shift than is the manner in which risk is identified and key functions are sustained. According to Wikipedia, "Social media refers to the means of interactions among people in which they create, share, and exchange information and ideas in virtual communities and networks." Google, YouTube, Twitter, and Facebook are just a few of the more popular communication resources and are increasingly used to notify team members that their plans have been activated and to keep them informed about the status of the event, to pass situational awareness from the incident or community to team leaders or to the emergency operations center, and for personnel accounting where all members of an organization can check in after a disaster to let leaders know whether they are uninjured and available to work. Social media can also be used for plan orientation and training. It is a source to track public opinion and disseminate crisis management information to the public or shareholders. As a communication tool, it serves as a redundancy to normal modes of communication (although for many, this *is* the normal mode of communication).

1.2.15.2 Rise in public–private partnerships

Before September 11, 2001, public–private partnerships (PPP) generally meant that business mangers wanted from the government access to their real-time situational information during an emergency, and government wanted from business access to their financial resources. Businesses were beginning to work closely with local emergency services agencies such as the fire department to understand their response capabilities and acquaint potential responders with the individual hazards and layout of the business facilities.

The 9/11 Commission's finding that most critical infrastructure is controlled by the private sector emphasized the need for cooperation between government and the business community to work together to develop strategies for resilience. September 11 and Hurricane Katrina "made it no longer a question of whether the private sector had a role to play in national security and disaster management, but a question of what that role should be, and how effective PPP for these purposes could be established (Abou-bakr, 2013)."

1.3 MANY DEFINITIONS

Like the history of BCP, its definition has evolved to reflect the perspective of its varied stakeholders and the current flavor of the times. Early definitions emphasized the creation of a plan and not a business continuity management program. These and other early definitions promised a return to a minimum level of operation. Some managers still confuse a BCP with that of a simple emergency action plan (first aid, fire response, etc.). Today we speak of organizational resilience, the "systematic and coordinated activities and practices through which an organization manages its operational risks, and the associated potential threats and impacts therein," as defined by the ASIS Standard.

ISO 22301 defines business continuity as the "capability of the organization to continue the delivery of products or services at acceptable predefined levels following a disruptive event," and business continuity management as a "holistic management process that identifies potential threats to an organization and the impacts to business operations those threats, if realized, might cause, and which provides a framework for building organizational resilience with the capability of an effective response that safeguards the interest of its key stakeholders, reputation, brand and value-creating activities." This definition minimizes the point that an activity that may not in itself create value may be a downstream dependency of one that does create value. It leaves little room for the consideration of functions whose services can or should operate at a reduced level of service, such as the reduction of custodial services to trash removal only, although in this case one could argue that the individual workers can empty their own garbage. The former is similar to the definition of business continuity management offered by the Disaster Recovery and the Business Continuity Institute. NFPA 1600 defines business continuity as "an ongoing process to ensure that the necessary steps are taken to identify the impact of potential losses and maintain viable recovery strategies, recovery plans, and continuity of services." Although it does not define business continuity management, it goes on to describe "continuity" as a "term that includes business continuity, continuity of operations (COOP), operational continuity, succession planning, continuity of government, which support the resilience of the entity." Succession planning, the process of grooming internal candidates within an organization for advancement, may have a different meaning to a seasoned business manager. Although cross-training is an important concept in business continuity management, used in this context, succession planning may be outside the scope of business continuity management. In the context of the standards, it is used simply: Develop a list of personnel who are next in line should the primary person become incapacitated or unable to fulfill his duties as a result of the disaster.

The ASIS SPC.1-2009 standard similarly says continuity is the strategic and tactical capability, preapproved by management, of an organization to plan for and respond to conditions, situations, and events to continue operations at an acceptable predefined level. It defines a disaster as an "event that causes great damage or loss," whereas social science maintains that a disaster is a condition destabilizing the social system that manifests itself in a malfunctioning or disruption of connections and communications of a social unit, partial or total destruction, making it necessary to take extraordinary or emergency countermeasures to reestablish stability (Kreps, and Kroll-Smith/Gunter in Quarantelli 1998). The definition of a disaster from the Emergency Management Standard (2007) is simpler: a severe or prolonged incident which threatens life, property, environment, or critical systems.

The term "disaster recovery" or "disaster recovery planning" in the past was used synonymously with the term "business continuity," but in practice today "disaster recovery" is often used as a subset of business continuity management to refer specifically to the recovery of data or telecommunications systems. Information technology practitioners often refer to business continuity as the "people" part of the equation, or the umbrella term that encompasses the remainder of the risk management/comprehensive emergency management components.

Business continuity is the management of a sustainable process that identifies the critical functions of an organization and develops strategies to continue these functions without interruption or to minimize the effects of an outage or loss of service provided by these functions. It develops the capability and the plans to implement the strategies and lists the resources necessary to support these operations. It is part of the emergency and risk management process of prevention, mitigation, preparation, response, and recovery. Examples of business continuity strategies include alternate worksites, data backups, and network server replacement.

Business continuity is not a project. Its initial creation may be managed as such when planning and constructing its various components, but ultimately it becomes a cycle of validation, reexamination, improvement, practiced execution, and readiness. When viewed from the perspective of an outside consultant, the goal should not be to produce a plan but to establish a business continuity management system that goes beyond the department level (IT, for example) to encompass a company-wide program of sustainability. This moves it beyond the historical practices of driving the process from the bottom up. The future state is not BCP but business continuity management, a term that is quickly replacing BCP. The thought that, "Oh, we got to have a plan" is becoming (and always has been) myopic.

Not to be confused with continuity of government planning, in which executive succession is defined, business continuity management from the government perspective is referred to as COOP. According to the Emergency Management Standard (September 2007), it is the capability to continue essential program functions and to preserve essential facilities, equipment, and records across a broad range of potential emergencies. The concepts of COOP are basically the same as business continuity management, and its emphasis is directed more toward the operations of the governmental entity and less on the recovery of the surrounding community, although they can be related. The recovery of the tax base, for example, may have a direct effect on the recovery of the governmental operations. Because of the various regulations, government agencies may have less flexibility than a business entity in the methods and format of their planning documents (FEMA provides COOP plan templates). National Security Presidential Directive-51 and Homeland Security Presidential Directive-20 national continuity policy requires all federal executive departments and agencies to develop an integrated, overlapping continuity capability. The Federal Continuity Directive (FCD 1) was developed to provide guidelines for developing these plans and programs. Although not required for state and local jurisdictions, or for nongovernmental organizations (critical infrastructure), it can also be used by these agencies as their planning model. The goal is the continuation of *national essential functions* (NEFs). The planning steps are similar to BCP, but with different terminology. These steps include:

- The three categories of essential functions: NEFs (the eight functions the President and the nation's leadership will focus on to lead and sustain the nation during a catastrophic emergency); *primary mission essential functions* (PMEFs) (agency mission essential functions that must be performed to support the performance of NEFs before, during, and after an emergency); and *mission essential functions* (MEFs) (agency-level government functions that must be continued throughout, or resumed rapidly after, a disruption of normal activities), are identified
- *Orders of succession* are developed
- *Delegation of authority* is predetermined
- *Continuity facilities*, i.e., alternate work locations and strategies, are identified

- *Continuity of communications* is planned and maintained
- *Vital records management* in which documents, files, and other materials vital to the agency and its operations are protected and available after disaster
- *Human capital* involves cross-training, communication, and guidance to staff to perform essential functions
- *Test, training, and exercise* to ensure readiness
- *Devolution of control and direction.* Devolution is the transfer of statutory authority and responsibility for PMEFs and MEFs from an agency's primary operating staff and facilities to other employees and facilities in case the original facility is unavailable
- *Reconstitution operations* that transition from continuity status to normal operations, execution of plans for reconstitution of operations and facilities, and return from an alternate facility to a new or restored facility.

1.4 REVIEW

Business continuity is the management of a sustainable process that identifies the critical functions of an organization and develops strategies to continue these functions without interruption or to minimize the effects of an outage or loss of service provided by these functions. It develops the capability and the plans to implement the strategies and lists the resources necessary to support these operations. Its effective implementation depends on the comprehensive emergency management components of prevention, mitigation, preparation, response, and recovery. A BCP, or a plan to manage an emergency or crisis situation, is only one element of the business continuity management process. Although the IT department may refer to the term "disaster recovery" as the efforts to continue or recover the technical operations of the data center or telecommunications systems, emergency managers understand the meaning of the term "disaster" to represent a severe or prolonged incident which threatens life, property, environment, or critical systems. Business continuity management from the government perspective is referred to as COOP.

The history of business continuity management brings with it the perspectives and skills of each of the disciplines that contributed to its current form. The two major perspectives, one from the militaristic, emergency management side of the house with its strict adherence to the dogmas of disaster management, and the other from the data center, which focused internally only on the recovery of IT, combined to bring BCP to its current state. Understanding these perspectives allows the business continuity manager to evaluate new ideas as truly representing progress and better work with those who hold these different outlooks.

The goal within the IT department to create a disaster recovery plan or a business continuity plan with the help of a loss control consultant in response to the suggestion or requirement of the organization's insurance carrier has evolved from a project-oriented practice into a sustainable management process that aligns with the goals of the organization and helps to ensure the resilience of the entire organization. This is accomplished in part by considering the effects on people, resources, and infrastructure through a better understanding of the social, political, and physical constructs of disasters, both regionally and distances apart. Today, the plan is secondary to the business continuity management process.

BIBLIOGRAPHY

Abou-bakr, A.J., 2013. Managing Disasters through Public–Private Partnerships. Georgetown University Press.

Alexander, D., 1993. Natural Disaster. Chapman & Hill, New York.

Alexander, D., 2005. From What is a Disaster: New Answers to Old Questions. Xlibris, Bloomington.

Dynes, R.R., 1993. Disaster Reduction: The Importance of Adequate Assumptions About Social Organization. Sociological Spectrum 13, 175–192.

Haddow, G.D., Bullock, J.A., 2003. Introduction to Emergency Management. Butterworth-Heinemann, Amsterdam.

Lord Jr., K.W., 1981. The Data Center Disaster Consultant, second ed. Q.E.D. Information Services, Inc., Wellesley, MA.

Mileti, D., 1999. Disasters by Design: A Reassessment of Natural Hazards in the United States. Joseph Henry Press.

Quarantelli, E.L., 1998. What is a Disaster? Perspectives on the Question. Routledge, London.

Tinery, K.J., 2003. Disaster Beliefs and Institutional Interests: Recycling Disaster Myths in the Aftermath of 9-11. Elsevier, New York.

UNDERSTANDING THE STANDARDS

CHAPTER SUMMARY

The application of a management system as defined by the process improvement requirements of the Deming cycle or PDCA (Plan, Do, Check, Act) and adopted by the International Organization for Standardization 22301, American Society for Industrial Security SPC.1–2009, and National Fire Protection Association 1600 standards is not well understood by many business continuity professionals. This chapter discusses how PDCA, also known as the Shewhart cycle, is applied to the inputs and outputs of business processes to produce risks management outcomes that form the basis of a business continuity or organizational resilience management system. A discussion of how standards are developed reminds the reader that these consensus standards provide "what" is required to build a system that is effective, sustainable, and that allows for continuous improvement, but not "how" this is accomplished. An overview of the requirements of the standard's clauses is explained.

KEY TERMS

ANSI standards; Business Continuity Management System; Business continuity standards requirements; Consensus standard; Deming wheel; Horizontal management; ISO standards; Organization of the standards; Organizational resilience; Plan, Do, Check, Act; Process approach; Shewhart cycle.

KEY POINTS

- The standards are consensus standards developed by technical committees
- Distinction between ISO and ANSI standards
- ISO implements a process approach
- How the Deming cycle applies to the Business Continuity Management Systems
- Organization of the standards
- Overview of the standards' requirements
- The standards emphasize documentation and continual improvement

2.1 INTRODUCTION

Written to address the needs of all sizes and types of organizations, the business continuity standards provide auditable criteria to help ensure the rigor of the business continuity planning capability is sufficient to ensure success during and after a disruptive event. They are designed to integrate with similar standards and management systems that may already be established within the organization.

International Organization for Standardization (ISO) standards are developed by technical committees of subject matter experts after an industry need for the standard is identified and a proposal is made by the industry to, and accepted by, the standards organization. The request is initiated by a consumer group or a professional association such as the American Society of Safety Engineers. The subject matter experts on the technical committees can include members from academia and from the relevant industry, but also from the government or nonprofit organizations. Participants on the committees, who are recommended by members of ISO, negotiate all aspects of the standard, including its scope, key definitions, and content. This results in a draft standard.

The draft is then reviewed by ISO's members, who submit their comments before an approval. If a consensus is reached, the draft becomes an ISO standard; if not, it goes back to the technical committee for further edits. Hence, they are called consensus standards.

Both American Society for Industrial Security (ASIS) SPC.1-2009 and National Fire Protection Association (NFPA) 1600 are American National Standards Institute (ANSI) standards. Although ANSI does not directly develop standards, it oversees their development and use in the United States (US). It promotes and facilitates the development of voluntary consensus standards and ensures their integrity. As the sole US representative member of ISO, it often takes standards to the international organization for adoption. ANSI also accredits programs that assess conformance to the standards.

2.2 PROCESS APPROACH

Many of the ISO standards, including 22301 and ASIS SPC.1–2009, are management systems that use a process approach. ISO defines a process as a set of interrelated or interacting activities that transforms inputs into outputs. Its purpose is to enhance an organization's efficiency in achieving its objectives. A process approach is the application of a system of processes within an organization, together with the identification and interactions of these processes, and their management to produce the desired outcome. Types of processes can include:

- Organizational management. Examples include strategic planning, establishing policies, goals, and objectives, ensuring communication, resources, and continual improvement.
- Resource management. These processes relate to the provision of the resources necessary to meet the organization's goals.
- Realization processes. Processes that deliver business results more consistently and predictably.
- Measurement, analysis, and improvement processes. Processes that include performance analysis, trending, and continuous improvement are included here.

Steps that ISO standards use to implement the process approach include:

- Identify the processes of the organization. Determine all processes needed to produce the intended outputs, how they are sequenced, and how they interact with other processes. To do this effectively, an understanding of the needs of customers (stakeholders), both internal and external, must be identified, understood, and documented. Process owners are also identified.
- Process planning. Define the activities within the process and how performance is to be monitored and measured, determine resource requirements, and confirm that the characteristics of the process are consistent with the organization's objectives.

- Implementation and measurement of the process. The processes are implemented, controlled, and measured as intended.
- Analysis of the process. Performance is quantified and compared to its goals and expectations. Process improvement is identified and reported to management.
- Corrective action and improvement of the process. Methods for improvement of the process are defined when correction is needed. The Deming wheel (see below) can be used as process improvement.

The process approach used by many ISO standards emphasizes a horizontal management system. Contrasted with the more common vertical management, in which organizations are structured into individual departments arranged according to functional units with corresponding layers of management, a horizontal structure has few or no levels of middle management between staff and executives, allowing the organization to better focus on its overall goals and customer needs. The component parts of the organization can be better understood in how they relate to each other, avoiding the silos often encountered in a vertical management system. Employees in a horizontal organization may work in teams that are cross-functional, allowing quicker decision making and a better view of the end product (some experts say that decision making in a vertical structure is often quicker than in a horizontal or flat structure, as it is also known). Managers in horizontal organizations may have a better understanding of how to manage risk to the organization and can better see how the inputs and outputs of all functions interrelate. As a result, problem solving can be accomplished in a more holistic manner. Newly formed companies often start with a horizontal structure but find that a vertical structure is necessary as their company grows. A hybrid of the two structures may exist in a well-managed organization.

ASIS and ISO 22301 do not require an organization to adopt a horizontal structure. The use of the process approach and the management system supports a consistent integrated implementation with other related management system standards while keeping a focus on continual improvement.

Wikipedia defines a management system as "the framework of processes and procedures used to ensure that an organization can fulfill all tasks required to achieve a set of related business objectives." A management system can include the organization's structure, roles and responsibilities, planning and operation, etc., across the entire enterprise or its individual functions and components. It is the set of interrelated or interacting elements of an organization to establish policies and objectives, and the processes necessary to achieve those objectives. It can address a single or multiple disciplines. This is essentially the same as the definition of a process approach, as mentioned in this chapter.

2.3 PLAN, DO, CHECK, ACT

ASIS uses Plan, Do, Check, Act (PDCA) to "structure the Organizational Resilience (OR) process" and refers to it as its OR management system that takes inputs and uses PDCA to produce "risks management outcomes" that fulfill the requirements of the standard. ISO 22301 says basically the same thing by focusing on the standards (requirements for continuity management) and interested parties (ASIS substitutes this with "stakeholders") as inputs to produce continuity outcomes to meet its requirements. The PDCA model is used in ISO's management standards. It tells the manager how to establish the elements of a Business Continuity Management System to better manage risk to the organization.

PDCA is an iterative four-step process typically used in business process improvement and decision making. Known as the Deming wheel, Deming cycle, or Deming circle, it was developed by Dr. Walter Shewhart at Bell Laboratories in 1920. Shewhart was known for his work on statistical quality and process control. An engineer and physicist, he based his Shewhart cycle on the scientific method of hypothesis, experiment, and evaluation, thus leading to Plan, Do, and Check.

Dr. William Edwards Deming refined Shewart's methods and in the 1950s he helped Japan rebuild its economy and positioned it as a world leader in quality products. Later, his teachings in management and quality brought the Ford Motor Company from billion-dollar losses to the top in the industry. Deming is credited with the birth of the total quality management revolution and is considered to be the father of modern quality control. Deming and others expanded the Shewhart cycle into PDCA. Variants include PDSA ("Study" in place of "Check," because Deming believed it better emphasized a formal process to analyze results and to compare them against the expected goals) and OPDCA. Observation (O) is added to represent the need to understand the current condition of a process.

2.3.1 PLAN (ESTABLISH, OR IN THE ASIS VERSION: ESTABLISH THE MANAGEMENT SYSTEM)

ISO 22301 describes "Plan" as the establishment of the business continuity policy, objectives, targets, controls, processes, and procedures in accordance with the organization's policies and objectives. ASIS further defines "Plan" to include these elements in terms of managing risk and improving security, incident preparedness, response, continuity, and recovery.

All processes start with an input that serves as the driver for the planning phase. Inputs can be derived from outputs of a dependent or upstream process (an exercise seasoned business continuity managers recognize), the results of root cause analysis, benchmarking, compliance, or from process mapping, to name a few. The beginning of a new iteration of the cycle (see below) can also be an input. Define problems or gaps and investigate or strategize to determine requirements and objectives. If appropriate, identify the process owner including their responsibilities and accountability, resource requirements, and outputs or customer requirements.

2.3.2 DO (IMPLEMENT AND OPERATE)

Execute (implement) the processes identified in the Plan stage. This is where most of the traditional Business Continuity Planning steps are found. Putting in place preparedness, response, and mitigation programs, conducting the risk and business impact analysis (BIA), developing and instituting continuity strategies and resources, as well as documenting plans are assigned to this stage.

The implementation of certain processes may involve a separate independent PDCA cycle. For example, under Plan, you identify the need to conduct a BIA, but when it comes to implementing the BIA, there is a separate planning and execution (and of course, Checking and Acting) structure to its realization.

2.3.3 CHECK (MONITOR AND REVIEW)

Management consultant Peter Drucker is credited with saying: "If you can't measure it, you can't manage it." Develop metrics and track performance (audit) against goals, objectives, or milestones for the implemented processes and report progress to management on a regular basis. As implied above, this does not mean that you simply check to see whether the process is implemented. Key performance indicators, resource allocation, management reviews, surveys, testing, data analysis, heat maps, and charts can be developed so that actionable trends and data that support managerial risk control and other actions are identified.

When progress toward the goals is less than expected or desired, understand the causes and devise improvement plans (devising improvement plans can be placed under Act). The type of process you study will dictate the type of metric that is the most appropriate.

2.3.4 ACT (MAINTAIN AND IMPROVE)

ASIS defines "Act" as taking corrective and preventative actions based on the results of the internal management system audit and management review to achieve continual improvement of the management system. This is required under ISO 22301.

This is the step where you close any gaps discovered in the Check (Monitor and Improve) stage or improve on things that may be working well. If things are operating as expected, adopt it as the procedure and keep checking. Consider abandonment of the procedure or repeat the PDCA cycle if corrective actions are not effective and sustainable (or devise better corrective actions).

PDCA is an iterative process because the cycle repeats once completed, thus ensuring continuous improvement of a process or of the entire system, building on the knowledge and experience gained in the previous iterations to reach a more perfect state.

The PDCA model is applied at the strategic level by defining the overall development of the Business Continuity Management System and at the tactical level by the application of PDCA to each of the processes within the system. ISO standards are arranged by clauses and sub-clauses. At the strategic level, the main headings (the high-level steps to develop a Business Continuity Management System) in ISO 22301 are aligned with the PDCA components (Table 2.1).

To illustrate how PDCA might work in practice, consider that ISO 22301 requires top management to appoint one or more competent persons who have the authority and accountability to implement and

Table 2.1 ISO 22301 Clauses Associated With PDCA Steps		
PDCA	**Clause**	**Description**
Plan	4	Context of the organization
	5	Leadership
	6	Planning
	7	Support
Do	8	Operational planning and control
		Risk assessment
		Business impact analysis
		Business continuity strategy
		Establish and implement procedures
		Exercising and testing
Check	9	Performance evaluation
Act	10	Improvement

maintain the Business Continuity Management System. It also requires the organization to determine what level of competency is necessary for anyone with responsibility within the Business Continuity Management System, and what level of education, training, and experience will satisfy this requirement. This applies also to any contracted personnel working within the system. Mentoring or professional development can be used to reach the appropriate level of competence, but actions taken must be evaluated for their effectiveness. All of the evidence that demonstrates competence, of course, must be documented. PDCA can be used at the tactical level to hire a Business Continuity Management System Manager (Table 2.2).

Table 2.2 PDCA: Example for Recruitment of BCM Manager			
Process: Hire Business Continuity Manager			
Plan	**Do**	**Check**	**Act**
Develop list of required skills and qualifications	Publish job opening	Does manager meet goals and objectives	Professional development
Obtain approval for position	Develop interview questions	Are goals and objectives met on a timely basis	Participate in professional organizations
Determine minimum educational requirements for position	Establish interview schedule	Does manager maintain professional credentials	Subscribe to professional journals
Establish level of experience necessary	Interview candidates	Obtain feedback from peers and customers	Obtain additional professional credentials
Determine if special training is required	Check references and credentials	Audit effectiveness of program	Reevaluate requirements
Develop job description	Make offer		Merit raise or employee improvement plan
Agree on reporting structure	Schedule new hire orientation		
Conduct salary survey	Order business cards		
Source candidates	Locate and set up office space		
Develop budget	Order office equipment		
Develop expectations and timelines	Explain expectations top management has for business continuity		

2.4 ORGANIZATION OF STANDARDS

As we mentioned earlier, the ISO standards are arranged into different sections or clauses.

Clauses 0–3: Introduction, Scope, Normative References, Terms, and Definitions

Clauses 0–3 do not contain requirements to develop the Business Continuity Management System. The Introduction (Clause 0) summarizes the concept of a Business Continuity Management System. It describes key components and essential considerations necessary to build the management system. It maps how the stakeholders and interested parties, and business continuity (or the organizational resilience management system) requirements and expectations act as inputs into the PDCA cycle with its resulting outputs to stakeholders and interested parties that manage business continuity and risk.

ISO 22301 identifies the remaining clauses (4–10) according to its alignment with PDCA. The ASIS standard includes an explanation of the process approach. It goes on to say that "compliance with this standard can be verified by an auditing process that is compatible and consistent with the methodology of ISO 9001:2000, ISO 14001:2004, and/or ISO/IEC 27001:2005 and the PDCA Model." ISO 9001 is the quality management systems requirements standard that establishes the requirements of a quality management system. ISO 14001 is the standard on environmental management and ISO 27001 is the standard on information security management that contains clauses on business continuity management.

The scope (Clause 1) of ISO 22301 explains the standard's intent as described above and lists some reasons why an organization may want to adopt the standard. ASIS does basically the same, but better explains that it does not intend to require the "how' of the required elements allowing organizations to fit the requirements of its and its stakeholders needs into their management system as appropriate. ASIS also expresses its scope more in terms of risk/risk control, a resilience culture, and the protection of critical assets to the extent of the organization's risk tolerance. It "covers all phases of incident management before, during and after a disruptive event."

Clause 2 lists the normative references, which are documents that the reader must comprehend or reference to better understand the standard. ISO 22301 says that there are no normative references; however, ASIS refers to several documents that include ISO's guide 73:2002 (risk management vocabulary), ISO 9001, ISO 14001, and ISO 27001, as mentioned above, and includes ISO 28000:2007, specification for security management systems for the supply chain.

Terms and definitions are included in Clause 3. Although most of the pertinent terms needed to understand and work with the requirements of the standards are explained, it is important to highlight the following definitions because they guide the manager to select the most appropriate subclauses to match the level of planning necessary for the scope of the business continuity management effort. Some terms may be new to the seasoned business continuity professional; we will describe these in later chapters. Taken from the ISO rules for the structure and drafting of International Standards:

- "Shall" is a requirement that must be followed without modification or deviation
- "Should" means that the clause is a recommendation that is not necessarily required or that a certain course of action may be chosen over another
- "May" is used to indicate that something is permitted
- "Can" is used to indicate that something is possible

As described above, Clauses 4–10 are aligned with PDCA and contain the actionable steps required to build a Business Continuity Management System.

Clause 4: Context of the Organization

Understanding and controlling internal and external risk, and therefore positioning an organization for resilience cannot be effectively achieved without knowledge of its mission, its operational environment, and what constraints may be placed on the delivery of products and services as the result of an adverse event. Clause 4's sub-clauses of understanding of the organization and its context, including the needs and expectations of interested parties, along with the consideration of relevant legal and regulatory requirements, are used to characterize the context of the organization. The criteria to define and document the scope of the Business Continuity Management System, including any exclusions, are listed in this section. It also mandates the establishment and continuous improvement of the Business Continuity Management System and supporting processes according to the requirements of the standard.

ISO 22301 lists a number of specific requirements (shall) and its guidance document (ISO 22313:2912) lists a number of suggestions: for example, a list of who would qualify as an "interested party" that includes competitors and pressure groups. The great majority of the requirements are satisfied through the completion of a robust risk and business impact analysis, as described in Clause 8, but its mandate to document the links between the business continuity policy with the organization's objectives and other policies and with its overall risk management strategy is typically not identified until later in the business continuity management processes.

Clause 5: Leadership

The content of the sub-clauses of Leadership and Commitment, Management Commitment, Policy, and Organizational Roles and Authorities emphasizes the need for all levels of management to integrate support, active involvement, and continuous improvement in a manner that ensures the success of the Business Continuity Management System and its processes. This is in part demonstrated by management's communication and enforcement of the business continuity policy, compliance with the standards and regulatory requirements, and participation in steering committees. Organizational responsibilities and authorities for Business Continuity Management and related positions must be assigned and communicated throughout the organizations.

Clause 6: Planning

Clause 6 refers back to Clause 4 and with its two sub-clauses, Actions to Address Risks and Opportunities and Business Continuity Objectives and Plans to Achieve Them, directs the organization to determine what is required, i.e., the planning steps necessary to implement the Business Continuity Management System. Impediments to the implementation are considered and strategies to prevent or mitigate the impediments are designed into the plan in a manner that integrates this into the management system processes. Methods to check the effectiveness of the strategies along with the inclusion of a continual improvement loop are built into the system and documented.

Depending on the complexity or scope of the Business Continuity Management System, a simple or detailed project plan based on the goals and objectives that assign responsibilities, resources required (see Clause 7), and milestones of the tasks, many of which are included in Clause 8, is documented. A simple listing of the objectives may suffice for a small project, or it may be necessary to use more advanced project planning tools such as a Gantt chart.

Clause 7: Support

Seasoned professionals may confuse the requirement in Clause 7 to determine and provide resources required to meet the business continuity policy and objectives with the resources required to implement individual business continuity strategies, the latter is the more common reference in their experience.

Clause 7 speaks to the need to ensure that all of the resources necessary to put the program in place are identified, including those resources needed to maintain and continually improve the program, but the guidance document refers to all resources necessary that include people, communication, financing, facilities, and infrastructure that some may interpret to be resources necessary for strategy implementation.

It goes on to require that those who have responsibility to affect the program's performance must meet a level of education, training, and experience determined by the organization. When the level of competency is less than adequate, the organization must provide the means to increase the level of competence while documenting its effectiveness. The use of proficient outside consultants, such as a person skilled in Business Impact Analysis, for example, can satisfy some of these requirements. The competency requirement may prove difficult for some large organizations that use a team approach to continue or recover the operations based on functional lines.

These same persons are required to have an understanding of the business continuity policy, their responsibilities under the program, and how their assigned duties contribute to the effectiveness of the business continuity management program as a whole. Awareness of responsibilities under the program should go beyond their scripted duties to include how their participation contributes to a culture of business continuity.

Related to awareness is the sub-clause of Communication. Here the organization is required to figure out what and when it needs to communicate, both internal and external to the organization. Procedures must be developed for both technical and non-technical communication that relays and receives relevant information to or from (non-inclusive):

- Employees and other interested parties within the organization
- Customers and suppliers
- Media
- Community

The systems used to communicate must be tested and available during a disruptive event, i.e., resilient or redundant. A means to receive and act upon threat warning systems must also be incorporated into the system as appropriate.

Finally, Clause 7 spells out the documentation required by the standard and by the organization that it believes is necessary to increase the effectiveness of the Business Continuity Management System. A formal document control system is not necessary, but the standard specifies basic requirements for what to document and how the documents are identified. Title, date, author, and reference number are some of the requirements referenced in the standard. Documents must be available when needed, confidential information must be protected, and some system of version control should exist so that obsolete information is not used. Access to documents and the ability to change them must be controlled and steps taken to prevent the accidental deletion of information. In other words, if documents are electronic, security and access levels should be assigned.

Clause 8: Operation

Clause 8 represents the "Do" component of PDCA and introduces the main work tasks required to develop a Business Continuity Management System. This is accomplished by implementing the processes to manage risk that were developed in Clause 6. Clause 8 again requires some type of documented and managed control over the criteria for the processes, their implementation, milestones, and verification of effective implementation. It introduces the need for a change control process that takes into account the documentation of unintended changes and any corrective actions taken to mitigate them. This is outlined in its first sub-clause, Operational Planning and Control.

The next sub-clause, BIA and Risk Assessment, requires the documented completion of both, giving the manager the option of conducting the risk assessment in accordance with ISO 31000, Risk Management–Principles and Guidelines. ISO 22301 comments that depending on the methodology used for the business impact analysis and risk assessment, they can be completed in any order. The guidance document, however, states that the risk assessment identifies the risks of disruption to the organization's prioritized activities, but this prioritization should be the result of the business impact analysis.

Sub-clause 8.3, Business Continuity Strategy, defines the next operational step by devising continuity strategies and the necessary resources to implement the strategies, based on the results of the business impact analysis and risk assessment. Listed as a strategy, and not part of the business impact analysis, is the requirement to evaluate the business continuity capabilities of suppliers. There is no clarification in the guidance document about whether this applies to all suppliers or to just single source or critical suppliers. Other portions of the sub-clause reference the mitigation and response to impacts.

Documented instructions to competent persons with the authority to carry out the tasks necessary to implement the business continuity strategies are combined with an incident response structure that includes escalation procedures under Sub-clause 8.4: Establish and Implement Business Continuity Procedures. The identification of an incident and how internal and external communication regarding risks and impacts resulting from an incident are emphasized. In other words, this is the organization's written business continuity plan. A crisis management plan (i.e., a public relations plan) and procedures to return to normal operations are required.

Although Sub-clause 9 (Performance Evaluation) refers back to the Sub-clause 8 Exercising and Testing section, the ISO standard spells out the requirements for the organization to conduct regular scenario-based exercises and tests that validate and improve the effectiveness of the Business Continuity Management System. As we will discuss in upcoming chapters, exercising and testing is the best method to train stakeholders in their duties and responsibilities under the Business Continuity Management System and one of the most important steps in the business continuity management process.

Clause 9: Performance Evaluation

In the past, many business continuity managers evaluated the performance of their plans simply by the fact that all plans were completed and updated. Successful testing, often evaluated by subjective criteria, indicated to many of these managers that the plans would work during a real incident. The sub-clauses of this section include: Monitoring, Measurement, Analysis, and Evaluation; Evaluation of Business Continuity Procedures; Internal Audit; and Management Review. Clause 9 forces a higher level of management by establishing metrics to assess the effectiveness of the Business Continuity Management System, developing an internal audit process to ensure its requirements are effectively implemented and maintained, and implementing a system of ongoing management review to monitor its adequacy and effectiveness.

Exercises and audits almost always identify areas of opportunity for improvement and the ISO standard mandates that identified deficient performance results in formal corrective actions. Deficient performance is defined in many ways in the standard and can include nonconformity to the standard, near misses, and adverse trends.

Many business continuity plans include the task to perform an after-action evaluation and report after the plan has been activated owing to an actual incident and to circle back and make improvements based on the results of the review. ISO 22301 requires this step in the management system.

Clause 10: Improvement

Most deficiencies identified in the Business Continuity Management System resulting from an audit, exercise, incident, or re-analysis of the BIA and risk assessment are corrected, but few organizations have a formal corrective action process. Clause 10 requires the organization to retain documented evidence of the nature of the deficiency and the results of any corrective actions. It does not require a corrective action plan per se, but a process that helps the organization take compensatory measures, identify and eliminate the causes of any issues, and search for the extent of the condition, and one that mandates effectiveness reviews of the corrective actions will help to make the task consistent and sustainable.

The ultimate goal of Clause 10, the "Act" element of PDCA, is to continually improve the adequacy and effectiveness of the Business Continuity Management System.

The ASIS standard spells out many of the same requirements, but in differing language and with a different level of detail in what it calls the Organizational Resilience (OR) management system. It views risk and resilience from the reference of threats and risk scenarios and specifically calls out the requirement to establish and maintain strategic programs for the elements of Comprehensive Emergency Management. It is more direct in its approach because it places less emphasis on project planning versus implementation, most of which is included in its Clause 4, OR Management System Requirements (Table 2.3).

Table 2.3 ASIS Clauses Associated With PDCA Steps		
PDCA	**Clause**	**Description**
Plan	4.1	General requirements
	4.2	Organizational Resilience management policy; management commitment
Do	4.3	Planning: Risk assessment and impact analysis; legal and other requirements; objective, targets, and programs
	4.4	Implementation and operation: Resources, roles, responsibilities, and authority; competence, training, and awareness; communication and warning; documentation and control of documents; operational control; incident prevention, preparedness, and response
Check	4.5	Checking (evaluation): Monitoring and measurement; evaluation of compliance and system performance; nonconformity, corrective action, and preventative action; control of records; internal audits
Act	4.6	Management review: Review input and output; maintenance; continual improvement

The 2010 edition of NFPA 1600 was the first release of the standard that aligned its requirements with the PDCA model. It expanded its chapters to include leadership and commitment, requirements for defining performance objectives, and new requirements for records management. Evaluations, corrective actions resulting from the evaluations, and continuous improvement were also blended into the standard. Some of the language in NFPA 1600 is not business friendly. Terms such as "enabling authority" in reference to the development of policy and its requirement to implement a strategy to revise legislation when the organization believes there are limitations in applicable laws may not fit into the organization's existing systems or business mindset.

Similar to the ASIS SPC.1-2009 standard, NFPA 1600 calls for prevention, mitigation, and response strategies. Past issues of the standards have required the use of the Incident Command System (ICS). Unfortunately, elements of ICS (incident action plans and management by objectives) are required under the Incident Management chapter that applies these principles to recovery operations.

2.5 REVIEW

ISO standards are developed by technical committees of subject matter experts after an industry need for the standard is identified. They provide auditable criteria to help ensure the rigor of the business continuity planning capability is sufficient to ensure success during and after a disruptive event. Written to address the needs of all sizes and types of organizations, ISO 22301 and ASIS SPC.1–2009 are designed to integrate with similar standards and management systems that may already be established within the organization. Both ASIS SPC.1–2009 and NFPA 1600 are ANSI standards. ISO 22301, ASIS, and NFPA 1600 are consensus standards.

A management system is "the framework of processes and procedures used to ensure that an organization can fulfill all tasks required to achieve a set of related business objectives." The Deming wheel or Deming circle (PDCA) is an iterative four-step process typically used in business process improvement and decision making. It tells the manager how to establish the elements of a Business Continuity Management System to better manage risk to the organization. The PDCA model is applied at both the strategic level by defining the overall development of the Business Continuity Management System, and at the tactical level by the application of PDCA to each of the processes within the system. All processes begin with an input and end with an output. The PDCA uses these inputs to produce risks management outcomes that fulfill the requirements of the standard (Figure 2.1).

Clauses 0–3 of the ISO and ASIS standards do not contain requirements to develop the Business Continuity Management System. ISO 22301 identifies the remaining clauses (4–10) according to its alignment with PDCA. It defines the "what" that is required to build a business continuity or OR management system, but does not specify how it is to be accomplished.

The ASIS standard spells out many of the same requirements as ISO 22301 but is more direct in its approach to developing its version of the Business Continuity Management System, or by its term, an OR management system. It places a greater emphasis on the treatment of risk from the reference of threats and risk scenarios.

NFPA1600: 2010 and 2013 are now aligned with PDCA and a continuous improvement model, but terms such as "enabling authority" and other similar requirements may not be business friendly.

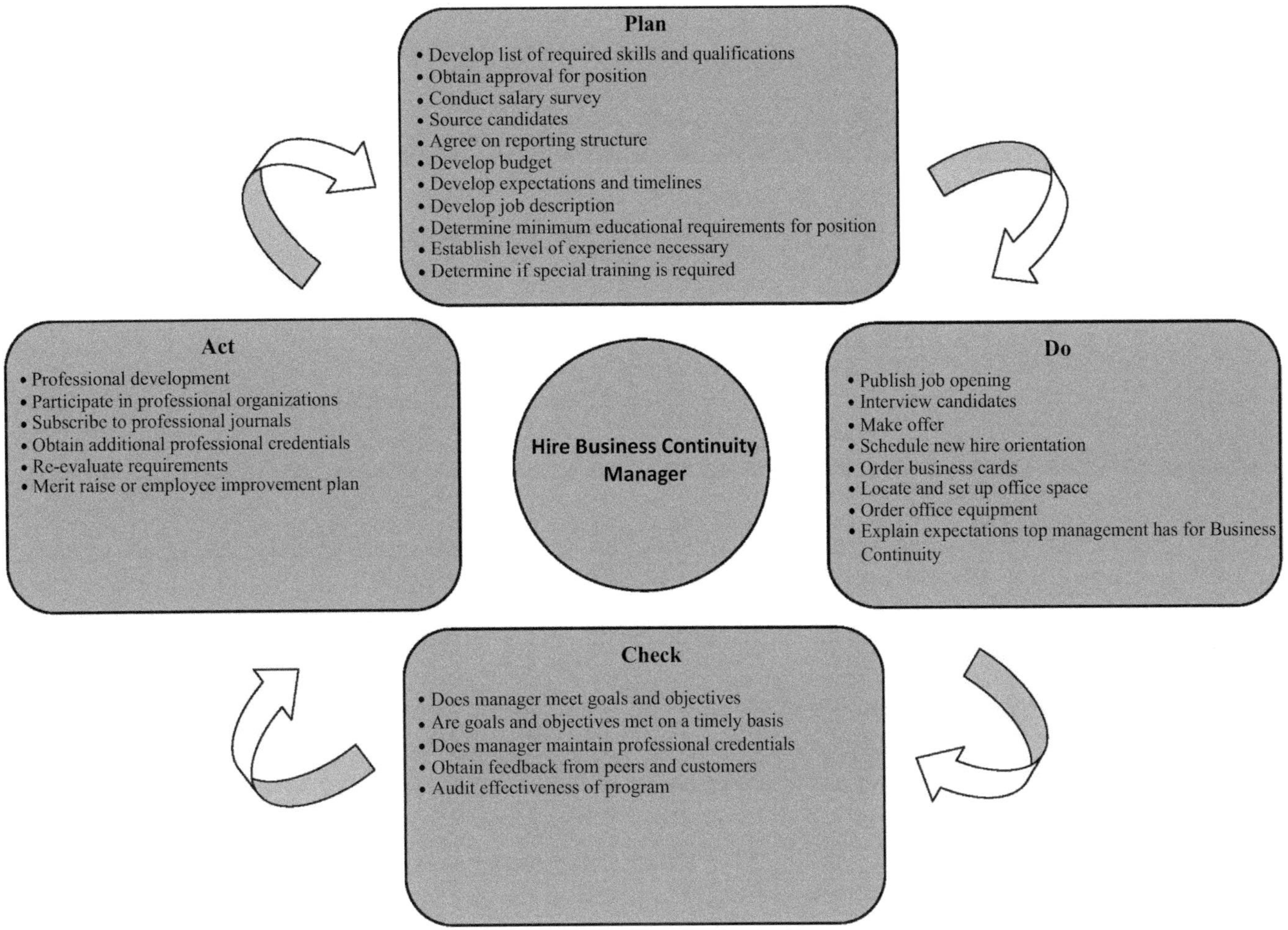

Plan

- Develop list of required skills and qualifications
- Obtain approval for position
- Conduct salary survey
- Source candidates
- Agree on reporting structure
- Develop budget
- Develop expectations and timelines
- Develop job description
- Determine minimum educational requirements for position
- Establish level of experience necessary
- Determine if special training is required

Do

- Publish job opening
- Interview candidates
- Make offer
- Schedule new hire orientation
- Order business cards
- Locate and set up office space
- Order office equipment
- Explain expectations top management has for Business Continuity

Check

- Does manager meet goals and objectives
- Are goals and objectives met on a timely basis
- Does manager maintain professional credentials
- Obtain feedback from peers and customers
- Audit effectiveness of program

Act

- Professional development
- Participate in professional organizations
- Subscribe to professional journals
- Obtain additional professional credentials
- Re-evaluate requirements
- Merit raise or employee improvement plan

Hire Business Continuity Manager

FIGURE 2.1

PDCA wheel: example for recruitment of business continuity management manager.

BIBLIOGRAPHY

International Standard ISO 22301:2012 Societal Security – Business Continuity Management Systems – Requirements.

NFPA 1600 Standard on Disaster/Emergency Management and Business Continuity Programs, 2010 and 2013 editions.

Organizational Resilience: Security, Preparedness, and Continuity Management Systems – Requirements with Guidance for Use, ASIS SPC.1–2009 American National Standard, ASIS International.

BUILDING A BUSINESS CONTINUITY CAPABILITY

3

CHAPTER SUMMARY

Business continuity management identifies risk and the steps taken to treat the risk in a manner that makes the organization resilient to events or conditions that cause disruption. It develops strategies to continue the operation of its functions and keeps its members trained and ready to follow the detailed plans to implement the strategies. It ensures the necessary resources to accomplish these tasks are available when needed.

Before this can materialize, the framework for the business continuity management system (BCMS) must be established. Fundamental to the success of any business continuity management effort is a strong and demonstrated commitment to the program by the organization's top management and the selection of the correct scope and objectives of the program. A complete understanding of the context of the organization by the business continuity staff that leads to the development of policy and procedure that is communicated and enforced is key to putting this process in place. Establishing the method to control the implementation of the management system through the use of project planning and a Gantt chart is best decided at this early stage in the management system's development. The project plan should identify risk to the program. A statement of applicability or a link between the risk assessment and business impact analysis and the controls that are needed to control risk are identified. An RACI (Responsible, Accountable, Consulted, Informed) matrix can illustrate where the communication of roles, responsibilities, and authority throughout the organization are required. Competence and awareness that are commensurate with the level of responsibility are examined and gaps corrected.

Although not all of the standards require the use of a steering committee, a properly selected and chartered steering committee can help to develop and streamline approval of necessary elements of the program and to demonstrate management commitment. It also helps to better integrate the BCMS with all of the organization's business processes.

Part and parcel to building an auditable BCMS is the implementation of an effective document control system. The standards require the maintenance of certain documents and auditors will use them to verify that the BCMS is set up effectively and meeting all of the requirements of the standard. The rigor of the documents must match the complexity of the organization or the scope of the BCMS. The manager should concentrate less on the document control system itself and more on the sufficiency of the creation and maintenance of required documents to ensure the success of the BCMS.

KEY TERMS

Awareness; Business continuity policy; Business continuity working group; Competence; Context of the organization; Documentation; Management commitment (leadership); Project planning; RACI chart; Scope of business continuity management system; SMART business continuity objectives; Statement of applicability; Steering committee.

KEY POINTS

- A strong management commitment must be demonstrated
- Roles, responsibilities, and authority must be communicated

33

- The context of the organization provides the necessary perspective to design the management system
- Competence and awareness should be commensurate with responsibility
- Properly defining the policy, scope, and objectives will help ensure success
- Risk to the management system must be identified and mitigated
- Project planning can be used to track and control the implementation of the program
- Documentation must be adequate to ensure the success of the management system

3.1 INTRODUCTION

Business continuity management identifies risk and the steps taken to treat the risk in a manner that makes the organization resilient to events or conditions that cause disruption. It develops strategies to continue the operation of its functions and keeps its members trained and ready to follow the detailed plans to implement the strategies. It ensures the resources necessary to accomplish these tasks are available when needed.

Before this can materialize, the framework for the BCMS must be established. Management commitment (leadership), selection of the correct scope and objectives of the program, and the development of policy and procedure are key to putting this process in place. Establishing the method to control the implementation of the management system is best decided at this early stage in the management system's development.

3.2 LEADERSHIP

In the recent past, the starting point to build a business continuity capability was to obtain management support. This generally involved getting an agreement from top management that a business continuity plan was a good thing for the organization to pursue. This came with the assumption that management would provide the program with the necessary resources and communicate this support throughout the organization. Generally, the business continuity program manager or the person tasked with developing a business continuity capability would find a member of top management to act as his or her sponsor to champion the business continuity program, armed with justification for the program from the results of a business impact analysis, a regulatory requirement, audit findings, or a customer requirement. Although most people in an organization acknowledge that a business continuity capability is a good thing to have, it was thought that without the backing from top management, participation from individuals responsible for their part of the program would be lacking owing to the limited time resources that many face in today's organizations. Except for occasional (i.e., every few years) emergency operation center or management team exercises, top management awareness and participation in the program were minimal.

Business continuity managers can, but most often in limited ways, be successful in developing a business continuity capability for portions of the organization without a high degree of buy-in from top management, but for the purposes of the standards, this is not sufficient. The standards require a much higher level of active involvement in the BCMS (or the organizational resilience management system) by all levels of management, but in particular top management. This is not a big leap for organizations that already monitor and manage risk on a regular basis and that have an innate understanding of the value of a resilience capability. Absent this understanding, the question of how one goes about gaining the necessary level of top management commitment and support is often asked by those responsible for developing a BCMS. Understanding the relevant driver that supports the need for a program is a key answer to this question. The justifications for a program might include survivability or the prevention of loss as demonstrated by the risk and business impact analysis or to meet a regulatory obligation, but the need or desire to take the program to a higher level required by the standards may also be based on a customer requirement or strategic marketing decision. The risk and business impact analysis are best completed when management support is already established, but before this the help or direct involvement of the organization's risk manager or chief financial officer, who could act as an ideal sponsor, could be solicited. In any event, it is important to communicate to top management from the beginning, either directly or through a sponsor, the breadth of tasks they will be asked to perform. This will require a solid understanding of the scope of the program, its financial and operational consequences, high-level resource requirements, and their responsibilities. For example, top management under International Organization for Standardization (ISO) 22301 is required to some degree to engage in tasks that they may consider to be operational in nature, such as establishing a business continuity policy (in large organizations they usually ratify policy developed by the business continuity manager) and ensuring that internal audits of the BCMS are maintained. They must monitor and ensure the success of the program through the integration of business continuity requirements into all business processes and review metrics and corrective actions to ensure continuous improvement as a regular agenda item at management meetings.

When we speak of management support, we are really speaking of the commitment to business continuity by the entire organization. The requirement that top management and managers included under the scope of the management system demonstrate leadership by motivating and empowering persons to effectively fulfill their responsibilities for business continuity management is demonstrated in a number of ways. Although many of the requirements are satisfied through the normal course of management commitment, the challenge may be in how this is documented. One way to demonstrate the support of top management is by documenting how management assigns responsibility for the management system and how it ensures policy and procedure are carried out. It can exhibit support by active participation in the steering committee, participation in exercises, and by reaffirming the mandate to follow the requirements of the program through communication of the importance of an effective management system in plan introductions, Web pages, policy statements, and other printed documents (financial, marketing, etc.).

3.3 BUSINESS CONTINUITY MANAGER

Top management is also tasked with ensuring that roles and responsibilities along with the requisite authority to support the BCMS are assigned and communicated throughout the relevant parts of the organization, i.e., within the scope of the management system. An RACI chart may be a good way to document the roles and responsibilities. According to the guidance document for ISO 22301, a member of top management should be tasked with the overall responsibility and accountability for the BCMS. This seems to indicate that the intent of the standard is not to task top management with operational duties, but remember that the guidance document does not contain auditable requirements. This person, as well as the entire top management team, is responsible for the organization to meet the goals of the management system.

Depending on the size and complexity of the organization, one or more persons are selected to manage the program. Although these positions can be shared with other responsibilities, they must have the authority to implement and maintain the management system. The ideal competence of a person assigned or hired to this position will include, again depending on the complexity of the organization, managerial experience, certification in business continuity management (see Chapter 1), experience in managing emergency and/or crisis situations, risk management, project planning, and a knowledge of quality management principles, i.e., continuous improvement. A successful manager will have exceptional people and leadership skills and is comfortable working in the high-stress situations likely present if called upon to manage through a disaster. For those not experienced in high-stress emergency circumstances, thorough planning and participation in regular exercises are key to building confidence when needed at the time of a disaster. Attention to detail is also important. Technical knowledge, such as a deep understanding of computer systems, is helpful, but a good manager can rely on the expertise of the subject matter experts. A number of business continuity departments are composed of one person whose predominant experience is risk management or emergency management and another whose background is from information technology.

A written position description (in addition to an RACI chart) as suggested by National Fire Protection Association (NFPA) 1600 should designate the leader of the program as a managerial position. Not only does this assume it will attract a more competent person to manage the program, it is much easier to gain cooperation from those who are too busy or, despite top management's directives or culture change efforts, do not believe in the need for the program.

A number of universities offer business continuity and emergency management programs and many of the business continuity trade organizations provide classes and workshops that feature vendor exhibits so attendees can keep current on the latest knowledge and resources available to manage an effective program. Experienced business continuity managers take advantage of these opportunities to stay abreast of the latest knowledge and ideas, but they are also a great venue for the less experienced.

3.3.1 UNDERSTANDING THE CONTEXT OF THE ORGANIZATION

One of the first tasks for a new (or current manager) is to understand and to document the context of the organization so that he or she is in a position to make decisions or recommendations that position the business continuity or organizational resilience management system for success. This means that the manager must have a deep knowledge of how the organization works that includes its culture, products and services, supply chains (external issues), and technology, risks, and risk tolerance to set up, implement, and continually improve the BCMS. This level of knowledge is generally not gained until the completion of a comprehensive business impact analysis and risk assessment—processes that are not conducted until later in the development of the BCMS. In the end, the business continuity manager should be one of the few people in the organization with the most knowledge of how it actually works. Policy and procedure development and the scope of the management system depend on this knowledge because the standards require they consider organizational goals, the regulatory environment, and legal/regulatory obligations.

Meet initially with the insurance and risk manager to gain an understanding of the organization's risk management strategy and risk appetite. Your manager should be a good source of information on the organization's objectives, especially about how it is to relate to the BCMS. The head of procurement can give the manager a good account of the organization's external requirements and third-party obligations. The legal representative, safety and security, and the human resources manager can complete the initial picture of the legal and regulatory requirements the business continuity manager will need to use to help develop the scope of the BCMS. These meetings are a good way to introduce your program and gain initial support going forward. Marketing materials and financial publications such as stock reports and disclosures are also good sources of information to help understand the context of the organization, its legal and regulatory requirements, and the needs and expectations of interested parties that are relevant to the establishment of the BCMS.

Later in the process, we will be asked to determine the risks and opportunities for the context of the organization that need to be addressed to prevent or mitigate unacceptable risk and to ensure the management system can be effective.

3.4 SCOPE OF THE BCMS

If not already decided, one of the first steps the business continuity manager should take is to determine what the scope of the BCMS will cover and potentially what it will exclude. In other words, what will and will not apply. In a smaller organization, the answer may be simple. One of the keys to constructing an effective business continuity capability in a timely manner is to build on success. Trying to do too much with too little staff in a large, complex organization will likely lead to failure. Granted, the standards mandate top management to allocate resources to support the program, but adjusting the scope of the effort to use a phased approach where necessary could help foster the development of a successful program and to build a positive business continuity culture. Devising the scope of the BCMS is a critical step. A properly defined scope will help to avoid failure by keeping it focused on what is important to the BCMS and will serve as one of the roadmaps auditors will use for review or certification.

This is not to say that a program cannot be developed for a larger organization all at once or that the scope cannot include all of the internal and external requirements of the organization. When I worked for a Fortune 100 company with operations in most continents of the world and with close to 20 subsidiary companies, the Business Continuity Department consisted of a staff of two professionals and one administrative assistant. The operations of the company were highly centralized (not a good business continuity strategy). Long before the international standards were developed, we successfully scoped our approach to one that developed a BCMS for the corporate offices and nearby data center, and then rolled out our program to the remainder of the world by setting up, of all things, planning and audit standards that the country managers were tasked by top management to carry out.

The scope can be narrowed to a division of the organization, a geographical location, or functional areas such as revenue producing departments—something small enough to allow for a positive outcome, but understand that upstream and downstream dependencies (inputs and outputs) that may appear to reside outside the chosen boundaries will necessarily become part of the scope. Often these dependencies such as supply chain risks and other resource needs are not identified until completion of the business impact analysis, a process that occurs later, but initial investigation as described above in Section 3.3.1 is necessary to better decide how the scope needs to be adjusted to include any internal and external dependencies, business functions, legal or contractual requirements, or outside interests. The scope should always consider the context of the organization and address the elements of comprehensive emergency management, especially if using the American Society for Industrial Security (ASIS) standard, but this is probably best addressed in the policy statement. Circle back and refine portions of the scope based on the results of the business impact analysis, although a major adjustment to the scope at that point could be problematic.

Other reasons to narrow the scope can include a desire to implement the BCMS in phases, concentrate on a specific division or product line of the organization, prioritize according to risk or value streams, or simply choose a portion of the organization upon which to build success. An overly complex organization, or the need to quickly put a program in place, limited funding, or a strategic decision to limit costs or to reduce the cost of auditing are also reasons to narrow the scope. A caution on limited funding is in order: An auditor may look at the exclusions to determine whether they retard the effective implementation of the in-scope BCMS, but more importantly, use caution that your scope limitation does not add cost in the end if the scope is later expanded. Your goal (and we are aware of the business constraints) is to make your organization resilient to risk. Even if the scope is narrowed to something that does not apply the BCMS to the entire organization, it must still incorporate and describe internal and external obligations, business objectives, and risks associated with functions, processes, and resources that remain under the more focused effort.

The scope of the BCMS is sometimes included as a part of the policy and procedure document. The scope must be succinct and accurate and, for the purpose of the standards, describe what is excluded from the scope and why it was excluded. The ultimate intent is to design an effective and sustainable BCMS. Lengthy or complex scope or policy documents are less likely to be read in detail, providing an opportunity to miss an important point. ISO 22301 appears to require in the scope statement an explanation of why things were excluded, but this may be better accomplished with a separate document if the justification of the exclusions is lengthy. In writing the scope, focus on high-level descriptions unless it is important to narrow the scope. In other words, "XYZ Corporation's business continuity management system applies only to location X and not to location Z…" Ideally, the scope statement should be one to three paragraphs and can reference other documents.

ASIS requires a statement of applicability that defines "the strategic weighting of *security management* [emphasis our own], preparedness, emergency management, disaster management, crisis management, and business continuity management in developing the management system, based on the risk assessment and impact analysis." Note that the original name of ASIS International was the American Society for Industrial Security.

3.4.1 STATEMENT OF APPLICABILITY

ASIS requires a statement of applicability in its scope of the organizational resilience system. A statement of applicability is familiar to an information technology security professional who has had experience with the implementation of ISO 27001, the standard for information security management systems, but it may be a new concept to the business continuity professional. It is a document, often a spreadsheet or in tabular form, that describes the controls and control objectives that are relevant to the BCMS. In ISO 27001, it records which security measures (controls) were selected from a list in its annex. The control objective is what the organization intends to achieve through the application of a control. Controls are countermeasures for vulnerabilities and risk. The reasons why the controls were chosen, and why the others were excluded must be justified. There is no equivalent annex in the ASIS standard or in ISO 22301 (and this requirement is not mentioned in ISO 22301 or NFPA 1600). The statement of applicability is a link between the risk assessment and business impact analysis and the controls that need to be implemented to eliminate or mitigate the identified risk. It can also list controls that are already implemented or the results of a gap analysis in controls that have not reached maturity.

The statement of applicability is also a document an auditor may use to assess the organizational resilience management system so just enough detail should be included, but not too much to send the auditor in an unnecessary direction. External legal and regulatory requirements, and contractual requirements may need to be considered, but these should naturally be identified in the business impact analysis. It can also be used as, or combined with, a project planning document. It can be signed as adopted by the business continuity manager, the top management representative, or the steering committee and should reference the date of the latest analysis. It can, in its introductory statements, refer to the organizational resilience management system policy and to management's commitment.

Because the statement of applicability is tied to the risk and business impact analysis, and because risk and objectives can change, it must be a living document, updated on a defined basis, likely paralleling the periodicity of the above.

Because the statement of applicability can be a lengthy document, a reference in the scope statement such as "This is in accordance with the statement of applicability dated February 14, 2015" is likely acceptable.

3.5 POLICY

Management commitment is also demonstrated by a strong written business continuity policy and procedure that is communicated, enforced, and understood throughout the organization. Methods to communicate the policy can include a restatement of the policy on a company internal business continuity Web site, discussion at the steering committee meetings, and annual review of the policy by the steering committee, and by making the policy available to outside third parties. Understanding of the policy can be demonstrated by inclusion in tabletop exercises coupled with an appropriate metric, metric reporting, and any necessary corrective action for improvement. A question and answer or FAQ section can be added to the Web page mentioned above.

Top management should therefore develop a business continuity management policy and procedure that aligns with the vision of the organization and that mandates the implementation of all elements of the BCMS, including the elements of comprehensive emergency management. It should affirm the organization's pledge to the protection of life, property, and the environment. It must contain language that enables and directs workers to contribute to the effectiveness and to the continual improvement of the program, especially those in other leadership or managerial positions that affect the BCMS. It should briefly spell out how continual improvement is to be achieved such as the establishment and review of metrics and corrective actions.

ISO 22301 also directs management to show its commitment to the program by making resources available to support the program. This requirement is best stated in the policy but the wording in the standard does not, until later, qualify any limits on what resources it needs to provide. The level of resources that includes funding for the program can be that which is necessary for the effective implementation of the BCMS, but I do not believe it is intended to be an open checkbook. The guidance document later refers to an "appropriate" level of funding as appropriate. An appropriate level is ultimately what is decided by top management, partially determined by the goals stated in the policy and procedure document and should be based on the level of risk they are willing to tolerate and on the recovery time objectives (see later chapters) and the strategies to meet them.

The policy and procedure should follow the organization's normal policy and procedure development process, but for the purposes of the standards, it should provide for the development of business continuity objectives. Any vision or mission statement should also align with that of the organization and can include a discussion of the scope or limitations of the management system, authorities, and delegations, including who is responsible for the management system, and should be signed by a member of top management. It should also define the purpose of the BCMS, as all good policy and procedure documents would normally do. Reference to other documents, standards, policies, or regulations that the management system must follow can be included. Reference to the standard such as "XYZ Corporation's business continuity management policy will conform to the provisions of ISO 22301…" may be acceptable.

The policy should be reviewed for relevance on a regular basis (annually) or when significant changes occur that affect the organization, risk, or BCMS.

Similar to ISO 22301, the ASIS standard also requires a "commitment [within the policy] to comply with all applicable legal requirements and with other requirements to which the organization subscribes." It also directs the policy to consider the nature of the organization's risks but the standard itself, not the guidance document, frames the policy within the scope of the organizational resilience management system. It commands the policy to identify its commitment to life safety, both within and outside the organization as the first priority. The policy should speak in terms of enhanced organizational sustainability and resilience and lists policy ownership and/or a responsible point of contact. ASIS says that the policy should ensure the determination of and documentation of risk tolerance. We believe this to mean verbiage that requires risk and business impact analysis.

Despite the requirements for top management policy, the business continuity manager will invariably encounter someone in the organization who will ask where it is written in policy that he needs to do what you ask. Keep these people in mind when crafting the policy and procedure. Managers who encounter such questions have a long road ahead in their effort to develop a positive business continuity management culture.

3.6 BUSINESS CONTINUITY OBJECTIVES AND PROJECT PLANNING

As part of understanding the context of the organization, ISO 22301 directs the manager to identify external and internal issues within the scope of the management system that could affect the organization's ability to accomplish the goals and objectives of the BCMS. External issues can include legal and regulatory requirements, supply chain risk, partnerships, other interested parties such as customers, and external hazards that can cause disruption. Internal issues could involve risk to products and services, or impediments to the implementation of a continual improvement process or to other activities of the organization. Again, much of the risk is identified through initial interviews and research and ultimately from the results of the risk and business impact analysis.

Many organizations include an objective statement as part of their policy document. Also called strategic priorities or key result areas, these are clear and concise high-level statements of what is to be achieved, generally by whom, and within a timeline that leads the organization toward the resolution of a particular issue. Words such as "explore," "discuss," "commence," "seek," and "encourage" generally do not produce a clear and concise objective. Objectives, as we will learn when we discuss corrective actions, must be SMART: Specific, Measurable, Attainable, Relevant or Realistic, and Timely. They should be consistent with the policy statement. The guidance to ISO 22301 says that something similar to the following business continuity objective may meet the standard's requirements: "By December 31, 2018, XYZ Corporation will have a business continuity program in place that meets our obligations to key customers."

Detailed goals and objectives can be expressed as a project plan (Gantt chart) used to build out the program. This becomes the implementation plan. This is a good point in the process to plot such a plan because the manager can begin to organize other requirements mandated by the standards. A BCMS is not a project but its creation and management can be broken down into a series of projects, some that have no end dates. Be careful that project plan documents reflect the intent to list goals reflected in its title or produce separate documents that retain the requirements mentioned below. Goals and objectives could represent the project tasks (i.e., what needs to be accomplished) such as "complete business impact analysis," "set up steering committee," or "establish continuity teams" and apply as well to any subordinate tasks. As with all good project plans, responsibility is assigned, milestones and due dates are established, risks to the project are examined, and resources are put in place. When assigning responsibility, consider including the RACI. Criteria that will indicate success are documented and metrics are developed where appropriate. The assignment of responsibility will help satisfy the requirement that the business continuity objectives are communicated to the relevant parties (as will the proper distribution of the risk and business impact analysis report and recommendations). The goals must be specific and actionable; using a project planning approach will help avoid poorly focused goals such as "recover after a disaster" or "achieve business continuity." If not already a skilled project planner, this may be a professional development opportunity for the business continuity manager.

Do not miss the point made above: Risk to the project must be identified and documented steps be taken to prevent or mitigate their effect. This and a project plan that lists goals and objectives are archival documents and are updated as things change.

Use caution that embedded goals such as recovery time objectives, risk mitigation projects, or any minimum acceptable service levels are captured and communicated. The recovery time objective, as we will later discuss, is the agreed-upon time frame by management that data or business processes must be reestablished after an outage, and is generally identified in the business impact analysis.

Milestones should be monitored in some manner (metric) such as regular reporting to top management and the steering committee and any resulting corrective actions implemented. This allows the project plan to act as an operational planning and control tool to manage most of the steps required to implement the BCMS and to meet necessary requirements of the standards.

The high-level steps and underlying detailed steps necessary to implement the BCMS are listed, predecessor steps (time ordered) are identified, the expected completion dates are estimated, and the responsible persons are assigned in the plan/chart. This helps to establish criteria for the various processes, but in some cases additional documents to describe such criteria such as the business impact analysis will be necessary. Progress toward the milestones and deliverables is tracked and reported as described above. Because outsourced processes must be controlled, they should be added to the project plan. The Gantt chart can help to track if progress is carried out as planned.

If a Gantt chart is not used, heat mapping to show progress toward a milestone or metric is an effective way to motivate individuals to reach their goals or deliverables (the heat map can, of course, be used in conjunction with a Gantt chart). A heat map can also show that processes have been carried out as planned (keep supporting documentation). In this application of heat mapping, red, yellow, or green is assigned to represent progress. Blue is often used to show the completion of a task in place of green, which is used to indicate that progress is within expectations or on schedule. This practice is especially effective when displayed to a group of peers or top managers. People simply do not like to see a red mark next to their name. It helps to easily visualize progress (or lack of progress) toward the goal and can therefore help to keep projects and assignments on track.

The project plan should cover the entire scope and objectives of the program. Preparedness, response, mitigation, risk and business impact analysis, and so on should be plotted. Adjustments to timelines will be made as conditions and circumstances warrant. Changes to the plan must be checked and monitored to ensure that they do not cause adverse effects.

The resources identified in the project plan will help to show resource requirements that management will need to support to make the program successful. It will help to justify capital and expense budgets going forward to fund the management system and its requirements, including that needed to administer the program.

3.7 COMPETENCE AND AWARENESS

As the manager is developing the project plan and assigning responsibility for each step or action, this is a good time to begin deciding and documenting the level of competence that is required for the responsible parties to carry out their obligations under the BCMS. By looking at a project plan, you should be able to identify most of the people, both specifically and in general, who have responsibility under the plan. The manager can then determine what competencies are required for these groups of participants. A matrix can be developed to show this relationship. Once the manager has identified the required competencies, he or she must see how they align with the actual skills and experience of those persons tasked with carrying out their responsibilities. Obviously, this is a continuing process as the management system matures. The assistance of the human resources department may be able to supply information on individual experience and training or the manager can ask for verification of experience directly from those involved. Any gaps are filled through an appropriate level of awareness, training, or mentoring, or by finding someone better suited for the tasks. Qualified consultants can also be engaged to fill any gaps. In a large organization, the creation of a personal development program could be a daunting task unless the manager can delegate this task to other managers or to team leaders to administer training against a list of required competencies and classes. Because competence and understanding must be demonstrated, written examinations or practical evaluations must be maintained. Some managers argue that it would be a simpler task, especially in organizations with a high level of employee turnover, to just assume nobody has the required level of competence (apart from their normal duties) and begin the training and awareness program from that perspective.

Competence should be commensurate with responsibility. Therefore, the business continuity management leader and staff must maintain a high level of competence. Any consultants retained to augment or to advise staff should share a similar requirement. Those responsible for the BCMS should come into the organization with strong experience (at least 5 years) in management and in the technical aspects of managing a business continuity program, a business continuity certification such as the Certified Business Continuity Professional (see Chapter 1). Experience in the ISO certification process is a plus if that is the intent of the program. See the Appendix for suggested qualifications.

In general, everyone in the organization will need to have an awareness of the existence of the policy and their responsibilities under the plan during and after a disaster. This applies even to people who are not assigned duties. They will need to know how information is communicated to them to stay at home, come back to work, or report to an alternate site, and the status of the organization as it responds to an emergency.

Because disasters tend to occur during the off hours, all members of the organization should be aware of home preparedness to help ensure the safety of themselves and their families, and to better ensure their ability to return to work in a timely manner. Home preparedness is a new requirement under NFPA 1600:2013.

Training and awareness can be delivered in a number of ways depending on the subject and audience (Figure 3.1). Examples include:

• Business continuity management system Web page	• Classroom training
• Monthly business continuity professional (BCP) newsletter	• On-line classes
• 1:1 Meetings, mentoring	• Help desk
• BCP orientation presentation	• Disaster fairs
• Exercises: Tabletop, relocation, full-scale	• Posters
• Educational games highlighting BCP	• Discussion in staff meetings
• Membership in professional organizations	• Attendance at professional workshops
• Subscription professional publications	• Help files/FAQ
• Business Impact Analysis (BIA) interview meetings	• Professional certification classes
• Response to unplanned incidents	• Computer based training
• Timely subjects presented to steering committee	
• Local seminars and training (Red Cross, Community Emergency Response Team (CERT))	

3.8 DOCUMENT CONTROL

Part and parcel to building an auditable BCMS is the implementation or alignment with an effective document control system. The standards require the maintenance of certain documents, and auditors look closely at how well the documents are protected against loss, misinterpretation, use of outdated versions, and disclosure of confidential information or tampering with the document irrespective of the type of media in which the documents reside (i.e., paper, electronic, photographic). Auditors will also use them to verify that the BCMS is set up effectively and meeting all of the requirements of the standard.

The business continuity manager should use any document control system already established within the organization as long as it contains the following elements. The information technology or manufacturing functions may already have a usable system in operation. The document control system should also follow the organization's achieving requirements or become consistent with any regulatory retention obligations. If one is not in use, the following should be incorporated into a new system for all documents, including those received from outside the organization that are relevant to the BCMS:

- All documents include title, name, date, author number, version, or revision control
- Reviewed and approved by signatures
- Type of media used and approved. If the documents reside in a software program, include version number and language
- Available when needed. This may cross over from document control into business continuity management by ensuring teams have access to information on a variety of media in alternate locations, i.e., redundancy through paper, cloud, tablet, etc.
- Protected from loss (i.e., backed up), inadvertent change (read-only), deletion, or breach of confidentiality

Training requirements matrix (roles across the top, training topics down the side):

Training Topic	Human Resources Team	Purchasing Team	BCP Professional Staff	Document Management	Plan Maintenance	Software Program	Resilience at home (individuals)	Cross trained individuals	Management	EOC Team and Support	Emergency Response Team	Remote workers (alternate site)	IT Support Team	Continuity team Members	Continuity Team leaders	Steering Committee	Customers	All employees	New employees
New Hire Orientation																			X
RTO, RPO, Etc.									X					X	X	X		X	X
Risk Appetite			X						X	X	X	X		X	X	X	X	X	X
Crisis Communication			X						X	X	X	X	X	X	X	X	X	X	X
Initial Damage Assessment			X					X	X	X	X	X	X	X	X	X	X		
Disaster Fairs			X								X	X		X	X	X	X		
Plan Maintenance			X	X	X				X	X	X		X	X	X	X	X	X	X
Continual Improvement		X	X	X	X			X	X	X	X	X	X	X	X	X	X	X	X
First Aid / CPR		X	X	X				X	X	X	X	X	X	X	X	X	X	X	
Emergency management / ICS		X	X				X				X	X	X	X	X	X	X	X	X
BCP Software Tools			X		X	X			X		X	X	X	X	X	X			
Technical Communication		X	X						X	X	X	X	X	X	X		X	X	
BCP Basics		X	X	X	X				X	X	X	X		X	X	X	X	X	X
Risk Analysis			X							X					X	X	X		
Business Impact Analysis			X		X				X		X		X	X	X		X	X	
Supply Chain Monitoring		X	X		X				X		X			X	X		X	X	
Pandemic Planning			X					X	X	X	X		X	X	X	X	X	X	X
Plan Activation		X	X	X	X			X	X	X	X	X	X	X	X	X	X	X	X
Roles and Expectations under the BCMS		X	X	X	X				X	X	X	X	X	X	X	X	X	X	X
Benefits of Program		X	X	X	X				X	X	X	X	X	X	X	X	X	X	X
Consequences of Nonconformance		X	X	X	X	X			X	X	X	X	X	X	X	X	X	X	
Communication with the EOC/Teams		X	X	X	X	X					X	X	X	X	X	X	X		
Plan Orientation Meetings		X	X	X	X				X	X	X	X	X	X	X	X	X	X	X

FIGURE 3.1

Training requirements matrix example.

- A version control process that also prevents the use of obsolete information
- Access control (physical and electronic)
- Review, update, and reapprove as applicable

The manager should concentrate less on the document control system itself and more on the sufficiency of the creation and maintenance of documents to ensure the success of the BCMS.

The rigor of the documents must match the complexity of the organization and the scope of the BCMS. If your goal is certification, you may have satisfied each requirement perfectly and have in place a world-class management system, but if this is not apparent in the documents, your goal will fall short. A cynic may argue that detailed documentation is the most important element of the program. For example, the manager must document the context of the organization. Subject headings might include, depending on the size and complexity of the organization, the following:

1. Introduction
   a. Management commitment
   b. Purpose of the document
2. Description of the organization
   a. Overview of the organization
   b. Type of organization, structure, and other vital statistics
   c. Geographical areas covered
   d. History of organization
   e. Mission, vision, outlook
   f. Culture of the organization
   g. Activities
   h. Technology
   i. Products and/or services, customers
      – Rank or describe by revenue
   j. Partnerships and third-party relationships
   k. Supply chain dependencies and/or critical vendors
   l. Major functional areas (Organization chart)
3. Policies and objectives
   a. Business policies
   b. Objectives
   c. Business continuity requirements
4. Organizational risk
   a. Risk philosophy and risk appetite
   b. Business obligations
   c. Internal risk
      – Risks to BCMS
   d. External risk
      – Regulatory environment
      – Natural hazards
   e. Impacts of disruptive events
   f. Risk mitigation

5. Purpose and scope of the BCMS
   a. Exclusions
   b. Capital and expense budget
6. Other requirements and information

Software programs and templates are available on the Internet to assist with the completion of the documentation requirements.

3.9 STEERING COMMITTEE

A properly selected and chartered steering committee can assist the business continuity manager to develop and streamline approval of necessary elements of the program. It helps to demonstrate management commitment through the inclusion of top management membership and to better integrate the BCMS with all of the organization's business processes because it is often composed of members from major functional units. Sometimes called the business continuity advisory board or advisory committee, it can help to design and approve policy, scope, and objectives. It will discuss and approve high-level strategies, mitigation efforts, and procedures thus helping with buy-in from all of the participants because they have had a chance discuss the pros and cons of issues brought before it, arriving in the end at a consensus going forward. A steering committee can add consistency to the process because each member will receive the same message and direction and provide a conduit for communication of business continuity information throughout the organization. Both ASIS and NFPA 1600 mandate the use of a steering committee (ISO 22301 recommends it through its guidance standard).

Many managers believe that steering committees are necessary evils that must be led by a strong manager. Personalities can get in the way of decision making, causing unnecessary delays especially if the manager is not an experienced leader. Scope creep, overanalysis, or taking a wrong direction that an influential member believes is correct can also delay progress. One advantage of a steering committee is it can sustain momentum for the program, but if poorly managed, it can have the opposite effect. One of the biggest reasons business continuity programs fail is the loss of momentum. Some corporate cultures are simply not conducive to steering committees.

The committee should be composed of the organization's power brokers (some would argue with this premise) and representatives from most major functional units, but use caution so that the committee is not so large that it becomes difficult to make decisions or so small that the advantages described above are negated. Decisions made by the committee must consider the environment and needs of all the affected business units within the scope of the management system.

The steering committee can be tasked with the oversight of all plans and activities of the management system or simply as a forum for decision making in the selection of strategies, exercise schedules, policy development, and resource approval, such as which software tool to use.

The committee should have a charter and its members should be individually chartered by top management or by the most senior member of the workgroup. The charter will describe duties or objectives of the committee, under whose authority it is formed (member of top management), and designate a top management person who is the committee sponsor (person accountable). It can include a problem statement and list deliverables. It can mention a scope but it should be worded in a way that does not restrict the business continuity manager from making decisions without committee approval, especially if such a decision is required when the committee cannot meet. It can also mention who is to participate. Project charters typically have an end date, but the business continuity steering committee should be never-ending.

A charter for each participant, specifically naming the individual, can have an end date, usually after a 1-year period. If the organization or individual wishes to continue after this time, it can be renewed. Chartering an individual to participate on the committee signals the importance of the assignment to the committee member and to the member's management that the time required to participate has been approved by the organization.

The business continuity manager should lead the committee and schedule regular meetings in advance with discussion topics and deliverables selected well ahead of time. Designate a nonparticipating member as the scribe who will forward meeting minutes to the committee and top management. The meetings can include subject matter experts and outside speakers.

3.9.1 BUSINESS CONTINUITY WORKING GROUP

There are a number of ways in which the business continuity manager can facilitate the development of the management system and the resulting continuity capability. One common method is to task each team leader to develop the instructions to the team that implement the agreed-upon strategies and to list the resources necessary to support resilience. Another method often used is to form a business continuity working group composed of team leaders that acts as sort of a subgroup to the steering committee. The members of the working group can better understand the tasks they are asked to complete through discussion with members from other functional units, which allows them to maintain consistency with the other units. Although this may not produce results as quickly as other methods, it provides an opportunity to develop the competence of the team leaders by selecting a monthly topic, providing training and discussion on how the teams can apply the topic to their plans, and then returning in a month to discuss the completed results. Topics will follow the established project plan and can include planning elements such as the accountability of employees after a disaster, management succession within their functional units, vital records, document control, and so forth.

3.10 REVIEW

Fundamental to the success of any business continuity management effort is a strong and demonstrated commitment to the program by the organization's top management. When developing a BCMS under the standards, the level of participation by top management is heightened. Top management must monitor and ensure the success of the program through the integration of business continuity requirements into all business processes, review metrics and corrective actions to ensure continuous improvement, and empower all participants to carry out their tasks. Much of the management participation can be absorbed by a single member of the top management team who is tasked with the overall responsibility for the program.

Competent business continuity staff with the authority to implement the management system is selected. This can be a single person with duties other than business continuity, depending on the size and complexity of the organization.

The manager must understand the organization and how it works, including its culture, products and services, supply chains (external issues), and technology, risks, and risk tolerance. This allows the manager to keep the proper organizational perspective when designing, implementing, and improving the program.

Defining the scope of the BCMS is an important step because it is an element that can help to enable success or failure of the program. The description of the scope of the management system that is often included as part of the policy and procedure document should be succinct, accurate, and high-level, and describe any exclusions, i.e., what is out of scope.

A statement of applicability is required by the ASIS standard. This is a document that describes the controls and control objectives that are relevant to the BCMS. In ISO 27001, it records which security measures (controls) were selected from a list in its Annex. The control objective is what the organization intends to achieve through the application of a control. The reasons why the controls were chosen and why the others were excluded must be justified. The statement of applicability is a link between the risk assessment and business impact analysis and the controls that need to be implemented to eliminate or mitigate the identified risk. It should be referenced in the scope statement.

Management commitment is also demonstrated by a strong written business continuity policy and procedure that is communicated, enforced, understood throughout the organization, and available to third parties. It should align with the vision of the organization and mandate the implementation of all elements of the BCMS, including the elements of comprehensive emergency management. It should affirm the organization's pledge to the protection of life, property, and the environment and must contain language that directs workers to contribute to the effectiveness and continual improvement of the program. It should briefly spell out how continual improvement is to be achieved. It must show that resources necessary for the program's success will be available. Reference to other documents, standards, policies, or regulations that the management system must follow can be included. The policy and procedure must be reviewed and updated as appropriate on a situational or regular basis.

The manager must identify external and internal issues within the scope of the management system that could affect the organization's ability to accomplish the goals and objectives of the BCMS. But on a higher level, goals are often included as part of the policy and procedure document. Detailed goals and objectives that identify operational planning and control can be documented with a project plan. Risk to the project must be identified and documented steps taken to prevent or mitigate their effect. A Gantt chart and heat mapping can be used to act as an operational planning and control tool to manage most of the steps required to implement the BCMS and meet necessary requirements of the standards.

Competence should be commensurate with responsibility. The level of competence that is required for the parties responsible to carry out their obligations under the BCMS must be identified and any gaps between the requirements and individual competence closed. Competence and understanding must be demonstrated. In general, everyone in the organization will need to have an awareness of the existence of the policy and their responsibilities under the plan during and after a disaster. This applies even to people who are not assigned duties.

The standards require the maintenance of certain documents, and auditors look closely at how well the documents are protected against loss, misinterpretation, use of outdated versions, and disclosure of confidential information or tampering with the document irrespective of the type of media in which the documents reside (i.e., paper, electronic, photographic). Auditors will also use them to verify that the BCMS is set up effectively and meeting all of the requirements of the standard. The manager should concentrate less on the document control system itself and more on the sufficiency of the creation and maintenance of documents to ensure the success of the BCMS. The rigor of the documents must match the complexity of the organization and the scope of the BCMS.

A properly selected and chartered steering committee can help to develop and streamline approval of necessary elements of the program and demonstrate management commitment by including a member of top management on the committee. It also helps to better integrate the BCMS with all of the organization's business processes. There are advantages and disadvantages to steering committees, but they are required under most of the standards. A business continuity working group can be used to help implement portions of the BCMS.

BIBLIOGRAPHY

NFPA 1600. Standard on Disaster/Emergency Management and Business Continuity Programs, 2010 and 2013 editions.

EMERGENCY MANAGEMENT— PREPAREDNESS AND RESPONSE

4

CHAPTER SUMMARY

Fundamental to a successful business continuity management system that makes the organization resilient to disaster is the application of the elements of emergency management: mitigation, prevention and preparedness, response, and recovery (continuity). Organizations that are prepared are better positioned to respond to disruptive events. A documented and tested emergency response capability can prevent a situation from becoming a disruptive event. The standards treat these elements in different ways, both directly and indirectly. We focus here on prevention and response.

An emergency is almost always a very visible event that will have both short- and long-term ramifications for all stakeholders affected by the emergency. The lack of a coordinated response can result in regulatory and civil liability to the organization. The slow government response to Hurricane Katrina and the aftermath of many other disasters has demonstrated that organizations and households cannot depend on the services we would normally expect for a number of days after the event. Organizations that prepare their employees to meet the challenges of a disaster through awareness and training by sponsoring citizen emergency response teams, stockpiling resources ahead of time, and preparing home disaster plans such as those found on the American Red Cross or Federal Emergency Management Agency Web sites enable employees to return to work sooner to begin continuity or recovery operations.

Managers must prepare for their response to emergencies by identifying foreseeable situations, understanding their cause and effects, and devising emergency response plans and procedures (emergency plan implementing procedures) ahead of time. Using these plans, well-trained groups of volunteer employees are organized into emergency response teams (ERTs) whose purpose is to stabilize the effects of an emergency or, on a limited basis, act as the primary response to emergencies if the response by governmental agencies such as fire or medical services is delayed for extended periods of time.

The ERTs can organize themselves under the incident command system (ICS). The standards allude to its use both for emergency response and business continuity planning, and in some cases the use of ICS is a regulatory requirement. Even if the organization decides not to use the ICS, emergency response leaders and the business continuity system manager must be aware of how ICS works because they will likely interface with government response services who use this tactical incident management system.

KEY TERMS

American Red Cross; Citizen emergency response teams (CERT); Emergency management; Emergency plan implementing procedure (EPIP); Emergency provisions; Emergency response plan; Emergency response team; Go bags; Incident command system; Preparedness; Response; Training and awareness.

KEY POINTS

- Organizations that are prepared are better positioned to respond to disruptive events
- An effective business continuity management system considers all of the elements of emergency management

- Businesses organizations must be prepared to provide their own emergency services after a regional disaster
- An emergency response capability is required by the standards
- An emergency action plan is a regulatory requirement
- Emergency response teams can help to stabilize the effects from an emergency situation
- The incident command system is used to respond to an emergency or to structure business continuity

4.1 INTRODUCTION

Organizations that are prepared are better positioned to respond to disruptive events. A documented and tested emergency response capability can prevent a situation from becoming a disruptive event. Prevented or mitigated hazards can eliminate many of the risks that lead to disruption. The elements of emergency management—prevention, preparedness, mitigation, response, and recovery—combine to maximize the resilience of the organization. Business continuity managers who understand and apply these elements to their management system are the most successful in developing a program that will meet the above objectives. The standards treat these in different ways, both directly and indirectly. Regardless of what the standards do or do not require, an effective business continuity management system must consider all of these elements. We will discuss prevention, mitigation, and recovery (continuity) in later chapters.

The response to an incident is almost always a visible event that will have both short- and long-term ramifications for the organization, responders, the business continuity or emergency manager, and any victims injured as a result of the incident. An emergency response capability of some degree is increasingly becoming a regulatory requirement and the liability to the organization in civil court for the lack of a program can be serious. The reputation of the organization and business continuity manager will run parallel to the success or failure of the response.

4.2 PREPAREDNESS

Preparedness, according to the American Society for Industrial Security (ASIS), is the "activities, programs, and systems developed and implemented prior to an incident that may be used to support and enhance mitigation of, response to, and recovery from disruptions, disasters, or emergencies." It strengthens the plans we put in place to respond to and recover from all types of events. Preparedness on the governmental level encompasses all of the steps taken by national, state, and local organizations to protect its communities, assets, and delivery of services. The business continuity manager must be aware of the government's preparedness efforts, especially those on the national level, to ensure their planning considers and, as applicable, coordinates with their efforts.

Some preparedness will be built into the continuity strategies. Developing plans for on-site child day care in the likely case that schools will be closed after a regional disaster will allow caregivers to return to work instead of staying home to supervise children is an example of preparedness that can be part of the human resources continuity team plan.

Examples of what could be a long list of preparedness include:

- Design and installation of warning systems
- Travel advisories
- Public–private (government–business) partnerships

- Preplanning in general
- Setting up intelligence functions
- Establishing lines of communication with suppliers
- Agreements and memos of understanding with third parties
- Planning and plan documentation
- Purchase, training and testing of two-way radios, satellite phones, and other forms of redundant communication
- Cameras for damage assessment and documentation
- Safety equipment for in-house emergency response personnel such as safety glasses, gloves, and handheld toxic gas detectors

The basic components of preparedness are planning, equipment and resources, training and education, and exercises. It could be said that all of the effort to set up the business continuity management system leading up to the point of emergency response or activation of the continuity plan is preparedness.

Preparedness also relates back to the risk and business impact analysis in which the relevant hazards and risk are identified. In other words, those organizations located in the Midwest of the United States would not want to devote time and resources to prepare for a tsunami. The analysis can also reveal the current level of preparedness, allowing the manager to take steps to close any gaps, especially from the perspective of equipment and other resource needs.

The standards require management to devote resources to support the management system and this may include preparedness related to continuity strategies. Materials, supplies, and services needed to respond to an event must be in place and ready for use. These must be preidentified and available for use at a time when materials or services will be in short supply and in high demand.

Specific training and awareness is preparedness. Many local fire departments hold classes that prepare residents to react to emergencies and disasters because, after a regional disaster, the community will not be able to depend on help from governmental services including the police, fire, and medical services for a number of days to weeks. These classes allow the formation of citizen emergency response teams or neighborhood emergency response teams to conduct light rescue operations, tend to the injured, and practice basic fire safety and control. Conditions to expect postdisaster, home preparedness, and hazard mitigation are also included in the curriculum. Organizations should encourage or sponsor the formation of these teams because the training an employee receives has a direct benefit to the organization after a disaster.

Disasters are more likely to happen during the nonworking hours (assuming we are working an 8-hour shift) so preparedness at home is an important aspect of the business continuity management system. Home preparedness is required under National Fire Protection Association (NFPA) 1600:2013. The fewer issues employees must deal with at home means they are able to return to work to begin recovery operations, or if the event occurs during working hours, they are more likely to remain at work when they know their families and property are safe. The organization should establish a business continuity intranet Web page that includes links to sites that support home preparedness. These sites include the Red Cross, the Federal Emergency Management Agency's (FEMA) www.ready.gov, and some state emergency services agencies. Local utilities may also have safety information on their Web pages. The business continuity management staff must be well versed in these resources and the steps workers need to accomplish to make their home environment resistant to disasters and terrorist acts. Basic topics can include (many of these topics also apply to the work environment):

54

- Resources for children and the elderly
- Care for pets after a disaster
- Special consideration for the handicapped
- Instructions for emergency contact and meeting locations. During a disaster it may be easier to make phone calls out of the area. If family and friends are separated at the time of the disaster, a phone number out of the area that members can call to leave messages about their status and location is reassuring. Wallet cards can be issued by the organization that contain emergency phone numbers and Web addresses for company disaster information and instructions. A field for employees to write in their out-of-area emergency contact number and meeting location can be included on the card. Also if separated, a predetermined meeting location that is generally safe and central to where members may be located can serve as a get-together place if it is not practical to meet at home
- Emergency supplies (food, water, medical, and sanitary)
- Structural and nonstructural mitigation
- Insurance and disaster finance considerations and documentation
- Fire prevention and control
- Shelter-in-place instructions
- Home disaster plans
- Warnings and media sources
- Evacuation routes

Many large cities have disaster preparedness departments that can be a resource to the manager to help craft home preparedness programs.

Exercises and drills are also a form of preparedness (we cover this in a later chapter). These are especially important for high-risk or high-consequence physical response requirements such as rescue, fire control, and first aid/CPR. As we will say later, the tasks we will require participants in the management system, including the emergency response teams (ERTs), to carry out must be repeatedly practiced in varying forms.

Preparedness used to be thought of in terms of the stockpiling of emergency provisions and supplies to last for a 3 or more day period. Hurricane Katrina and other disasters taught us to expand this period to a 5- to 7-day supply and some emergency managers suggest a 2-week or more supply at home. During or after a regional disaster, certain employees may need to remain at work, or many may be trapped at work owing to impassible roads or other conditions that require the need to shelter in place. The organization will be liable for the care and safety of these employees. After a regional disaster, food and water could be in short supply and time-consuming to transport. Electricity may be out affecting gasoline pumps, point of sale terminals, and bank ATM machines. One approach organizations use to prepare for this contingency is to stockpile food, water, tents, and rescue equipment in large shipping containers placed in the parking lot or other location on their property. This makes sense for large and nonperishable items but food and water must be replaced roughly every 3–5 years, a process that can be expensive. Also, placing all of the supplies in one location makes them more vulnerable to damage, theft, or sabotage. This approach cannot provide for the needs of individual employees. Another approach, one that does provide for the needs of individual employees, is to issue each employee a carry bag, often referred as a "go bag" of supplies, when they are hired. These bags can carry the company logo and contain food bars, water, light sticks or flashlight and battery, basic first aid supplies, thermal blanket, and other simple supplies. Laminated instructions for employees to use subsequent to a disaster can be included in the bags (be sure to list this as an item in the awareness document). Employees are encouraged to personalize the contents with items such as reading glasses, prescription medication (remember to change out to retain freshness), pictures of family, old tennis shoes (in case you want to hike home), and clean underwear (after the 1989 Loma Prieta Earthquake, despite a ship full of supplies sitting off the coast, the top requests of the near-epicenter city of Watsonville, California was for a shower and clean underwear). A copy of an old utility bill that contains the name of the employee is also useful in case proof of residence is required to pass through road closures or areas restricted to local residents only. These go bags are kept in the employee's desk or trunk of the car. There are many Web sites that contain a list of suggested contents of the bag as well as companies that make them available to the employer.

The business continuity manager should make use of in-house training professionals and perhaps marketing professionals to ensure preparedness material is presented in a manner that the organizational population will find relevant and actionable. Interest in preparedness training is usually high, but in the end, few take action on what they have learned. Intentions are good, but the daily hazards of everyday life and the lack of an imminent hazard tend to de-prioritize the necessary action. This is one reason why frequent reminders in various forms are necessary. Positive incentives such as a raffle for a vacation trip for those who can verify that they have purchased or put together a home disaster kit along with a simple home disaster plan can produce the desired results. Participants at a disaster preparedness fair were given a list of 10 questions they could answer by visiting the booths and reading information posted around the room. Questions ranged from what local radio station provides 24-hour news and emergency information to the organization's emergency information number, and what to do if they find a downed electrical wire. The questionnaires with all correct answers were placed in a basket for prize drawing for local products and services. We made the questions fun and a bit difficult, so we were liberal in correcting the answers. We made sure everybody scored 100%.

4.3 RESPONSE

The standards view response in different ways. One view is that incident response is the immediate actions to control a disruptive event such as a fire; the other view is of the action the continuity teams would take to continue or to recover their operations. One could also look at response from the information technology perspective if a critical piece of technology fails or the network is under attack. ASIS is clear on this issue, with its requirement to establish and maintain one or more strategic programs for emergency response: "the initial response to a disruptive incident involving the protection of people and property from immediate harm," but it also mixes incident response with continuity operations. NFPA 1600 is more expansive with its definition: "the immediate and ongoing activities, tasks, programs, and systems to manage the effects of an incident that threatens life, property, operations, or the environment." ASIS goes on to say that "an emergency is usually a disruptive event or condition that can often be anticipated or prepared for, but seldom exactly foreseen." This is an interesting comment because courts and regulators are increasingly holding organizations liable for the absence of effective emergency response plans for foreseeable incidents. Many business continuity situations start with some type of emergency, be it a fire, flood, hurricane, or terrorist incident. Organizations must therefore be in a position to respond to situations they can reasonably anticipate during normal conditions and conditions that result from a disastrous event. Action taken to control an emergency will reduce injuries, protect assets or mitigate their loss, help protect the environment, and position the organization for a rapid recovery. Ultimately, an effective response to an emergency, like good mitigation efforts, may prevent the escalation to a continuity situation.

Emergency response is generally intended to stabilize an incident until the arrival of governmental services such as the police, fire department, or paramedics. But, as mentioned above, organizations are the last on the government's response priority list after a regional disaster, the logic being that organizations have the resources to take care of themselves. Organizations must develop the capability to protect their population and assets during these times that can range from days to weeks.

The manager must identify foreseeable hazards that can affect the organization and its population. The manager must have a higher level of understanding of the characteristics of the hazards than non-professionals so that effective prevention, mitigation, and response programs are operational and effective. The manager must also understand any warning systems associated with the hazards. In addition, they must understand how people do and do not react to emergency situations. Hazards are identified through the risk and business impact analysis that will allow the manager to make decisions about the probability and consequence of their occurrence. This includes identification and examination of past emergencies, incident reports, and hazards experienced at similar types of organizations. Typical hazards generic to most organizations, depending on location, include:

- Bomb and terrorist threats
- Chemical or biological attack
- Earthquake
- Evacuation planning
- Fires
- Floods
- Hazardous materials incidents
- Hurricanes
- Severe weather
- Power failure
- Serious injury or illness
- Workplace violence

The publication *Risk Analysis and the Security Survey*, 4th ed. (James F. Broder and Eugene Tucker, Elsevier, 2012) contains an extensive chapter that lists descriptive information on many hazards along with detailed steps the manager can take to prevent and mitigate, prepare for, and respond to an emergency created by the hazard. It also contains some recovery steps typically associated with the hazard.

4.3.1 EMERGENCY RESPONSE PROGRAM AND PLAN

An emergency response program begins with the commitment of senior management to support the program and the assignment of responsibility for the development of the program. Document this responsibility in the plan. This can be the business continuity manager, security or safety manager, or other position that makes sense to the organization. Along with the responsibility is the delegation of authority to manage the emergency, which may mean the ability to direct personnel of higher rank within the organization. The manager or a planning team will then:

- Identify the foreseeable hazards as mentioned above that could affect the organization's population, assets, and operations within the scope of the program. The process of the hazard identification must also identify any legal, regulatory (code) requirements associated with the response to the hazard after the risk they pose has been treated. Consider hazards posed by nearby third-party operations
- Establish the response system or emergency organizational structure appropriate to the size and complexity of the response based on the identified risk. This can be as basic as a floor warden system for evacuations as long as clear lines of management and response authority are established, or it can be a full ERT that is structured under the incident command system (ICS)
- Ensure that the identified hazards are mitigated or prepared for if not done previously
- Investigate the opportunity for public–private partnerships or the need to work with local response agencies. Coordinate response protocols and if possible, interoperability of communications. Share hazard information, prefire plans, floor plans, contact information, and staging areas. Print identification cards for the response team members, signed by the local police chief or county emergency manager, that allow them to cross police lines to respond to an emergency from outside the site
- Identify how affected individuals are notified of an emergency. This applies to the organization's general population and to the ERT. Public address announcements, notification via two-way radio, and push notifications to desktops and text messages to cell phones are some examples. An announcement over the public address system to a fictitious name such as "Paul Bunion report to location X" could be used to alert the team to a problem at location X without announcing too much information that may disrupt operations of the organization or to cause unnecessary crowds of onlookers. The business continuity manager and ERT leader must understand how hazard warnings are communicated from public agencies
- Develop and communicate plans and procedures (response guidelines or response protocols, sometimes called an emergency plan implementing procedure (EPIP)) for the response team for each type of situation the team is expected to control. There should be a general instruction for the appropriate people to notify outside emergency services (i.e., dial 911 in the United States). EPIPs should include other notification instructions related to the particular incident. Management should be informed of the occurrence of certain incidents on a graded basis. Human resources and the safety department should be immediately informed of injuries (after the notification of emergency services, of course), but not necessarily senior management unless the injury is of a serious nature. On the other end of the scale, a bomb threat or a toxic material release that affects the surrounding community demands senior management notification. The EPIP may also direct those notified to either activate their continuity plan to notify third parties of the incident or expected degradation of services as a result of the incident
- Plans must consider the needs of the impaired or disabled
- Develop a procedure or means to activate business continuity or the crisis management team (such as the public relations team) if the situation escalates into a more serious matter
- Create, train, and equip an emergency response organization
- Orient (awareness) employees to the content of the plan and their responsibilities in an emergency situation. This orientation should occur when the plan is first introduced, when they are initially hired or transferred into an area with different exposures, or if the plan changes. Personal responsibility and the safety of responders must be emphasized
- Drill, drill, drill (we will repeat this later)

Response planning must be accomplished in light of the expected scenarios and cause and effect situations. A hazardous materials incident can be associated with single or multiple injuries, an earthquake can cause injuries, structural damage, fires, localized water damage from broken pipes, exposed electrical wiring, and so on.

Emergency response plans do not substitute as a business continuity plan or management system, a mistake many business owners make. This will become obvious after just a cursory review of the standards. In the United States, all organizations must maintain emergency action and fire prevention plans. These plans must be in writing if there are 10 or more employees, and certain types of organizations such as hazardous waste generators must have additional plans. The degree of planning required for most organizations is relatively simple but must all consider the applicable regulations and foreseeable hazards.

These emergency action plans in the United States are required by the Occupational Health and Safety Administration (OSHA) to contain the following elements:

- The plan must be kept in the workplace and available for inspection
- It must contain procedures for reporting a fire or other emergency
- The name or job title of the person who can provide information or explain employee duties under the plan
- Procedures for employees who remain behind temporarily during an evacuation to operate critical systems
- The types of evacuations (full evacuation, partial evacuation, or floor relocation) and how to account for employees who have evacuated
- Any rescue and medical duties for those who are to perform them
- Emergency alarm systems that have a distinctive signal for each purpose

The emergency response program should be documented. Many of the requirements for an emergency response plan parallel those for a business continuity plan. It can be blended into the business continuity plan, act as a separate plan appended to the business continuity plan, or exist as a standalone document. Although a solid emergency response capability supports business continuity, a standalone document is likely the best approach. Because it contains emergency response information, i.e., information that may need to be immediately accessed, it should not be buried inside a larger document. For this reason, an abridged version can be produced that contains the operational procedures for the response team and a separate emergency guide directed toward the employee population. If combined with a larger document, consider coloring the page edges red for easy identification and location of information.

The unabridged version of a response plan should contain a commitment by the organization to protect life and the safety of its employees, contractors, and guests; to protect property; and to protect the environment. Organizations with more complex risk or a larger response need (or governmental organizations) may need to structure their plans according to the framework of FEMA's *Comprehensive Preparedness Guide CPG 101: Developing and Maintaining Emergency Operations Plans*. See Appendix C, Table of Contents of Campus Emergency Plan, for an example of what a plan for a large quasi-governmental campus may look like. Its contents could be overkill for most organizations but it gives the reader the breadth and detail that such plans may contain. Because the example in the Appendix is from a government-oriented plan, items such as "Authorities," in which the enabling legislation or regulation is listed, would be disregarded by a nongovernmental agency.

An emergency response plan should have the following characteristics:

- Clean and easy to follow. Operational plans such as the EPIP should not contain unnecessary verbiage
- Organized in a logical sequence
- Detail emergency contact information including off-hour phone numbers if applicable, and other alternate numbers (i.e., in addition to listing 911 in the United States, list the direct number to the local emergency dispatch center)
- Use action-oriented instructions that are specific, focused on the effects of the hazard, but flexible. "Grab fire extinguisher," "Pull pin," "Squeeze handle" are examples of action-oriented instructions
- Avoid acronyms
- Operational instructions should be complete but not overly detailed
- Training material or excessive explanation is eliminated from operational instructions
- Superfluous information is also eliminated
- Never contain an instruction to avoid panic or control panic. People do not panic before, during, or after an emergency except under specific circumstances. Requiring responders to control panic, unless they have received specific and qualified training to accomplish this difficult task, could incur liability if panic were to develop and someone was injured as a result. Instructing employees or a responder not to panic demonstrates that the planner has not researched the hazard sufficiently to understand its nature
- Provides for incident reporting and after action evaluation. The corrective action system set up for business continuity and continuous improvement should be used

The plan should follow the format of the organization's normal document control processes (see Chapter 3) and at the least contain a provision for approval and sign-off.

4.3.2 EMERGENCY RESPONSE TEAM

An ERT is an internal organization of employees designed to respond to and control emergencies before the arrival of public agencies. After a disaster, it may become the organization's primary source of medical, fire control, and hazardous materials cleanup within the scope of its training and equipment. ERT members are typically volunteers, because if they are paid they may lose their Good Samaritan protection and the organization may become responsible for the provision of other requirements (see below).

Required in nuclear power plants, hospitals, and many high-rise buildings, an ERT can help the organization to:

- Intervene and stabilize emergencies before they have the chance to escalate
- Increase the survival of injured or sick employees through the rapid application of life-saving devices and first aid protocols
- Manage the complete and orderly evacuation of employees and guests from the building
- Prevent adverse publicity by preventing escalation of an emergency
- Demonstrate management concern and support for the safety of employees
- Minimize the impact on the environment
- Help comply with regulatory requirements (US OSHA, the Uniform Fire Code, and the Environmental Protection Agency) to mitigate hazardous materials incidents

- In remote locations away from normal emergency response services or when a prompt rescue is required or the responding agencies do not have the technical capability to quickly effect a rescue, the ERT will serve this purpose
- Reduce property damage and loss
- Become the sole response in a disaster situation when public agencies do not have the ability to respond

The effective and safe operation of an ERT involves a large commitment of time, money, and resources for planning, training, and equipment. The time required for training even a small ERT in a low-hazard environment should be no less than 12 hours each quarter—much more in a larger, risk-intensive environment. The type of hazards to which the team may respond will also affect the minimum training and equipment requirements. Teams involved in hazwoper (hazardous waste operations) require a minimum of 40 hours of specialized training. Defining the scope, or to what type of incidents the team will respond, will also define the recruitment standards, equipment requirements, and amount of training necessary. This decision should be a natural result of the hazard identification analysis. The scope can (and in some cases, such as fire response, should) speak to the level of response (i.e., the team responds only to small fires in the incipient stage). The training must fit the scope of the team's duties and regulatory requirements. It may be necessary to bring in outside consultants or to have the local fire department assist with training. Consider the following ERT training subjects:

- Roles and responsibilities of the ERT
- Hazards within the scope of the response
- Notification and communication
  - Reporting emergencies
  - Activation of team
  - Technical communications (two-way radio operation, satellite phones, and room and building markings)
  - How to communicate information effectively (nontechnical)
- Incident command structure/incident management
- Basic fire science and control (fire extinguishers and hoses), fire systems (preaction systems, sprinkler head activation, risers, post-indicator valve operation, and deluge systems)
- First aid, Cardiopulmonary Resuscitation (CPR), automated external defibrillator, and triage
  - Management of injuries and illnesses, and notification
- Evacuation, floor warden duties, and accounting for individuals evacuated
- Basic search and rescue
- Hazardous materials response and/or cleanup
- Shelter-in-place procedures
- Weapons of mass destruction recognition and response
- Workplace violence
- Bomb threat management and search
- Flood/water control
- Emergency supplies and equipment
- Preservation of evidence for investigation
- Scene and response safety
- Location of shut-off valves

Budget for short-term and long-term equipment and resource needs. Equipment may include (noninclusive list):

- Reflective vests with identification such as ERT or Incident Commander (IC)
- Hardhats
- Safety glasses
- Chemical spill kits
- Two-way radios
- Police and fire scanners
- Clipboards, pens, chalk, paper, or electronic tablet with hazardous materials locations, shut-off valves, floor plans loaded onto it. It can also contain copies of EPIPs
- Yellow caution tape or red danger tape
- Bullhorn with built-in siren
- Backpack for responder equipment
- Heavy gloves
- Cribbing
- Hand tools
- Flashlight and batteries and/or light sticks
- First aid supplies
- Duct tape
- Badges, ERT arm bands, first aid/CPR/hazmat pins, hardhat decals
- Television, radio, and social networking
- Unending supply of pizza for meetings and training sessions

Team members should be recruited in sufficient numbers to field full teams for all shifts, to meet the staffing demands of each type of incident, and to allow for a reserve force to substitute for sick or injured team members. Although membership in the team is usually voluntary, provide incentives to create interest, but be careful that the incentives do not create a de facto situation where the team is no longer considered volunteer. A team compensated for its participation may require a much higher degree of prescreening, medical examination and inoculation, training, and increased liability. ERT members should not be critical members of a business continuity recovery team and certainly not the recovery team leader or alternate team leader. The timeline from the onset of an emergency that leads to a continuity situation will likely overlap the activation of the continuity teams. If the ICS is not used, a team leader and alternate with an established chain of command is selected and documented along with the leader and alternate's name and job title. Most managers do not like to list individual names because organizations with high turnover may need to update their plans more often, but the requirement to list names is spelled out in some regulations and standards. Team leaders must be able to evaluate the situation and make decisions on the appropriate response actions and resource requirements to control the situation in a manner that protects people, property, and the environment. In other words, they need the competence to manage the incident.

Let employees and the organization's community know about the existence, authority, and capabilities of the team. This will increase confidence in the organization's ability to respond to emergencies, and it should elicit better cooperation from employees during an emergency. Identify the team members in newsletters, Web pages, and special identification as an ERT member placard on the office door or cubical entrance. This identification should contain a picture of the team member and identify any special training (Figure 4.1).

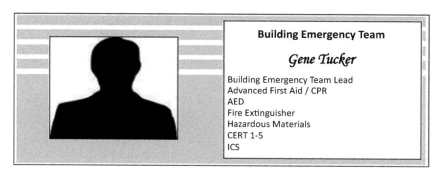

FIGURE 4.1

Example of cubicle/office emergency response team (ERT) identification display.

Finally, conduct and document regular drills. Practice, practice, practice. See Chapter 9 on Exercise Planning. Arrange joint drills with public agencies.

4.3.3 INCIDENT COMMAND SYSTEM

The standards do not directly require the use of the ICS when responding to an emergency or to building a business continuity structure. ASIS briefly mentions ICS and NFPA 1600 refers to it in its explanatory material under its specification for incident management. Past versions of NFPA 1600 have directly referenced its use. International Organization for Standardization (ISO) 22301 accreditation training material does, however, discuss the use of ICS both for emergency response and business continuity.

The ICS is a hierarchical management system used by governmental agencies, fire departments, and the police to structure the tactical field response to an incident. It is also used in the emergency operations center (EOC). The ICS is a subset of the National Incident Management System (NIMS), as described in the National Response Plan that specifies how governmental resources will work in concert with state and local governments and with the private sector to respond to "incidents of national significance." NIMS is a command and control structure (as is ICS) that provides a template for the coordination of efforts to prevent or respond to threats and incidents of all sizes and complexity. NIMS consists of the following components:

- Preparedness
- Communications and information management
- Resource management
- Command and management (ICS)
- Ongoing management and maintenance

Homeland Security Presidential Directive-7, Critical Infrastructure Identification, Prioritization, and Protection identified a number of entities that comprise the critical infrastructure to the nation that must be protected from terrorist attack. Water districts, medical facilities, transportation, food production and distribution, and critical manufacturing are included as critical infrastructure. Most of these entities are controlled and operated by the private sector (i.e., not the government). These entities may wish to develop their response system under ICS. OSHA requires all organizations that handle hazardous materials to use ICS. In any event, it is important that the business continuity manager and the members of the ERT understand at least the basics of ICS because they will likely need to interface with outside agencies responding to their emergency. Certain concepts of operation, even if not using ICS, are useful for structuring the organization's management of an incident. The rules to establish a command post are a prime example.

ICS solves a number of problems experienced in the past when multiple agencies responded to an area wide emergency, and in many cases between agencies of the same jurisdiction by forcing common multiagency operating procedures, terminology, communications, and management among all agencies. Its modular structure allows for a consistent and coordinated response to incidents of all types and complexity.

The ICS uses the management system of management by objectives. Response objectives that are designed to protect life safety, stabilize the incident, and protect property and the environment are set by the IC and delegated to the subordinate positions after agreement that the objectives can be met. By using this approach, the IC can coordinate the response to complex and technical incidents without unreasonable expectations.

The ICS structure is also sensitive to the span of control to limit the ratio of supervisors to subordinates. If the incident is small and the response is relatively simple, the ratio is eight subordinates to one manager. If the crisis expands and becomes more complex, the span of control is reduced by adding additional supervision to provide the most effective leadership. Some believe the span of control in an emergency situation should be five subordinates or fewer.

The ICS is divided into five major functional units referred to as sections (Figure 4.2). The fire service version is expandable to 36 positions, but most are not relevant to business response. The five units are:

- Incident Command
- Operations
- Planning and Intelligence
- Logistics
- Finance and Administration

It is not necessary to establish all sections of the ICS when responding to a small-scale incident. In this case, the IC will directly manage or assume the duties of each of the sections or activate the sections as additional personnel arrive according to operational needs. Each section is headed by a section chief and the sections may be further divided into subsections as required by the complexity of the incident or need to maintain the proper span of control. The subsections are called branches and are headed by a director. Further division is possible with corresponding titles, but this level of detail is usually not required in a business environment.

4.3.3.1 Incident commander

The IC assumes overall responsibility at the incident or event. A distinctive vest that contains the words "Incident Commander" is worn as identification. When used inside the EOC, the identification vest will usually just say "Command." The IC determines objectives and establishes priorities based on the nature of the incident, available resources, and agency (or company) policy. The role of the IC is usually filled by the first responder to arrive at the scene, who may be relieved of this duty when a more senior responder or a designated IC arrives. A formal handoff of responsibility is completed when the changeover occurs.

FIGURE 4.2

Basic incident command system.

A Command post (CP) or an incident command post is set up at a safe distance near the location of the emergency where the IC and its staff will manage the response. Once established, the CP should not be moved unless the conditions of the emergency pose a threat. It can be located in the field, at a vehicle, inside an office, or where reliable communications (electronic and verbal) and security (access control) can be maintained. When appropriate, it should be within view of the incident, but away from noise or activity that may interfere with the command efforts. Often the CP is located in a building lobby if the incident occurs inside such a structure. The CP may be identified by the display of a blue and white square.

In a business environment, management must delegate ahead of time to the IC the authority to make the tactical decisions necessary to stabilize or end the emergency without interference by those who would normally possess some degree of authority within the organization, as mentioned above. Management's role, as part of the management or crisis management team, is in the EOC to make strategic decisions based on the events or to allocate resources among multiple incidents, generally not at the scene of an incident. Reliable communications between the EOC and IC or CP are essential. The IC follows preexisting policy set by management and will use standard forms and checklists (EPIPs) to ensure that all tasks are completed. Software programs are available to aid in the management of the emergency in the field, but for these tools to work effectively, as we will point out later, they must be practiced and reside on systems that can withstand field conditions where the possibility of limited resources such as electrical power or extra batteries may exist.

Some of the specific duties of the IC include:

- Overall field management and responsibility for the control of the emergency
- Situational analysis
- Setting objectives and priorities
- Coordination with the EOC or other ICs (unified command). The IC of the firm's ERT should co-locate with the fire or police department IC if they will allow
- Ultimate responsibility for the safety of responders
- Approval of all incident action plans (IAPs) and resources
- Delegating authority as necessary
- Primary responder until others arrive

In addition to the section chiefs (general staff), three other positions report directly to the IC depending on the size of the emergency. Also wearing distinctive vests, the command staff consists of the information officer, safety officer, and liaison officer.

4.3.3.1.1 Information officer
The information officer, or public information officer (PIO), is responsible for providing situational awareness information and progress on the control of the event to the news media. He or she also obtains information from and provides information to the planning section. In a government structure, the PIO releases information about the incident that is approved for release by the IC. In a business environment, the public relations representative will fill this role. If the crisis management team is activated, the PIO may be located in the EOC and not in the field. Depending on the organization, in a business application, the PIO may or may not be subordinate to the IC and would release information based on the professional judgment or the decision of the management team.

4.3.3.1.2 Safety officer
The safety officer ensures that legal and regulatory compliance is maintained, and develops measures to ensure the safety of all assigned personnel. Working primarily with the operations section, the safety officer is responsible for monitoring and evaluating changing conditions and has the authority to withdraw responders or to suspend an operation without clearance from the IC. This authority to suspend operations and remove responders from an unsafe condition must be firmly communicated to all responders.

4.3.3.1.3 Liaison officer
The liaison officer assists the IC on larger incidents in which representatives from other agencies may respond by coordinating their involvement and providing them with information on conditions, objectives, and resources. The liaison offer can also reside in the EOC to perform the same duties or to act as the liaison between the EOC and business continuity team leaders.

4.3.3.2 Operations section
The operations section implements the IAPs and objectives issued by the IC. Operations determine tactics and resources to achieve the objectives and directs the tactical response. These are the worker bees of the response. They participate in the selection and reality-checking of goals and direct all resources necessary to carry out the response. A constant flow of situational information and milestone achievement is communicated back to the IC. Operations can be subdivided into the functional or geographical groups (divisions as described above) as needed. Examples of these divisions include first aid, search and rescue, and hazmat cleanup. Operations typically expand from the bottom up and may need staging areas for equipment and resources.

4.3.3.3 Planning and intelligence section
The planning and intelligence section develops the IAPs to implement the goals and objectives of the IC. As part of their plans, this section also determines what resources are needed to accomplish each task. Members of this section must gather information about the incident before they can devise a meaningful plan. In a large-scale incident, this section will accomplish the following:

- Collect intelligence (situational analysis: analyze conditions and the scope of the incident)
- Project or predict changing conditions

- Prepare action plans
- Prepare contingency plans in case conditions, events, or resources change
- Track resources available, in service, and used
- Maintains incident documentation (chronology of events)
- Development plans for demobilization

Technical advisors (subject matter experts) are included in the planning section to provide expert advice when needed. Chemists, safety engineers, toxicologists, industrial hygienists, meteorologists, radiological technicians, and structural engineers are examples of the types of experts that might be included in the response.

According to FEMA, every incident must have an IAP despite the size of the incident. The intent of the IAP is to:

- Understand the situation
- Establish incident objectives
- Develop the plan
- Prepare and disseminate the plan
- Execute, evaluate, and revise the plan

The IAP should:

- Specify the incident objectives
- List the activities necessary to achieve the objectives
- Define a specified time frame, called an operational period. The operational period can be for a work shift, 24-hour period or whatever makes sense under the circumstances
- Be either oral or written. Templates for written IAPs are found on the Internet

Every IAP must answer the following questions:

- What do we need to achieve?
- Who is responsible to achieve the action?
- How do we communicate with the parties involved in its achievement?
- What are the safety procedures?

4.3.3.4 Logistics section

The logistics section obtains all resources and services needed to manage the incident. This section orders and delivers personnel, equipment, food and supplies, restroom and shower facilities, and so forth. The logistics section simply supplies resources. The planning section is responsible for resource management and use.

4.3.3.5 Finance and administration section

The finance and administration section projects, tracks, and approves expenditures by the logistics section, and completes a final cost analysis of the response. It is responsible for:

- Contract negotiation and monitoring
- Timekeeping
- Cost analysis

- Documentation for reimbursement from other agencies under any memorandum of understandings

4.4 **REVIEW**

Fundamental to a successful business continuity capability and management system that makes the organization resilient to disaster is the application of the elements of emergency management: mitigation, prevention and preparedness, response, and recovery (continuity). The standards treat these in different ways, both directly and indirectly.

Preparedness, according to ASIS, is the "activities, programs, and systems developed and implemented prior to an incident that may be used to support and enhance mitigation of, response to, and recovery from disruptions, disasters, or emergencies." The basic components of preparedness are planning, equipment and resources, training and education, and exercises—all of the efforts to set up the business continuity management system. Preparedness applies to both the work and home environment.

The response to an incident is almost always a visible event that will have both short- and long-term ramifications to all parties involved in the incident and is increasingly becoming an issue for civil liability. A response capability is a regulatory requirement for certain types of organizations.

Emergency response is generally intended to stabilize an incident until the arrival of governmental services, but business organizations are the last on the government's response priority list after a regional disaster. Organizations must develop the capability to protect their population and assets for days to weeks after a regional disaster.

The manager must identify foreseeable hazards that can affect the organization and must have a higher level of understanding of the characteristics of the hazards than nonprofessionals so that effective prevention, mitigation, and response programs are effective. The manager and appropriate personnel must also understand any warning systems associated with the hazards.

The emergency response program that is compatible with the level of risk should be documented. Many of the requirements for an emergency response plan parallel those for a business continuity plan. Response planning must be accomplished in light of the expected scenarios and cause and effect situations.

An ERT is an internal organization of trained volunteer employees designed to respond to and control emergencies before the arrival of public agencies. After a disaster, it may become the organization's primary source of medical, fire control, and hazardous materials cleanup. The team should be composed of personnel from all shifts and should not include business continuity team leaders. It protects the safety of itself and the organization's workers and guests, property, and assets, and minimizes the effect of the emergency on the environment.

The ICS is a hierarchical management system used to structure the tactical field response to an incident but is also used in the EOC and to structure business continuity implementation. It is led by the IC and the command staff of the public information officer, the safety officer, and the liaison officer. The general staff consists of four sections: operations, planning and intelligence, logistics, and finance and administration. The fifth section is command.

BUSINESS IMPACT ANALYSIS

5

CHAPTER SUMMARY

The Business Impact Analysis (BIA) is a key activity necessary to develop the Business Continuity Management System and to satisfy major requirements of the Business Continuity Standards. It identifies the financial and operational loss of the organization's business functions and processes over periods significant to the individual organization regardless of what caused the loss by examining their impact on service objectives, financial position, cash flow, regulatory and contractual issues, and competitive risk. Information useful to understanding the context of the organization and the collection of resource requirements necessary for the implementation of the business continuity plans are often included in the analysis.

The information developed from the analysis allows management to make decisions concerning their Maximum Acceptable Outage (MAO) or the Maximum Tolerable Period of Disruption (MTPD). Another similar term, the Maximum Tolerable Downtime (MTD) is used as the maximum downtime or length of time a process can be unavailable before the organization experiences significant (unacceptable) losses. The impact can be stated as both financial or operational loss. Operational loss is used when it is difficult to characterize the loss or degradation of a function in financial terms, assigning a subjective severity level from one to five or Low to Critical. This then allows management to set Recovery Time and Recovery Point Objectives (RTOs and RPOs) for each critical or prioritized business function. Work Recovery Time (WRT) is another concept developed by the analysis. Based on this information, business functions are designated as critical or noncritical to the goals of the organization. The upstream and downstream dependencies of each function within the scope of the analysis are highlighted.

The data for the analysis is collected through a combination of workshops, questionnaires, and interviews with functional managers from all components of the organization that are within the scope of the analysis. Detailed sample questions allow the analyst to identify gaps in the prevention, preparedness, response, mitigation, and recovery of each business function's resilience and include recommended corrective actions to close gaps suggested by the answers revealed on the questionnaires or during the interviews. Pandemic flu preparedness and response, supply chain risk, and legal and regulatory compliance are addressed.

The manner in which the BIA is documented is important to auditors and to management so that the objectives of the analysis are clearly illustrated. It should identify the MAO/MTPD and RTO for each process, product, or service, and internal and external dependencies. The BIA and its documentation must outline an understanding of the negative impacts over time that the failure to provide these products, processes, and services would have on the organization. It describes the risk to the organization of not resuming its business activities. BIA documentation should be regarded as confidential, controlled information.

KEY TERMS

Business Impact Analysis; BIA documentation; BIA project planning; Business impact analysis questionnaire; Financial impact of risk; Maximum Acceptable Outage (MAO); Maximum Tolerable Downtime (MTD); Operational impact of risk; Pandemic planning; Recovery Point Objective (RPO); Recovery Time Objectives (RTO); Supply chain risk; Work Recovery Time (WRT)

KEY POINTS

- The Business Impact Analysis (BIA) is necessary to develop the Business Continuity Management System
- The Business Impact Analysis is key to understanding the context of the organization
- The Business Impact Analysis identifies the financial and operational loss of the organization's business functions over time
- The Business Impact Analysis provides data to establish the Maximum Tolerable Downtime (MTD), Recovery Time Objectives (RTO), and the Recovery Point Objectives (RPO)
- The BIA presents management with a financial basis for selecting the most cost-effective continuity strategies
- Identifies gaps in prevention, preparedness, response, mitigation, and recovery

5.1 INTRODUCTION

The Business Impact Analysis (BIA) is a key activity necessary to develop the Business Continuity Management System. It is necessary (apart from the requirement in the standards) because it defines almost all aspects of the business continuity program. This process allows the Business Continuity Manager and other important key players including interested parties to understand the context of the organization. It identifies which business functions and processes are critical to the survival of the organization.

The International Organization for Standardization (ISO) defines BIA simply as the "process of analyzing activities and the effect that a business disruption might have upon them." ASIS does not seem to define the BIA. The BIA identifies the financial and operational loss of the organization's business functions over periods significant to the individual organization regardless of what caused the loss by examining their impact on service objectives, financial position and cash flow, regulatory and contractual issues, and competitive risk.

The BIA process will help to establish the importance of each of the organization's functional units in a manner that avoids the bias of opinion by the functional leader (i.e., if you simply ask the leader of a function how valuable his or her operations are to the organization you may receive the useless response "Of course all of my functions are the most critical to the operation of the organization"). This allows the ranking of functions by importance and tells the Business Continuity Manager exactly which functions need to be recovered and at what level they need to continue without interruption, that is, which functions are the most mission critical and at what times of the business cycle they are the most critical. In many of today's lean organizations, however, few business functions can be deferred for any period, or, in other words, few are not critical. It will identify which data processes and computer applications are the most important to the resilience of the organization and to the continuity of its key business objectives. The ranking produced by the analysis will show where to concentrate funds and resources and in what order the functions need to be recovered if not included in a high-availability category. It will also

- Identify the financial and operational consequences of a function's loss over time
- Highlight interdependencies from one process or function to another and to any third party relationships
- Establish the Recovery Time Objectives (RTOs), Recovery Point Objective (RPO), and the Maximum Tolerable Downtime (MTD)
- Aid in the understanding of where to focus risk treatment

- Refine the scope of the Business Continuity Management System
- Identify critical resource requirements to support the management system and to implement the continuity strategies
- Determine the legal, regulatory, and contractual obligations related to business continuity or to the failure to provide a service or product
- Serve as a venue for the awareness of the business continuity management system
- Reveal potential inefficiencies in normal operations. The results of any LEAN initiatives that produce process mapping can be incorporated into the BIA and provide a deeper level of "understanding the organization"
- Begins the process of continuity strategy development and allows the organizations to select the most cost-effective strategies
- Understand where to set escalation levels for IT or other support systems and potentially when to activate the business continuity plan

The BIA presents management with a financial basis for selecting the most cost-effective continuity strategies. The BIA of a Fortune 500 company with worldwide operations located on the west coast of the United States showed that a disruption of their product supply would cause the loss of prime product placement space on the shelves of supermarkets resulting in a tremendous loss of sales over a short period. Shopper's eyes naturally look first at certain locations on shelving and tend to select products in this space over others. Once this prime placement is lost, it is difficult and time-consuming to get back. The main computer operations for the entire company were concentrated in a single location, less than a mile from the predicted epicenter of a future major earthquake. The company decided the best strategy was to build a second, backup data center in the Midwest at a cost of $6 million. All data going to the primary data center would be mirrored in almost real time to the backup center. As this plan was in the implementation phase, the economy suffered a sustained downturn imposing a significant financial hardship on the company and placing the completion of the second data center in jeopardy. However, they were able to return to the BIA and used its information to better prioritize the continuity of their business systems resulting in a revised strategy that mirrored only *critical data* and implemented a less expensive solution for data processes that did not need to be restored for days to weeks. By better focusing on the results of the BIA, the company was able to save $3 million in their second data center strategy.

The BIA also highlights times throughout the business cycle when certain business functions, processes, or service objectives are more critical than others allowing the Management Team to adjust strategies or resources based on the timing of the disaster. Not all business functions need to be continued without interruption or recovered all at once. Some are more or less dependent on seasonal variances. The BIA will show these variances.

5.1.1 RECOVERY TIME OBJECTIVE AND RECOVERY POINT OBJECTIVE

The information in the BIA from the example above showed that not all business processes need to continue without interruption. The RTO is established for each business function and the processes that support the function. The standards define the RTO as the period following an incident within which a product, service, activity, or resource must be resumed or recovered. ASIS defines it more precisely by saying it is the goal for the restoration and recovery of functions or resources based on the acceptable downtime and acceptable level of performance in case of a disruption of operations. The RTO is the amount of time by which the organization would like to have the process or function back in service after an outage. It is based on the Outage Tolerance, a term replaced by the Maximum Acceptable Outage (MAO) or the Maximum Tolerable Period of Disruption (MTPD), which is the time it would take the loss or degradation of a business function or process to have an adverse impact on the organization's objectives such as the delivery of a service or product. Another similar term, the Maximum Tolerable Downtime (MTD) is used as the maximum downtime or length of time a process can be unavailable before the organization experiences significant (unacceptable) losses. The impact can be stated in both financial or operational loss. The RTO, MAO, and MTD are ultimately a management decision based on the results of the BIA and the agreement between the process owners and management about what level of loss or impact is acceptable. This tolerance can be zero, hence the terms "continuity," "high availability," "0.9999% up-time," and so on. Alternatively, the organization can decide that a minimum acceptable level of production, service, or delivery of product is adequate to remain under the MAO over time. In determining the RTO, consideration must be given to the goal to have processes reestablished before the point is reached at which the outage begins to cause unacceptable harm or, in other words, before the MAO is reached.

The RTO of each business function is a major deliverable of the BIA. As the above example illustrates, the RTO will guide the organization toward the selection of the most cost-effective continuity strategy. The strategies necessary for the lowest RTO, that is, those with the least tolerance for an outage, are usually the most expensive to implement, a longer RTO will allow for the selection of lower cost options.

The RPO, also referred to as the Maximum Data Loss, is the point at which information used by an activity must be restored to enable the activity to operate after its resumption. In other words, how much loss of data or loss of records is the organization willing to accept or how current does the data need to be to start the recovery? In many cases, the tolerance for data loss is near zero, but at what point do you begin the reconstruction or reentry of records? This is often used to decide what form of backup strategy is used. Tape backup, for example, would mean a day or more of lost data. Similar to RPO, the Work Recovery Time (WRT) is the time necessary to catch up from any backlog created by an outage.

5.2 BUSINESS IMPACT ANALYSIS PROCESS

The biggest predictor of the success or failure in the development of a Business Continuity Management System that will actually meet its objectives at the time of a disaster is the amount of demonstrated management support for the program. Without this, many business continuity programs take too long to develop often causing the entire effort to fail. A poorly constructed BIA, or the lack of one, is another contributor to failure, causing the misdirection of resources and decisions based on poorly defined risk.

Apart from the requirement of the standards for management commitment, it is the BIA and Risk Assessment that will help to solidify this support by demonstrating the financial and operational risk the organization could face. But how does one begin this process if the support is not yet solidified? After all, the BIA will require a large block of organizational time to interview process owners and have them complete informational questionnaires. In this case, the management sponsor can be used to introduce the program and to motivate all process owners to participate in the analysis. In addition to management's support, the following major elements of the BIA process include:

- BIA project planning
- Data collection

- Data analysis
- Documentation and Communication of analysis
- Reanalysis

5.2.1 BIA PROJECT PLANNING

One way to avoid failure and to maintain the momentum of the analysis is through good project planning. The BIA should be completed in the shortest time possible to avoid the loss of momentum established by management. The loss of momentum can cause the effort to languish to the point that the information produced is no longer accurate or descriptive of the current state of the organization.

A project plan incorporated into a descriptive document that outlines the approach and methodology used to complete the analysis will show a third party, such as an auditor, that all elements of the analysis have been met. It is important to determine what method will be used to complete the analysis, especially how the data will be collected that must be illustrated in this document.

Just as important in the project planning phase is the understanding of the scope of the analysis. The scope will most often run parallel to the scope of the Business Continuity Management System, but often the scope of the former is not determined until the latter. The scope of the Business Continuity Management System, if already established, can be refined by the results of the BIA (many organizations will start with the BIA, examining all functions of the organization before they decide on the scope of the management system). As we mentioned in a previous chapter, use caution that an out-of-scope dependency of something that is in scope must be included in the analysis and therefore included in the management system.

After management commitment and a definition of the scope of the analysis are established, the next step is to review any previous BIAs. If one was recently completed, it may simply become a matter of revision and update (see Reanalysis below). If not recent, it should provide valuable information about products, process, process owners, and acceptable risk. It could provide clues about a presentation and report format acceptable to management that can be used for the current BIA. If no previous analyses exist, review the organization's marketing data, stock reports, or other regulatory filings. Insurance reports and financial audits are also good sources of information. Examine the results of any Lean Kaizen initiatives where process flow charts such as Fishbones or Value Stream Mapping may have been produced (this information is gained from an interview with manufacturing or quality managers). An organizational chart is also a valuable tool to assist the manager with planning the BIA. The results of the BIA should provide much of the same information in the end, but it is useful to at least have a basic understanding of the organization before its start. This understanding will help the analyst ask more pertinent questions during the data collection or process-owner interview phase.

Decide what data to collect. Information that helps the manager understand the organization, and that returns financial and operational information to establish risk and prioritized treatment of IT and functional processes is the main focus of the BIA. However, to minimize the need to meet with a number of individuals a number of times, Business Continuity Managers, and especially Business Continuity Consultants, will often combine the process of initial strategy and resource development with the BIA. Although one relates to the other, some managers separate these tasks for simplicity and for the expedience of not asking for too much information all at once when a need for an all-at-once approach is not demonstrated. If using an outside consultant to develop the program, combining these phases of program development will likely result in a less expensive effort. Strategies and resource information developed in this manner may need to be refined later. In our description of the BIA process, we will assume the analyst will follow the combined approach as is the common practice in the industry. BIA software programs are generally structured to follow this approach.

Next, decide how the information for the BIA is to be collected. Some managers rely on the CFO to provide the necessary financial information, but this practice does not allow the manager to effectively gain the level of understanding of the organization or serve to begin the orientation and training that functional leaders will need to gain the knowledge to begin the business continuity process for their areas of responsibility. The CFO is the person who may be legally responsible for the protection of financial data so would likely be a valuable resource to the BIA. The results of the BIA must not only be acceptable to an auditor but ultimately must be acceptable to senior management. The credibility of the information is vital especially if developed by an outside consultant. The advantage of obtaining the data from the CFO is that it is more readily accepted because a top-down approach produces data from those closer to senior management, but has the disadvantage of less interaction with others in the organization to orient them to the concepts of risk ranking and initial strategy development. The CFO can help to clarify or refine the contents of the analysis. The CFO can also provide the analyst with an idea of the general time frames in which risk becomes unacceptable or what the Recovery Time Objectives will look like—information useful to the analyst when developing the financial impact profiles; in other words, will an outage become unacceptable after just a few minutes or after one to two weeks? Other managers rely purely on the distribution of questionnaires sent to functional leaders to collect the data. This method can produce results in a greater amount of time than other methods, but also does not carry the advantages described above. Ideally, the collection of the data is best accomplished through a combination of personal interviews with the functional owners and through the distribution of a list of questions before the interviews take place. This gives the functional leader time to understand what the analysis is looking for and to formulate a more complete answer. When the questionnaires are returned to the analyst prior to the interview, he or she will be better positioned to ask follow-on or clarifying questions. Often, questions arise after a review of the written response that would not have occurred to the analyst to ask initially or the functional leader may identify important areas for discussion that are not addressed in the questions.

Determine what functions or business processes are within the scope of the analysis and who within these functions need to be interviewed. This generally includes the functional or process leaders. The trick is to avoid going too high in the organization (but speaking with these people is not a mistake) because persons in these positions may be too far from the day-to-day operation of the functions under their control, but also avoid going too low in the organization as these people will not likely understand how their jobs map to others or are unaware of the function's interdependencies. When selecting groups to interview for the BIA, try to think ahead about what business functions will have continuity or recovery teams. Continuity teams are groups of employees and/or third parties that will implement the continuity strategies. The teams are generally aligned along functional groups such as the Human Resources Team, IT Infrastructure Recovery Team, the Customer Support Team, and others. Teams are segregated by separate alternative work areas, differing continuity strategies, different resource requirements, and the like. This, however, will not likely be the case if organized under an Incident Command System structure.

One word of caution: some literature suggest that the manager only meet with and interview the owners of "critical" processes, but it is the BIA that helps the organization to decide what is critical to the continued operation of the organization and what is not. Do not make the mistake of including in the analysis only those functions you or management believes up front are critical. All functions within scope of the analysis should be analyzed to decide what is critical, and to what degree other functions are not critical to the continued operations of the organization.

5.2.2 DATA COLLECTION

As described above, decide how the data are to be collected. We believe the best method is to identify the functions in scope and develop a set of questions to send to the function owners prior to a meeting to discuss the questions and data that are required for the analysis. As we will explain later, the questions sent to functional leaders must be accompanied with detailed instructions, but some business continuity managers prefer to conduct a short orientation session with all of the functional leaders as a group to introduce the process and outline the expectations of their participation in the analysis.

List those functions that are within scope. This may include every function within the organization, but may also include third parties outside of the organization (see the interview questions for Purchasing/Procurement for example). Consider:

- Customer Service
- Engineering
- Facilities, Real Estate, Custodial
- Finance (Accounting, Accounts Payable, Accounts Receivable, Payroll, Cash Management, Order Entry, or others that may be pertinent to your organization. These functions, depending on their complexity and relations to the others, may be treated separately or combined. This will also apply to functions listed below.)
- Human Resources, Benefits
- Information Technology (Desktop systems, Servers, Infrastructure, Environment, Security, Disaster Recovery)
- Insurance, Risk Management
- Legal
- Marketing
- Operations, Manufacturing
- Public/Media Relations
- Purchasing or Procurement, Supply Chain
- Research and Development
- Sales
- Security, Safety
- Shipping, Receiving, Distribution, Mailroom
- Telecommunications
- Warehouse, Stores

Once the functions are identified, prepare the questions you will need to ask during the interviews. At a high level, the questions are designed to:

- Understand risk to the functional unit and ultimately to the organization
- Understand the organization. What are the primary service objectives of the business unit or function, how does the function fit into the overall mission of the organization, and what are the

function's dependencies? What other functions are dependent upon its continued operation are questions that should be answered

- Rank functions to determine criticality (RTO, RPO)
- Identify gaps in prevention, preparedness, and mitigation
- Serve as a beginning for strategy development (we will discuss strategies in a later chapter, but for now remember that continuity strategies generally consist of an alternate work site, an alternate location where IT functions are available, and a means to connect the two. On a lower level, each business function may have additional specific strategies to continue its functions, such as a plan to collect and deliver mail to relocated workers)

The questions and the subsequent meeting are also designed to orient functional owners, who later may become team leaders, to the program. This is an opportunity to build interest and support for the program at the midmanagement level. If the business continuity manager or consultant combines the BIA process with strategy and plan development, questions are also designed to provide information that the planner can cut and paste or electronically import into planning software to include in the individual continuity team plans.

The questions consist of two major categories. The first contains questions common to all functions, and the second are questions focused specifically to each function. Sections included in the common questions are descriptive of the function, a discussion of risks to the function, information on potential alternate locations, team leaders, and alternates, and sections that ask for financial and operational risks that list legal and contractual dependencies. The focused questions may also seek information related to resource needs for the continuity teams that can start with initial strategy development and implementation. Resources needs include the continuity team list and contact numbers, internal and external contact numbers, forms and supply needs, software requirements, and vital records. Implementation can be addressed by asking the question "What are the first 30 things your team would need to do if access to the building was denied for 2 weeks?" See Appendix D for sample questionnaires.

The questions are then combined (general and function specific) into a questionnaire that is distributed to functional leaders in either paper or electronic form. An electronic form can consist of a simple word document or spreadsheet or an executable toolkit questionnaire produced by a commercial BIA software program. These programs allow the completed toolkits to upload into the program for compilation and varying degrees of analysis, graphing, and reporting. The rigor of the final reports produced by the software is not likely to be sufficient for certification, but can be a good start. If a commercial software program is used, ensure that it is compatible with the IT systems in use within the organization. Users who have difficulty with the installation of the program, especially if the difficulties are widespread, will likely not become champions of the process. Be prepared to assist with the installation of the software. If a group meeting is held to introduce the BIA process as described above, this may be a good venue to walk users through, with the help of IT representatives, with the installation of the software, especially if laptop systems are used. If the questionnaire/toolkits are sent in advance of the interviews, as we recommend, an explanation of the intent and expectations must be included. Detailed instructions, especially if commercial software is used, must also be sent to the recipient. Expect the recipient to know very little to nothing about what you expect or how to answer the questions, especially those that pertain to financial and operational impacts. Consider using screen captures and examples in your instructions. This can also be accomplished verbally in an orientation meeting.

Meetings with each functional leader are then scheduled roughly 2 to 3 weeks or more after they receive the questionnaires, but not so far that they become deprioritized. Reasonable timelines should be established and progress reported to management on a regular basis. Functional leaders may not understand what you are asking and return information that is off the mark. In addition, information returned may not be as complete as necessary. Tracking the tasks in a project plan or via a heat map is an important metric that will help to illustrate progress toward the milestones the manager established. When establishing timelines, consider the workload constraints of the organization. Beginning the BIA at the start of a seasonal rush or product introduction will lead to a higher degree of difficulty to achieve on-time results. Typically, once the communication describing the project and tool kits/questionnaires are distributed, allow for a two-week period for completion or before scheduling the first interview or group of interviews. Two to three weeks, depending on the norm for the organization, should be sufficient for functional owners to return any necessary information. It is more important that complete and accurate data is obtained, and continuity strategies well considered (if asking for this type of information at this phase) than it is to require the return of information quickly, but use caution because longer response times will add delays to the analysis.

The duration of most interviews is usually an hour in length, but one should allow at least an hour and a half for Facilities and potentially two hours for Information Technology. A memo or email should describe the intent and expectations of the interview, and if an outside consultant is used for the analysis, an introduction and brief biography with the consultant's affiliation should be included. Consider having a member of senior management sign the memo or send the email under their name to ensure that all requested functional leaders participate in the analysis. Some leaders may believe their presence will not add value to the program. Open the interview with a discussion of the Business Continuity Management program and an explanation of the BIA. At the end of the interview, inform the participants of the next steps and the timelines agreed upon. This is in general good meeting etiquette but worth repeating. It may be appropriate at the beginning of the interview to mention any scope limitations. Managers often preface the meeting by asking the participants to think about a worst-case scenario when answering the impact questions and when developing their continuity strategies. Although this is arguably the correct thing to do, bear in mind that a worst-case scenario can cause some participants to feel overwhelmed or to take the attitude that nothing can be done after the asteroid strikes the earth, so why plan a response? A better approach might be to propose a very serious but credible regional disaster scenario (but remember that we are concerned with the loss of functionality, not the cause of the loss, although we will change this focus when we discuss mitigation). Nevertheless, the analyst should frame questions that are applicable to different types of disasters. For example, in an area subject to earthquake risk, many are aware of the consequences that are associated with such a hazard. However, speaking about earthquakes may not give the proper perspective when asking questions about reputational damage due to securities fraud. As appropriate, ask questions based on the consequences or conditions expected from different threat scenarios.

During the interview, encourage the function owners to describe how their function and processes work and how they relate to the goals of the organization and to other units within the business. This is the opportunity to "understand the organization." Ask open-ended questions before moving onto the specific questions, allowing the functional owners to talk without interruption, noting any follow-up questions you may have. When asking follow-up questions (actually, keep this in mind when forming all questions), be careful to frame them in a manner that does not cause the manager to believe they need to justify their positions or the value of their functional units within the organization. For example, don't ask the manager how valuable their function is to the organization. Ask, instead, questions that elicit a value-oriented response:

- What would be the impact to the organization if your business unit could not function?
- How would this impact change over time?
- How would the loss of your business unit affect other functions within the organization—what other business units are dependent on the input or output from your unit?

Discuss the financial and operational impact questions early in the interview so that neither party feels rushed to provide answers that may be incomplete due to time constraints. Avoid conducting the interview in an office to eliminate any disruptions.

A summary report of the discussion, data obtained, strategies explored (including any that were discussed and rejected), and recommendations to close gaps identified in the interview and review should be sent to the interviewee for factual accuracy and acceptance of any proposed recommendations. Once accepted, the recommendations should be entered into a corrective action tracking system (this may require additional review and acceptance at a higher level). Selected content from these reports can later be collated into the final BIA report.

5.2.3 DATA ANALYSIS

Once the questionnaires are completed and the interviews finished, the analysis of the data can begin. Define Maximum Acceptable Outage (MAO), RTO, and RPO for each business process or function. Rank functions by their shortest RTO, greatest risk, greatest loss, or in the order that management agrees is the most critical after evaluation of the data. Once this is accomplished, the analyst then maps the software and data (IT) processes that support these functions to illustrate their criticality. Look at dependent functions to decide if their ranking should be elevated to match any associated functions that have been deemed critical. If a function is critical, generally all that supports that function becomes critical necessitating the adjustment of their RTOs or RPOs to a higher level. Identify gaps in prevention, preparedness, mitigation, and response revealed from the questions and develop recommended corrective actions to close the gaps. Keep the following in mind when analyzing the data:

- RTOs, MAO or Maximum Tolerable Outage (MTO), and criticality ranking are not simply a function of the raw data. It is an agreement with senior management. The loss of function "A" or product "A" may pose the greatest risk to the organization's goals or cause the greatest loss, but management may decide that in light of future plans, they may want to shift emphasis onto function or product "B." Before the analysis and the selection of strategies are finalized, meet with management to ensure they are in agreement with the BIA's conclusions
- Establish MAO, RTO, and RPO within the normal business cycles and within any peak cycles (some managers simply use the peak cycle, which is what ISO 22313 suggests). For example, the peak cycle for a retail toy manufacturer could be the months just prior to the holiday season.
- Account for impact only once, that is, watch for duplication. This can be a problem, for example, if the impact of the loss of order entry is duplicated inside a separate loss estimate for Accounts Receivable, or Accounting in general

- Do not deduct insurance or anticipated claims reimbursements from loss estimates. Claims can become a matter of litigation and in the end may not be realized in total, or the delay in reimbursement may cause cash flow difficulties that can be fatal to a small- or medium-sized organization. Figures adjusted for expected reimbursement cannot consider these uncertainties
- Combine the financial loss data by exposure over time (see example #1). Some of the suggested BIA questions ask for the financial loss for each day of an outage. The data is then further combined into a cumulative loss by function over time (see example #2). This will allow the manager to say "if we were to go cold and dark for three days, we would lose X amount of money."

BIA software programs will help to establish the MAO, operational impacts, and future resource requirements. Without the software, financial impacts are combined (totaled) into the financial impact table used to collect the data (see Table 1 Financial Impact Spreadsheet in Appendix D). Note that the next table will now list the functions themselves and not the breakdown of the loss categories (although a compilation of these losses may be included in the BIA report).

Meet with the steering committee, the sponsor, or with top management to agree on the MAO and RTO after the data is compiled and the report is in draft form. Include these agreements in the final report. In addition, matrix the operational impacts and RPO for the BIA report.

Most of the questions asked in the interview pertain to preparedness, response, and strategy development gaps that are designed to prevent and limit the impact of the disaster, resulting in recommended corrective actions included in the BIA report. Consider at this juncture developing the cost estimates for the implementation of the corrective actions. If less expensive alternates are available, also consider a discussion of these options.

5.2.4 DOCUMENTATION AND COMMUNICATION OF ANALYSIS

The results of the analysis are combined into the BIA report that is often combined with the Risk Assessment report. The manner in which the BIA is documented is important to auditors and to management, so the objectives of the analysis must be clearly illustrated. Although the standards do not specify a particular format for the report (remember the document control requirements), it is important that the report describes the business (its products, processes, and services), processes that support products, and services that enable the goals of the organization ("understanding the organization"), the MAO/MTPD for each process, product, or service, and internal and external dependencies. The BIA report is one of the most important documents within the Business Continuity Management System. It must provide an understanding of the negative impacts over time that the failure to provide these products, processes, and services would have on the organization. It describes the risk to the organization of not resuming its business activities.

The report can begin with an introduction that describes the purpose of the analysis and must describe the business impact analysis process, including the processes used to analyze the data to arrive at the assigned priorities. The scope of the analysis is discussed and should include a high-level list of products, processes, or services that were excluded from the scope of the analysis. The rationale for any exclusion should also form part of the discussion. If the list of exclusions and the rationales for their exclusion are extensive, consider including the detail in an appendix. A list of all personnel and/or third parties who were interviewed or participated in the analysis should be listed along with their titles or positions. If an outside consultant was used, their affiliation can also be listed. Significant documents reviewed can be summarized with the detail (if lengthy) included in an appendix.

Because this can be a lengthy report, it is important that an executive summary is compact but complete and, as most executive summaries are, included early in the report. Describe the nature of the organization, but from a high level in the summary with the appropriate amount of detail in the body of the report. Also, discuss the overall impact to products and services and the overall impact of the organization's inability to meet its goals after a disaster, listing the most vulnerable functions or those with the greatest gaps with a description of the risk and financial and operational impacts. Tables that illustrate the risks and rankings can supplement the discussion. The MAOs and RTOs, and potentially the RPOs, should be highlighted. A list of recommended corrective actions can also be included in the summary (be careful not to preface the recommendations in a findings or recommendation format, leave this to the body of the report).

The body of the report should contain an expanded description of the functions that support products, processes, and services within the scope of the analysis and items from the Executive Summary, focusing on a detailed treatment of the impacts of potential loss. First describe and illustrate the major impacts (and risks if a combined report) revealed in the analysis. For example, an excerpt from a BIA that discussed its impacts (and later illustrated in a combined table of impacts) describes the impact of the loss of their call center:

> The loss of the call center could result in the failure to realize about $1 million per day in direct sales. Many strategies have been discussed to continue their operations but call center managers disagree about their effectiveness. The existing strategy to use the presentation room on the first floor of the San Diego facility will take some time to prepare and can only accommodate less than one quarter of the total call center volume. Work-at-home strategies, although expensive to implement and maintain, have been successfully tested. Other strategies discussed involve transferring call volume to other present and future call center locations.

The discussion should then focus on the following, in no particular order:

- Combined financial loss of each function over time (but list the function in place of the loss category)
- Operational loss by severity and function
- Maximum Acceptable Outage (MAO) (or other measures) by function
- Recovery Time Objectives (RTOs)
- Recovery Point Objectives (RPOs)
- IT systems associated with functional rankings
- IT applications (software) associated with functional rankings
- List dependent functions
- List alternate locations by function
- List of internal and external dependencies (upstream and downstream dependencies)
- Initial strategies by function
- Key resources necessary for continuity
- Other significant measures from the analysis

Although the organization can arrange the information in any manner it wishes, some simple examples include (some tables have been abbreviated by the number of weeks and number of functions represented) (Tables 5.1–5.8):

Table 5.1 Example of Financial Loss over Time by Exposure

Exposure	Day 1		Day 2		Day 3		Day 4		Day 5		Week 2	
	Min	Max	Min	Max	Min	Max	Min	Max	Min	Max	Min	Max
Processing												
Royalty overrides	10,000	14,000	10,000	14,000	10,000	14,000	10,000	14,000	10,000	14,000	0	0
Total	10,000	14,000	10,000	14,000	10,000	14,000	10,000	14,000	10,000	14,000	0	0
Salaries												
Records administration	2830	2830	2830	2830	2830	2830	2830	2830	2830	2830	28,300	28,300
Refunds and repurchase	2269	2269	2269	2269	2269	2269	2269	2269	2269	2269	22,690	22,690
WW training	958	958	958	958	958	958	958	958	958	958	9580	9580
Royalty overrides	4457	4457	4457	4457	4457	4457	4457	4457	4457	4457	44,570	44,570
Statistical analysis	1400	1400	1400	1400	1400	1400	1400	1400	1400	1400	14,000	14,000
Sales awards	472	472	472	472	472	472	472	472	472	472	4720	4720
Dist. services admin.	912	912	912	912	912	912	912	912	912	912	9120	9120
Total	13,298	13,298	13,298	13,298	13,298	13,298	13,298	13,298	13,298	13,298	132,980	132,980

Table 5.2 Example of Financial Loss over Time by Function

Function	Day 1		Day 2		Day 3		Day 4		Day 5		Week 2	
	Min	Max	Min	Max	Min	Max	Min	Max	Min	Max	Min	Max
Sales/call center	1.2	1.5	2.4	3.0	3.6	4.5	4.8	6.0	5.0	7.5	10.0	14.0
Sales/direct	0.7	1.0	1.4	2.0	2.1	3.0	2.8	4.0	4.5	5.0	9.0	10
Royalty overrides	0.1	0.1	0.2	0.2	0.3	0.3	0.4	0.4	0.5	0.5	1.0	1.0
Total ($million)	2.0	2.6	4.0	5.2	6.0	7.8	8.0	10.4	10.0	13.0	20.0	25.0

Table 5.3 Example of the Severity of Operational Impacts

Impact	Dist.-Royalty Overrides	Distributor Services	Human Resources	Medical Affairs	Reception/Operators	Records Admin.	Refunds &Repurchase	Sales Awards (WW)	Scientific Affairs	Statistical Analysis	Training (WW)	Average
Customer service	5	4	5	1	4	5	5	5	4	4	5	4.2
Legal obligations	5	1	4	5	1	5	3	1	1	1	3	2.7
Regulatory	5	1	5	1	1	5	3	1	4	1	3	2.7
Industry image	3	1	5	1	1	5	4	3	4	1	3	2.8
Public image	2	1	4	1	3	5	4	1	0	1	3	2.3
Increase in liability	3	1	4	1	1	5	3	1	4	1	1	2.3
Financial reporting	5	1	1	1	1	4	3	1	1	1	1	1.8
Cash flow	5	1	1	1	1	1	1	1	1	1	1	1.4
Shareholder confidence	3	1	2	1	1	4	1	1	3	1	3	1.9
Vendor relations	3	2	1	1	1	2	1	2	4	1	1	1.7
Financial control	4	1	2	1	1	2	1	1	1	1	1	1.5

Table 5.4 Example of Operational Loss by Function

Impact	1 (Low Impact)	2	3	4	5 (Severe Impact)
Cash flow	Human resources Reception/operators Medical affairs Scientific affairs Records administration Refunds and repurchase Sales awards Statistical analysis Dist. services admin. Training				Order administration Royalty overrides
Competitive advantage	Reception/operators Medical affairs Refunds and repurchase Statistical analysis	Training	Human resources Royalty overrides Sales awards Dist. services admin.		Scientific affairs Records administration
Customer service	Reception/operators Medical affairs			Statistical analysis Dist. services admin.	Human resources Royalty overrides Records Administration Refunds and repurchase Sales awards Training
Financial control	Reception/operators Medical affairs Refunds and repurchase Sales awards Statistical analysis Dist. services admin. Training	Human resources Records Administration		Royalty overrides	

Table 5.5 Example of Risks and Single Points of Failure by Function

Function	Risk	Mitigation
Distributor services–call center	Loss of the call center could result in the failure to realize about $1 million per day.	Build out extra capacity in Dallas, develop failover procedures.
Global supply chain	Losses could increase backorder shipping costs by $11 to $20.	Equip members to work remotely, migrate to Agile [a new software program].
Licensing	Recall of product and suspension of sales, possible imprisonment of country manager, fines and penalties.	Records duplicated and stored in fire-resistant containers, equip selected team members to connect to data systems from remote location.
Organizational development	Delay in program milestones.	Equip members to work remotely, establish offsite training locations out of disaster affected area.
Royalty overrides	Potential FTC fines of $10,000 per file Inability to produce records for civil and criminal proceedings Inability to service 2500 new distributors	Redundant data center, records protection. Records are scanned and archived off site. Store work in progress in fire-resistant containers.

Table 5.5 Example of Risks and Single Points of Failure by Function—cont'd

Function	Risk	Mitigation
Scientific affairs	Loss of clinical trial could delay product introduction by one year or more and possibly the loss of the monetary investment in the study. Adverse event files are not duplicated and stored off site	Ensure trial sites maintain tested business recovery plans certified under ISO 22301 or ASIS SPC. 1-2009. Scan critical adverse event files into an electronic form and archive off site. Store work in progress in secure, fire resistant cabinets.

Table 5.6 Example of Initial Recovery/Continuity Strategies by Function

Function	Alternate Location	Recovery Headcount	Continuity/Recovery Strategy
Business development	Any, home	6	Work from home
Distributor services	Los Angeles, Dallas	25	Continue Century City Backup until Dallas center is built out
Distributor/royalty accounting	Los Angeles distribution center	5	Overstock supplies and store in secure location off site
Human resources	Los Angeles, Dallas, home	6	Work at alternate location until replacement facility established
Internal audit	Near audit locations	7	Wait for recovery
Legal	Home, contract law offices	8	Connect remotely
Organizational development	Home, any alternate location	2	Schedule sessions off site at alternate location
New technologies	Contract labs	8	Salvage equipment, use contract or partner labs
Payroll	Payroll contractor, Los Angeles	2	Pay 80 hours and adjust later
Royalty overrides	Any alternate location	27	Remote connect to systems
Records	Any alternate location	5	Remote connect to systems
Refunds and repurchase	Canada, any alternate location	5	Canada to pick up load
Supply chain planning	Home, any alternate location	8	Alternate, but more expensive shipping modes, carriers, and ports
Transportation	Shipper, any alternate location	12	Redundant and alternate modes, overstocking
Treasury	Home, any alternate location	2	Maintain ability to communicate with financial institutions.
TOTAL		137	

The results of the questionnaire and interview questions are summarized in the report by department, process, or function. The summary, where applicable, should include products, preparedness, vulnerabilities and impacts, alternate work-space strategies, and initial continuity/recovery strategies, along with any special resources or needs required to implement the strategies (this does not mean the number of pencils Human Resources would need if they were to work from

Table 5.7 Example of Maximum Acceptable Outage (MAO) and Business Cycle Criticality by Function

Function	Maximum Acceptable Outage	Critical Business Cycle
Legal	Immediate	Quarter and year end
Risk management	Immediate	None
Corporate communications	1 hour	None
Facilities	1 hour	None
Investor relations	4 hours	End of month, SEC Filings
Licensing	1 day	None
Finance	2 days	7–14th each month
Human resources	4 weeks	None
Employee benefits	2 days	None
Distributor services–call center	2 days	All
Order processing	2 days	End of month
Distribution	2 days	End of month
Treasury	2 days	None
Royalty overrides	3 days	Middle of month
Records	1 week	All
Royalties	3 days	Middle of month
Refunds and repurchase	3 days	Middle of month
All other royalty override functions	1 month	None
Internal Audit	3 months	None

Table 5.8 Example of Recovery Time Objectives for Business Applications

Application or Process	Used By:	Recovery Time Objective
Share point	Investor relations	2 hours
Company track	Licensing	4 hours
	New technologies	3–4 months
	Supply chain management	2 days
CAPS	Distribution	1 day
Clear orbit	Supply chain planning	1 week
	Distribution	1 day
e-Time	Finance	1 day
HRIS	Human resources	1 day
Oracle	Distribution	1 day
	Transportation	3 days
Paybase	Finance	1 day
Phoenix	Finance	1 day
Remote desktop	Royalty overrides	1 day
PAIRS	Supply chain planning	1 week
Genesys	New technologies	3 months

Distribution – Process Improvements and Operations Technology
---

The Distribution – Process Improvements and Operations Technology department utilizes software within Oracle and other technologies to improve productivity, to better manage loads, and to work with suppliers to implement technology. The department is also responsible for product life cycle management.

This group has about 70 employees at the San Diego distribution center and 100 employees at the Nashville distribution center. There is also a distribution center in the Netherlands and one is under construction in Mexico City, Mexico. The Chicago distribution center includes about 10,000 square feet of space but will be used only for direct sales to distributors.

About 30% of the product volume is distributed during the last two to three days of every month. Each distribution center keeps about a two month supply of their top 20 products and about a 30 day supply of the remainder. Turns occur about 3–4 times per year. Inventory value worldwide equals about $100 million, with Amsterdam accounting for $40 million, Nashville $35 million, and San Diego $25 million.

If a disaster occurred, this group could produce about 40% of their current workload and they could work a second shift by executing manual picks. If this function could not be performed for a lengthy period of time, the impact would be the suspension of sales of affected products, loss of revenue, and loss of company reputation. Lead time for replacement of distribution center equipment is about 30 days. The replacement of Operations Technology would occur first, Process Improvement could be out of service for 30 days with minimal effect.

The department has hardcopy files of order forms and shipping documents that are stored in regular filing cabinets.

Personnel from this department could work from home or from any location with a telephone and VPN connection. Their plan is to relocate to other Distribution Centers. These personnel would need access to the corporate network data and Clear Orbit that is the interface with vendors used to place and schedule orders. It is maintained on their servers and supported by the IT department. The department director is the only person with a laptop and VPN access at this time. If Clear Orbit is lost, they "would be blind" but could follow up by telephone. Their CAPS system downloads inventory information from Oracle and then re-uploads when completed. It is maintained by IT, but servers reside at the distribution center. The loss of this system would not cause any lost orders since they can work in manual mode, but orders, except for walk-ins, would not go out the same day. This department would take the lead in the restoration of their server. There are no service level agreements, but IT has a drop shipment agreement.

There are several sole source contracts with suppliers for various products. These contracts state that the suppliers must provide an alternate source for XYZ Corporation and the department has asked for copies of their business continuity plans for review.

Recommendations

▫ Distribution Management should store order forms and shipping documents in secure fire-proof filing cabinets.
▫ Distribution Management should investigate the redundancies and other protections built into the Clear Orbit and CAPS server. Upgrade equipment to include the redundancies and other protections where lacking.
▫ If not included in the IT disaster recovery procedures, Distribution Management should include tasks and resources required to rebuild these servers in the business continuity plan.
▫ Distribution Management should ensure continuity/recovery team members have the resources necessary to connect to IT systems from alternate locations.

FIGURE 5.1

Example of Business Impact Analysis Results of Interview Questions.

home, but this might be listed in the Human Resources Team Plan under Resource Requirements. It refers to higher-level necessities, such as high-speed data connections at home (which most people these days already have) to enable Virtual Private Network (VPN) connections, any special software necessary on the home computer and any associated licensing requirements. For each gap in prevention, preparedness, response and mitigation, obligation, and the like identified in each functional description, a resulting corrective action or recommendation should be listed. Suggested vendors or product cut sheets, if the recommendation involves the purchase of a product or service, should be included in an appendix (see Figure 5.1).

5.3 REANALYSIS

The introduction of a new project, function, or process should include an analysis of the impact of its loss. This helps to foster a culture of business continuity and keeps the BIA fresh. Likewise, any major change in the organizational structure, risk appetite, or strategic direction of the company would necessitate an update of the analysis. Otherwise, the expectation is an annual review of the BIA, and reanalysis every 3–5 years.

5.4 CONFIDENTIALITY

Because of the sensitivity of the information revealed in the BIA, it should be treated as a confidential document. It is appropriate to distribute the full report to top management and to distribute the individual departmental (functional) results and recommendations to the functional leaders for review. Tables of RTO, RPO, and MAO may be included in the Business Continuity Plan, which should also be a controlled document.

5.5 REVIEW

BIA identifies the financial and operational loss of the organization's business functions over periods significant to the individual organization, regardless of what caused the loss, by examining their impact on service objectives, financial position and cash flow, regulatory and contractual issues, and competitive risk. It is necessary to develop the Business Continuity Management System and is essential to understanding the context of the organization. To meet the requirements of the standards, the BIA must identify the functions that support the delivery of products, processes, and services. The BIA process must also be documented.

The information developed as a result of the analysis allows management to make decisions concerning their MAO or the MTPD, which is the time it would take the loss or degradation of a business function or process to have an adverse impact on the organization's objectives, such as the delivery of a service or product. Another similar term, the Maximum Tolerable Downtime (MTD) is used as the maximum downtime or length of time a process can be unavailable before the organization experiences significant (unacceptable) losses. This then allows management to set

RTO and RPO, respectively, for each critical or prioritized business function. The information consists of financial loss impacts in addition to operational or subjective loss impacts in which it is difficult to characterize the loss or degradation of a function in financial terms.

Based on this information, business functions are designated as critical or noncritical to the goals of the organization. The functions are prioritized based on the level of criticality, and continuity or recovery strategies are cost justified based on the results of the analysis. It also identifies the upstream and downstream dependencies of each function within the scope of the analysis and highlights internal and external resources to ensure its resiliency.

The data for the analysis is collected through a combination of workshops, questionnaires, and interviews with functional managers from all components of the organization that are within the scope of the analysis. The scope of the analysis should parallel the scope of the Business Continuity Management System, but the scope may be improperly limited unless the entire organization (within reasonable constraints) is analyzed. Information that will be useful later in the planning process, such as an evaluation of the minimum number of personnel required at alternate worksites, is often included as part of the analysis.

The manner in which the BIA is documented is important to auditors and management, so the objectives of the analysis must therefore be clearly illustrated. It should identify the MAO/MTPD and RTO for each process, product, or service, including internal and external dependencies. It must provide an understanding of the negative impacts over time that the failure to provide these products, processes, and services would have on the organization. It describes the risk to the organization of not resuming its business activities. The BIA document should also identify gaps in the prevention, preparedness, response, mitigation, and recovery of each business function's resilience and include recommended corrective actions to close gaps suggested by the answers revealed on the questionnaires or during the interviews. BIA documentation should be regarded as confidential, controlled information.

Business impact should be understood with the introduction of any new process, product, or service and reevaluated when a significant change occurs in the organization's structure or strategic direction.

RISK ASSESSMENT

6

CHAPTER SUMMARY

The standards allow the selection of a number of quantitative and qualitative methods to systematically assess risk to critical processes, systems, and products identified by the Business Impact Analysis or by independent examination of the risk to organizational and business continuity objectives through the risk assessment process. Departing from a strictly pure risk methodology in its approach to risk assessment, ISO 22301's suggested use of the ISO 31000 Risk Management Standard enables the analyst to look at speculative risk to these objectives, systems, and processes that include financial and reputational risk. Using an Enterprise Risk Management framework, the context of the analysis is established through communication and consultation. The Risk Assessment then systematically identifies, analyzes, and treats the risk of disruption to the organization's prioritized activities in accordance with the organization's risk appetite.

If a hazard is not identified, the risk it presents cannot be prevented, prepared for, or treated. Hazard identification is aided by a healthy degree of paranoia, knowledge of history, research, and the extrapolation of cause and effect. Once identified, the likelihood and consequence of the hazards are analyzed and entered into the risk registry for treatment or monitoring. Depending on the type of analysis used, an Annual Loss Expectancy (ALE) could be used to help prioritize treatment of risk and residual risk through risk avoidance, risk control, risk transfer, or risk assumption.

The assessment and the methodology used to conduct the assessment are documented and communicated to management and to third parties as appropriate. The organization's risk appetite, risk registry, and process for the monitoring and review of risk are important components of this documentation.

KEY TERMS

Annual loss expectancy (ALE); Enterprise risk management; Hazard identification; ISO 31000; ANSI Z690.2; Qualitative risk; Quantitative risk; Residual risk; Risk analysis; Risk assessment; Risk management standard; Risk registry; Risk treatment.

KEY POINTS

- A formal and documented process is required by the standards for a risk assessment
- Risk assessment comprises risk identification, risk analysis, and risk evaluation
- The risk assessment will help ensure that threats are fully understood and treated in the appropriate manner
- Risk is the effect of uncertainty upon objectives
- Risk appetite is the amount of risk an organization is willing to accept in pursuit of its objectives
- Risk analysis provides the basis for risk evaluation and decisions about risk estimation and risk treatment
- Risk is treated primarily through acceptance, avoidance, control, transfer, and financing

6.1 **INTRODUCTION**

Similar to the Business Impact Analysis, a formal and documented process is also required by the International Organization for Standardization (ISO) and ASIS for a risk assessment that helps to ensure that the business continuity management system aligns with the objectives of the organization and with its stakeholders, as well as providing guidance to the selection of business continuity strategies. The National Fire Protection Association (NFPA) 1600:2013 now requires a Risk Assessment. The Risk Assessment must systematically identify, analyze, and treat the risk of disruption to the organization's prioritized activities in accordance with the organization's risk appetite. This means anything within scope that supports the Business Continuity Management System—its products, processes, services, and resources. NFPA also associates the purpose of the risk assessment (and the Business Impact Analysis) to "develop required strategies and plans" and to determine priorities for the application of the elements of Emergency Management (prevention, preparedness, mitigation, response, and recovery).

Although all three standards acknowledge there are different ways to conduct a Business Impact Analysis and Risk Assessment that will determine the order in which they are conducted, the task of the prioritization of activities is generally a function of the Business Impact Analysis. ISO 13000 lists the Business Impact Analysis as an example of a type of acceptable risk assessment method and technique. Prior to the standards, many Business Continuity Professionals would analyze risk to all assets of the organization before the Business Impact Analysis is conducted (as suggested by professional practices). Now the standards, except for NFPA, say to conduct the analysis on prioritized activities.

ASIS guidance suggests analyzing cyber security risk and the level of resilience of each hazard or threat to each asset. This methodology is common to the assessment schemes developed by the United States Department of Homeland Security. ASIS also suggests that the organization assess the physical and psychological harm to employees and interested parties, the devaluation in the share price of stock, the cost of the loss of image and reputation, indirect impacts to the regional economy including losses to the tax base, and the degradation to the environment, including endangered species, as the result of impacts that may affect the organization. It is not clear in the standard if this is intended to be part of the Business Impact Analysis or the Risk Assessment. NFPA requires an evaluation on the impacts of regional, national, or international incidents that could have cascading (synergistic) effects. This is a sound requirement as demonstrated by the March 2011 9.0 magnitude Tōhoku, Japan, earthquake that caused the tsunami responsible for the meltdown of the three reactors at the Fukushima Daiichi Nuclear Power Plant. Ninety-two and a half percent of the casualties died from drowning and not by the earthquake (which occurred offshore). The health effects and other impacts of the radiological contamination are yet to be fully realized. Earthquakes also produce landslides, fires, floods from damaged dams, extended power and utility (water, natural gas) outages, building and roadway bridge collapse, liquefaction, sandboils, train derailments, and hazardous material releases. NFPA uses this earthquake as an example of supply chain disruption (perhaps a better example would include the 7.2 magnitude Great Hanshin earthquake of 1995 in which cranes on the docks in Kobe and Osaka Japan were damaged causing significant supply chain disruptions). This earthquake resulted in more than 6000 deaths and over 30,000 injuries. Fires following the earthquake incinerated the equivalent of 70 US city blocks and with the shaking from the earthquake destroyed over 150,000 buildings, leaving 300,000–600,000 people homeless. The economic loss resulting from this earthquake was around $200 billion. The seismology of the region is very similar to that found in California.

Assets can represent physical structures and equipment, as well as people, processes, services, infrastructure, and products. NFPA 1600:2013 also requires the risk assessment to identify, evaluate, and monitor the impacts of hazards on the health and safety of "persons in the affected area" and then uses the wording "personnel responding to the incident." This appears to indicate the need to include those outside your organization for which operations and processes, such as the use of toxic materials, could affect the broader community or the environment. It goes on to include the analysis of impacts to the continuity of operations, services, supply chain, reputation, and regulatory and contractual obligations. Included without explanation is the requirement for an analysis of "economic and financial conditions." NFPA 1600:2013 directs the organization to monitor the hazards it identifies. According to ISO 31000 (see below), monitoring is defined as the continual checking and critical observation to identify change.

Experienced business continuity professionals may also notice that a risk assessment, not a risk analysis as was required in the past, is mandated by the standards. The Risk Assessment, if executed properly, can be as involved as the Business Impact Analysis. Many Business Continuity professionals minimize the Risk Assessment process mostly because they are not well versed in its requirements or believe that very general estimates of risk based on their knowledge of hazards and their experience are sufficient to understand where to focus resources to treat the risk. This is most often a mistake because the risk assessment will help ensure that threats are fully understood and treated in the appropriate manner. Strategy development and implementation, prevention and mitigation measures, and the development of the organization's risk appetite are often expensive endeavors that cannot be left to the manager's or the organization's intuitive guess, especially if the goal is certification under the standards.

ISO 22301 specifically calls out ISO 31000, the Risk Management Principles and Guidelines, as an acceptable (but not required) process that can be used to satisfy the risk assessment requirement. Related to ISO 31000 is ISO Guide 73:2009, Risk management—vocabulary that provides definitions relating to the management of risk, and ISO/IEC 31010:2009, Risk management that focuses on risk assessment concepts, processes, and the selection of risk assessment techniques. ANSI Z690.2-2011 is the adoption of ISO 31000 in the United States and was sponsored by the American Society of Safety Engineers (ASSE). Although not a management standard, it establishes an Enterprise Risk Management framework for the organization. This standard is not intended for certification in the manner of certification under PS-Prep.

The Risk Management standards spell out an enterprise risk management framework that integrates risk management into the entire organization. The serious Business Continuity Manager should become very familiar with this standard. The framework begins with and requires communication and consultation (the involvement of stakeholders, both internal and external, combined with a process that considers all opinions on the treatment of risk) throughout all stages of the process and ends with continual improvement and feedback. This surrounds the process of risk assessment and risk treatment. Risk is also assessed within the context of the organization and with the risk management process and assessment method or methods selected under 31000.

6.2 UNDERSTANDING RISK

Risk is not necessarily bad or something that needs complete elimination. According to the ASSE Risk Assessment Institute Website (http://www.oshrisk.org/), risk is the combination of the probability of occurrence of harm (injury or damage to the health of people, or damage to property or the environment) and the severity of that harm. This speaks to pure risk: situations that present the opportunity for loss but no opportunity for gain. In opposition to pure risk is speculative risk: uncertainty that could produce either a positive or negative outcome such as gambling, or investing in the stock market. The Security, Safety, and the Business Continuity Manager historically would analyze and treat only for pure risk, but the standard allows consideration of speculative risk. Increasing risk to take advantage of an opportunity is an example. Risk reduction to establish the organization's resilience used for business development or in response to a requirement from a customer is also considered a speculative risk.

Some risks are more important (i.e., those that have a greater effect on the achievement of objectives) than others or those that become increasingly or less important in a different context. Going boating on a windy day presents a certain risk to your new hairdo but the consequences are far less (an acceptable risk) than when the context is windblown hair while going on a first date (a risk that now needs some treatment because the objective is to look good).

ISO and ASIS define risk as the effect (a positive or negative deviation from the expected) of uncertainty on objectives. This definition implies that the objectives are clearly articulated. Objectives can be both macro and micro, including those of the organization, a function, process, or product. Risk is not one-dimensional. It is the combination of the probability of the effect of potential events and the consequences if it does occur. A pure risk results from a peril such as a fire, flood, or earthquake. Hazards contribute to perils (see Risk Analysis and the Security Survey, 4th ed., Broder and Tucker, Butterworth Heinemann 2012).

Risk appetite is the amount of risk an organization is willing to accept in pursuit of its objectives. It defines limits around the amount of risk the organization is willing to pursue so that the success of achieving its goals is better ensured. Ideally, all top-level decisions and strategic initiatives should consider not only the risk appetite of the organization, but potentially the risk attitudes of outside interests. An example of a low-risk appetite would be the decision of an organization not to pursue a business venture with a high potential for profit but one that carries a great deal of risk through consistent offshore supply chain disruptions and labor issues. Although this sounds like a simple concept, it can be difficult to characterize for the organization as a whole because differing levels of risk acceptance can exist within the organization. Whereas it is most often not the Business Continuity Manager's role to establish the risk appetite for the organization, he or she may be responsible for a portion of its documentation and communication under the standards. Overall risk appetite statements are often found in annual reports and financial statements, strategic plans, and marketing reports. These are generally broad statements but must be measurable and time dependent. Some organizations might include statements about the risk appetite for each major class of organizational objectives or categories of risk.

6.3 RISK ASSESSMENT

According to ISO 31010, Risk Assessment comprises risk identification, risk analysis, and risk evaluation. NFPA's definition is essentially the same thing but also refers to hazard identification, the analysis of probability and vulnerability, and an evaluation of their impact. ASSE also refers to hazard identification but adds the need to evaluate controls and conclude with a statement of risk.

Risk assessment allows the organization to characterize the risks they face and how these risks may affect their objectives, to evaluate the adequacy of controls already in place, and to put risks in the proper perspective for later risk treatment.

Many assessment methods (at least 32) suggested by ISO/ANSI can be used that range from brainstorming to Multi-Criteria Decision Analysis (MCDA), each of which are explained to some extent in ISO 31010/ANSI Z690.3-2011. They can be used singularly or in combination with others, and some are better than others at developing the components of risk assessment (risk identification, risk analysis, and risk evaluation). The standard also identifies which methods can provide quantitative output. The Risk Assessment tools include:

• Bayesian Statistics and Bayes Nets	• Hazard Analysis and Critical Control Points (HACCP)
• Bow Tie Analysis	• Hazard and Operability Studies (HAZOP)
• Brainstorming	• Human Reliability Analysis
• Business Impact Analysis	• Layer Protection Analysis (LOPA)
• Cause and Consequence Analysis	• Markov Analysis
• Cause-and-Effect Analysis	• Monte Carlo Simulation
• Checklists	• Multi-Criteria Decision Analysis (MCDA)
• Consequence/Probability Matrix	• Primary Hazard Analysis
• Cost/Benefit Analysis	• Reliability-Centered Maintenance
• Decision Tree	• Risk Indices
• Delphi Technique	• Root Cause Analysis
• Environmental Risk Assessment	• Scenario Analysis
• Event Tree Analysis	• Sneak Circuit Analysis
• Failure Mode Effect Analysis (FMEA)	• Structure What if? (SWIFT)
• Fault Tree Analysis	• Structured or Semi-Structured Interviews
• FN Curves	

Understand what methods other similar organizations use, or are required to use, and what advantages and disadvantages they pose. Some United States government agencies specify the use of specific risk assessment tools, such as Hazard Analysis and Critical Control Points (HACCP) for the food distribution industry or VSAT for water and wastewater facilities, that are consistent with the 2007 United States Risk Analysis and Management for Critical Asset Protection framework.

NFPA 1600:2013 suggests the following method to conduct the Risk Assessment:

• Determine the methodology the organization will use to complete the assessment that aligns with the expertise of those responsible for its completion
• Assess the vulnerability of the organization's assets from identified hazards using internal or external experts
• Categorize assets by type
• List threats and hazards. The standard provides a good list of natural, human-caused (accidental and intentional), and technological hazards. Nevertheless, it is the responsibility of the analyst or assessment team to develop additional hazards that are pertinent to the organization (Appendix G)
• Evaluate the hazards and identify risk
• Assess the effectiveness of any existing controls (prevention and mitigation) for credible threats

- Calculate (categorize) threats, hazards, and potential incidents by their frequency and severity considering how they may differ under varying combinations and how the hazards may trigger collateral risk
- Evaluate residual risk (risk that may still remain after risk treatment controls are implemented)

6.3.1 HAZARD IDENTIFICATION

For many managers, the identification of hazards could be the most difficult part of the risk assessment process. Most of us know that a box of matches in the hands of children presents a potential hazard, but the significance of the absence of shear walls that create a soft first story is not a situation most, apart from those with training or research in the effects of earthquakes on the built environment, would identify as a problem. The remainder of the risk assessment process is relatively simple math (depending on the analysis method chosen) and collaborative decision-making.

If a hazard is not identified, the risk it presents cannot be prevented, prepared for, or treated. The ability to identify hazards is a state of mind, based on a healthy degree of paranoia, knowledge of history, research, and information about cause and effect or the extrapolation of cause and effect to identify what NFPA calls a cascade of events, such as that described in the earthquake effects from Japan mentioned previously.

As many hazards as possible (within reason) that can affect your operations, facilities, workers, or other assets should be identified. Within reason means, for example, hazards will include the rejection of the possibility that a band of roving monkeys would enter a department store and cause havoc within, a scenario that would be considered in Thailand (this actually happened) but not in a major North American city. Likewise, planners in San Francisco or Seattle should not list hurricane as a threat because the adjacent ocean water is too cold to support such an event (if you did not know this, it would be listed, researched, and rejected). Some would argue that it should be listed anyway to show an auditor that all foreseeable events were considered. Caution must be used so that hazards are not too quickly rejected without analysis.

Natural hazards and their effects are relatively easy to identify because they tend to recur on a roughly cyclical basis in the same general region. The March 22, 2014, Oso, Washington mile-wide mudslide that killed almost 45 residents in its path was known by locals and revealed in public records to be an area of instability since the late 1930s. Although no major business interruptions resulted from this incident, it is important to understand the hazards in the community surrounding the organization. Despite this knowledge, Emergency Managers in the area stated that the slide was "completely unforeseen" (http://en.wikipedia.org/wiki/2014_Oso_mudslide). Similar statements were made about the unpredictability of the September 11, 2001, method of attack, but documents found in the Philippines detailed al-Qaeda plans (Bojinka Plot) to crash an airplane into the headquarters of the United States Central Intelligence Agency in 1995. An examination of historical records would have revealed that. Although a manufacturing facility in the midwestern United States was located on high ground, a local river periodically overflowed its banks, flooding the town's sewage treatment plant and causing the otherwise unaffected business to shut down for health reasons. Previous hazards in the community can be identified in newspapers, libraries, previously declared disasters, civil and geological surveys, and interviews with long-time residents. Insurance loss control runs are another good source of historical information.

Hazards are also identified through a complete physical inspection of the organization's facilities, grounds, and surrounding environment. Locate surrounding organizations and determine if their operations could pose a hazard to your organization. Include an examination of the area's crime statistics.

If your offices are in the same building as a government agency such as the Internal Revenue Service, you may want to evaluate the risk of a bombing or protest. During your inspection, identify structural hazards, fire hazards, and the adequacy of the fire control system, non-structural hazards such as bookcases not bolted to the wall, or sensitive and expensive equipment not sitting on seismic damping mats if located in an area subject to earthquakes. Look at conditions, equipment, and processes and imagine what could go wrong, how employees could be injured, or what can shut down operations. Analyze how what you see can fail. Watch for regulatory compliance issues such as the lack of secondary containment around storage tanks. The collapse of a 50-foot-tall storage tank in Boston, Massachusetts, sent a 25-foot wall of molasses down a street and killed 21 people and injured 150 in 1919. Earlier, in 1814, 135,000 imperial gallons of beer similarly drowned eight people in the surrounding community.

Checklists and surveys can help the inspection process by giving the inspector clues about what to look for. The checklist should contain items that answer the following questions under normal and disaster conditions:

- How can employees or the community be injured?
- How can critical systems be damaged?
- What single points of failure exist?
- What hazards can disrupt operations?
- How can hazards affect the environment?
- What hazards can have a public relations impact?
- What hazards might generate regulatory issues?

Completed checklists should be retained as archival documents and consideration given to inclusion in the Risk Analysis report.

Examine processes and critical equipment to understand their failure modes. What is the life expectancy of equipment or its "Mean Time Before Failure." Are procedures in place to monitor the precursors to equipment failure? Hazard and Operability studies (HAZOP), Failure Mode Effects Analysis (FMEA), both risk assessment tools mentioned in the ANSI standard, and Preliminary Hazard Analysis (PrHA) are some engineering tools that can be used to identify hazards to equipment and processes. Manufacturer maintenance and operating manuals and their support personnel may also be a good source of risk to the safety or failure of their equipment. Interview process owners who generally have a good understanding of the hazards and risk that their operations face.

Similar to history, research is a primary source of hazard information. The internet contains a wealth of data often pinpointed to very specific locations. The discovery of this information is often constrained only by the manager's ability to conduct the keyword search.

Hazardous Materials Management Plans are required of all organizations that store or use hazardous materials above threshold quantities defined by local regulations. These plans can be found on the internet and are a good source of information about the risk posed by nearby operations. They generally contain listings of the hazardous materials in use, often with dispersal data and maps. In place of the internet, the jurisdiction's Emergency Services or Fire Department can provide information about where to find these plans.

The United States Disaster Mitigation Act of 2000 requires all communities to prepare mitigation plans designed to improve the planning, response, and recovery from disasters by requiring state and local entities to have all hazard mitigation plans in place by November 2004. Referred to as Local Hazard Mitigation Plans, they will list the hazards and risks faced within the jurisdiction and often include detailed maps that pinpoint areas of varying impact for natural hazards, sometimes technological hazards, and human-made hazards. These plans can also be found on the jurisdiction's (city, county, state) emergency services or fire department web pages. Likewise, a phone call to one of these departments may produce the needed information if the internet search is not successful.

The United States government and governmental agencies maintain many websites that contain hazard information on natural phenomena and other types of hazards, including those posed by terrorist acts. Although some of the following websites may change over time, look at the following noninclusive list in Appendix F to help develop hazard information.

In cases in which the above sources do not cover certain locations, or in which information is insufficient, a phone call to the nearest university's earth or atmospheric sciences department can reveal very specific and detailed hazard information not found in searchable databases.

The use of outside experts can also aid in the identification of hazards. Engineering firms can identify structural and nonstructural performance under seismic or storm conditions. Insurance loss control consultants are often skilled fire protection engineers. Enlist Information Technology and Telecommunications experts to help identify hazards to their equipment and to internal and external networks. The Steering Committee or a risk assessment team can also be tasked with hazard identification.

Review literature (or webpages) about hazards to understand how they develop, how they may be triggered, and what their cascaded effects may be that could affect your risk assessment (and ultimately your assets). For example, floods can trigger fires, snake bites, hazardous materials releases, and the growth of toxic mold. Just some of the effects of an earthquake that can be revealed from literature or the internet include:

- Structural damage and displacement
- Post-traumatic stress
- Loss of utilities (gas, water, electrical power) and other infrastructure
- Disruption of communications
- Transportation difficulties
- Inflated prices for goods and services (in a cash economy)
- Human resource problems
- Cash economy
- Overloaded and nonresponsive governmental services
- Victims trapped under structures and debris
- Mass casualties, shortage of hospital beds and medical assistance
- Disruption of routines
- Loss of housing
- Difficulty obtaining food, water, and other basic needs
- Uncontrolled fires
- Increased illnesses
- Damaged or destroyed products and raw materials
- Canceled orders
- Loss of vital records

A primary goal of security, business continuity management, and hazard identification is to anticipate the unexpected (Broder and Tucker, 2012). Combine the knowledge of history, inspections, and research and use brainstorming or scenario planning to anticipate the cause and effect of what conditions, human acts, or natural phenomena will create a hazard, or associated risk generated by a hazard. This is an especially useful tool when trying to anticipate the actions of a terrorist. A major goal of organized terrorism is the disruption of our economy and therefore our business and infrastructure. The threat of terrorist acts is one that Business Continuity Managers must be adept at assessing, or have the ability to work in conjunction with Security Professionals to properly identify and characterize these threats. Brainstorming can be an individual or group endeavor. Here is the chance to let your imagination go wild; free-flow thinking is desired upfront. Similar to brainstorming is scenario planning. Scenario planning is the development of descriptive models of how the future might turn out. It is used to identify potential situations and impacts and to devise strategies based on future variables or changing conditions. It is also useful to understand how additional hazards or incidents can cascade or take different pathways (risk interaction) from a trigger hazard. Scenario planning can be applied to natural, technological, and human-made hazards including risk to the organization's brand. Subject the hazards to analysis under changing conditions. An example of scenario planning for the flood potential of a nearby river might examine how the flood risk would change under the following conditions:

- Climate change
- Economic downturn that reduces the tax base and the ability of the jurisdiction to continue flood control measures
- Dam failure
- Ice jams
- Landslide
- Beaver dams
- Landfill
- Change in flow from previous floods
- Mitigation completed or proposed
- Changes in the built environment
- Water rights litigation
- Tropical storm
- Emergency dam releases to support fish survival
- Changes in the community response plan
- Road changes that could retard evacuation
- Rapid snow melt

6.3.2 RISK REGISTRY

Once the hazards are identified, they are entered into the first columns of the risk log, most often referred to as the risk register or risk registry. A risk registry is a summary of identified risks and their ranking, and how they are to be treated. It can serve as the reference to the remainder of the risk assessment. It can exist in the form of a spreadsheet, database, or descriptive document. The contents of the registry vary, but the Project Management Institute's 2013 version of its Project Management Body of Knowledge suggests that when analyzing risk to a project, the hazards are listed along with a description in as much detail as is reasonable of the associated risks. A consistent format for the description should be used, for example, one that outlines the event that results in an impact and consequence. The detail included should correspond with the level of risk and the degree of risk treatment, concentrating on high and moderate risks. Low-priority risks are included on a watch list within the registry. The standard allows risks to be screened to concentrate on the most significant risks or to exclude minor risks based on the context of the analysis, but the manager faces a certain degree of risk without going through the analysis process for all risks. Any exclusion should be completely explained and justified in the report. The registry should also include:

- Unique risk number for each one identified
- Name or title of team member responsible for the risk (risk owner)
- Controls currently in place
- Information used to assess and prioritize risks (Probability, Severity, and Overall Risk based on the risk analysis method used)
- Ranking
- Budget and schedule necessary to implement risk treatment
- Risk treatment strategies
- Residual risks (any risk not addressed that remains after treatment)
- Secondary risk (additional or new risk created by the treatment of the primary risk)

The cause of the risk (may include risk triggers and may be included in the risk description), a statement of risk appetite, and third-party stakeholders may be referenced in the registry. Although the risk registry is a working document, it should be included in the risk assessment document and included in the periodic management report.

6.3.3 RISK ANALYSIS

The analysis of risk, that is, how risk is quantified, can be approached in many ways and can be either quantitative or qualitative, but it is generally a quantitative method that returns the most reliable, auditable, and actionable data. The more important the risk or the more complicated the risk may necessitate using a quantitative approach, but keep in mind, like the Business Impact Analysis, some risks are better (or easier) characterized in a qualitative manner, especially when reliable data is lacking about the hazard or process analyzed (which often is the result of inadequate research). When a need exists to justify an expensive treatment of the risk, the use of a quantitative method such as Bayesian Theory, which returns a numerical value for the risk, may have more chance of acceptance by upper management. A mixture of the two is acceptable if the circumstances warrant.

According to the standard, risk analysis provides the basis for risk evaluation and decisions about risk estimation and risk treatment. It is a process to understand the nature of risk and to determine the level of risk for an event, opportunity, or objective so that the proper amount of resources are justified and directed toward its treatment over others of lesser consequence.

Quantitative risk analysis estimates the probability (defined in the standard as "likelihood") that the event or condition will occur and estimates the impact or consequence if it does happen. It is represented by the formula:

$$\text{Risk (R)} = \text{Probability (P)} \times \text{Consequence (C)}.$$

However, this equation is challenged by some as not representative of the true risk at the extremes of the scale, that is, low probability and high consequence versus high probability and low consequence. It does not consider the speed of the onset of a risk. The probability represents the chances of the event happening and can be expressed in terms such as for every 10 annual rainstorms, the river will flood its banks once making it a one in 10 chance of flooding each year (or .10). Consequence is the positive or negative outcome of an event, or range of events that affects objectives. Consequence can be quantitative or qualitative but whenever possible use quantitative values, that is, the cost of the impact. Remember that consistency in comparisons across the organization is important.

Consequence can be expressed in financial terms using the Annual Loss Expectancy (ALE). The ALE returns a value that management can better understand and use to justify the commitment of resources when applied to mitigation and continuity strategies. It is the probability times the value of the loss or

$$ALE = 10^{(f+i-3)}/3.$$

From Risk Analysis and the Security Survey, the following values may be used to estimate risk (Table 6.1):

Table 6.1 Values for Frequency and Impact			
Estimated frequency	**Value of "f"**	**Cost of impact**	**Value of "i"**
Once in 300 years	1	$10	1
Once in 30 years	2	$100	2
Once in 3 years	3	$1000	3
Once in 100 days	4	$10,000	4
Once in 10 days	5	$100,000	5
Once per day	6	$1,000,000	6
Ten times per day	7	$10,000,000	7
One hundred times per day	8	$100,000,000	8

Qualitative risk analysis characterizes the risk as high, medium, or low and is the most commonly used method of analysis in Business Continuity Management. It carries the advantage of ease and speed of use and often produces a table or graphical output. A common method is to plot Likelihood on a vertical axis and Consequence on the horizontal after values are assigned to each. Assigned values should be meaningful to the context of the analysis and are generally scaled from a value of one to five. A scale of 10 or something less than five generally does not return meaningful comparisons. Similar to Table 6.1, scales for Likelihood and Consequence are found in Tables 6.2–6.4, respectively, and can include:

Table 6.2 Sample Likelihood Scale		
Scale	**Likelihood**	
5	Almost certain (Frequent)	81–100%
4	Likely	61–80%
3	Possible	41–60%
2	Unlikely	21–40%
1	Rare or very unlikely	1–20%

Table 6.3 Sample of Consequence Scale

Scale		Impact or consequence
5	Extreme	Financial loss between $X and $X Major loss of reputation, market share Significant regulatory fines, prosecution, or incarceration of senior staff Fatalities and/or third party liability Spill or release with direct health effects to people or lasting effect on environment
4	Major	Financial loss between $X and $X Sustained negative public relations attention, loss of market share Formal investigation by a regulatory agency Major or multiple injuries, especially to third parties Contamination causing stress on environmental systems or wildlife
3	Moderate	Financial loss between $X and $X Significant public relations, reputational damage Regulatory finding that requires formal analysis and corrective action Recordable injury that requires hospitalization Spill or release over regulatory limits
2	Minor	Financial loss between $X and $X Minor public relations, reputation issues Simple filing of report to regulators Minor first aid injuries to employees or guests Minor spills cleaned by normal means
1	Incidental	Financial loss up to $X amount Public relations (reputation) issues easily resolved No regulatory impact No injuries to employees or guests No damage or effect on the environment

Table 6.4 Sample of Risk Matrix

	Certain	Likely	Possible	Unlikely	Rare
Extreme	High	High	High	High	High
Major	High	High	Medium	Medium	Medium
Moderate	High	Medium	Medium	Medium	Low
Minor	Medium	Medium	Medium	Low	Low
Incidental	Low	Low	Low	Low	Low

The likelihood scales can be expressed in terms of the life of an asset, project, working career of an employee, or a 30-year period, the service life of real property.

The United States Federal Emergency Management Agency, Department of Homeland Security considers risk to be a function of Consequence (C), Vulnerability (V), and Threat (T) represented as $R = f (C,V,T)$ when analyzing risk to critical infrastructure. They have refined the formula to

R = (T*V)*C to arrive at a total risk value. The phrase (T*V) represents the likelihood. Threat is defined as the likelihood that a particular asset, system, or network will suffer an attack or an incident such as a natural disaster. Threat is a function of intent and the capability of an adversary or, in the context of a natural disaster, based on the probability of occurrence. Vulnerability is a characteristic that renders an asset, system, or network susceptible to destruction, incapacitation, or exploitation. Numerical values are assigned to each depending upon the percentage of impact of risk criteria to natural, technological, and human-made hazards to arrive at a diagram that plots likelihood against consequence.

6.4 RISK TREATMENT

Once the risks have been analyzed and prioritized, it is now time for management to do something about the risk that considers the organization's risk appetite. A key consideration is that all risk treatment must be cost-effective. There are many ways to treat risk, but the primary methods for our purposes are:

- Risk Avoidance
- Risk Control
- Risk Transfer
- Risk Acceptance
- Risk Financing

Risk Avoidance is by far the most effective (but not necessarily the most cost-effective) because the source of pure risk is eliminated. If your facilities are located next to a river that floods every year, move the operations to a location on higher ground. However, the location next to the river may carry advantages such as ease of receiving raw materials, shipping finished product, water to cool production machinery, and so on. Another example is the avoidance of opening an office in a high-crime district, but this must also be weighed against the opportunity of the potential revenue that may be generated by the new office (other forms of risk treatment can be utilized in this case). ANSI Standard Z10, the Occupational Health and Safety Management Standard's Hierarchy of Controls (see next chapter) refers to Risk Avoidance as Risk Elimination.

Risk Control is the steps taken to reduce and manage the risk to within acceptable levels. Prevention, preparedness, mitigation, response, and continuity strategies are examples of risk control. Risk Control can be administrative through the implementation of policy and procedures or it can be an engineered solution such as the construction of dikes in flood-prone areas.

Risk Transfer is passing the risk to a third party, generally considered insurance coverage to protect against the risk. However, the manager must remember that obtaining insurance against a risk does not reduce or eliminate the risk, only that reimbursement to the organization for the loss may be available. The danger here is that not all risks are covered, reimbursement can be delayed at a time that cash flow for the organization may be of concern if the loss was due to a larger disaster, and the insurance carrier may dispute the claim if the organization cannot sufficiently prove the loss. Risk transfer can also occur with contracts, outsourcing, joint ventures, or partnerships.

Risk Acceptance or Risk Assumption means the organization has determined that the risk is not sufficient to warrant additional controls (such as residual risk) or it is impossible to eliminate the risk.

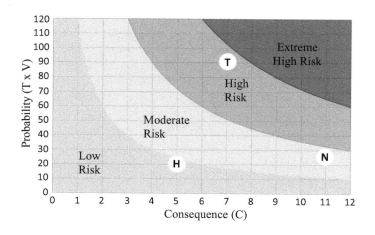

FIGURE 6.1

Example of Homeland Security Risk Assessment Diagram (U.S. Department of Homeland Security, 2009).

These may include some of the risk identified in the lower right squares in Figure 6.1. In accepting the risk, the organization decides to make itself liable for the loss that may be incurred. No additional effort is taken to manage the risk, except perhaps through risk financing. The organization should document and justify all assumed risk by adding to the risk register as part of the watch list for future monitoring.

Risk Financing is a form of self insurance in which the organization sets aside and manages (read invests) funds to cover a future potential loss. Risk Financing is often used for liability and worker compensation reserves.

6.5 RISK ASSESSMENT REPORT

Similar to the Business Impact Analysis report, the risk assessment report must, of course, detail all of the requirements called out in the standard and comply with its document control mandates that includes a description of the report authors and management approval. It must describe the assessment methodology and, if not one listed in ISO 31000, describe briefly what makes it a valid method. This is not required by the standards, but could save future grief.

One of the outcomes of the report is to communicate the risk to interested parties, so the process of risk identification, analysis, and treatment need to be fully explained. Identified hazards, and if appropriate how they were identified, are listed. Remember to include hazards and threats for financial, reputational, natural, human-made, and technological hazards that include any downstream threats to people and processes that support critical activities. The analysis of the hazards is explained in a manner that generates the risk ranking. Explain just what the impact of each threat has on the organization's objectives. The treatment applied to each risk is detailed or proposed. A copy of the risk registry, or updated version that resulted from the analysis should help to make a clear statement of these requirements. All of this is framed around the context of the analysis and of the organization's risk appetite, which should be completely outlined in the report. An overall risk evaluation that summarizes the primary risks and how they intend to be managed through risk treatment or business continuity strategies should be demonstrated.

The report must be kept up to date (i.e., the process repeated or reviewed as appropriate) and confidential.

6.6 REVIEW

Risk is the effect (a positive or negative deviation from the expected) of uncertainty on objectives. Pure risk is the combination of the probability of occurrence of harm (injury or damage to the health of people, or damage to property or the environment) and the severity of that harm. A pure risk results from a peril such as a fire, flood, or earthquake. Hazards contribute to perils. The standards allow for the inclusion of speculative risk in the assessment. Risk appetite is the amount of risk an organization is willing to accept in pursuit of its objectives.

The Risk Assessment must systematically identify, analyze, and treat the risk of disruption to the organization's prioritized activities in accordance with the organization's risk appetite. It is a formal process that systematically identifies hazards (i.e., what may happen and why), what is the likelihood of the hazard, and what are the consequences if it should happen. All identified hazards are analyzed, prioritized, and the appropriate risk treatments in accordance with the organization's risk appetite are implemented.

ISO 22301 specifically calls out ISO 31000, the Risk Management Principles and Guidelines as an acceptable (but not required) process that can be used to satisfy the risk assessment requirement. This standard spells out an enterprise risk management framework that integrates risk management into most aspects of the entire organization.

A primary goal of hazard identification is to anticipate the unexpected. Combine the knowledge of history, inspections, and research and use brainstorming or scenario planning to anticipate the cause and effect of what conditions, human acts, or natural phenomena will create a hazard, or associated risk generated by a hazard.

A risk registry is a summary of identified risks and their ranking, and how they are to be treated. It can serve as the reference to the remainder of the risk assessment. It can exist in the form of a spreadsheet, database, or descriptive document and is a document updated and reviewed by senior management on a regular basis.

Risk analysis provides the basis for risk evaluation and decisions about risk estimation and risk treatment. It is a process to understand the nature of risk and to determine the level of risk for an event, opportunity, or objective so that the proper amount of resources are justified and directed toward its treatment over others of lesser consequence. Quantitative risk analysis estimates the probability (defined in the standard as "likelihood") that the event or condition will occur and estimates the impact or consequence if it does happen. Qualitative risk analysis characterizes the risk as high, medium, or low and is the most commonly used method of analysis in Business Continuity Management. It carries the advantage of ease and speed of use and often produces a table or graphical output.

Consequence can be expressed in financial terms using the Annual Loss Expectancy (ALE). The ALE returns a value that management can better understand and use to justify the commitment of resources when applied to mitigation and continuity strategies.

Risk Avoidance is by far the most effective (but not necessarily the most cost-effective) means of risk treatment, because the source of pure risk is eliminated. The steps taken to reduce and manage the risk to within an acceptable level is risk control, which is another way to treat risk. Other risk treatment methods include Risk Transfer, Risk Financing, and Risk Assumption.

The risk assessment report must detail all of the requirements called out in the standard and describe the assessment methodology used and how it was used and its results. One of the outcomes of the report is to communicate the risk to interested parties, so the process of risk identification, analysis, and treatment need to be fully explained. Identified hazards, and if appropriate how they were identified, are listed. An overall risk evaluation that summarizes the primary risks and how they intend to be managed through risk treatment or business continuity strategies should be demonstrated.

BIBLIOGRAPHY

Broder, J.F., Tucker, E., 2012. Risk Analysis and the Security Survey, fourth ed.Butterworth-Heinemann.

A Guide to the Project Management Body of Knowledge (PMBOK Guide), fifth ed. 2013. Project Management Institute, Inc, Newtown Square, PA.

Enhanced Threat and Risk Assessment Training Support Package 2009. U.S. Department of Homeland Security, Texas A&M Engineering Extension Services (TEEX).

Oso Mudslide, 2014. http://en.wikipedia.org/wiki/2014_Oso_mudslide.

MITIGATION AND BUSINESS CONTINUITY STRATEGY

CHAPTER SUMMARY

Continuity and recovery strategies are cornerstones of a Business Continuity Management System but their need to be mapped to the results of the Business Impact Analysis and Risk Assessment is often unrecognized by many Business Continuity Managers. The failure to recognize this relationship results in strategies that may be less than cost effective, may not completely achieve the goal to continue the activities of prioritized functions, and will not meet the requirements of the standards.

Strategy development is best accomplished by the process owners or continuity team members, not by the steering committee or consultant, although their input can add a broader perspective to proposed continuity solutions. Strategies that are technically feasible, aligned with the Recovery Time Objective of the functional unit and supply chain vendors, and minimize changes to routine and organizational structure are the most effective. Organizations with active Business Continuity Management programs utilize a high-level strategy of a backup Information Technology capability, offsite alternate workspace, and a means to connect the two. Individual functions implement strategies specific to their goals and objectives that supplement the higher-level strategies, which include the protection and recovery of vital resources. This chapter lists typical strategies employed by common business functions including Supply Chain Risk Management. Many business continuity strategies are actually a form of mitigation, an important element of Emergency Management.

The mitigation of risk to critical functions can reduce the impact of an incident to the point that response or recovery is minimal or not even necessary. This is accomplished in part through the implementation of general controls that include redundancies, divergence, and service level agreements. Mitigation for specific hazards can be addressed by following the Hierarchy of Controls' risk treatment methodology of Substitution, Engineering, Administrative Controls, and Personal Protective Equipment.

KEY TERMS

Administrative controls; Business continuity strategy; Divergence; Engineering controls; Hierarchy of controls; Mitigation; Redundancies; Substitution; Supply chain continuity; Supply chain risk management (SCRM); Supply chain threats; Vital records.

KEY POINTS

- Business Continuity Strategies must be based on the results of the Business Impact Analysis (BIA) and Risk Assessment
- Alternate work locations and access to Information Technology (IT) systems compose the primary strategies
- Mitigation and Business Continuity Strategies share many attributes
- Mitigation is often cost-effective and can eliminate or greatly reduce the impact of an incident
- Mitigation should be based on the Hierarchy of Controls

- Strategies are most effective when developed by the process owners
- Strategies are designed to continue the prioritized activities of critical functions

7.1 INTRODUCTION

Most organizations with a Business Continuity Management program rely on a high-level strategy of alternate data systems should the original fail or meet with destruction. They establish an alternate location from which to work should the facilities become damaged or access is restricted, and create a means to connect the two so that relocated employees can continue, with the proper resources, to carry on their work. Individual business functions implement strategies that are specific to their goals and objectives and that supplement the above.

According to the standards, Business Continuity Strategies must be based on the results of the Business Impact Analysis (BIA) and Risk Assessment. Indeed, many of the gaps identified in the BIA and Risk Assessment are translated into mitigation or Business Continuity Strategies. For the purposes of certification against the standards, this relationship must be clearly demonstrated and approved by top management.

A fine distinction commonly exists between mitigation and business continuity strategy. Mitigation applies more directly to strategies to protect the organization from the impacts of hazards, and business continuity strategies protect against the impact of risk to prioritized activities of the organization. A Business Continuity Strategy is defined by the DRI International as "a strategic approach by an organization to ensure its recovery and continuity in the face of a disaster or other major incidents or business disruptions" (International Glossary for Resiliency, DIR International, 2013). Mitigation is sustained action that reduces or eliminates long-term risk to people and property from hazards and their effects, although NFPA 1600 (2013) requires interim action in addition to long-term measures. Under NFPA 1600, mitigation strategies are required when the hazard cannot be prevented.

7.2 MITIGATION

Mitigation is a primary element of Emergency Management and often considered its first phase, but it is not a linear process. Mitigation in some form is integrated into all of the other elements of Emergency Management. After the continuity or recovery efforts have been completed, the cycle returns to mitigation because it is an opportune time to build mitigation measures into repair or reconstruction projects while money and interest are available.

Examples of mitigation include diversion dikes to prevent flooding, bolting book cases and file cabinets to the wall in seismically active areas, installing automatic fire sprinkler systems or smoke detectors, establishing a "defensible space" around the perimeter of the building by removing flammable vegetation, removing debris from nearby creeks, and strengthening the wind resistance of facilities.

Mitigation can eliminate or greatly reduce the impact of an incident to the point that response or recovery is minimal or not necessary. It can allow for a smoother and more rapid response and recovery.

Mitigation is cost-effective, but use this blanket statement with caution. It is generally accepted that for every dollar spent on mitigation, three dollars are saved on costs avoided because of a disaster. Mitigation can increase the cost of new construction by 1–5%, but the cost of earthquake retrofitting can reach five times the cost of the original construction. A bank in Southern California spent $17.00 to prevent the loss of $3000 desktop computer systems, estimating a 4–5% mitigation cost versus replacement cost, saving $30 million after a major earthquake.

The outputs from the identification of hazards and risk to critical functions (BIA and Risk Assessment) are examined. The most practical, cost-effective strategies to reduce or eliminate their impact are selected and approval for funding is obtained from management. Once the measures are implemented, they are maintained and monitored to ensure they are functional when needed at the time of a disaster.

After the hazards are identified, it is important that the effects of the hazard are fully understood so that all of the risks posed by the hazard are anticipated and adequately treated. Knowledge of the maximum and anticipated potential of the hazard, its rate of onset, the geographical area that could be affected, and what populations and assets are at risk will help avoid surprises at the time of the disaster by applying appropriate measures to mitigate their effects.

Although not required by the Business Continuity standards, mitigation (and business continuity) strategies should follow the Hierarchy of Controls as defined in American National Standards Institute (ANSI) Z-10, the Occupational Health and Safety Management Systems Standard (Figure 7.1). The Hierarchy of Controls establishes a set of actions to consider in a descending order of effectiveness to resolve hazardous situations by designing risk mitigation (controls) based on the highest achievable order. In other words, reasonable attempts are made to mitigate a hazard or hazards using the highest order in the hierarchy before considering the next lowest order—a lower step is not chosen until all practical applications of the preceding higher levels are exhausted. These levels of controls consist of

- Elimination
- Substitution
- Engineering Controls
- Administrative Controls
- Personal Protective Equipment (PPE)

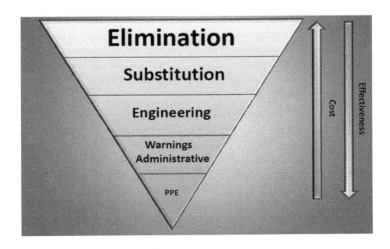

FIGURE 7.1

Hierarchy of Controls.

Elimination, Substitution, and Engineering are the most effective and most sustainable controls because they rely least on human intervention or performance but in general are the most expensive to implement. The remainder rely greatly on human performance and are therefore considered the least effective controls.

The elimination of the hazard (risk avoidance) is the preferred and most effective means to mitigate a hazard. The elimination of the hazard removes the risk so no potential for harm remains. Relocating your facility to higher ground or out of the flood zone should eliminate the main risk from flooding.

Substitution replaces a hazard with a process or substance that is not hazardous or with one that is less hazardous. Outsourcing or using a non-toxic chemical in place of a toxic chemical are examples of substitution. Substitution may involve a tradeoff between expense and efficiency, but often in the final analysis, organizations find the control that provides the higher level of safety is the most cost-effective.

Engineering Controls are the next best form of mitigation apart from the elimination or substitution of the hazard. Engineering Controls change the tool, process, or built environment to permanently prevent exposure to the hazard. These controls are built in and require no attention from the user or organization—they don't generally rely on human intervention or action. Engineering Controls isolate the exposure from the hazard; in other words, it provides a barrier that separates the hazard from the risk. Flood diversion dams or dikes, bomb-blast-resistant designs, and earthquake bracing are examples of engineering controls.

Administrative Controls are typically policies and procedures or regulatory controls such as codes and standards. Building codes, land use permits, and evacuation procedures are examples of Administrative Controls. This is considered one of the least effective of the hierarchy because it is dependent on human intervention, understanding, and compliance. Therefore, use caution when designing mitigation based on administrative controls because codes and standards often represent minimum requirements and not necessarily best practices. In addition, the controls may be poorly communicated to those who need to understand or implement the control.

PPE relates predominantly to worker safety by providing some type of barrier between the worker and the hazard. PPE places the protection directly on the workers' body. It is considered the least effective, again because of the reliance on human intervention to identify the need, and because the equipment must be maintained in a usable condition. PPE applies to business continuity through the protection of emergency responders and in a pandemic situation, which requires the use of respiratory protection and gloves.

Other forms of mitigation include:

- Service Level Agreements
- Redundancies and Divergence
- Separation of Hazards

Service Level agreements include contractual obligations for the repair or replacement of equipment or the delivery of services or products within an agreed upon period, usually within 24 hours. Emergency replenishment of diesel to backup generators, overnight replacement of damaged equipment or replacement parts, and the delivery of a number of workstations preconfigured with the organization's software image to an alternate location are examples.

Many lean organizations of today strive to eliminate redundancies, but the decentralization of facilities, equipment, and systems adds resilience to the organization. Diverse functionality of equipment and processes, or processing locations will help mitigate the loss of equipment or processing capacity. The use of multiple modes of emergency communication, for example, such as two-way radio, satellite radio, cellular service through multiple carriers, and amateur radio communications will help ensure against the loss of one or more modes of communication. Diverse routing of data communications will build protection against cable cuts or central station outages largely avoiding single points of failure. A second data center with the capacity to absorb critical processing can prove to be a cost-effective form of mitigation.

Critical equipment, processes, and personnel should be separated from hazards as much as practical. Large amounts of hazardous or flammable materials, for example, should not be stored in the same building as the data center. The design of the facility, site, and processes should consider the risk posed by nearby hazards and steps taken to protect one from the other.

7.2.1 COST EFFECTIVENESS

Similar to Business Continuity Strategy, mitigation must be cost-effective, technically feasible, and must not create additional hazards. Few organizations devote unlimited funding to Business Continuity Management needs so it is important that resources are directed to the most at risk, impactfully prioritized exposures. Mitigation can be a "big-ticket item," often necessitating capital project-level funding. Other mitigation measures may need to be prioritized and spread out over several budget cycles. The experienced manager will identify, if possible, alternate or interim measures in case funding is not approved for the original plan. Risk tolerance is also important because an "extremely unlikely" threat may fall within the risk acceptance category.

Funding for the mitigation plan may be secured in part by demonstrating the return on investment (ROI) or the amount of losses avoided by the implementation of the proposed measures. For example, calculate the cost of the failure or damage to the facility, its contents subject to damage, and any displacement costs that would occur if the mitigation actions are not implemented. The BIA should supply values for the loss of revenue that may be necessary to add to the loss estimate. The costs associated with the implementation and maintenance of the mitigation should be demonstrated. Include subjective (operational) losses such as regulatory or contractual compliance to supplement the cost justification. According to Risk Analysis and the Security Survey (Broder and Tucker, 2012):

Displacement costs represent the dollar amount required to relocate a function, or a building's functions, to another location on a permanent or temporary basis. Consider moving costs, replacement costs if not included above, costs to prepare the new space, lost subleases, and other expenses as required. If moving to a temporary location, include the costs to move back to the original or to a permanent facility. One possible shortcut to determine the expected future loss based on a past incident for which the previous impact is known is to multiply the impact (dollar loss) by the increase or decrease in exposure. Adjust the resulting figure for inflation.

A building or facility replacement cost is usually expressed in terms of cost per square foot and reflects the present-day replacement value. The cost may be offset by insurance, but be careful because that coverage may include only "present value" (depreciated value) and not total replacement. Include the cost to demolish a damaged facility, especially if there is some type of overriding expense, such as asbestos removal. Anticipating management's decision to replace a facility exactly as previously configured, or to use the opportunity for expansion, is probably best not attempted. Determine if repairs to the current building, if not replaced, will require expensive building code upgrades.

Projected repairs may be predicted by multiplying the replacement cost adjusted as necessary by the percentage of damage. It may be advantageous or useful to understand the value of the functional loss of a building or facility. One method to make this determination is to add the budgets (or appropriate percentage of the budgets) or annual sales of the groups located within. You may need to determine the content value of an entire facility if it is completely destroyed. Businesses may or may not have complete inventories listed by location. The Purchasing or Risk Manager may be the best source of content data. Depending on your intended use (business impact analysis or mitigation analysis), you may need to use depreciated values or replacement values.

Mitigation specific to individual hazards, along with a list of preventative measures for each hazard, can be found in the 4th edition of Risk Analysis and the Security Survey.

7.3 BUSINESS CONTINUITY STRATEGY

Business Continuity Strategy is the core around which the Business Continuity Management System is built. Strategies are most effective when developed by the process owners or continuity team members, not by the steering committee (unless the committee manages the recovery), Business Continuity Manager, or consultant, although their input can add a broader perspective to the range of strategies considered. It is often the thought process or discussion with the team about how best to enable their functions to continue uninterrupted in the face of adversity that returns a greater value than simply having the functional continuity team read through a list of tasks after the disaster. What are not included in a task list are the results of strategies proposed and rejected during the discussion. This knowledge behind the task list will, of course, diminish over time, but can be designed into training and exercises later. Strategies are developed by a partnership between the functional owner and the Business Continuity Manager usually during the BIA interview or at separate meetings called for that purpose. Strategies should be approved by top management.

Strategies are designed to continue the prioritized activities of the organization's critical functions. They must:

- be cost-effective
- be technically feasible
- consider the output of the BIA and Risk Assessment
- be aligned with the RTO, RPO, and MAO
- adhere to any assumptions in the plan
- minimize any changes to routine
- not establish unfamiliar organizational structures
- not require extensive post-disaster training

Cost versus benefit is an important consideration in the selection of continuity strategies. The example used in a previous chapter in which the organization planned to design and develop a second data center for $6 million was not cost-effective because they could accomplish the needs identified in the BIA by using a combination of strategies at half the cost (data mirroring of only critical information, tape backup of lesser important data). The cost to implement continuity strategies must be understood and tracked by the Business Continuity System Manager.

Strategies must be realistic and technically feasible. A strategy may be workable under normal circumstances, but after a regional disaster resources may became scarce, transportation systems compromised, and deliveries delayed. Although unique solutions are acceptable, ensure that solutions are workable. Strategies must meet the objectives of the function and of the organization as a whole.

The standards consider business continuity strategy as the implementation of the findings of the BIA and Risk Assessment that prevents disruption to its prioritized activities. This is an important consideration for those looking for certification under the standards. Not all viable continuity strategies, however, flow from the BIA, but gaps identified in the analysis should be addressed through mitigation and other forms of risk treatment.

The strategies must be aligned with the RTOs and other constraints identified in the BIA. Remember that in some, if not most circumstances, certain solutions must be in place before the RTO expires to allow for processing or production to begin or to reach expected capacity. Use caution when dealing with multiple strategies or dependent processes that contain embedded RTOs that are of a shorter duration than expected. Understand any restrictions on the timely delivery of needed resources.

Strategies should align with any assumptions listed in the plan and not create any unrealistic expectations. They should also consider the scope of the plan. Any necessary deviations should be completely explained (and potentially justified) in the overview to individual team plans.

Disaster situations place a good deal of stress on workers. Routine activities can become difficult due to distraction, fear of the unknown, and concern for family and personal property, and potentially the disruption of relocation. The best way to mitigate these problems is to implement strategies that make as few changes from normal routines as possible. Different or unfamiliar organizational structures, changes in leadership, or new job functions can add additional roadblocks to success in the achievement of the continuity objectives. Unfortunately, this advice is counter to the requirements of the Incident Command System.

Learning a new job can be difficult, especially under disaster conditions. Cross training is an important tool for business continuity, but any necessary training must occur predisaster. This training must be repeated often, a luxury few organizations can afford. Strategies that depend on training for new tasks should be minimized, or the manager should ensure that those who need to implement the strategy are well versed in its requirements. Job rotation is a possible solution to this potential problem.

Gaps identified in the BIA can be translated into opportunities for mitigation or serve as the basis for continuity strategies. The following suggested strategies (noninclusive) are common (and some not so common) to major organizational units. Not all are required under the standards and their use will not apply in all circumstances. Depending on the assignment of responsibilities of varied functions within different organizations, strategies listed under one function may actually belong to a different function. In addition to redundancies, divergence, and the avoidance of single points of failure, a resource requirement common to all functional areas is the protection of, and access to, vital records.

7.3.1 VITAL RECORDS

The primary cause of an organization's failure to recover after a disaster is the loss of its business records. Most of the regulations pertaining to business continuity are largely concerned with the protection of financial records. The loss of accounts receivables, customer lists, and asset inventories can severely affect cash flow, future sales, and insurance reimbursement. Whether on paper or electronic media, functional units often depend on certain records and documents to carry out their normal operations. These records and documents must be protected and available to the continuity teams in a timely manner, often at an alternate location.

The insurance industry refers to vital records as "important papers." This helps to distinguish from the more commonly usage of the term to mean birth and death information. Records are defined as vital if they are important to the continued and future operation of the organization or that would provide a burden to the objectives of the functional unit if they were lost. Examples include the following as applicable:

- Accounts receivable
- Articles of incorporation
- As-built drawings
- Asset lists
- Banking statements
- Business continuity plan
- Bylaws
- Clinical trial results
- Contractual agreements
- Corporate minutes
- Customer lists
- Deeds
- Food and Drug Administration filings that support regulatory requirements
- Food and Drug Administration security files
- Human Resource records
- Insurance policies
- Laboratory notebooks
- Leases
- License agreements (including software licenses)
- Memorandums of Understanding
- Negotiation records
- Nondisclosure agreements
- Other corporate financial records
- Patents and trademarks
- Payroll and benefits information
- Research and development
- Securities and stock records
- Tax documents
- Treasury records

Remember that the standards require the maintenance of certain documents, and auditors look closely at how well the documents are protected against loss (see Chapter 3). Backup copies of these records should be duplicated and stored offsite a distance that is outside of the area that could be affected by the same disaster. Work in progress or documents not yet copied and sent offsite should reside in locked fire-resistant cabinets. Commercial records storage companies will pick up and store documents, and deliver them upon request to an alternate location. If these services are used, be sure to audit the security, fire safety, and rapid retrieval of the documents. A records management system that identifies which documents are forwarded to the storage company is necessary and the location of the pertinent records recorded in the business continuity team plans.

Not all documents require backup and offsite storage if they can be quickly and reliably recreated from the originals that are in the possession of vendors, customers, or regulatory agencies. Ensure that these entities have a robust vital records protection program in place.

7.3.2 ACCOUNTING, FINANCE, AND PAYROLL

Most finance departments are highly dependent on access to their data systems, although in smaller originations some manual methods may be possible. Manual methods are used when it is possible to record transactions on paper for later entry into the data systems as they become available. Manual methods, in our high dependency on technology, may require a degree of training, assuming the proper forms necessary to record the data still exist (normal screen images are often used as the input form). Strategies should include working from an alternate location, possibly from home in some instances, and connection to the backup data systems.

- Issue credit cards for those business continuity members who may need to make purchases to support the continuity of their functions. This should, or course, be issued before the disaster.
- Increase the amount of petty cash held in reserve or bring in cash from out of the area. Banks may be closed after a regional disaster.
- Monitor, forecast, and report the financial health of the organization during continuity operations.
- Request payroll services to duplicate the previous payroll run and resolve discrepancies on an exceptional basis. Encourage direct deposit.
- Work with the Human Relations department to establish policy for payscale adjustments for workers assigned to different duties and for furloughed workers.
- Streamlined approval for funding requests and expense reimbursement.
- Maintain contact with banking and financial institutions and any regulatory agencies; file reports as required.
- Ensure check stock, special printer ink for checks, and other resources are available and sent to alternate locations.
- Transfer all operations, if applicable, to locations within the organization that are outside the affected area of the disaster.
- If not already established, develop a program to list and track assets.
- Establish ledger accounts ahead of time to track disaster-related expenses and time. Communicate account numbers to continuity team leaders or write them into the plan.
- Design strategies that prevent financial damage in the short and long term, and that monitor the financial obligations of the organization.
- Revise contracts or include Force Majeure clauses in new contracts as applicable.

7.3.3 CUSTOMER SERVICE/TECHNICAL SUPPORT

Strategies to continue customer or technical support are part infrastructure dependent and knowledge based on particular product lines. If redundant support centers do not exist in other geographical locations within the organization, consider the use of a commercial center to be used at the time of the disaster. Ideally, the failover in communications to alternate centers should be rapid and seamless.

- Ensure all customer service centers are capable of handling all products or have plans in place to relocate product engineers to alternate locations
- Expand hours of alternate centers to accommodate all time zones serviced
- Ensure resiliency in the ability to transfer calls to other in-house or contract service centers
- Increase call capacity of backup service centers as necessary
- If cost and risk are justified, have telecommunication lines enter the facility from opposite directions (divergent routing)
- Relocate technical support engineers to major customer locations
- Increase staffing at alternate centers as necessary

7.3.4 FACILITIES

The Facilities or Maintenance function often plays a major and varied role in continuity and recovery and can be highly dependent on the use of outside resources. The provision of utilities, fire protection, repairs, and maintenance of buildings and grounds, custodial and other functions necessitate a variety of continuity and recovery strategies.

- If the loss of electrical power will have a serious impact (and it usually does), consider bringing in a redundant power feed from a different grid. This will prevent power losses caused by local conditions, such as lightning strikes or downed lines. Feed the power from a different direction and to a different part of the site. Consider the same for other vital utilities such as natural gas and water lines.
- Install backup electrical generators that are tested monthly under load conditions. Enter into a service level agreement with fuel suppliers for prioritized delivery when demand for fuel may be high due to a regional disaster. Smaller generators mounted on trailers can be rented and brought on site. If this is the strategy selected, consider the installation of a "quick fit" device (transfer switch) outside the building. This device would be hardwired to the electrical distribution panel; the generator is simply plugged into the building, saving many hours of connection time.
- Maintain listings of alternate facilities that can be occupied while the original is rebuilt or refurbished. As appropriate, enter into agreements with real estate firms for the emergency or low-cost (guaranteed) floor space or replacement facilities to be used if the current workspace is damaged or destroyed.
- Register with a restoration service provider and write the appropriate procedures into the plans. If structurally sound, most organizations will remain in their original facilities after a fire or flood. Smoke from a fire is acrid and corrodes sensitive electronic components, even after the fire is out. The odor of the smoke is powerful and difficult to remove. Water from sprinklers or firefighting hoses can damage documents and cause dangerous molds to grow. The removal of odors and the drying and dehumidification of buildings requires specialized equipment and techniques that most general contractors cannot offer. These services are provided by "restoration" companies, which either do the work themselves or subcontract to companies that specialize in the following areas:
  - Salvage and debris removal
  - Electronic component cleaning and repair
  - Soot removal
  - Dehumidification and drying
  - Document drying and recovery

- Reconstruction (painting, plumbing, masonry, and drywall)
- Water extraction and moisture control

It can be expensive to scrap damaged equipment, especially if it is unique or replacement lead times are extensive. Insurance policies may not pay the full replacement value of the damaged equipment. According to companies that specialize in the decontamination of equipment, restoration can save up to 75% over replacement costs, and restoration can be completed in a few weeks instead of the months potentially needed for replacement.

- Maintain as-built drawings of utilities and other facilities support systems.
- Ensure public address systems and warning communication devices are secured from damage and connected to backup power systems.
- Maintain disaster-related tools and materials (plywood, glass cleanup brooms, shovels, etc.).
- Prequalify service and maintenance contractors, preferably from outside the area affected by a disaster to provide supplemental personnel after a disaster.
- Develop a damage assessment checklist that lists inspection of critical utilities, HVAC, and life safety systems.
- Train facilities staff in rapid building-damage assessment.
- Determine if the local jurisdiction will allow for internal or contract engineers to evaluate structures according to the Applied Technology Council (ATC 20) guidelines and Green/Yellow/Red tag the structure in place of the jurisdiction's evaluators. The local inspectors may be pressed for time due to a need for many inspections and unnecessarily red tag your building.
- License staff and purchase amateur radio equipment to use for the emergency summons of services if normal communications are disrupted. This can be more easily addressed by sourcing amateur radio operators within the organization. Many local fire departments monitor and use amateur radio as a backup form of communications. This may be a function of the Emergency Operations Center, but is sometimes assigned to Security or the Facilities function.
- Establish agreements with transportation providers to move workers to and from alternate facilities, home if normal modes of transportation are not possible, or to other locations as appropriate.
- Prequalify and sign agreements with moving companies for prioritized treatment if needed after a regional disaster.
- Identify locations within the organization that can be utilized as temporary workspace if other portions of the site become unavailable for use. Devise plans ahead of time to accommodate relocation.
- Establish a program, in conjunction with the local fire department, to identify equipment or materials for quick removal after an incident. Some departments will remove critical materials if clearly marked or briefly allow workers into portions of the building to remove material.

7.3.5 HUMAN RESOURCES

Strategies for Human Resources during a disaster situation typically center on accounting for the welfare of each employee and the need to continue to provide staffing. Often, the Human Resources function is responsible for the general dissemination of information about the closure of the facility and instructions to workers, apart from direct contact by a continuity team leader, concerning alternate reporting for duty. NFPA 1600:2013 requires that the organization account for the wellbeing of every employee after a disaster and that it develop strategies for the temporary or long-term housing, feeding, and care of those employees displaced by an incident. According to its guidance, employee assistance should also apply to family and significant others.

- Develop a plan for pandemic flu that minimally contains the following elements:
  - Monitors developing pandemics around the world.
  - Tracks absenteeism to identify trends that may indicate the need to implement a pandemic plan.
  - Incorporates "trigger points" and thresholds for implementing different levels of response activities as described by the World Health Organization and the United States Center for Disease Control.
  - Maintains policy and procedure to restrict travel (such as video conferencing or delayed travel) to areas of the country or world where communicable disease outbreaks are active.
  - Considers cross-training and the recall of retired workers to fill in for absent key workers.
  - Arrangements executed with temporary personnel firms to supply individuals to fill in for absent workers.
  - Encourages, provides, or sponsors annual influenza vaccination for employees.
  - Establishes policies to remove workers from the site who exhibit the signs of an illness (influenza), that is, immediate mandatory sick leave. Establish policy to require employees to remain at home when sick.
  - Establishes policy for employee compensation and sick-leave absences unique to a pandemic including policies on when a previously ill person is no longer infectious and can return to work after illness. This may include extensions of family leave, vacation time, and employee assistance programs.
  - Enables telecommuting where possible.
  - Trains employees in the recognition, prevention, and steps to minimize the spread of a pandemic such as influenza.
  - Stockpiles prevention and hygiene supplies such as alcohol-based hand sanitizers, tissues, and closed receptacles for their disposal at convenient locations, including gloves and N-95 face masks.
  - Considers the stockpiling and use of antiviral medications.
  - Develops procedures to continue operations if social isolation is necessary.
- Establish processes and procedures to warn the public of any hazards created by the organization and ensure these warning systems are tested and resilient. The community must be aware of the actions to take when a warning is issued (if applicable and if it is the responsibility of the Human Resources function).
- Provide out-of-the-area voice-mail boxes, toll-free hotlines, web pages hosted outside the area, and other forms of information repositories to post information about the status of the organization. Include arrangements with local radio news stations to broadcast relevant information. Train workers to contact these resources to obtain information about what they are to do after a disaster (such as site is open for business, remain home until advised, report to alternate location). This is often a shared responsibility with the Emergency Operations Center.
- Examine the need to revise payroll policies for payscale adjustments for workers assigned to different duties and for furloughed workers.
- Decide what limits and develop policy and guidelines to cover the cost of the temporary relocation of family members at an alternate location (i.e., if a worker has children or is the caretaker of an older adult, will the company pay to house and feed children or the adult at the alternate location?).

- Decide if the organization will establish temporary on-site day-care centers after a disaster or to change policy and allow children in the workplace.
- Consider the expansion of Employee Assistance benefits to increase the allowable subsidized visits to Posttraumatic Stress counselors. Consider plans to bring counselors on site after a disaster or traumatic event.
- Devise a strategy and procedure written into the plan(s) to account for the wellbeing of every employee in the organization after a disaster. Include information on their ability to return to work (or go to alternate site), assistance needed, and report this to management through the Emergency Operations Center. This can be accomplished through phone trees, direct visit to residence, electronic check-in using social media or the internet, toll-free voice-mail boxes (mentioned previously) and the like.
- Match employees who need home assistance with furloughed volunteer employees.
- Prequalify home repair contractors and publish this list to workers who need assistance.
- Ensure clear lines of succession are written into the plan or included in official organizational documents.
- Discuss the need for a mass casualty plan in high-risk locations where, after a serious regional disaster, the coroner's office may become overwhelmed and not able to pick up bodies in a timely manner. The purchase of body bags, provision for cold storage, security, and the notification of relatives would be included in the plan.
- Develop strategies for the temporary or long-term housing, feeding, and care of those employees displaced by an incident.

7.3.6 INFORMATION TECHNOLOGY

IT consists of software (operating system, business applications), hardware (desktops, servers, or mainframe), infrastructure (routers, cabling), and its supporting environment (air conditioning, fire control). Physical protection and mitigation are directed toward these elements (user training and data security notwithstanding). Continuity strategies, again based on the results of the BIA, depend greatly on the type of system configuration in use. Service level agreements, arrangements for alternate processing locations, and timely access to data can become essential to the recovery or continuity strategies during a disaster, especially if it is a regional disaster when resources may be impossible to obtain even if premium prices are paid.

IT recovery strategies include hot sites, spare or underutilized servers, the use of noncritical servers, duplicate data centers, replacement agreements, and transferring operations to other locations. Data policies and procedures will help to prevent "disasters" caused by users. To recover data systems, identify the critical applications and prioritize the order in which they are restored. If applications or operating systems are dependent on others, restore them first. Once the applications are prioritized, identify where these applications reside. This will tell you which server or system to recover first.

Servers that are on the same network (or can be easily connected) and that have excess capacity can be pressed into service to rescue a server that has failed. Some organizations keep spare, preconfigured servers in storage for immediate replacement if a primary fails. Unfortunately, this is a very costly strategy, and most organizations prefer not to have "idle assets."

Duplicate systems—capable of processing normal operations, installed within the organization, and used to run test programs or other noncritical processes—can be pressed into service if a main system fails. Few managers, however, can justify the expense of such duplicate systems, but the supply of commercial hot sites is limited and could easily be oversubscribed after a regional disaster, leaving the organization without a recovery system or location.

- Establish a data backup policy and procedure in accordance with the RPO, RTO, and MAO. Data backup is likely the most common form of business continuity strategy in use by most organizations. This primarily involves the backup of each day's transactions onto some sort of magnetic tape. Backup strategies include:
    - Nightly incremental backup of the server
    - Weekly full backup
    - Monthly archiving
    - Annual archiving
    Backup tapes should be sent offsite each day to a commercial facility that specializes in the safe and secure storage of computer backup media. Offsite storage facilities should be audited annually to ensure the following:
    - Good physical security
    - Authorization lists are up to date and enforced
    - Fire prevention systems are to code
    - The building is structurally sound
    - Tapes and manuals can be found and delivered to an alternate location in a reasonable time
Alternately, store tapes in a fire-resistant cabinet located in a separate building. During an evacuation, take the tapes (or whatever media used) with you, if practical and only if this can be done safely.
- Devise and implement a strategy for alternate processing (we mentioned previously the use of internal equipment, such as a test server that could be converted to a production server in the case of equipment failure or use of the same at an alternate location within the organization). Options for alternate processing include locations outside the area that could be affected by a disaster but one still within a relatively convenient travel distance for workers to relocate.
    - Secondary data centers are generally a redundant site within the organization where data transactions are mirrored in near real time and failover to the second site rapidly and invisibly to the user. Everything done on the primary system is duplicated on the mirrored site. This strategy is by far the most expensive of the other options and is used when the results of the BIA indicate and any data loss would be costly to the organization. As discussed in the text, there can be different levels of backup strategies using a second data center when lesser levels of critical processes are backed to tape sent to the second data center. A mirrored system is often referred to as a high-availability solution.
    - Load balancing distributes processing throughout a network of systems internal to the data center or through varied offsite locations. This can add resilience to the system because the failure on one server in the network will have minimal effect on the processing as a whole.
    - Commercial hot sites are alternate locations that house mainframes or server farms and related equipment of the same manufacturer and configuration as your equipment. Hot sites typically include a limited number of workstations and both data and voice communications infrastructure, enabling the organization to relocate employees temporarily. Organizations pay a subscription fee to the hot site vendor and, when the hot site is needed, pay an additional "declaration fee"—to declare a disaster and reserve a system and space ahead of other possible claimants (although you have paid a subscription fee, it is still a first-come, first-served basis.

Some vendors will not guarantee a particular location, assigning the use of equipment at any one of their sites at the time of the disaster. This can make planning and logistics more difficult. This has necessitated the strategy followed by some organizations to declare a disaster after a regional event before they have completely determined the need to use the hot site, thus potentially absorbing the fee if use is not needed). The organization ships or electronically transfers their backup data to the site, loads its programs, and resumes operations at the hot site. In addition to the subscription and declaration fee, daily use fees are usually payable as long as the hot site is occupied. Other problems include the reluctance by some employees to travel great distances from their homes to occupy the hot site. For employees who relocate, it is often useful to give them a packet of services available in the general area to make their stay easier. Some hot sites have already prepared useful information to distribute to relocated workers. If a hot site is used, the business continuity plans should detail the step-by-step instructions to transfer operations and list the employees who are expected to occupy the site. Authorizations, contact and declaration numbers and passwords should also be written into the plan. Important documents such as contracts and other agreements should be treated as vital records. Modes of transportation should be considered ahead of time and travel details written into the plan.

- Cold Sites (sometimes referred to as a Dark Site) are empty facilities or leased space at which computer hardware, infrastructure, telecommunications, and furniture would be delivered to construct a temporary data center from scratch. A cold site has nothing or little prewired or ready for immediate operation. It could be a practical solution if only a portion of a facility is damaged that includes the data center, but sufficient space remains in the undamaged portions. This strategy, although most often the least expensive, could be constrained by the RTO.

- A Warm Site is some arrangement between a hot and cold site where some degree of infrastructure is in place or even spare servers in operation. Most organizations do not wish to have idle assets in use, but a strategy could include the placement of preconfigured servers at the warm site ready to be pressed into operation.

- Mobile Sites (mobile recovery units) are self-contained trailers delivered to your site or to an alternate location that house computer, telecommunications, and work stations. If their use is anticipated, space must be designated ahead of time and the necessarily logistics preestablished.

- Reciprocal arrangements with other organizations for the use of server or mainframe capacity are possible but like those arrangements with manufacturing strategies, ensure that your disaster does not cause a disaster for the host organization. A clear and documented (read contractual) understanding of obligations and cost must be defined. Agreements must include arrangements to test and validate processes and procedures. The protection of proprietary information may need consideration. All bets may be off, however, if both facilities are affected by the same disaster.

- Cloud computing in which the servers, applications, and storage of third parties over the internet perform the actual processing can replace the need for a second data center and allow near real-time recovery of systems for the small or midsized (or perhaps larger) organizations.

- Service Level Agreements, although considered as mitigation by some, may be considered as a recovery strategy by others. Some extended service agreements may include quick ship arrangements in which after the loss of a building full of desktop computers or servers, the vendor will ship a number of systems preconfigured with your software image.

- Maintain as-built and configuration information as vital records in case the data center must be recreated.

7.3.7 INSURANCE AND RISK MANAGEMENT

The primary strategies for Insurance and Risk Management are awareness of the exposures before the disaster and understanding the limitations of coverage and reimbursement so that the treatment of risk is better aligned with the risk appetite. After the disaster, it is important that each continuity team document all damage and expenses related to the incident for subsequent reimbursement.

- Ensure gaps in coverage are addressed ahead of time
- Ensure measures are in place to mitigate exposure when coverage is lacking or risk is assumed
- Devise plans to document expenses, damage, and loss and to collect this information for insurance reimbursement
- List claims procedures in the plan

7.3.8 LEGAL

Strategies for the legal function, if one exists within the organization, are to continue litigation in progress, ensure that regulatory, contractual, and other obligations of the organization are met, and to act as advisors to the Crisis Management Team on issues that may have legal ramifications.

- Recover any work in progress if destroyed or access is denied
- Review and approve any contractual arrangements that stem from continuity operations that were not executed before the disaster
- Ensure required notifications and filings to regulatory agencies are submitted on time or file for extensions (after a regional disaster, some obligations may qualify for deferments, but if the incident is localized to only the organization, deferments may not be an option)
- Work with law firms for support to continue litigation and to use as alternate work space for staff
- Monitor the status of the courts to determine if dockets, filing locations, courier services, law libraries, or other services are available
- Monitor regulatory, contractual, and other obligations to ensure they are met in a timely manner
- If part of the legal function's responsibilities, determine needs and apply for any permits required by relocating functions

7.3.9 MANUFACTURING

Strategies for the continuation of manufacturing are varied and sometimes difficult because just-in-time manufacturing keeps inventories low, thus increasing the risk to the loss of inventory or disruptions in the supply chain. The standards suggest keeping an inventory of materials to support its prioritized activities, but do not qualify how much. Management may be reluctant to increase inventories, especially if stored at diverse locations. Many high-technology and biotechnology processes use equipment that is large, requires a lot of resources to operate, has lead times for replacement of six months or more, or recreation of its operating environment is difficult or time-consuming. In such cases, prevention and mitigation (target hardening) becomes a primary strategy.

Responsibility for supply chain management may reside with the manufacturing function or it may reside with the Purchasing function. Here we will discuss supply chain continuity strategies under Purchasing. Some of the strategies suggested here can apply to other functions as well.

- Relocation strategies include the use of manufacturing lines within the same facility or other locations within the organization that are undamaged. It may be possible to temporarily set up manufacturing at convention centers or empty warehouses—similar to a cold site.
- If some degree of capability remains after damage to facilities or equipment, or if manufacturing can be transferred to other parts of the organization, working extra shifts with the existing workforce or contracted temporary personnel is a simple strategy to continue operations especially if employees are cross-trained to perform multiple functions.
- Rescheduling production compliments the above strategy by suspending some product lines to concentrate on the manufacture of others if capacity is affected.
- Third-Party Manufacturing may be used if there is a loss of manufacturing equipment, facilities, or personnel due to labor action, pandemic flu (although they may suffer from the same problem), or natural disaster. Contract manufacturing firms exist to produce or assemble products for others. Arrangements are best made before the need to use their services. Consider using these vendors to supply a small portion of your regular production to check quality, reduce ramp-up time, and familiarize the vendor with your operations and expectations. Forward all production change control diagrams to the vendor as they occur. This strategy is generally not available if the organization uses unique manufacturing equipment.
- If equipment is damaged or destroyed, many plans call for their temporary replacement with rentals, which is an obvious strategy, but ensure that this equipment and its sources are listed in the plan along with any special support requirements or configuration parameters. Remember that other organizations may be after the same equipment, so have alternate or out-of-town sources available. Arrange for priority service agreements when cost-justified.
- Some organizations have the ability to use virtual manufacturing if their in-house production is damaged or destroyed. This is a variant of contract manufacturing in which different parts of the product are assembled by a number of manufacturers that together make up the whole of the product, shipping the work in progress to the next manufacturer to add their portion of the whole. The process is repeated until the product is complete and then drop-shipped to the customer.
- The rebranding of products from competitors can be used when the manufacturing capability is disrupted for either a short- or long-term period. The failure to deliver product can cause the loss of valuable shelf space in markets as discussed in a previous chapter, or allow a long-standing customer to change their loyalty to the competitor's product. Rebranding the competitors product and resold at a lower price, along with some type of note to explain any change in quality, can help to prevent the loss of customers until normal production is restored.
- Reciprocal Agreements with manufacturers in similar industries or with competitors to use their excess production capacity can be used if the organization is unable to find capacity within the organization. As outlined in IT strategy above, the protection of proprietary information and fluctuations in the host's excess capacity can make this a difficult strategy.

7.3.10 PUBLIC RELATIONS

The Public Relations function ultimately protects against the loss of market position, devaluation of the company, and diminished reputation. The value of the organization's brand is often its most valuable asset. Public Relations, along with Marketing or Marketing Communications in some cases, serves to control the release of information in a manner that best serves the organization. It keeps interested parties (customers, regulators, community, vendors, and employees) informed of the situation so that rumors and misinformation are avoided. It exists to control the impact of the negative effects on the goals of the organization. Its planning and response framework fits well with that used for Business Continuity Management and therefore should be included as part of the Management Team or Crisis Management Team plan within the Business Continuity Plan.

Crisis Communications or Crisis Management is part of the Public Relations responsibility as it is often associated with a major emergency or disaster but not necessarily caused by a natural or technological failure. Crisis Management follows the elements of Emergency Management—once the threats are identified, preventative measures such as tamper-proof product containers are developed and implemented. Material for the media and position statements are prepared ahead of time and, when an issue becomes public, the spokesperson responds with the collection and dissemination of information designed to prevent escalation or to minimize the negative impact of the situation. Recovery includes strategies to restore confidence in the organization.

- Include the top Public Relations Manager as a member of the Crisis Management Team in the Emergency Operations Center. The company spokesperson, if a different person, could be located in the field to interface directly with the media.
- Monitor the indicators of an impending crisis so that the organization may prevent or prepare for their impact. Indicators can include subtle signals in trade journals, increase in customer service calls, social media, or a rise in terrorist threats. Threats can include:
  - Accusations against or the arrest of a company official
  - Boycotts
  - Data security breach or loss of personal information
  - Demonstrations
  - Errors and omissions
  - Fines and penalties imposed by regulatory agencies
  - Missed production milestones
  - Good neighbor policies and community concern
  - Hazmat and environmental issues
  - Health of key executives
  - Hostile takeover attempts
  - Human error
  - Insider trading
  - Kidnap and ransom
  - Labor disputes
  - Major injuries or fatalities
  - Mismanagement
  - Negative research or a death from clinical trials
  - Patent infringement
  - Product liability
  - Product recalls and defects
  - Product tampering
  - Reorganization
  - Rumors
  - Terrorism

- Third-party crime (assault, rape, robbery)
- White-collar crime
- Workplace violence
- Develop, communicate, and enforce policy that restricts contact with the media to only those authorized such as the company spokesperson. Ensure the spokesperson has received on-camera media training.
- Ensure that any public warning systems are operational, maintained, and resilient and that necessary action is understood within the community.
- Consider the preparation of media kits (company brochure and description, biographies, favorable news articles, awards, civil recognition, contributions) and background roll ("b-roll") for distribution to the media that contains video snapshots of the organization, products, or services. Some public relations professionals, however, argue that news media today are not interested in such materials because they will simply use footage they film on the spot with little preparation or editing for broadcast.
- Have pre-prepared preapproved statements that cover foreseeable incidents so those authorized as spokespersons can respond to inquiries prior to the intervention by the main spokesperson. Have similar statements in HTML format ready for publication on the organization's web page.
- List media and other crisis contacts in the Business Continuity Plan.
- Control any news briefings by setting up conference or meeting rooms for the media. Ensure access control, explain ground rules before the start of the conference, and keep any victims separated from the media. Record all conferences.
- Consider the need to increase telephone switchboard capacity and staffing if an increase in communications traffic is anticipated. Log all incoming calls, referrals, and disposition.
- Although potentially a responsibility of the sales or marketing function, devise a process to keep customers and other interested parties informed on the extent of the situation and on the continuity and recovery efforts. This may include the community and regulatory agencies as required.

7.3.11 PURCHASING/PROCUREMENT

Purchasing is highly dependent on its data systems so IT strategies that continue access to its data are important. Supporting the resupply of damaged or destroyed equipment, raw materials, and the provision of business continuity services become critical functions after a disaster. Mitigation is also a primary duty. The standards emphasize the requirement for the organization to evaluate the resiliency of its suppliers and that they are able to respond within the RTO of the functions they support. Note that the requirement refers to "suppliers," not critical or sole source suppliers. The risk assessment should examine threats to the supply chain, and to subtiers of suppliers and the appropriate risk treatment applied. This is accomplished by mapping the supply chains. Some of these threats include:

- Loss of local transportation modes. Hurricane Katrina and its floods closed ports, barge traffic, roads and bridges, rail lines, and air traffic.
- Loss of shipping due to disaster (docks and cranes were severely damaged in the Kobe Earthquake), labor disputes and protests have closed ports on the entire west coast of the United States (package delivery was also stopped by labor actions), and hijackings.
- Theft in transit or product diversion.
- Loss of inventory in warehousing due to disaster (global, regional, or localized).
- Physical and cybersecurity threats.
- Political instability.

- Financial health of the supplier.
- Ethical practices of the supplier.
- Map the supply chain, tiered suppliers, and, based in part on the results of the BIA, prioritize suppliers according to their criticality to the organization, ease of replacement, and overall risk.
- Develop a program and process to monitor and assess the health of suppliers and to respond to any changes that might increase risk to the supply chain.
  - Develop and communicate trigger levels
  - Train responsible individuals in the recognition of impending issues and take the necessary action to mitigate any increased risk
  - Map critical or sole source suppliers by geographical location and monitor these locations for regional disruption
  - Associate shipping modes for critical or sole source suppliers and monitor for disruption
  - Ensure that adequate resources are devoted to this effort
  - Escalate issues to top management or to the Crisis Management Team if warranted
- Maintain open and ongoing communications with suppliers.
- Ensure supply chain requirements of the organization are written into agreements.
- Identify and monitor purchasing-related contractual and other third-party obligations and ensure they are met in a timely manner. Escalate any issues or pending issues to the Crisis Management Team.
- Identify sole source suppliers and take action to find alternatives far ahead of problems.
- If the operation uses "just in time" manufacturing, arrange to warehouse a sufficient quantity of material to allow for delay caused by a disaster or contingent interruption. Some distributors will warehouse materials at your location, retaining ownership until the material is removed and used.
- Physically audit the security and resiliency of suppliers and their tiered suppliers. Take action to close gaps.
- Write into the plan instructions to notify suppliers of alternate locations so they can redirect shipments to the proper locations. Ensure they are capable of shipping to the alternate location.
- Include critical suppliers as participants in joint business continuity exercises.
- Include the Supply Chain Risk Manager on the Steering Committee.

7.3.12 SALES AND MARKETING

The main strategies for Sales and Marketing are to communicate with customers, forecast changing needs created by the disaster, and work with public relations to help repair any damage to the organization's reputation.

- Notify customers of the situation and when normal delivery of product is expected to resume. This is accomplished by direct notification, web pages, media advertising, and even social media. Communication with customers may be a good strategy even if the organization has not suffered any disruption but may be located near a regional disaster or when there may be a perception the organization is affected by a disaster.

7.3.13 TELECOMMUNICATIONS

Even if telecommunication systems are undamaged after a disaster, the phone systems both wired and cellular can become overloaded and inoperable. Strategies for telecommunication systems are very similar to

IT strategies because the type of equipment used is essentially the same. These include emergency service and replacement agreements, divergent routing, radio systems (radio frequency and microwave), mobile switches, third-party call centers, and hot sites. Most switch vendors offer emergency service and replacement agreements. Divergent routing in which communications are divided over geographically separated locations should be examined closely with a carrier representative. Mobile satellite transmission can be used as a backup or as a form of diverse routing. Microwave transmission is a method to add redundancy to connections between buildings of a campus or across town. The simplest way to ensure the continuity of inbound communications is to transfer all calls to another company location if the equipment can accommodate the extra volume and if a sufficient number of knowledgeable operators are available to answer the calls. Commercial call centers are available to handle overflow traffic or to act as a substitute for your operators. Most call centers operate like data center hot sites, with similar fee structures. Their operators can take messages, forward calls, explain the situation, or if qualified, take orders and answer technical questions.

- Where telecommunications is especially critical, consider bringing phone and data lines into the building or site from two different directions. This is referred to as a "dual entrance facility." A cable cut, fire, or other type of incident may leave the lines entering from the other direction intact.
- Write circuit numbers, routing, and other topographical information into the plan. Many systems will allow the rerouting of numbers from a remote location.
- Build as much redundancy into the system as justified by the BIA. Multiple cell carriers, two-way radio, satellite phones, and the like could become vital after a regional disaster.
- Telecommunication distribution frames should be contained in secure, limited access areas.
- All telecommunication systems should be connected to backup power systems and to uninterruptible power supplies.
- Ensure any failover systems are tested on a regular basis.

7.3.14 ALTERNATE LOCATION

A few other considerations to keep in mind when managing relocated workers:

- Ensure alternate locations are geographically separated to be unaffected by a regional disaster but close enough that transportation or relocation is not onerous. Provide clear instructions (airline schedules, maps, directions) in the plan.
- Notify the post office of the need to temporarily forward mail to alternate locations.
  - Establish procedures to distribute mail and package delivery to relocated workers if not direct from the post office.
- Track and publish the location and contact numbers of relocated workers. Remember that multiple alternate locations can include those working from home.
- Publish contact information of all relocated functions, especially those working from home.
- Another common strategy is to simply relocate from one part of a damaged building or site to another. Executive suites, hotel rooms, convention centers, client and vendor offices, empty warehouses, or mobile home trailers are other options to consider to relocate some or all of your business functions. The use of circus-type tents as an alternate workspace is generally not a good strategy. Major hotels such as casinos and convention centers can be a good choice for an alternate work location because rooms, check-in services, and food are available. They are generally located close to major airports. However, these locations may be completely sold out at certain times of the year.

- Staff-issued laptop computers should be instructed to take them home each day so they are available for relocation if access to the organization's facility is not possible.
- Business Continuity Management may be responsible for the update of web pages, voice mail, and other forms of the communication of the status of the organization. They may also be responsible as the liaison with the news media (if not Human Resources or another function) to deliver messages to employees about the status of the organization, and what alternate locations have been activated.
- Remember that relocation strategies must be executed in time to allow the functions to meet their RTOs.

7.4 REVIEW

Mitigation is action taken to eliminate or reduce the impact of a natural, technological, or human-caused hazard. Mitigation and a mitigation plan, although important elements of the Emergency Management cycle, are required by the standards and guidelines. Before a mitigation strategy can be developed, the hazards must be identified. An understanding of the nature and effects of hazards will provide a reasonable basis for mitigation planning. Cost-effective strategies are developed, presented to management for approval and funding, and systems maintained in a ready state. The purpose of mitigation is to reduce the likelihood, duration, and impact of a disruption to the organization's critical processes, products, and services. Often, the difference between mitigation and strategy is difficult to distinguish. The Hierarchy of Controls can be used to select the most effective mitigation strategy.

Business Continuity Strategies must be based on the results of the BIA and Risk Assessment. Alternate work locations and access to Information Technology (IT) systems compose the primary strategies, but individual functions will have other strategies designed to continue the prioritized activities of their critical functions. They are most effective when designed by the process owners or continuity team members. Strategies must be cost-effective, technically feasible, aligned with the Recovery Time Objective (RTO), Recovery Point Objective (RPO), and Maximum Acceptable Outage (MAO), adhere to any assumptions in the plan, minimize any changes to routine, establish familiar organizational structures, and not require extensive post-disaster training.

The primary reason organizations fail after a disaster is the loss of business records. Most of the regulations pertaining to business continuity are primarily concerned with the protection of financial records. These records and documents must be protected and available to the continuity teams in a timely manner, often at an alternate location. Relocation strategies must be implemented in a timely manner that enables workgroups to meet their collective or individual RTOs.

BIBLIOGRAPHY

Broder, J.F., Tucker, E., 2012. Risk Analysis and the Security Survey, fourth ed. Butterworth-Heinemann.
International Glossary for Resiliency, DIR International, 2013. dirr.org.
NFPA 1600 Standard on Disaster/Emergency Management and Business Continuity Programs, 2013 edition.

BUSINESS CONTINUITY PLANS AND PROCEDURES

8

CHAPTER SUMMARY

The emphasis of business continuity managers in the past was to produce "the plan." Achieving the goal of developing a broader business continuity management program in too many instances became secondary if the need for a program was recognized at all. The standards correctly place the focus on developing a business continuity management system, but the business continuity plan still holds its place as the most critical document in the effort to continue the critical operations of the organization and to recover from the effects of a damaging incident. Based in part on the all-hazard, Multihazard Functional Planning structure recommended by the U.S. Federal Emergency Management Agency, a "basic plan" describes the pertinent parts of the business continuity management system that the responsible individuals must know to achieve the objectives of resiliency. The basic plan is supplemented by specific team plans in which the instructions and resources needed to implement the organization's continuity and recovery strategy are listed. A management team or a crisis management team oversees the entire incident response effort. They are typically located in the emergency operations center. Important information about how and when to activate the plan ("invocation of the plan"), the order of succession if a key member of the organization is unable to perform their duties under the plan, and a description of the execution of its high-level data and relocation strategies are found in the basic plan. It describes how this information is communicated internally and externally, how damage is assessed, and how financial or purchasing policy may change during an incident. The business continuity plan should be brief and to the point, but it should encompass enough information to implement the strategic objectives and resource requirements of the organization and of the individual continuity or recovery teams at a time when stress and physical and mental exhaustion are elevated. Plans are maintained in a manner in which they can be accessed offsite, are flexible, and their security and the confidentiality of their contents respected.

KEY TERMS

All-hazard planning; Alternative workspace; Business continuity communications; Crisis management team; Damage assessment; Emergency operations center; Invocation; Multihazard functional planning; Order of succession.

KEY POINTS

- Importance of business continuity plans
- Fundamental attributes of continuity plans
- Plan organization and structure
- How the continuity response is activated
- Order of succession
- Communication within the business continuity structure
- The emergency operations center is a focal point for situational information and strategic decisions

8.1 INTRODUCTION

The emphasis in the past was focused toward building a business continuity plan, or at the very least, filling out the blanks in a template plan. Today it is to build a business continuity management system that enables resilience for the entire organization. However, the business continuity plan is still a vital and necessary piece of the process.

The plans list the detailed instructions (procedures) to the continuity team members that implement their strategies and define their roles and responsibilities. Communication and other resource information, internal and external interdependencies, activation criteria (now referred to as invocation criteria), and relocation information are included to assist the team to accomplish their tasks. A flexible response and control structure and the purpose, scope, and objectives of the business continuity management system are described in the plan. It documents many of the processes required by the standards.

Continuity plans must be "lean and mean" but complete, executable documents. However, the standards make this difficult because each plan must contain certain information that is not necessarily geared toward direct incident response. Remember that the standards also do not draw solid distinctions between planning for emergency response and business continuity. Business continuity plans typically consist of two separate documents, the top document or "base or basic plan," which outlines the overall incident organization, its policies, scope, assumptions, and lines of authority, and the team plans, which are similar to the government's Functional Annexes that list the specific instructions and resources for each individual continuity team. The basic plan contains information pertinent to all teams and interested parties, and the team plans focus on the business function. Rather than repeating the information required by the standards, the manager may consider a single plan with the team plan as simply additional chapters. Although the standards allow for a single or multiple plans, this approach may or may not be agreeable to an auditor. However, the requirement to repeat basic information can be wise if plans consist of subplans based on a corporate, divisional, or regional basis.

The type of plan described above is known as Multihazard Functional Planning according to the U.S. Federal Emergency Management Agency (FEMA) and fits well the recovery team methodology suggested in this text. It uses "all-hazard emergency operational planning" and is based on the premise that although the causes of incidents and disaster can vary, almost three-fourths of them produce common response requirements. Task-based plans are developed around these requirements rather than using contingency planning, which calls for the listing of response procedures for each individual hazard or risk.

8.2 FUNDAMENTAL ATTRIBUTES OF THE PLAN

Absent regulatory requirements, the plans can exist in several formats, but they should be consistent within the organization and follow its, and the standards', document control procedures (The plan must conform to the requirements for document control as described in Chapter 3). Plans exist on the cloud, on webpages, in portable electronic devices, in laptop computer systems, on thumb drives, and DVD and other electronic forms, but in case all else fails, it should also exist on paper. Paper plans do not rely on batteries. No matter what format is used, plans should meet the following conditions:

- The plan must be organized in a logical sequence.
- It must be simple and easy to follow. The stress of the situation can add to the difficulty in finding important information if executable procedures are mixed with background, descriptive, or training information. Information that is difficult to find is useless.
- It must be complete but not overly detailed. The plan, both basic plan and team plans, should contain enough information to allow someone who did not participate in the planning process to understand and perform the instructions necessary to implement the strategies but referring detailed procedures to embedded or linked documents. Except for what is required by the standards, the plan should not contain information about how the plan was developed, hazard identification, or strategy development. If necessary, try to include this information in separate documents. Necessary documents can be treated as, and listed in, the vital records resource section of team plans.
- It must assign roles, responsibilities, and lines of authority. This is another requirement by the standards that are included in all plans. This can be accomplished at a high level in the basic plan by describing a continuity organization and more specifically in the individual team plans by identifying team leaders, team lead alternates, and the responsibilities (team task instructions) of team members.
- The plan should include a glossary of any terms used. Avoid or minimize the use of acronyms. Use plain, clear language.
- It must be flexible enough to respond to unforeseen issues and allow for midcourse correction and adaptation. Although most organizations exist in controlled, predictable environments where they can foresee the types of incidents they need to respond and recover from, the ability to react to unforeseen events must be written into the plan.
- It must state assumptions upon which the plan is based or constrained. Any additional assumptions contained in the team plans should be explained.
- Outline or proceduralize what and how pertinent information is communicated to internal and external stakeholders, among teams, and to the management team/crisis management team and emergency operations center (EOC). This requirement must exist in all plans.
- Specific resources and the tasks required to perform recovery or continuity operations are included in the plan. These are typically included in the individual team plans.
- Each plan must contain implementation procedures. These are mostly found in the individual team plans, but activation procedures can also reside in the basic plan.
- Consider including information that is subject to frequent changes as an attachment to the plan, and not part of the body of the plan. This will facilitate the ease of updates. The use of single-sided pages will also make updates easier.

8.3 PLAN ORGANIZATION AND STRUCTURE

If not using the Incident Command System (ICS), the business version of the basic plan and individual continuity team plans form a viable set of plans that, as part of the greater business continuity management system, will help ensure success of the continuity effort. The basic plan contains administrative and descriptive details to properly manage the continuity activities in a focused, constructive manner. It contains information that is of interest to all continuity team members.

The plan, depending on the needs of the organization, should contain the following sections:

- Table of contents
- Statement of policy
- Purpose
- Scope
- Objectives
- Assumptions
- Damage assessment
- Invocation (activation) criteria, procedures, and authority
- Order of succession and delegation of authority
- Continuity organizational structure
- Communication of information
- Emergency telephone numbers
- EOC
- Alternative locations and space allocations
- Recovery priorities or recovery time objectives (RTOs)
- Internal and external dependencies
- Documentation of expense and activities
- Additional information
- Plan distribution
- Orientation and training
- Exercising and testing
- Plan maintenance
- Confidentiality
- Appendix

8.3.1 TABLE OF CONTENTS

After the title page that conforms to the requirements listed in the standards, the plan should contain a table of contents. If the plan is in an electronic format, then it is useful to link each subject heading to its location within the document.

8.3.2 STATEMENT OF POLICY

The plan should outline, but not necessarily duplicate, the business continuity policy. The pertinent elements of the policy should be emphasized. The plan should tie the achievement of business continuity goals and objectives to performance evaluations and bonuses. Statements from the policy that illustrate management's support for the program should be emphasized.

8.3.3 **PURPOSE**

The purpose of the business continuity management system and that of the plan must be completely defined. This is one of the required elements of the standards and applies to each documented procedure (i.e., plan—the plan can consist of a single document or collection of multiple documents).

8.3.4 **SCOPE**

The dimension of the business continuity management system encompassed by the plan is briefly but completely discussed. If the plan pertains to a single building or site, then refer to it by building numbers, site name, and exact street address. Inform the reader of any pertinent functions, locations, or contingencies not included in the plan. If the scope of the plan is a subset of a higher or broader plan, or part of a phased approach, then explain this in the appropriate detail. Explain very briefly what is excluded; why it was excluded; and, if necessary, reference a more complete document. If the business continuity system is designed according to the ASIS International standard, then include a Statement of Applicability (see Chapter 3).

8.3.5 **OBJECTIVES**

The objectives of the business continuity management system and those of the plan should also be described. What will the plan accomplish, by whom, and within what timeline? Objectives must be SMART (Specific, Measurable, Attainable, Relevant or Realistic, Timely) and consistent with the scope and policy statement. Objectives are another required plan element. Objectives can include the following:

- The organization will meet all legal, contractual, and regulatory requirements throughout the duration of the incident.
- Continuity teams will implement all strategies in a manner that meets their RTOs.
- The human resources team will account for the location and welfare of all employees within 24 hours of an incident with the potential for mass causalities.

8.3.6 **ASSUMPTIONS**

List assumptions upon which the plan is based or constrained. It is nearly impossible to plan for the absolute worst-case scenario in which everything ceases to exist. Assumptions must be realistic and can describe things out of the organization's control. Assumptions can also include something pertinent that cannot be mitigated. Common assumptions include the following:

- Facilities will be either partially or totally damaged or inaccessible for a period of 30–60 days.
- Key personnel identified in the plan are available after a disaster. However, incidents that have a national impact such as the September 11 attack when air traffic was grounded may necessitate a different assumption. Pandemic situations may use the assumption that key personnel may not be available.
- Alternative facilities identified in the plan are available for use after a disaster.
- Backup data and valuable papers located in offsite storage will be readily available.
- Critical resources will be available.
- Employees are trained in facility evacuation and relocation procedures.

8.3.7 DAMAGE ASSESSMENT

The strategies for damage assessment to facilities, building contents, and equipment and the methods to document and report the damage (generally to the EOC) are described in the plan. Damage assessment can include an estimation of any reduction in production capacity and estimates of the time needed to recover. Damage to facilities and infrastructure can be the responsibility of the facilities team, contract structural engineers, or a trained damage assessment team. The assessment will include an estimate of the time required to repair and re-occupy the facility. Some strategies call for a rapid assessment to be forwarded to the EOC, followed by a more detailed examination. This will help to decide if relocation to alternative facilities is necessary.

Individual continuity teams are often tasked with conducting their own assessment of the damage to their equipment, resources, or ability to deliver services. This is also documented and forwarded to the EOC.

8.3.8 INVOCATION (ACTIVATION) CRITERIA, PROCEDURES, AND AUTHORITY

Another required element that must be defined in the plan(s) is the criteria to use to determine when the plan (i.e., the response or continuity effort) is to begin. A major earthquake when lights and computer systems go dark, pieces of the building start to fall to the ground, and the potted plant above your desk is now resting on top of your head should signal the need to invoke your plan. However, what if the earthquake is of a much lesser magnitude? Some disasters or major incidents can develop gradually. List the triggers and invocation criteria, procedures, and activation authorities in the plan.

This will include the people or circumstances that have the authority to invoke the entire plan, individual team plans, or multiple team plans. Typically, any member of the management or crisis management team, or the business continuity system manager, can invoke the entire plan or any portion of the plan, whereas team leaders can independently invoke only their individual teams with notification to the business continuity system manager, management team, or EOC. The plan may be activated in whole or in part when the operation of a department, critical function, machine, or system component fails to operate, is damaged, is unable to meet its operational objectives, or access to it or to the facilities is restricted.

Many plans allow for a graduated invocation (Level I, II, III), and some, in an effort to get to the head of the line when competing for space at a hot site, will let the type of disaster dictate how the plan is invoked. For example, after a localized disaster such as a fire in the data center, the team will first assess damage before declaring a disaster. However, if the disaster is regional, such as an earthquake, and the data center is damaged, the person with the invocation authority will immediately declare a disaster to the hot site, pay the declaration fee, and then assess the damage. Only then they will decide whether there is a need to relocate to the hot site.

Organizations must develop invocation sequences that make sense for their situation. Disaster levels can be defined as follows:

Level I disaster: A Level I disaster is one that results in facility inaccessibility or loss of power or other critical services for an expected period of up to 48 hours (this time factor should change according to the RTO and maximum allowable outage). Damage from a Level I disaster is not large scale. It may consist of minor damage to one or more buildings, lack of access due to weather or city infrastructure conditions, or hardware and software problems not addressed by normal short-term support.

Level II disaster: A Level II disaster exists when the outage is expected to last between 2 and 5 business days. Damage from a Level II disaster is more serious than that from a Level I disaster, and it may result in more serious loss to equipment and documentation (files, reports, contracts) due to a serious or prolonged event, such as a fire or local flooding.

Level III disaster: A Level III disaster is one in which the effects of the incident are expected to last in excess of 5 days; cause severe damage to reputation; or have serious legal, contractual, or regulatory implication(s). A Level III disaster is severe and could include the total destruction of one or more buildings, requiring significant facility restoration or replacement.

Information technology (IT) team plans may use a different activation sequence, each of which may involve a specific response by a different group of people. If an IT disruption is expected to last less than 2 hours, then a "Stage 1" situation is declared, the team leader or shift supervisor is notified, and instructions are implemented by the on-duty technical support or repair personnel. If the outage is not resolved within this time frame, or if it is apparent that more time is required, then the response will escalate to Stage 2 or 3. This will invoke an additional set of instructions, notifications, or full recovery team activation.

A process to determine when and how teams are to deactivate (i.e., stand down their continuity and recovery operations) should also be include in the plan.

8.3.9 ORDER OF SUCCESSION AND DELEGATION OF AUTHORITY

National Fire Protection Agency (NFPA) 1600: 2013, as does governmental planning, requires the documentation of lines of succession for top management of the organization. The term "succession planning" is included in the NFPA's definition of continuity, but the manager should understand that the use of this term carries a meaning broader than simply listing who is next in command when the primary person cannot fulfill their duties and responsibilities under the plan as a matter of choice, death or injury, or inability to respond. Succession planning is a human resources function (typically) that identifies workers within the organization who have the potential to advance into senior management positions. It implements a long-term program of training and mentoring its future leaders.

In the event that a member of top management is unable to perform their duties under the plan, then an order of succession with the associated delegation of authority to act in the successive position is followed according to the plan. This is often included as a portion of the organization's Articles of Incorporation or in other legal documents. An example of an order of succession includes the following:

This order of succession and delegation of authority is authorized by the president and is valid until the succeeded manager becomes available, is changed by the president, or is permanently replaced by the organization. The successor will have the full authority to act in place of the original (Table 8.1).

There is no requirement in the standards to go three deep or more on the "Replaced by" or "Alternate Replaced by"; it is completely up to the organization as to how many replacements it wants to list.

8.3.10 CONTINUITY ORGANIZATIONAL STRUCTURE

The plan should succinctly describe the structure of the business continuity incident response. Is the achievement of continuity operations accomplished according to the ICS or according to a continuity team methodology? Identify the elements of the organizational structure, its purpose and goals, authority, and communication.

Table 8.1 Order of Succession

Position	Replaced by	Alternate Replaced by	Alternate Replaced by
President	Executive Vice President	Vice President Operations	Vice President Finance/CFO
Executive Vice President	Vice President Operations	Vice President Finance/CFO	Director of Manufacturing
Vice President Operations	Vice President Finance/CFO	Director of Manufacturing	Director of Human Resources
Vice President Finance/CFO	Finance/Treasury Director	Accounting Manager	Purchasing Director

Most plans and continuity structures are based on a continuity team concept. This means that all required continuity or recovery actions are the responsibility of designated teams with specific instructions and resource requirements contained in their section of the continuity plan. Each team will be responsible for performing a series of tasks and procedures to continue or to facilitate the resumption of their unit's business or systems processes.

One member of each the team is designated as the team leader. The team leader, who may or may not be assigned unique tasks within the team plan, will act as the liaison (communication) between the management team or EOC and other team leaders and is responsible for the continuation of the team's critical functions (i.e., the tasks designed to implement the team's business continuity strategies). The team leader has the authority to modify their team task instructions to adapt the strategies to any unique demands of the disaster or to adapt them to any strategic decisions issued by the management team/EOC. Each team leader should have an alternate team leader. See Recovery Teams for more information.

A flow chart or organizational chart can help to clarify the relationships among the management team, team leaders, and those responsible for the implementation of assigned tasks. See Figure 8.1 for an example of the continuity organizational structure.

Figure 8.1 represents an organization with multiple worldwide locations, the business continuity structure of which consisted of several continuity teams for which the team leaders reported to the local crisis management team. Part of their management strategy provided for support of senior managers from the corporate offices—a management strike team if you will. The business continuity manager acted as the EOC leader with the management team located in the EOC. The Corporate Strike Team had the ability to stay in the EOC or to provide support in the field as needed.

Communication to and from the EOC was accomplished through the team leaders. Communication from one team to another was also accomplished through the team leaders.

8.3.11 COMMUNICATION OF INFORMATION

The communication requirements of the standards call for the receipt of information to identify impending incidents, to warn the community of hazards created by the organization, and to identify how the organization will communicate to other stakeholders.

A description of how the organization will communicate internally with members of the organization as well as externally with interested parties (e.g., emergency responders, the community, and the media) is written into the plan. The procedures to detect, monitor, document, and respond

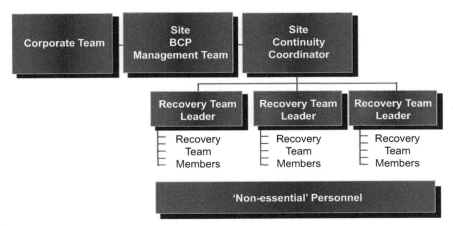

FIGURE 8.1

Example of continuity organizational structure.

to an incident, including national or regional advisories, must also be written into the plan. Some of this information can reside in individual team plans, such as the requirement for procedures to operate a communications facility that could be included in the EOC plan. However, despite the goal to minimize information in the plan that is not executable, methods to ensure the technology of warning and communication systems are survivable during an incident are explained. Redundancy of communications and interoperability of communication among responding agencies (i.e., all can all talk on the same radio channel using common terminology) are best left to the purchasing department, but they can be placed in this section of the document, especially if specific radio channels must be selected.

How and what will be communicated to the employee population is listed. This does not preclude individual teams from developing supplemental communication means. If applicable, indicate that in all cases, the telephone is intended to serve as the primary means of notification and communication. Cellular phones can act as an alternative. The organization's emergency notification and communications systems will be used to notify and provide instructions to staff, visitors, and guests. In addition, each team will maintain emergency contact numbers for each of its team members. Other modes of communication the organization may use in an emergency include:

- Commercial emergency notification systems: These firms will send prerecorded messages over the phone system or send text messages to all phone numbers in their database after activation by a single call.
- Call trees.
- Two-way radios: List channel numbers to use in an incident.
- Satellite phones (usually found in the EOC).
- Public address system.
- Warning siren.
- Amateur (Ham) radios (specify a frequency and other necessary parameters).
- Telecommunications network.

- Websites: Similar to the toll-free number described below, a webpage should be available via an outsourced, offsite hosted webserver, www.status.organization.com, located in a third-party data center outside of an area that could be affected by the same incident. The site provides status information in the event of a disaster as updated by the business continuity manager, public relations, EOC, or a support team. List the URL in the plan.
- Organization-wide e-mail messages.
- Bullhorns.
- Voicemail boxes hosted outside of the area to leave messages or instructions.
- Toll-free numbers: The toll-free numbers should connect to messages and instructions that will inform workers, customers, and other parties about the status of the organization. The number can be printed on employee security badges, webpages, and training materials. The instructions on how and when to update the message should be contained in the public relations or EOC plan. List the number in the plan.
- AM/FM/TV stations: Local news stations can be contacted to broadcast messages to workers during a disaster. List the frequencies in the plan and instructions in the team plan that tell team members how to contact the stations. Many jurisdictions maintain emergency radio stations that can be listed in the plan. Train employees to monitor these stations for information.

This section of the plan can also be used to inform responsible individuals how to communicate with other team members, team leaders, and internal emergency responders, but remember to minimize any verbiage in the plan that is purely training in nature. To the greatest extent possible, communications should be documented.

8.3.11.1 Emergency telephone numbers

As a separate section, or a subsection of communication of information, include a list of emergency notification telephone numbers that would be common to multiple teams. Include primary and alternative numbers. In the case in which 911 (112 in Europe, 999 in the United Kingdom, 000 in Australia, etc.) is used to notify the police, fire, and ambulance, include the direct dispatch number as the alternative. Some emergency numbers to consider for the plan include:

- Police, fire, and ambulance
- Office of emergency or disaster services
- Local hospital
- Local medical clinic
- Electric, gas, and water utilities
- Taxi and transportation
- National or local weather service
- American Red Cross or other relief agency
- Poison control center
- Applicable regulatory agencies
- Fire and security alarm company
- Local and long-distance phone carriers
- Traffic information and road closures
- Coast Guard or other appropriate rescue agency
- Department of Homeland Security

8.3.12 EMERGENCY OPERATIONS CENTER

A brief description of the EOC and its primary and alternative location is included in the basic plan. Directions to the EOCs are detailed. The management or crisis management team members are instructed to report to this location when the plan is invoked or when a situation warrants activation of the EOC. Some plans call for a third alternative location outside of the area. Primary telephone numbers of all EOC locations are listed.

8.3.13 ALTERNATIVE LOCATIONS AND SPACE ALLOCATIONS

Describe the strategies for relocation to alternative data processing sites and for alternative workspace. Include complete details that instruct team members where to go, how to get there, and what to do when they arrive. The name of the relocation facility, address, and special instructions are written into the plan. Maps and directions should be included in the appendix along with air transportation schedules and any special reservation instructions. Also included in an appendix are any instructions on how to connect to data systems once the teams arrive at the alternative work area. A relocation assistance team can be formed ahead of time to help with travel arrangements, other transportation needs, lodging, check-in, and orientation at the alternative location. If the organization has an in-house or onsite travel department, then they are good candidates for this task. Of course, this does not apply to work-at-home strategies (one would hope).

Relocation strategies can be based on different scenarios. The corporate offices of a company based in the San Francisco Bay Area are located about 20 miles north of its worldwide data center. Their strategies directed critical functions to relocate to the data center if the corporate offices were rendered unusable. If the corporate offices and the data center were damaged by the same event (a credible scenario), then IT was to relocate to a hot site and the business systems (continuity teams) were to relocate to a hotel in Reno, Nevada.

Although the organization may have an overall relocation strategy, certain teams may choose to relocate to different locations. All alternative locations should be listed in this section of the plan along with the associated contact phone numbers.

It is important to train all team members who may be required to relocate in the details and expectations of the plan. It is more important to conduct exercises that actually call for the physical relocation to their alternative location and practice logging onto the alternative data systems. In the above example, a relocation exercise was held and the team members were asked to make their way from the corporate offices to the data center. Detailed maps and directions were distributed to the data center that was adjacent to a major interstate highway with an off-ramp less than one-quarter mile away. Forty percent of those who participated in the exercise could not initially locate the data center.

Space allocations can also be listed for each alternative location. Allocation refers to the number of team members that will relocate. Not all employees may be needed during the initial phases of a continuity or recovery operations. The allocation will indicate how many employees or team members are needed so resources and space can be anticipated. Some planners include the total head count and the short- and long-term space requirements (square footage) in this section, but this may be best left in the facilities, real estate, or other team plans.

The plan should describe from a high level how it will return to its original location after repairs are completed or how it will transition from the alternative location into a new facility. The details of the return may reside in the facilities, IT, and/or other team plans.

8.3.14 RECOVERY PRIORITIES OR RTOS

RTOs, recovery point objectives, and the maximum allowable outages should be discussed in the overview for each team plan, but it is useful to list this information by critical function in the basic plan for easy reference when resource reallocations need to be made at the time of the disaster. Some would argue that this information is better placed in the management team or EOC plan.

In the order of importance (criticality) as determined by management agreement on the basis of the business impact analysis and risk assessment, also list any times of the year (quarter, month, or other business cycle) during which the loss of these functions is especially critical.

8.3.15 INTERNAL AND EXTERNAL DEPENDENCIES

Probably best recorded in the team plans or in an appendix, some managers will list each function's upstream and downstream dependencies in the basic plan. The advantage to listing in the basic plan is the provision of a better view of the interrelationship between functions, and it allows the business continuity manager to better manage the incident.

Most functions require some sort of input into their processes such as raw materials or information to deliver their products or services. When completed, this product or work in progress then becomes the input for the next function until the finished product is completed. The accounts receivable function may depend on the output of the sales function in the form an invoice, and their output would be cash or a check for deposit. In other words, how does one function support or depend on another? Likewise, the facilities department in a research institution may support the survival of laboratory animals by ensuring that their life safety support systems remain functional during an incident. This is an example of a downstream dependency for the Facilities Department.

8.3.16 DOCUMENTATION OF EXPENSE AND ACTIVITIES

Instructions directing each participant in the business continuity process, or at the very least each continuity team leader, to document all actions and expenses during and after an incident should be emphasized in the plan. This practice is of such importance that the instructions bear repeating in all team plans. A log of the actions performed by team members can be used later for an after-action report to identify lessons learned, verify that important steps were completed, defend the organization in litigation, or to demonstrate that regulatory compliance was achieved. It demonstrates to management and to auditors that the plan was executed as intended. The log, along with photographs and receipts, provides additional documentation to insurance claims adjusters that the expenses were in fact incurred.

The activities and expenses should be entered as they happen because the stress of the moment will likely result in forgotten entries or unreliable detail. A process should be developed and written into the plan that describes how and who is to receive the completed logs on a daily basis (potentially the risk and insurance management team) and how this information is to be collated and reported. It is not unreasonable to copy the business continuity manager or EOC support team because they can be used to help craft a daily status report on the progress of the continuity operations.

A form for this purpose should be developed and appended to the plan. The form can ideally exist in an electronic format in which entries are easily transmitted and collated. See Figure 8.2 for a sample log form.

APPENDIX X

Continuity Action and Expense Log

INSTRUCTIONS: Use this form to record all recovery related events, actions, expenses, and decisions. Provide as much detail as possible. Insurance Reimbursement will be completed at a later date.

Team Name: _____

ITEM #	DATE / TIME	EVENT, DESCRIPTION, COMMENTS, ETC.	AMOUNT	COST CENTER	VENDOR	INVOICE NUMBER	LOGGED BY	INSURANCE REIMBURSEMENT

FIGURE 8.2

Appendix continuity action and expense log.

8.3.17 ADDITIONAL INFORMATION

Other pertinent information that most, if not all, teams need to know that is specific to the recovery or continuity operation should be listed, potentially under separate headings. For examples, emergency financial or purchasing procedures (expedited purchasing or changes in approval levels) or changes in policy under emergency conditions should be agreed to beforehand and explained in the plan.

8.3.18 PLAN DISTRIBUTION

Again, paying strict attention to the document control requirements of the standards and of the organization, list the plan recipients in this section. If a separate means to track document ownership and version control exists, then this section could become redundant and therefore would be eliminated. Large organizations will not list in the plan every person who is entitled to receive a copy. Senior members may be listed by name and the remainder by title or generic description such as "team leaders" and "team members."

The entire plan is not distributed to every continuity team member. Complete distribution is appropriate only for the business continuity manager and staff, offsite vital record storage, and the management team (EOC). There may be others who need the "phone book" version of the plan, but team members must receive only the information they will need in a continuity or recovery situation. This will help them to remain focused in their duties, locate important information in a stressful situation, and maintain security of the confidential information contained in the plan. This is accomplished by distributing only a copy of the basic plan and the individual team plan to the team members. Some business continuity managers argue that the team members should receive only their team plan, excluding the basic plan.

As mentioned above, most plans today will exist in some type of electronic format. However, paper plans are still useful and necessary—when all else fails, the ultimate business continuity planning tool, the pencil and eraser, becomes the base element. Remember that the standards require the documents to be available when needed. Maintaining the plan in varied forms and locations will help to ensure this requirement is met. To facilitate version control and updates to the plan, print paper plans on single sheets, not double-sided sheets. This may also allow comments and notes to be written for later improvement opportunities.

Team members will maintain paper and electronic copies of the plan with at least one copy secured offsite at all times. All team members with laptop systems should ensure that their team plans are regularly replicated to their system or other portable devices.

8.3.19 ORIENTATION AND TRAINING

Normally a description of the program that provides orientation and training to those who have responsibility under the business continuity management system is included in the plan, but when planning under the standards, the details of the training program will likely reside in a separate document. The plan can still define and reference the requirements to conduct orientation (initial training on the contents and expectations of the plan) when it is first introduced and to all new members of the organization. It can also include an overview of the ongoing training program with possibly a training schedule or training requirements included in an appendix. Orientations should emphasize the confidential nature of the plan's contents.

8.3.20 EXERCISING AND TESTING

Similar to orientation and training, the exercising and testing section should contain a high-level description of the testing program or exercising strategy, but the actual exercise plans should exist outside of the basic plan. Testing and exercising requirements are described in a subsequent chapter. The types of exercises, drills, and tests along with their expected frequency can be included in the plan. Specific requirements for all tests, such as the need for an after-action report and corrective actions, may also be listed.

8.3.21 PLAN MAINTENANCE

As part of continuous improvement, the information contained in the plans must not only be updated on a regular basis, but the document control provisions of the standards also require that the use of obsolete information is prevented. Version control according to the organization's document control system, and converting the plan to a form such as a pdf, will help avoid the unauthorized deletion of information or modification of its content. Information contained online should be protected by adequate security access rights.

Information in the plan should be reviewed and updated on a regular basis, or as the International Standardization Organization requires for the management review (see Chapter 10), at "planned intervals." Ideally, when personnel changes occur, team assignments and contact information will be updated as soon as possible. Links to the human resources database could make this possible, or notification by human resources to the business continuity management team will help to expedite updates to the plan. Some managers send inquires to team leaders on a quarterly or biannual basis. Changes in team work area recovery, resource needs, and other important requirements such as contractual or regulatory changes are also examined and updated in the plan.

Any changes that result from the management review should also be updated in the plan and in other related documents. These changes could include revisions to policy, scope, relevant external issues, and the results of continuous improvement initiatives such as the implementation of corrective actions. The findings of internal or external audits, gaps identified in exercises and testing, updated business impact analysis and risk assessments, and lessons learned from after-action reports of actual incidents may also necessitate updates to the plan.

The plan should reflect the frequency and need to update any of the above as appropriate. Significant changes in organizational structure, strategy, or risk tolerance should also trigger immediate updates to the plan and to other relevant documents within the Business Continuity Management System.

8.3.22 CONFIDENTIALITY

The basic plan should be clearly marked on the cover sheet and on each subsequent page as a confidential document. It should also contain a statement outlining the confidential nature of the information contained in the document. Electronic copies of the plan should be secured against unauthorized changes.

8.3.23 APPENDIX

Forms for use by the recovery and continuity teams, supporting information such as maps and directions to alternative locations, and documents used by all teams can be appended to the plan. A glossary and list of acronyms are also included here, but the continuity effort is best served by repeatedly training responsible individuals and those who may become responsible individuals in the terminology they will need to use and by the elimination of the use of acronyms.

Large documents should also be minimized from inclusion in the basic plan to keep it to a manageable length and so that it does not become cumbersome to find necessary information at a time when stress may make the most obvious difficult to see. Team plans can also contain their own appendices; therefore, decide if the information resides in the proper location.

8.4 TEAM PLANS

Some organizations, especially those of a smaller size, rely on a single team of top executives and key employees to direct continuity operations during a major incident. They decide what individuals or departments within the organization will do at the time of the incident. Their decisions may be based on detailed preplanning or on a loose set of continuity strategies. Although the standards are designed to apply to any size organization, this approach will meet with difficulty under the standards and ultimately with achieving their business continuity goals.

Forming teams of employees, consultants, and interested parties with defined roles, responsibilities, and authority organized around departmental lines or from several departments with similar critical functions (and with similar recovery strategies) is a more efficient method to manage the necessary actions to continue and recover their critical functions. Complex functions or teams may contain subteams, support teams, or teams that focus on particular resources. This is more common to IT teams.

As described above, each team is composed of a team leader, one or more alternate team leaders, and essential personnel that are tasked with implementing the team's continuity strategies. In most organizations, few if any workers are not considered essential and are included on the team. The team leader (who is usually the functional manager anyway) is given the authority by top management to make and approve decisions within the team structure, direct expenditures within the limits of the business continuity policy, and alter the procedures contained in the team plans to better meet the particular circumstances of the incident. The team leader is responsible for managing the team members to ensure that all tasks are accomplished as intended and that these tasks are completed in a manner that will meet RTOs.

The qualities of a good team leader include the ability to take charge in an emergency or stressful situation, familiarity with the operations of the functions under their control, and freedom from other significant continuity duties that may interrupt their focus or attention to team management. An understanding of the organizational structure and how information is communicated up, down, and across the business continuity response structure is vital.

As mentioned above, team plans can be standalone documents or appended to the basic plan. They must be of a consistent format in the type of information they contain and how the data are presented. The team plan will obviously contain the name of the function; for example, "Human Resources Continuity Team Plan." The team plans should also carry a "Confidential" or "Company Private" warning.

The team plans should begin with a brief overview of the critical functions that are addressed by the team, which functions need to be addressed first (or in what order they need to be addressed), and the justification for the prioritized order. Some managers like to add a brief paragraph that calls attention to information in the basic plan and that the information in the team plans is supplemental. Other managers prefer to also outline the team's continuity strategies, but others argue that because the team task instructions (continuity procedures) are designed to implement the strategies, listing the strategies becomes redundant.

Some would argue that a paragraph outlining the objectives of the team is also redundant to the overview of the critical functions, but a restatement may be warranted to make it clear to someone responsible for its implementation who was not part of the planning process. However, remember that the standards require that certain elements, including purpose, scope, and objectives, are required on all plans.

Any activation criteria and authorities that are different from that described in the basic plan are listed under a separate heading that draws attention to the modified or additional requirements. Some functions specify that their teams will automatically activate after an earthquake of a certain magnitude (MM 6.2 or greater) or a pandemic declaration of a certain level.

Alternative workspace locations and relocation criteria are also outlined in the initial pages of the team plan. Provide only enough information in this section to alert team members and interested parties of the relocation strategy and how it is executed. It must be descriptive but not overly detailed, leaving maps and complex directions for the team plan appendix.

Other pertinent information is then listed under its appropriate headings. Other information can include flow charts, special communication requirements, brief description of upstream and downstream interdependencies (or internal or external requirements), and processes and procedures not included in the team task instructions. Remember that the introductory material for the plan should be minimized so that other important information is easy to locate without the need to dig through too many pages.

Finally, the actual names, not the titles, are listed for the team leader and alternate team leaders. Several managers prefer to bold face these titles in the plan. The duties and responsibilities of the team leader and how the team relates to the recovery or continuity operations may be discussed if not they are not included in the basic plan.

8.4.1 **TEAM MEMBER CALL LIST**

When the plan is invoked (activated), the first page in the plan that comes into use is the team member call list, especially if the incident occurs (as it likely will) after hours. Team members are selected according to the minimum number of persons necessary and with the expertise to perform the procedures to implement their continuity strategies. Generally speaking, these are the normal people assigned to the functions that the team represents. Business continuity managers speak of minimum staffing because space in a hot site or the need to relocate individuals to alternative workspace can be expensive. "Nonessential" personnel are assigned to other duties or to other teams as needed, or they are temporarily furloughed. Team members must have the ability and necessary resources to relocate. Ensure that the need to relocate is understood and agreed upon beforehand.

The team member call list is simply a list of the names and contact information of the team members. When the team members are notified that the plan has been invoked, typically by the team leader, they are instructed to report to their normal work area, to an alternative location, or to remain at home in a standby status as determined by the team leader, business continuity manager, or the crisis management team/EOC. However, the EOC is typically not yet operational by the time this step occurs. Another function of the team leader's call is to determine the welfare not only of the team members but also all members of his or her staff. This will necessitate that all of the function's workers are listed on the list. Any injuries, fatalities, or special needs are reported to the EOC or to the human resources team. Some plans call for full investigation of any calls that are not answered. Organizations will use other methods of welfare check-in that instruct all workers to account for themselves by direct phone contact to an out-of-the-area voicemail box or by any of the other proprietary or commercial web-based or smart-phone text systems. This voicemail box can also be used by the team leader to provide information to the team. Team member call lists can also be compiled into distribution lists for mass messaging via e-mail or text messages.

The call list should consist of the following:

- First and last name of team members: If using a spreadsheet or database, then consider placing first and last names in different columns for ease in sorting.
- Title of employee or position: This can be their normal title or that of their business continuity responsibilities.
- Home address of each individual that includes city, state, and zip code: The home address or at least the zip code can be used to sort employees and pinpoint those who may be most affected by a disaster by comparing the areas of most damage to the location of residences.
- Contact information: This is the work, home, cellular, and other alternative phone numbers that can be used to contact team members and employees. The more numbers the better. Included in contact information are work and home e-mail addresses and e-mail to text addresses (each carrier has a different address). Call tree assignments can be placed in this section. A call tree divides the responsibility for calling groups of team members.

It is possible that all team members will not be needed during the early stages of the continuity operations. Indicate at what phase or day they should be called by assigning a priority number and listing the priority key in the plan. Priority 1 could mean that the team member is needed immediately, Priority 2 is needed within 7 days, and Priority 3 is not needed for more than 7 days. Priority 4 could be assigned to any "nonessential" personnel.

The ability to notify and communicate with team members (and with the EOC) should have as much redundancy as possible.

8.4.2 TEAM TASK INSTRUCTIONS

The next section or pages of the team plan lists the checklisted instructions or tasks that the team members must follow that are designed to implement their continuity or recovery strategies and to respond to and manage the effects of the incident. These should match the continuity and recovery objectives identified in the business impact analysis. A separate list of instructions can exist for the team leader or for subteams assigned to the plan (subteams may require their own, separate plan). In the past, the checklists were sectionalized by listing those tasks that were to occur within 24, 48, and 72 hours or listed by phase (response, restoration, recovery), but this practice is now rarely used.

If using the ICS to manage continuity operations, the manager will find fundamental differences in the approach using the continuity team methodology as suggested here. Incident action plans (IAPs) are developed under ICS at the time of the response to the incident, whereas here we are developing the response instructions before the need. An IAP is necessitated in part because, in a large community or geographical region, it is almost impossible to anticipate response needs and resources at a microlevel. However, a business organization presents a more controlled, foreseeable environment, allowing a more decentralized, scripted approach. This allows the organization to make decisions beforehand on the basis of predicted situations or potential conditions that streamline its response and allow decision-makers in the organization's EOC to concentrate their efforts on situations that were not anticipated. In other words, tasks are more decentralized to the continuity or recovery teams than they are under ICS. As stated above, plans should permit the management team or team leaders to adapt recovery instructions as required to meet unique conditions as they occur and, in many respects, the team leader is acting as a quasi-incident commander or section chief. Although the instructions should not be changed without justification and knowledge of why they were created, assumptions and strategies may change sufficiently because the plan was developed to necessitate adaptation during the recovery.

The instructions are listed in the anticipated order of execution and should be prefaced by a comment that they do not necessarily list all of the activities that should take place during an actual emergency or continuity situation. The format used in many plans includes a check box, instruction number, the instruction, and a section to record the date and time completed in addition to who completed or signed off on the task. A section for comments can exist for each task to be filled in upon completion as necessary.

As stated before, these instructions should be brief and specific, eliminating any verbiage that is training oriented and focused on the effect of the incident. They should be understood by someone reasonably familiar with the type of operation the team is attempting to continue or recover; therefore, avoid technical terms, abbreviations, and acronyms. The instructions should minimize the need for decision-making after the disaster. Start the instruction with action words such as "notify," "collect," "decide," "determine," etc. The instructions should consider those actions necessary not only to achieve the team's objectives but also those that support internal and external interdependencies.

Because team members are more likely to use the executable team plan over the basic plan, certain instructions common to all teams should be included in each team plan. Noninclusive examples of tasks for team leaders that can be included in all plans are as follows:

- Begin logging all recovery/continuity-related events, actions, expenses, and decisions. Include the date and time team members are called, requests for assistance, etc. See Appendix X in the basic plan for a copy of the log form. Forward completed logs to the risk management team.
- If at work during the time of the incident, and if safety permits, power down all equipment and prevent further damage to critical functions.
- Obtain information about the disaster and the status of the organization's facilities. Dial 1-800-555-5555.
- Contact team members and inform them of the situation. Instruct them to report to their work area, to the alternative site, or to remain on standby. Determine the welfare of each employee and forward this information to the EOC.
- Notify the business continuity manager or the EOC (if established) that the plan has been activated.
- Prepare a damage assessment of your area. The report should include the extent of the damage, the salvageability of any equipment, vital records, and other essential items. Evaluate the amount

of time your function will be out of operation or the amount of reduced operation. Forward this report to the business continuity manager and the EOC.

- Photograph all damaged or destroyed materials, equipment, etc. If possible, record the date, time, description of the damaged items (include serial number), and a description of the damage on the photograph, or electronically record this information. If not possible, then record this information on the log. Forward logs and photographs to the risk management team leader.
- Identify the status of work in progress or lost information that must be reconstructed.
- Provide status reports each day no later than 4:00 p.m. on issues encountered and the on team's progress to the EOC for compilation of their daily progress report. Include in the report any roadblocks to meeting Recovery Time Objectives (RTO), Recovery Point Objectives (RPO), or the Maximum Acceptable Outage (MAO) within allotted times and what action the team has taken to mitigate the roadblocks.
- Debrief the team at the end of the incident and develop a list of lessons learned and corrective actions. Forward debrief report to the business continuity manager. Enter corrective actions into the corrective action or change management system.

Specific tasks for the team to follow would commence somewhere after "Identify the status of work in progress." Use caution when assigning tasks to team members if they are represented by a collective bargaining agreement. Ensure that they are authorized to do the work, or the work you are asking others to do does not conflict with the duties of other trades. In the initial stages of a major incident, organized labor typically may informally relax certain agreements, but never count on this unless formal agreements are reached ahead of time.

The duties imposed on the team members by the recovery instructions must closely match the members' normal skills and scopes of responsibility. If members are to perform special functions outside of their normal duties, then they should receive continual training in these new skills beforehand.

Although the basic plan may list a high-level process to stand down after the incident is over, the team plans should contain procedures to recover operations at the original or new facility as appropriate. A method to determine when the "return to normal" process is to begin and when the continuity operations are to cease should be written into the plan even if it is as simple as a direction to do so from the EOC.

8.4.3 INTERNAL/EXTERNAL CONTACT LIST

Critical vendors, suppliers, and service providers are included on the internal/external contact list. Governmental and regulatory agencies that have meaning to the team are good candidates for this list. Included here are also the names and contact information of those within the organization with which the team may need to communicate. This is a list that can become quite long; therefore, consider including only vendors used most often and either append the remainder or include it as a vital record. As many different contact methods as possible should be listed, including that of the vendor company, corporate office if different, and name and contact information for the representative. Addresses, phone, e-mail, text, and webpages should be included. Where necessary, include purchase order numbers or other useful information. Indicate what service or product the internal or external contact provides to the team or organization.

8.4.4 **CRITICAL RESOURCES**

Equipment requirements, forms and supplies, software, and vital records are the minimum types of resources that are listed in the team plan. Each will have its own section.

Resources listed in the plan must be sufficient to implement each team's continuity strategies. One of the standards would like to see a more formalized analysis of resource requirements. Resource requirements are usually validated through plan exercises and scenario planning. Unless the necessary resources are provided at a relocation site or taken offsite each day, assume nothing is available to the team at the time of the incident. In other words, if the building burned down while you and your team were at lunch, what resources (equipment, forms and supplies, contact phone numbers, software, and vital records) would be needed? If the team members are required to travel to alternative locations and purchase equipment, are they issued corporate credit cards, laptop systems, and communication devices? Answer the question: "What minimal amount of critical equipment will each team require to function after the disaster?" The completed forms used for resource data collection in the business impact analysis (see Chapter 5) can also be used to list the resources needed in the team plans.

8.4.5 **OTHER PERTINENT INFORMATION/APPENDIX**

After the resource needs, include any additional information that the team requires to attain their objectives. Telecommunication routing pathways and identifiers, flow charts, logon instructions, and the like are included last as an appendix to the team plan. Forms not included in the basic plan and potentially copies of contracts or agreements with vendors may also appear in the appendix.

8.4.6 **MANAGEMENT OR CRISIS MANAGEMENT TEAM**

The term "crisis management" carries specific meaning to top management and to other key players outside of the organization. They may define, as do many others, crisis management to mean the management of a situation that involves response to a situation that could damage the reputation of the organization through any of the triggers listed in the description of a crisis when we discussed the control of information through the public relations business impact analysis (see Chapter 5). The standards differ on their definition of crisis management. ASIS International considers it to be the management of the entire business continuity process, and NFPA 1600:2013 is closer to its generic definition. Although in this text we have referred to a management team and a crisis management team, our meaning has been that they are one in the same for our purposes of business continuity, although we prefer to use the term "management team."

The management team is the group of top managers who are charged with the overall management of the continuity and recovery but are primarily charged with strategic decision-making and action during and after the incident. In a larger organization, the EOC staff may be tasked with incident management and the management team with purely strategic management decisions and issues resolution. They may reprioritize functions, processes, or products; reallocate resources; change strategies; or approve exceptional expenditures or funding sources.

The chief executive officer, the business continuity manager (rarely does this happen), or the executive business continuity sponsor can act as the management team leader. A secretary or administrative assistant is included to log events, actions, times, and expenditures. As with the individual continuity teams, a complete and accurate record of events and decisions will help the organization wade through the inevitable legal, regulatory, and insurance problems once the crisis is stabilized. A corporate team may exist in organizations with many divisions or multiple geographical locations. The corporate team is responsible for making strategic business decisions and may direct the recovery process on a regional basis.

When an EOC is established, the management team generally will collocate with the EOC staff and work in tandem with them. The EOC staff will pass necessary situational information, decisions, and issues to be resolved to the management team and communicating management's decisions down to the individual functional team leaders. If a dedicated or separate EOC is not established or is not part of the plan, then the management team becomes the EOC and directly manages the incident according to the organizational structure documented in the plan.

When organizing team plans within the business continuity plan, the management team plan is often the first with the remaining teams arranged in alphabetical order. A call list of all of the functional team leaders is included in the management team plan in addition to their own call list as described earlier. The internal and external call list and other resource requirements are included in the management plan as they are with the other team plans. However, in practice, management will be less concerned with their resource requirements than they will be with decision-making; therefore, normal management support staff must also be part of the team and well trained in the expectations of their tasks.

Some tasks that the management team are responsible for and that can be written into their team task instructions include the following:

- Decide if the situation warrants activation of the EOC/management team (team leader or business continuity manager).
- Notify management team staff to report to primary or alternative EOC (team leader or business continuity manager).
- Collect information and initially assess the extent of the incident and its effect on facilities, operations, and the organization (team leader or business continuity manager).
- Provide a briefing to the team upon their arrival.
- Designate a record-keeper, and log decisions and actions. In addition, track time, associated costs, expenses, and purchases. Attach source documents to logs. Forward completed logs to the risk management team leader for archiving.
- If not already accomplished, decide to initiate warnings to the surrounding community and other interested parties of an emergency that could affect their health and safety. (Because the public relations team should be a subset of the management team, or at the very least the most senior public relations representative should be a member of the management team, the decision is made to contact local media outlets to assist with any alerts or warnings.)
- Decide which teams require activation
    - Contact team leaders via the varied modes of communication as necessary to activate teams if not self-activated.
- Determine if the incident affects external third parties and check if teams are addressing these issues in a manner appropriate to the goals of the organization.
- Determine the number of workers injured, missing, or killed.
- Monitor response/recovery activity teams through the team leaders. Ensure recovery teams are following appropriate procedures.
- Determine the need to review the strategic position of the company based on any change or expected change in financial position, production capacity, corporate image, or sales.

- Decide if operational or strategic priorities differ from those in established plans.
- Inform team leaders to modify team tasks to better conform to updated operational priorities or applicable decisions made within the management team or the EOC.
- Assist with the creation and distribution of operation schedules and procedures for business functions affected by the disaster.
- Project and track the financial impact of the disaster and take appropriate action to mitigate financial impacts.
- Coordinate requests for resources from team leaders as necessary. Resolve conflicts with the allocation of resource requirements among multiple sites affected by the disaster.
- Respond to and resolve issues as identified.
  - Communicate results to appropriate teams and/or to the EOC.
  - Document issues, decisions, and any resulting tasks communicated. Include time received and time communicated.
- Ensure the safety of all personnel; protect the environment and property to the extent that is practical.
- Monitor continuity expenses.
- Monitor and assist with building restoration, relocation, and the acquisition of any temporary or permanent replacement facilities.
  - On the basis of recovery strategies, support and monitor the progress of the organization's plans to refurbish the original facilities or to move to a new facility. Ensure that the organization and all teams develop plans to accomplish the "return to normal" operations in the original or new facilities. Ensure that these plans are completely documented.
- Work with the public relations director to develop messages and positions and communicate the necessary management decisions to the public relations team (i.e., activating the crisis management plan).
- Ensure that insurance claims are filed in a timely manner.
- Approve daily written synopsis of incident, progress, issues, and status as prepared by EOC support for distribution to stakeholders.
- Keep the board of directors updated on the position of the company and on the progress of the continuity operations.
- Prepare a critique and final report that describes the disaster, actions taken, actions deferred, results of actions taken, problems encountered, lessons learned, and corrective actions.

It is vital that management is intimately aware of their expected actions and has approved them ahead of time. The need for constant reminders to this group of the protocols imposed by the standards and by the business continuity management system cannot be understated. Some organizations include a brief discussion of business continuity at their regular staff meetings. In the absence of the approval and knowledge of what is expected for their response, people at this level of the organization tend to quickly make decisions. Their knowledge of the response organization and expectations will help to prevent uncontrolled spontaneous action.

8.4.7 EMERGENCY OPERATIONS CENTER

The EOC is a location where the management team members or emergency managers and their staff meet to direct or coordinate (i.e., manage) the response of the continuity teams or field operations to a large-scale incident. Although its primary function is strategic, the members of the EOC can make such tactical decisions such as the allocation of resources between competing teams as described earlier. It is a focal point for situational information and analysis. The EOC passes requests and information up, down, and across the structure of the continuity organization and outside of the organization as warranted.

The organization must anticipate the complexity of its response, continuity, and recovery, and it must design an EOC that accommodates its operational requirements. From the business perspective, the physical and operational layout of the EOC can be as simple as a conference or hotel room. Organizations that occupy a campus with many facilities or with numerous large sites in different geographical areas may need to design a dedicated theater-style area that has adjoining rooms and integrated audiovisual, computer network, communications systems, and support personnel. A theater-style room is used so that all of the EOC workstations can view the status boards, television news feeds, and other information feeds as if watching a movie of the incident. If this is the case, then separate documents, organizational structures, and training are in order and will likely not be included as a team plan. Large EOCs can internally use an ICS structure and configure the seating or workspace along ICS functional lines. In organizations in which a dedicated EOC is not justified, it is appropriate to list in the plan the requirements to set up the temporary EOC.

The EOC should be in a secure, structurally safe location that is central and easily accessible to its members even when transportation systems are likely disrupted. It is often located in a large conference room that is normally used by executive managers. An alternative EOC, such as a mobile trailer or hotel conference room, located an appropriate distance from the main site, should always be available. In today's highly mobile environment, virtual EOCs can accommodate those executives who are traveling out of the area or for those who encounter transportation difficulties getting to the EOC. The potential failures of a virtual EOC due to technological inadequacies caused by the incident and a lack of continued training and practice by the EOC members in the operation of the supporting software should be considered when planning for such an arrangement.

For most businesses, the EOC is a large conference room that has a sufficient number of phone and data connections; Wi-Fi; room for status boards; and workspace for the management team, support staff, and potentially the business continuity manager. The phone jacks should be wired to allow the firm's phone switch to be bypassed in case of power failure or the destruction of communications equipment. Extra phone sets and fax machines, as well as all supplies needed to operate the EOC (radios, extra batteries, overhead projectors, whiteboards, forms, and office supplies), should be stored in the room or close by. Duplicate supplies and equipment should be stored in the alternative EOC if possible. The need for supplies can be minimized by the use of EOC software residing on a dedicated server located in the EOC that is connected to laptop computers with backup power available. However, be aware that the use of technology carries the roadblocks described above. The operations chief in a recent incident took 45 min to log onto his system because he forgot his password, and the stress and workload thrown upon him in the initial moments of the incident contributed to his difficulties.

The flow of information from outside and within the EOC is critical to the decisions made during a crisis, especially in a large-scale incident. Technology, such as computer networks and large multimedia displays, will speed the delivery of accurate information to decision-makers and will greatly reduce fatigue. External information must flow between the incident commander (or continuity team leaders) and the EOC. Situational or conditional information reports must be available and updated on a regular basis. The standards require that the causes of an incident are continually monitored. Cable television, local news feeds, broadcast radio, and access to governmental information systems support this need. The EOC must have the ability to communicate with the outside world even when power and normal modes of communication are disrupted. Backup (redundant) communications, such as satellite telephones and amateur radio, should be utilized.

Other considerations for the EOC include the following:

- Do not overwork the management team or EOC staff. Decisions made under stressful conditions are often poor decisions. Add long hours to the stress, and the quality of the decisions can deteriorate even more. Shifts should not exceed 12 hours. Arrange for rest periods, breaks, professional massages, and plenty of food and water.
- Access control (security) is important, especially in a large EOC. Unauthorized visitors, including media personnel and managers not directly involved in the EOC operations, must be denied access to the EOC. Consider the use of a badging system to help control access to the EOC.
- Videoconferencing capability is useful, as is an ability to monitor amateur television (ATV) broadcasts. During a major flood, the local ATV club rented a helicopter and sent live video back to an EOC.
- All EOC operations, rooms, and equipment should be connected to backup power generators.
- The EOC must be "user friendly" with respect to comfort and functionality. Poor lighting, high noise levels, difficult-to-read visuals, poor ergonomics, and other negative "human factors" will tend to fatigue the staff sooner and adversely affect their ability to make intelligent decisions.
- Keep operations as quiet as possible. Establish separate meeting rooms and a soundproof radio room, deliver television audio through headphones or subtitles, and use telephones that flash a light instead of a ring.

An EOC support team should be recruited if a full-scale dedicated EOC is not used. When the management team is activated (invoked), this team is notified and prepares the area designated as the EOC for occupancy and use by the management team. Once the EOC is operational, the support team becomes responsible for answering phones, posting information to status boards, and attending to any ancillary duties. Instructions for the setup and operation of the EOC are written into the team plan.

The following EOC support team task instructions provide an example of what may be included in an organization's plan. The instructions used in the example were from a sub-EOC that coordinated the response of a large division of a campus with multiple diverse functions. The divisional EOC is referred to as the DOC (divisional operations center) and reported to the institution's EOC through a liaison located within in the EOC. The DOC was located in a large room with whiteboards attached to all of its walls and a large video monitor at the head or a large conference table. The EOC uses a software tool in which information is updated and available remotely according to security permissions. These instructions do not include the template team task instructions described in the chapter:

- Determine if primary DOC (Building 128, Room A-6) is safe to occupy.
  - Check http://status.organization.com, 1-800-555-5555, or after-hours security at 555-555-5555 for information on the incident.
  - Contact damage assessment team leader if necessary to evaluate safety of the building.
  - If primary not safe to occupy, determine same for alternative DOC.

- Inform team members to report to primary or alternative DOC.
- Notify all team leaders if alternative DOC is used (include contact information for DOC).
- Clean up any damage in room to make functional.
- Arrange tables and chairs according to Appendix A (Appendix A contained a diagram and additional instructions about how the room was to be arranged).
- Clear all voice messages from telephones in room.
- Set up web EOC on room's TV monitor.
  - Obtain laptop computer.
  - Connect laptop to TV monitor (see Appendix for instructions).
  - Log onto EOC software:
    - http://websoftware.com
    - Username: jsmith
    - Password: J531t = **
    - Locate and select current "issue."
    - Open "Boards": Significant Events and DOC Activity Log.
    - Arrange windows on screen adjacent to each other as pictured in Appendix B (screen captures of the desired arrangement were appended to the plan).
    - Monitor for pertinent information on Significant Events Board and alert DOC staff as appropriate.
    - Enter significant activity or activity of interest to the EOC on the DOC Activity Log.
    - Periodically enter "No updated activity" if more than 30–60 min of inactivity.
- Set up status boards. See Appendix C. (Appendix contained instructions to set up the boards.) (See Figures 8.3 and 8.4.)
  - Update status boards as information is received.
  - Query EOC about damage reports and post on status boards. Follow up (i.e., repeat query as necessary).
- Test phones and network. Inform EOC staff and team leaders of status.
- Obtain division radio/charger and set at control station to monitor Channel 6.
- Obtain building manager radio/charger and set at control station to monitor Channel 1. (An auditor may have difficulty with these two communication requirements, pointing out that there is insufficient interoperability.)
- Obtain materials from the supply room or previously cached location and distribute to each station (paper tablets, pencils, etc.). Include (print if able) supply of DOC communication forms.
- Inform EOC at x5555 (555-555-5555) that DOC is established at normal location or at alternative location.
  - Inform EOC of contact information. The phone extension in Room A-6 is x5555 (555-555-5555).
  - Obtain direct phone number from division EOC liaison (member of EOC operations section if and when that section is activated).
- Post sign on outside room door that reads "DIVISION OPERATIONS CENTER (DOC)—RESTRICTED ACCESS."
- Post issues on status board and verbally alert DOC of new issues.
- Receive daily summary reports from team leaders.
  - Schedule briefing with DOC staff.

DOC Status Boards

Setup the following status boards on the white board in a size that fits the available space and that is readable from the conference table. Draw sufficient lines below the heading examples below:

- Teams Activated / Relocated
- Building Status Board
- Damage Reports
- Resources Requested
- Problems / Issues

Teams Activated / Relocated

Team	Location	Phone #	Comment	Time Posted

Building Status Board

Facility / Building	Damage				Comments	Time Posted
	Major	Moderate	Light	None		

Other Damage Reports

Description of damage / access	Time Posted

Resources Requested

Resource Request	Amount	Requested by	Fulfilled	Time Posted

Problems / Issues

Problem / Issue	Disposition	Time Posted

FIGURE 8.3

DOC status board.

Status Board Instructions

When preparing status boards, draw grid lines with black, erasable marker pens on the white boards located around the room. Ensure each status board has the proper heading. Make grid and lettering large enough to be viewed easily by all participants, considering available space to construct the boards. Continue drawing cells below the heading to accommodate expected usage, i.e., if there are only eight teams, only outline 8 rows. If an alternate location is used and white or chalkboards are not available, use flip charts. Use blue ink to post the information. Posted information should not be released without authorization from the Management or DOC Team Leader. Information placed on boards is obtained from the DOC Communication forms.

Teams Activated / Relocated

- Team: List teams that have activated their plans
- Location: If a team moved to an alternate location list the location here
- Phone #: List an alternate phone number where the team leader can be reached
- Comment: Add any miscellaneous information as needed
- Time posted: record the time this information was posted to the board

Building Status Board

- As damage reports are received from the EOC or from the field, list the building number under the Facility/Building column
- Place a check mark in the Manor, Moderate, Light, or None (no damage) column
- Note in the Comment column the source or type of information, i.e., "Initial Assessment," "Dashboard Survey," etc.
- Time posted: record the time this information was posted to the board

Other Damage Reports

- List other pertinent damage reports received from informational resources
- Briefly but completely describe the type and extent of damage. Include any reports of restricted or denied access
- Record the estimated time the department, function, or process will be out of service (time estimated to recover)
- Time posted: record the time this information was posted to the board

Resources Requested

- Resource Request: List resources or other needs requested by team leaders or the EOC
- Amount: List the amount or number of items requested
- Requested by: Indicate the source of the request
- Fulfilled: If the request is still pending, leave blank. If the request has been fulfilled, record 'yes.' If a portion has been fulfilled, write what is still needed
- Time posted: record the time this information was posted to the board

Problems/Issues

- Problems: Record any problems or issues the DOC needs to address
- Disposition: Record the status, solution, or outcome of the problem
- Time posted: record the time this information was posted to the board

Important Note: The entries on the status boards should be transcribed onto paper or electronically. If necessary, photograph the content of the boards.

FIGURE 8.4

Status board Instruction.

- Provide daily written synopsis of incident, progress, issues, and status. Distribute to team leaders, EOC, and other stakeholders.
- Contact EOC for status information as required (weather reports, conditions, etc.).
- Arrange for food and water. Set up food and water station. Repeat this instruction for each day of DOC operation (the EOC logistics can assist with emergency provisions).
- If DOC is in operation more than 12 hours, develop schedule and staffing for additional shifts.
- Collect all completed DOC forms, logs, and other archival information and forward to DOC team leader for report preparation.
- Return room configuration to normal upon closure of DOC.

Some managers may criticize the sentence structure of the above instructions as "choppy," preferring to use complete sentences such as "Return the room configuration to its normal configuration upon the closure of the DOC."

In addition to the EOC displayed information, the DOC support team was tasked with posting certain information on whiteboards. They would record the information they obtained from two-way radio traffic, telephone calls, and other inputs onto a DOC communications form and hand it to a team member responsible for posting the information for the management team to see. Alternatively, this can be done electronically if connectivity is functional, but it is much easier to be able to scan this information all at once. See Figure 8.5.

8.5 PUTTING THE PLAN TOGETHER

Decide who is to complete the plans. The business continuity manager will construct the basic plan and review the team plans for completeness, consistency of format, and feasibility. In other words, will the procedures written for the teams to follow in their effort to achieve continuity or recovery meet the objectives of the team and of the organization as a whole? If the organization has many locations and divisions, then the business continuity manager may consider developing a template basic plan with instructions about how it is to be completed. The template is then forwarded to the various locations. We stated earlier that template plans should be avoided, but in this case the template is developed by and specific to the organization. Instructions for its completion can be located on the organization's business continuity webpage.

Team plans should be completed by the team leader or by the team as a whole. Although the plans should be written with the assumption that the authors will be long removed from the organization when the incident that triggers its need happens, it is the planning effort that returns a great deal of value. The process of thinking through what will work, what will not work, and what resources are needed will help to prepare team members for an effective response to the situation. This process also becomes a form of orientation and training for the team. When crafting complex team plans, portions of the plan construction can be assigned to different members or groups of members to expedite its completion.

The results from the completed business impact questionnaires should provide direct input into the team plans.

In Chapter 4, we mentioned that the emergency response plan can be part of the business continuity plan or it can exist as a separate document. Decide how the organization wishes to address this issue and follow the suggestions outlined in that chapter. As a practical matter, these should exist as separate but related plans.

DOC COMMUNICATIONS FORM

Referred by:_____ Call back #:_____

(Name/Title)

Date:_____ Time:_____ Taken by:_____

Situation Statement or Request:_____

_____

_____

_____

_____

_____

_____

_____

_____

Route to:

☐ Teams Activated/Relocated Board   ☐ DOC Team Leader

☐ Building Status Board   ☐ Management Team Leader

☐ Other Damage Reports Board   ☐ Other:_____

☐ Resources Requested board

☐ Problems/Issues Board

Posted by:_____ Date:_____ Time:_____

Disposition/Comments:_____

_____

FIGURE 8.5

DOC communication form.

8.6 REVIEW

The business continuity plans document the procedures necessary to manage the organization's conti-nuity objectives and that implement the continuity and recovery strategies of the individual continuity teams. It can consist of two documents. The basic plan describes the pertinent parts of the business continuity management system that the responsible individuals must know to achieve the objectives of resiliency. The basic plan is supplemented by specific team plans in which instructions and resources needed to implement the organization's continuity and recovery strategy are listed. These plans, especially the team plans, must be organized in a logical sequence; be simple and easy to follow; and must assign roles, responsibilities, and lines of authority. To the greatest extent possible, they must be executable documents, minimizing information not directly involved in the implementation of necessary tasks. The plans must be flexible enough to allow for the response to unforeseen issues and enable midcourse correction and adaptation of the plan.

The strategies for damage assessment, the conditions that necessitate activation (invocation) of the plan, and who has this authority must be explained. The documentation of lines of succession for top management of the organization is required by some of the standards. The plans will identify the elements of the business continuity organizational structure, its purpose and goals, authority, and communication methods. The communication requirements of the standards call for the receipt of information to identify impending incidents, warning the community of hazards created by the organization, and how the organization will communicate to other stakeholders.

Team plans identify the team leader, team member list, and methods used to communicate with the team. Contact numbers and other pertinent information, internal and external support vendors, and personnel are also listed in the team plan. Detailed instructions to the teams to implement their continuity strategies are highlighted, and the necessary resources to support their implementation are also listed. The management team oversees the entire incident response effort. They are typically located in the EOC.

ORIENTATION, EXERCISING, AND TESTING

9

CHAPTER SUMMARY

Business continuity plans are never proven effective until the "Re-opened for Business" sign is posted on the front door. Testing and exercises of increasing complexity allow the organization to validate the contents of the plans and to provide an opportunity for business continuity team members to practice their procedures without waiting for the next disaster. The middle of a disaster is not the time to discover that the backup infrastructure you put in place does not work. Once plans are developed, a documented program is established to validate the strategies, ensure the availability of resources, and to develop the proficiency of the responsible individuals to perform their tasks under the plans in conditions that will be less than ideal. Exercises and tests will identify poor or absent assumptions, reveal gaps and missing data in the plans, and will help ensure that the business continuity management system objectives can be achieved. Plans are executed during the exercise on the basis of the conditions imposed by plausible scenarios. As the business continuity management system matures, exercises begin with simple tabletop discussions using simple scenarios and graduate to more complex functional exercises and full-scale exercises that use more difficult scenarios to practice operational skills designed to satisfy the objectives of the business continuity program. Technology is also tested to ensure that it performs according to expectations and conditions that may be present in disaster conditions. Full-scale exercises demand a high degree of planning, control, and evaluation to simulate realistic conditions for multiple functions or organizations. The use of exercise controllers, evaluators, and simulators who inject situations into the exercise play for participants to solve will demonstrate the strengths and weaknesses in the plans and with the ability of the responsible individuals to meet the objectives of the program. The strengths and weaknesses identified in the testing and exercises are detailed in after-action reports and improvement plans that are reviewed and approved by top management so that corrective action plans are developed to ensure continual improvement of the business continuity management system.

KEY TERMS

After-action report; Controller; Evaluator; Full-scale exercise; Functional exercise; Inject; Scenario development; Simulation cell; System testing; Tabletop exercise.

KEY POINTS

- Business continuity procedures must be validated
- Procedures are validated by exercises of increasing complexity
- Exercise program risk is identified and treated
- Scenarios must be realistic and compliment the exercise objectives
- An exercise program and plan must be developed and documented
- Exercises must support continuous improvement

9.1 INTRODUCTION

The three most important elements of an effective business continuity management system are the affirmative and demonstrated support for the program by top management, the business impact analysis, and its exercise and testing program. Although never "finished" because of the need for continuous improvement, the adage that "a plan is not complete until it is tested" is insightful. Business continuity plans developed by some of the best professionals in the business that appeared to be perfect when peer reviewed by other professionals were found to have missed important details when simulated against a scenario.

All elements of the plans must be exercised, simulated, or tested. Although this is not practical to do all at once, the International Standardization Organization (ISO) allows progressive testing as long as the entire plan is ultimately tested. It has published a guidance standard, ISO/DIS 22398.2 Societal Security—Guidelines for Exercises and Testing, to assist with this process. It is a guidance document, not a requirements document.

Exercising and testing the plans will validate the effectiveness of strategies, ensure the accuracy of information, and increase the preparedness of the individuals who will execute the plans. It will pinpoint areas that need attention or improvement and reveal gaps in instructions, misplaced or absent assumptions, or the need for better strategies and tasks. It will help ensure that the business continuity management system objectives will be met. Exercises validate training, coordinate between functions or outside agencies, and identify communication and resource inadequacies. Although ISO refers to exercising and testing the organization's business continuity procedures, when we speak of exercising and testing plans, we really mean exercising and testing the business continuity management system.

Orientation and exercising, especially at the top management level, will help to prevent spontaneous action by those personalities, who are generally found in senior management positions, that are prone to quick and decisive action. Such actions, if not taken within the framework of the business continuity management system, can often derail agreed upon strategies and objectives. When the Twin Towers in New York were brought down in the terrorist attack, a senior manager of a major international company, who happened to be the organization's business continuity sponsor, made several decisions to close all operations near an airport, causing the loss of many dollars in production. Although some would argue that this was a wise decision to err on the side of caution to protect the safety of their employees, other criticized the ad hoc nature of his actions. The decision was made without understanding what at the time was known about the attack, including intended targets. The manager retired shortly thereafter.

A robust exercise program is a must and will help to demonstrate management support for the business continuity management system. However, bear in mind that the business continuity manager must demonstrate its value to top management. Many top managers will likely still hold the outdated mindset of a plan-centric program and not that of a management system. The result of this outdated thinking is that once the goal of producing the plan is complete, little more needs to be done. The cost and dedication of exercise resources is better invested in a careful reading of the plan at the time of the disaster. Experience has shown that type of thinking could prove disastrous without the validation and practice afforded by exercises.

In the past, we "tested" the plans to determine if the team members and procedures met expectations and the expected outcomes compared against the strategies were successful. The term "test" was replaced by "exercise" because "testing" carried a pass/fail mentality and managers believed their programs were better served by using a term that promoted a more positive outcome, thus not demotivating the exercise participants. In an exercise, failure was considered to be good because it highlighted opportunities for improvement by identifying weaknesses in the plan. Others still preferred the term "test" because it placed some degree of stress on the participants, thus creating a more realistic situation. Those in the middle of this argument used the word "simulation" in place of "test" or "exercise." ISO 22398.2 defines the term "exercise" as an "instrument to train for, assess, practice, and improve performance and capabilities in a controlled environment" and contrasts the term "test" as a type of exercise for which the objective is to include a pass or fail outcome. It notes that the terms should not be confused with each other. "Testing" applies more to the verification of the operation of equipment, technical processes, and infrastructure to ensure that it will operate as expected in a disaster or relocated environment. The backup electrical generator is tested monthly under load conditions. The ability of the telecommunications system to seamlessly and transparently transfer from one sales support center to another is tested on a scheduled basis. Other definitions are closer to the one found in the Disaster Recovery Institute (DRI) International Glossary for Resiliency that says an exercise is an activity that rehearses the plans to ensure they contain the appropriate information and produces the desired result when put into effect.

An exercise director or exercise coordinator (whatever the organization wishes to name the responsibility) should be identified in the exercise program or exercise plan in addition to describing their roles and responsibilities (this is not a requirement in the standards but is mentioned in the guidance). This responsibility could be filled by the business continuity program manager or in a large organization by a business continuity staff member dedicated to exercise planning and management. This person should, of course, be an exercise subject matter expert and understand project risk.

9.2 TYPES OF EXERCISES

Exercises are based on scenarios. The "players" in the exercise are asked to apply, walk through, or implement the tasks or procedures in their plans according to the parameters of a credible hypothetical situation. Exercises can be based on discussions or operations. Discussion-based exercises are designed to orient the team members and other responsible parties with the contents of their plans. It helps the members to understand how the plan works, what the communications protocols are, and how to obtain the resources necessary to complete their objectives. Operations-based exercises carry more of a "doing" component and primarily are designed to clarify roles and responsibilities; validate plan contents; and to identify gaps in the process, procedures, or resources.

The guidance document defines exercise types that describe the activity to be exercised by one or more of the exercise activities. The types include:

- Alerts: This type can test the technology to alert interested or responsible individuals to the need to invoke their plans and to report to their work location within an acceptable period of time.
- Start: The start exercise can be an extension of the alert exercise to see how quickly, once activated, the can team begin their continuity operations.
- Staff: Exercises interrelationships with other responsible individuals and internal processes.

- Decision: Practices the ability to make decisions to achieve objectives.
- Management: Combines many of the types of exercises with the emphasis placed on how roles and responsibilities interrelate with the management system.
- Cooperation: How the response elements coordinate with other teams, outside agencies, and the emergency operations center (EOC).
- Crisis management: Uses a scenario that exercises the crisis management plan.
- Strategic: Specific to major incidents on a national level when the organization must interface with local, regional, or national response agencies.
- Exercise campaign: A series of repeated exercises with a common methodology.

The guidance defines what most business continuity managers recognize as different types of exercises as "exercise methods:"

- Seminar and workshop: All exercises are considered to be training opportunities and awareness and training should always be a documented object of an exercise. A seminar and workshop are more of an orientation than an exercise. A seminar is defined as an informal discussion designed to orient participants to the contents of the plan and to the framework in which it is to operate. Seminars are led by a person knowledgeable in the business continuity management system and can be used to review lessons learned from a recent exercise.

  A workshop can be used by the individuals responsible for its implementation to initially construct their plans. They can also be used to develop exercise plans through the identification of exercise objectives and scenario development.

  Exercise risk is included as part of the exercise planning process. These two methods are considered to be low risk.

- Tabletop exercise: A tabletop exercise can take several forms or levels of complexity but begins simply as a discussion with the continuity team members while verbally executing their plan on the basis of a credible scenario. The team is given the scenario and asked to apply or walk through their plan tasks. This is often the first exercise for the team and too often serves as the initial level of training or orientation because it is the first time that team members have read the plan. The team will read through each of their assigned tasks and compare the task to the details and conditions of the scenario. The team then decides if the contents of the plan are sufficient to allow them to continue operations under the circumstances. The team leader should be instructed do just that—lead his team through the exercise. The exercise leader can act as the controller who runs the exercise and keeps it moving. The controller can change the parameters of the scenario as needed, but they should not do so unless he or she sees the need or advantage to go in a different direction to stimulate discussion or revise assumptions or resources. Depending on the scope of the tabletop exercise and the type of functions involved, the controller can break up the group into subgroups and pose several different questions to each group.

  At the beginning of the exercise, the controller makes it clear to the team members their purpose, the rules of the exercise (usually none), and the fact they are not there to find fault with the team or its members, but rather to validate their strategies and tasks. However, the guidance document does task the person responsible for the program to evaluate the performance of team members during exercises. Someone should be assigned responsibility to record the minutes of the exercise, noting what went correctly, what did not, and what action items result. The scribe should ideally not be part of the team.

- Games: The guidance lists two types of games: discussion and operations. A game is an exercise involving two or more teams in which the outcome will produce a victory over the other team or teams. A discussion-based game could involve answering several questions about the plans and the business continuity management system, and an operations game could involve competition to be the first or the highest percentage of team members to log on to a remote system and to start processing using live data. Some type of incentive such as movie tickets can be used that goes beyond bragging rights by the winners. When developing operational game exercises, be careful that the game does not compromise safety. Asking teams to drive to a nearby alternative location to log on in a competitive situation may encourage unsafe driving.

  A discussion game is rated as low risk and an operations game is rated as medium risk, but whenever an exercise works with live data, the risk may be elevated.

- Drills: A drill practices a specific operation or task by a single team or multiple teams and can include outside agencies or interested parties. Major objectives of drills are to apply new skills, review old skills, increase competence, improve coordination between groups, and identify procedural inadequacies. Drills are most effective when the instructions or protocols for action change significantly or when nonroutine tasks may be required in the future. The emergency response team members will conduct evacuation drills or will practice putting out pan fires (a controlled flammable liquid fire contained in a large pan or enclosure).

  Although the risk to the planning of a drill can be low to medium, the safety risk to participants and equipment can be high.

- Functional exercise: A functional exercise used to be considered the next step once tabletop exercises were completed. Something that actually tested the ability to physically accomplish a task was considered to be a functional exercise. This would include switching data processes to an alternative data site, testing communications, or a similar activity. The guidance document defines a functional exercise as one that practices a single function, but later in the document it defines a functional exercise with a governmental emphasis. DRI International's International Glossary for Resiliency uses the U.S. Department of Homeland Security's definition of a functional exercise as an exercise that "examines and/or validates the coordination, command, and control between various multi-agency coordination centers" (e.g., EOCs, joint field office). A functional exercise does not involve any "boots on the ground (i.e., first responders or emergency officials responding to an incident in real time)." The definition in the guidance document is very similar to DRI's definition. It goes on to say that functional exercises can be an extension of drills.

  It is considered to be a medium risk.

- Full-scale exercise: Similar to the functional exercise, a full-scale exercise continues the governmental, multiagency, multijurisdictional focus. This is a "boots on the ground" exercise in which actual operations are conducted in real time. An example of a full-scale exercise is when the fire department detonates an explosive device that starts a fire in an unoccupied (and hopefully condemned) structure, simulates multiple injuries so that area hospitals are involved, sets up incident command and the EOC, extinguishes the fire, and hands over management of the incident to the agencies responsible for the bomb investigation. Add a terrorist threat beforehand and you have by default potentially included the federal government in the exercise. A large business can participate in a full-scale exercise with city or regional governmental services to test the integration of operations, sharing of information and resources, or to exercise any number of emergency response issues. Many large businesses such as an oil refinery maintain their own fire departments, and this is a perfect situation to conduct full-scale exercises internally and with multiagency participation. Even entities with smaller response organizations can participate. A biotechnology campus participated in a city's full-scale exercise in which the scenario was a leaking hazardous materials tanker parked next to the campus producing a vapor cloud that affected a number of the campus buildings. The biotech's emergency response team participated on their side of the fence, sharing information with the city's EOC. The fire department dealt with the response on the city street. It is interesting to note that the emergency response team performed perfectly but the first fire engine to arrive drove directly into the "hot zone" and the exercise controller immediately declared the engine occupants "dead."

More directly related to business continuity, a full-scale exercise can include actually switching data systems to an alternative site or flying team members to a hot site to begin the restoration of information technology (IT) and other organizational operations. Most contracts with a commercial hot site provide some amount of time for exercises with the option to buy more time if needed. Unfortunately, if there are several real declarations while you are in the middle of an exercise, you may be asked to end the exercise without any reimbursement of your expenses.

A full-scale exercise involves a great deal of planning, coordination, documentation, and orientation. Sixty to ninety days of full-time work should be expected by the person planning the exercise. Pay close attention that budget constraints do not impede the success of the exercise.

Although not mentioned in the guidance document, other methods of exercises are commonly used. These include

- Desk check: A desk check is a review of the plan by a third party such as the business continuity staff, an internal auditor, the steering committee, the team leader's manager, or the critical function's owner. Accuracy of the information in the plan and agreement that the strategies are viable and that the procedures will enable the team to reach their objectives within the recovery time objectives are examined and validated. The desk check is usually part of the plan writing process, but it can be performed at any time, especially after updates have been applied to the plan.
- Call tree exercise: This is similar to the alert exercise (an exercise type as defined in the guidance) in which team members are contacted by the various means outlined in their plans. This is a good way to practice call trees if such a system is part of the notification process, but its intent is to test or exercise notification of team members no matter what method is specified for use. This exercise verifies that contact information is correct and that team leaders understand how to notify their team members of the need to invoke the plan. The call tree exercise can test any technology used to accomplish the notifications.

One organization issued pocket pagers to all business continuity team members and decided to use a call tree exercise to test the effectiveness of this form of notification (today we can substitute text messages, mass notification companies, or software notification packages, etc.). All team members were notified by e-mail of the exercise details and that there was a 100% expectation of success. We will discuss metrics in the next chapter. This could be a good metric to report. A banner was printed that contained the date of the exercise and brief instructions, and it was displayed at the building's main exit. Other reminders were issued. On the night of the exercise (after most had left the building), several different code words were transmitted to random groups of team members. They were instructed to report to a specific room the next morning between specific times and reveal the code in exchange for pastries, fruit, and premium coffee and juice. The members who did not report to the room were contacted and their reasons were analyzed.

The risk of this type of exercise should be rated as low because it is pretty straightforward. Those members traveling or who are ill may pose some risk to success, but these contingencies can be built into the system by allowing them to phone in the code.

- Relocation exercise: In Chapter 8, we described an exercise in which team members were asked to make their way to the organization's data center that was intended to be used as a backup work location if the corporate offices were damaged or unavailable. This is a relocation exercise. Only 60% of the participants were able get to the alternative facility, and several of those who did had difficulty remotely logging onto the mainframe computer. Because the relocated team members were asked to connect with their laptop computers from the remote location and accomplish work, this also could have been considered to be a functional exercise under the "old" IT centric definition. This exercise was conducted during normal hours, but if it was successful, the intent was to hold an additional relocation exercise after hours to practice their ability to find the data center from their homes and not from the corporate offices.

  The relocation strategy included a local team to provide check-in for the relocated corporate office members, assignment of available space, and helping to set up workstations. A temporary phone directory of the locations was established and published by this team.

  The risk associated with a relocation exercise can be considered to be low to moderate depending on if the participants will log on to the system and process live transactions.

- Offsite storage: Absent the request to deliver records, backup tapes, or other media to an alternative site as part of a larger test, the organization may elect to schedule a test of the storage facility's ability to deliver the complete or selected set of offsite storage boxes to an alternative location according to the agreements the organization has with the storage facility.

  This exercise could result in high risk because the organization is taking its backup material out of a safe environment and exposing it to the possibility of loss, damage, compromise, or destruction. The best strategy is to request the delivery of a less critical storage box. Some managers would argue that this type of test is meaningless because it will likely be conducted under ideal, and not disaster, conditions.

- Complex tabletop exercise: A higher level or next-step tabletop simulation can involve an exercise with one or more teams working together to test their ability to coordinate tasks, provide input or output to each other, or uphold communications. The complexity of tabletop exercises can also increase with the introduction of more complex scenarios, decision-based activities, and "injects" by the person controlling the exercise. An inject is a message, condition, or instruction "injected" into the exercise to support the scenario, change the direction of the exercise, or simply to keep the participants busy if for any reason the pace of the exercise slows. More commonly used in full-scale exercises delivered by the "simulation team," they can be used effectively in a tabletop exercise delivered by the person managing the exercise (but not by the exercise participants).

Exercises, especially in the beginning, should be simple and fun, minimizing the number of rules imposed on the participants. The author would start initial tabletop exercises by declaring that there were only two rules: (1) no spitting, biting, or yelling is allowed and (2) there are no other rules. This has a practical side in that it may make the participants more comfortable to make comments that seem to demonstrate that a written procedure will not work. Because this may be the responsible individual's first encounter with business continuity, a positive experience will help to build support for the program and emphasize the importance of the program to the team members. It is important to start simply and then graduate to more complex exercises to help ensure success.

9.3 SCHEDULING EXERCISES

An exercise schedule must be developed and maintained by the business continuity manager or person on his or her staff tasked with the responsibility of exercise development and management. The schedule should be mentioned at a high level in the basic plan with the possibility of appending it to the plan if not of excessive length. All portions of the plan must be eventually tested or exercised, increasing in complexity as the program matures while remaining consistent with the objectives of the business continuity management system. Exercising must be comprehensive to include all elements of the plans. The schedule can be represented in the project plan as a Gantt chart or in a form most appropriate to the organization.

When scheduling exercises, bear in mind the following:

- The time required to prepare the exercise, including scenario development, notification of participants, scheduling time and meeting rooms. Full-scale exercises should be scheduled well in advance, especially if outside interested parties will participate. Matching available dates becomes more difficult as the complexity of the exercise increases.
- Other commitments of those who will participate. In other words, try to schedule major exercises (full scale, hot site, or relocation) at times that do not conflict with other major events or business cycles that could cause conflicts.
- Time to conduct the exercise. Large-scale exercises will require 1–3 or more days in the case of a hot site restoration test.
- Time to evaluate the results of the exercise.
- Time to incorporate corrective actions or plan updates.
- Updating the exercise plan.
- Preparation of metrics and reports to top management.

Once the initial round of simple exercises is completed, decide when the next level of exercises is to be scheduled. ISO does not specify how often exercises must be scheduled, but they should occur at "planned intervals." Depending on the size and complexity of the organization and business continuity management system, a rule of thumb is each function (i.e., team) participates in an exercise no less than annually, ideally twice each year. More complex exercises can occur annually. Some government agencies require an annual full-scale exercise, but every 5 years they must invite outside agencies and jurisdictions to participate.

The original schedule does not need to be repeated in the same order as long as all relevant responsible individuals have the opportunity for regular practice. The focus for the next round of exercises can concentrate on, or prioritize those that carry the greatest risk, those whose initial performance was less than adequate or those who produced the greatest number of significant changes to their plans, which in some respects equates to an initial exercise of the revised plan. Major changes to the plan, changes in plan strategy, or major changes in the strategic direction of the organization may require a redirected exercise focus. The addition of new equipment or processes may also move testing higher on the schedule.

9.4 **ORIENTATION**

Before the start of an exercise, some type of orientation should occur. See Chapter 3, "Competence and Awareness," for a discussion on methods to train persons with responsibilities under the business continuity management system. All participants of exercises and test must undergo some level of orientation to:

- Understand the contents of the plan. Unfortunately, this is often the first time team members have heard of a plan; most will not have read it until the exercise is in progress. This is to be expected when first introducing the team plan at a tabletop exercise. Allow participants time to read through the scenario and the plan before the formal portion of the exercise is to begin. At higher levels of exercises such as a full-scale exercise, knowledge of the plan contents is expected, but typically the scenario is read to the group by the exercise director just before its start.

- Understand the purpose of the exercise. An explanation of the purpose of the exercise should depend on the type of exercise and its objectives. Care is taken not to reveal expected outcomes, but initially explain to participants that the purpose is not to find fault with individuals, but to validate the procedures and resources in the plan. In a tabletop exercise, the purpose is to prove and improve the instructions contained in the plan. In more complex exercises, one purpose could be to produce some degree of perspiration, but this goal is better left unstated.

- Understand their role and expectations of the exercise. If a player is selected to perform the duties as the logistics chair in the EOC, then we will assume that they have been previously trained in this role. In a full-scale exercise, controllers and evaluators may need detailed instruction in how to fulfill the needs of these positions before the exercise is to begin. Observers, simulators, controllers, and evaluators will likely require training on how to execute their duties and how to complete forms and reports.

- All participants must be made aware of the rules and exercise protocols. For example, exercise controllers will wear a brown vest and participants must follow their instructions. Questions may or may be directed to controllers. Exercise evaluators wear green vests, and participants should not be able to ask them questions or to interact with them in any way.

- Know the signal word to stop the exercise. Exercise designers must establish a code word that signals an immediate stop or cancellation of the exercise. This word is used if there is an actual emergency situation that develops at the time of the exercise and the exercise is discontinued or switched into real mode. All participants in the exercise, large or small, must be aware of the signal word. "Cowboy Blue" or "Paul Bunion" are examples the organization can use (it is more fun to make up your own, something that is more memorable under the circumstances).

- Become aware of any safety hazards and controls. Safety procedures, warnings, and rules are also emphasized to the participants. Any participant should have the power to stop the exercise and immediately take action to correct a hazard to life, property, or the environment or to remove themselves or others from the hazard. Nothing in the exercise plan should place a participant in harm's way or breach security protocols.

- Large-scale exercises will likely require communication among participants, the simulation team, field operations (incident command), and the exercise director and controllers. A simulated phone directory of pertinent agencies and internal and external contacts should be published and all participants instructed to use only the simulated directory. Printing the simulated directory on yellow or other colored paper can help identify the appropriate directory to use. As a precaution, the normal phone directories or call lists should be removed from the exercise location beforehand. Most of the phone numbers in the exercise directory will go to the simulation team who is located in the "Sim Cell." Participants should be instructed to state who they are calling so that the simulator knows who or what role they are to play unless there is a dedicated phone line for each possible position (mark each phone line to identify what position it belongs to). Calls are generally answered, "This is an exercise, how may I direct your call?" and then let the caller identify their need. The simulator can then begin to play the appropriate role.

Two-way radios are typically used to communicate with the incident commander, responders, and the exercise director. Communication channels and frequencies are determined as part of the exercise planning and written into the exercise plan. Before the exercise, participants and support staff are informed of the proper channels to use. They are also instructed that all participants involved in any communication via radio, telephone, or texting, including all communication with the Sim Cell, will be preceded and ended with the comment, "This is an exercise." This is an important issue that must be emphasized in the orientation and compliance monitored throughout. Radio traffic between the exercise director and the controllers generally will not need this warning.

- For example, if the scenario calls for the use of actors to simulate dead and injured persons, unruly or angry demonstrators, or aggressive news reporters, then there should be an orientation beforehand to explain expectations, safety, constraints, and other necessary information to the actors.

- Observers are often allowed to watch portions of a full-scale exercise. Observers do not participate in the exercise, nor do they perform any control or evaluation functions. Observers ideally view the exercise from a designated area and must remain within the observation area during the exercise. All observers must understand the above restrictions and must not in any manner interact with the exercise participants. Depending on who the observers are, they may or may not participate in the after-action evaluation and report.

All orientations should be accompanied by a sign-in roster that identifies the following:

- Date, time, and location of the orientation.
- Who conducted the orientation.
- Title of orientation.
- A complete description of the orientation (if lengthy, append the description to the roster). Include copies of any distributed materials or presentation slides (Power Point).
- Full names of attendees.
- Attendee signatures.
- If using outside participants, then include their affiliation.

The sign-in roster will become an archival document and may be appended to the exercise plan.

9.5 EXERCISE PROGRAM

A major intent of exercises is to progressively build the skills of the responsible individuals, to test and validate that strategies will meet their intended goals, and to progressively improve the plans and ultimately the entire business continuity management system.

The exercise program should be developed and documented to describe the organization's exercise process that fosters continual improvement by eventually exercising and testing all portions of the plan.

However, do not confuse the exercise program document with the exercise plan document. The progression from simple (walkthrough checks of plans) to the most complex (full-scale exercises with outside interested parties) should be detailed. The scale of the program will match the size and complexity of the organization. The program should include (noninclusive):

- The purpose and intent of the exercise program.
- The scope of the exercise program that is aligned with the scope of the business continuity management system. Exercises are designed to be consistent with how the organization plans to respond to an actual incident.
- The identification of the person responsible for the exercise program that includes their roles and responsibilities.
- All persons with responsibilities under the plans. Use caution that to most auditors, the word "all" equates to 100% and you may need to provide an accounting of this figure.
- The high-level schedule and types of exercises intended. Teams, plans, resources, and strategies are exercised. Equipment and systems, infrastructure, and connectivity in addition to automatic failover are tested. Add to this the progression frequency ("regular intervals," significant changes within the organization or its operational environment). The testing of warning systems should be completed on an accelerated schedule, usually on a monthly basis. Again, the schedule is dependent on the complexity of the program.
- Identification of risk to the program and to the normal operations of the organization and how they are mitigated (see below).
- Exercise design requirements that include realistic scenarios based on risk with clearly defined objectives.
- Documentation must be produced as a result of each exercise and who is to review and approve the reports. The type of reports will differ with the type of exercise (tabletop vs. full-scale exercise).
- Improvement process: Every exercise should result in some type of improvement plan that can range from the simple to the complex depending, again, on the type of exercise and on the extent of the findings. In the rare case in which no corrective actions were necessary, the procedures should require this to also be included in the documentation.
- Top management's role in the exercise program. Remember that the standards (ISO 22301 and others) require top management to be actively involved in exercise and testing, and evidence of this involvement is used to prove top management support for the business continuity management system. Top management involvement can also be demonstrated by their approval of exercise plans and after-action reports (AARs), including the improvement plan. Their review and monitoring of testing metrics, as well as their direct involvement in the exercising of their own management or crisis management team plan, serves as further evidence. Full-scale exercises should include some involvement by top management as players (within the scope of their plan). However, use caution that when designing exercises for top management, the scenario and management of the exercise is planned to a high level of efficiency. An exercise involving top management that is poorly designed and executed could be career limiting for the planner and can potentially diminish support for the program.
- Defines exercise program metrics and how they will be reported and monitored.

Similar to the requirement to identify risk to the business continuity management system, the same is accomplished for the exercise program to ensure that the objectives of the exercise are achieved. The standard suggests the use of ISO risk management standard ISO 31000 (see Chapter 6). Risks are identified and can be placed in their own risk registry for prioritization and treatment of the most likely and the most impactful risk. This should result in an exercise risk management plan that instills a risk management culture in the conduct of the exercises. The plan will describe how the risk is treated (the exercise plans should detail risk identification and treatment also where risk is identified).

9.6 EXERCISE DESIGN

To plan and conduct an exercise, follow these high-level steps:

1. Select objectives for the exercise. Objectives must be attainable, clearly stated, measurable, and test specific actions or specifications.
2. Detail the scope of the exercise. The scope will include who is to participate (single team, multiple teams, outside suppliers, outside agencies and jurisdictions). Will it be a single team or include suppliers? Will it include outside agencies such as the fire department? Include the type of exercise (see step 4 below), dates, location(s), and purpose in the exercise plan.
3. Decide what type of exercise to use (i.e., tabletop, relocation, full scale?). The type of exercise will depend on where the organization is in its exercise schedule, the objectives chosen, and the level of complexity desired on the basis of the maturity of the business continuity management system.
4. Develop a realistic scenario to exercise or test the objectives.
5. Design the exercise plan and supporting materials. The complexity of the plan and supporting materials will depend on the type or exercise chosen. Supporting materials for a tabletop exercise may simply be a copy of the scenario.
6. Distribute the appropriate notification to participants, describing the who, what, when, and where of the exercise. Ensure major groups or organizations are in agreement with the date of the exercise.
7. Select controllers, evaluators, and simulators, if applicable.
8. Orient the players, controllers, evaluators, simulators, and observers to the exercise rules, protocols, and expectations.
9. Conduct the exercise.
10. Discuss the results and prepare the appropriate reports.
11. Revise the plan on the basis of the lessons learned during the exercise.

Each exercise must have a documented exercise plan that describes the following. This is intended for a full-scale exercise, but it can be scaled back for less complicated endeavors.

9.6.1 CONFIDENTIALITY

Confidentiality by the exercise design team is vital. Have all exercise design participants physically sign a document that informs them they are trusted agents and cannot reveal any information about the exercise to any of the potential players. This will help protect the integrity of the exercise and offer proof of due diligence to maintain confidentiality if and when audited by an internal or external agent.

9.6.2 SAFETY

A safety officer should be assigned to a full-scale exercise or to one that includes field operations. The safety officer "reports" to the exercise director and has the authority to immediately pause, stop, or discontinue any action or the exercise itself. A recent full-scale exercise used a scenario in which the police and fire department were called to report a suspicious package left outside of the hazardous materials storage area of a company that produced toxic chemicals when an undetected device detonates a relatively short distance away. The bomb squad sergeant, who was a member of the exercise design team, offered to set off a recently confiscated M-80 firecracker to simulate the explosion. The prospect of using a live explosive seemed to motivate the design team. The team's disappointment when the exercise's safety officer nixed the plan was tremendous; however, this was for good reason. The safety officer should be a safety professional or a subject matter expert familiar with the type of operation that poses the greatest risk.

Although every participant in the exercise and member of the exercise staff is responsible for their own safety and for the safety of others, Controllers are often directly assigned the responsibility for monitoring the safety of the operations for their areas. One point of observation an evaluator could look for would be to see that the safety officer position within the incident command structure (if applicable) is established for any high-risk operations either simulated or in actual play.

9.6.3 EXERCISE RISK

Identifying, evaluating, and controlling the risks to the exercise program are among the duties of the person responsible for the exercise program (exercise program manager). This person should be tasked in the plan to monitor risk and ensure that the measures designed to treat risk remain effective. They are tasked to implement additional mitigation as new risks develop. However, apart from program risk, it is important to ensure that the exercise never intentionally or unintentionally disrupts the normal operations of the organization. Tests and exercises are always announced. They should never be a "surprise." It is completely unacceptable to walk into the data center and "pull the plug." One organization was testing their first aid response with the scenario of a workplace shooter when they used very realistic moulage to simulate a very bloody scene of severely injured employees shot in an elevator (a lift for our British friends). Unfortunately, the elevator cab was misdirected to the lobby, where a large group of employees was waiting for what they thought was an empty elevator. Thinking these were real injuries, the negative consequences of this mistake were long-lasting. Risk to the program can involve:

- Resources not available when expected
- Less than competent exercise management staff
- Last minute cancellation of a participating organization, agency, or jurisdiction
- Poorly devised scenario or exercise plan
- Performance objectives not adequately defined, observed, or captured and reported
- Changing conditions that may suddenly render the exercise unsafe (e.g., lightning storm)
- Community concern
- Mistaken belief that the exercise is a real event
- Premature disclosure of the details of the exercise
- Occurrence of a real emergency external or internal to the exercise (an emergency external to the exercise could be a nearby fire; one internal to the exercise could include an injured participant)
- Injury to participants (see above)
- The exercise does not stay substantially within scope
- Unrealistic expectations or insufficient staffing or volunteers to adequately manage the exercise and evaluate performance

- Ineffective or biased evaluation
- Loss or compromise of company private information
- Environmental damage
- Damage to physical assets or systems

9.6.4 EXERCISE OBJECTIVES

Exercise objectives are established before scenarios are developed. Writing scenarios can be fun but challenging, and it is often the step of exercise development that many inexperienced managers tackle first. They then try to fit the objectives into the scenario, but if developed in this manner, important outcomes may be missed and the exercise may have an unfocused outcome.

Objectives can include (in no particular order):

- Orientation and training of roles and responsibilities.
- Test the ability to install backup media at an alternative site.
- Build the confidence of responsible individuals.
- Identify gaps in the plan on the basis of the scenario.
- Progressively improve plans and the management system.
- Identify strengths and weaknesses in the handoff of inputs and outputs.
- Clarify roles and responsibilities.
- Verify that recovery time objectives are realistic.
- Confirm the abilities of key or sole source suppliers.
- Identify the need to invoke and execute relocation plans.
- Reinforce knowledge of procedures, systems, and equipment.
- Assess the ability to pass information throughout the business continuity management system (communication).
- Test the interoperability of technical communications systems (two-way radio).
- Improve individual performance.
- Identify missing or out-of-date information.
- Validate assumptions.
- Test the response of offsite storage facilities.
- Evaluate the skill of team leaders and team members.
- Comply with contractual and regulatory requirements.
- Assess the ability of teams to support interdependencies.
- Develop teamwork and cooperation between teams or outside agencies.
- Gain recognition and support for the business continuity program.
- Improve the ability of the team leader to analyze information and make decisions.
- Identify the ability of teams to manage resources.
- Test the ability of technology to meet expectations.
- Evaluate the ability of teams to relocate to an alternative workspace.
- Identify issues connecting to technology from remote locations.
- Test the effectiveness of warning systems. These systems should be tested on a more regular basis (monthly).
- The mitigation of threats identified in the risk assessment is effective.

Although not a hard and fast rule, limit the number of major objectives to no more than six. This will help keep the exercise focused and uncomplicated. For full-scale exercises, there are typically many more objectives or subobjectives, and each participating agency or jurisdiction may incorporate their own.

9.6.5 SCENARIO DEVELOPMENT

The exercise objectives tell the design team what "problems" or conditions they need to build into the scenario. A scenario is a story or situation that leads the players to achieve the exercise objectives. It is not enough to simply say our scenario today is an earthquake. If the objective is to practice the procedure to "duck, cover, and hold," then refine the scenario to read, "You are sitting at your desk and the building starts to shake violently."

Scenarios must be believable, realistic, and relevant. An asteroid striking the Houston Astrodome is entirely possible, but it is not realistic or relevant (unless you are an Astros baseball fan). The scenario must present a situation that causes an outage that tests tasks and resources and that satisfies the objectives of the exercise or test. They must be as simple as possible given the size of the exercise and be of a nature that does not overwhelm the players with too many possibilities. (Note: You may notice that we interchangeably use the terms "participants" and "players.") Make every attempt to include facts and accurate details in the scenario, excluding anything that cannot happen. The Richter magnitude of the earthquake listed in a simple tabletop exercise (see Appendix) was the exact magnitude predicted for that fault at the postulated epicenter. Scenarios may be based on the risks identified through the business impact analysis and risk assessment.

Scenarios can or should be written to achieve a goal to test or to increase the ability of team leaders and participants to analyze information and make decisions. A simple tabletop scenario included in the Appendix was designed to give the teams information that should have led them to the conclusion that relocation, or at least temporary evacuation, was necessary. They were not directly told in the scenario that the facility needed to be vacated; the situation presented should have led them to this conclusion. The author participated in a full-scale exercise at the Federal Emergency Management Agency's training institute as the business liaison and received an inject from the controller informing him that because of the hurricane (which was the scenario) 40,000 chickens at a nearby poultry farm were killed because of the severe flooding. Not having a great deal of experience with deceased birds, his first thought was to contact the local fried chicken outlet to inform them of a possible landfall in discounted raw materials. However, after a bit analysis of the situation, the realization was made that there was now a potential health hazard; therefore, the public health agency, the contact number for which was listed in the exercise phone book (good exercise planning), was contacted (the number was actually answered by a member of the exercise "simulation team," which we will discuss later).

Decide how to introduce the scenario to the participants. A scenario narrative that tells a story is typically developed as mentioned earlier. The scenario must have an initiating event, either described in the narrative or introduced by some other method. One EOC tabletop exercise in which the scenario was the detonation of a "dirty bomb" (radiological dispersal device) near the building was introduced by playing a very realistic recording of police radio communications that described a traffic stop of a delivery truck by a canine unit for which the bomb detection trained police dog alerted on the vehicle. A loud explosion was heard while the officer was talking when all communication by the officer stopped. The correct city police radio identifiers were used as well as the exact streets near the exercise location. The scenario narrative can also be introduced as a simulated newspaper article, prerecorded televised evening news broadcasts played on the exercise room's video display, or a tanker truck with a simulated spill of its contents to simulate the hazardous material. The initiating or triggering event is the detonation, earthquake, injury, or some event that starts the exercise. In a tabletop exercise in which the scenario is read to the team, the start of the exercise could be as simple as the person running the exercise saying to the team leader, "Please execute your plan now."

Some full-scale scenarios, especially those conducted by governmental agencies, summarize the preexisting conditions, initiating event, and response actions, and they conclude with exercise termination conditions. Scenarios for full-scale exercises should be crafted with a development team that includes, depending on the scope of the exercise, emergency management or representatives from outside agencies or other participating organizations, but be careful that the size of the team is not so large as to become unmanageable. The representatives must not include anyone who will participate in the exercise unless they are assigned to a support duty such as an observer or simulation team member. Do not forget to discuss confidentiality with these representatives.

Pertinent supplemental information can accompany the scenario narrative. This information is also included in the exercise plan and provided to the controllers, evaluators, and simulation team members. For example, in the case of a hazardous materials release, the simulated weather conditions such as wind speed and direction, humidity, and approaching storms can be listed so that a consistent message is delivered to the players and that information provided to them is sensitive to the outcome of the exercise. The dirty bomb exercise described earlier generated a radiological dispersal device fact sheet that described what a dirty bomb is and what the potential immediate effects it could have in the hot zone and surrounding area were. This was provided to the simulation team so that they could accurately respond to questions or to unanticipated situations.

After scenario information is developed, it is checked by the team or by a third party to ensure it is technically accurate, the situations are consistent with the initiating event and type of hazard, and that it enables the exercise participants to meet its objectives.

The standard discusses the use of ethnography to develop scenarios that have a greater impact based on the experiences of people who have lived through catastrophic events to provide realism and content to the exercise learning experience. This is achieved through unstructured interviews and research. Ethnography is defined as the systematic study of people and cultures.

9.6.6 TIMELINE AND MASTER SCENARIO EVENT LIST

Related to scenario development but geared more toward the conduct of a full-scale exercise is the timeline and master scenario event list (MSEL). A timeline of key scenario events details the activities that are expected to occur during the exercise. The timeline represents the upper-tier task that the participants must successfully complete to meet each exercise objective. It is a schedule of the major injects and interactions between participants and is used to help build the MSEL. It includes key events and the expected responder actions and, where possible, it correlates them with exercise objectives. It includes activities of controllers and some elements of exercise management. In other words, the timeline does the following:

- It lists the time sequence of significant events that are to occur during the exercise.
- It lists the major controller-initiated events and expected participant actions/response.

- It validates the details of the scenario.
- It helps to ensure that objectives are met.
- It indicates times in clock time (real time) or plus or minus the triggering event or exercise start time.
- It can be separated by location or organization if many are involved, but this may not necessarily simplify management of the exercise.
- It includes preexisting conditions and the triggering event. Notifications to agencies or other organizations before the start of the exercise should be scheduled on the timeline. Even if representatives of the police and fire department are participating in the exercise, dispatch should always be notified of the pending start and finish of the exercise to prevent a "false alarm" response. The media or the surrounding community should be notified of the exercise if it will produce any smoke, noise, or many marked response vehicles that might draw their attention. Any such notification should be cleared through the public relations spokesperson.
- It signals the positioning of controllers and evaluators.
- It signals the end of the exercise and the start of debriefing activities.

The MSEL provides the detailed exercise control messages, data, information, and expected actions by the participants. The time indicated in the MSEL is the number of minutes plus or minus the start of the exercise. The messages are numbered in sequential order. Some designers use the letter "C" after a message to indicate it is a contingency message to be issued to the controller(s) only when directed or if a specific event occurs. The message summary provides who issues the message, who receives the message, and an overview of the message content. The expected response provides the expected sequence of events that will occur in response to the incident. The MSEL does the following:

- It contains additional detail than that found in the timeline.
- It is the baseline list of all messages and injects that details the expected participant actions.
- It can be used by controllers, simulators, and evaluators (and of course the exercise director) as a checklist of messages and injects they are responsible to deliver or simulate.

See Table 9.1 for an excerpt from an MSEL.

9.6.7 MESSAGE INJECTS

Injects are the simulated information or directions used to drive the scenario and to trigger the actions designed to initiate a response by the participants that satisfy the exercise objectives. There are two types of injects:

- Informational: Informational injects provide the event messages, situations, or condition to the participants.
- Control: Control injects are used to run the exercise, such as starting or stopping the exercise.

Each type of inject can have a subset called a contingency message. The injects can be directed to the participants or to the field controllers. For example, a controller in the field may be instructed to reveal information contained in a fact sheet at a particular time during the exercise.

Some Sim Cells are issued an inject list that contains only the injects and not the full MSEL. The format of the messages follows that in the MSEL. The message number allows for tracking, control, or

Time	Number	Message Summary	Expected Action
		Table 9.1 Excerpt from Master Scenario Event List	
+02	11b	**From 911-actor to 911 center**: Second 911 call to report accident.	☐ Department of Transportation (DOT) help truck arrives at the scene.
	11c	**From 911-actor to 911 center**: Third 911 call to report accident.	☐ 911 dispatch directs city fire, police, and EMS to report to the scene.
+03	11d	**From 911-actor to 911 center**: Last 911 call to report accident.	☐ 911 dispatch notifies county emergency services (CES).
+04	12C	**From senior controller to fire department (FD) controller**: Release the FD assets from the exercise staging area 5 min after they receive the dispatch call. Use the sequence in the message for release.	☐ CES places EOC staff on standby. ☐ DOT assesses and reports the situation to include the radioactive materials. Assists ambulatory patients.
	13C	**From senior controller to police controller**: Release the police assets from the exercise staging area 5 min after they receive the dispatch call.	
	14C	**From senior controller to emergency management system (EMS) controller**: Release the EMS assets from the exercise staging area 5 min after they receive the dispatch call.	
+05	15	**From senior controller to truck driver**: Make call to base.	☐ Truck driver calls shipping company to report the accident. ☐ DOT begins initial traffic control.

reference to the message. The time the message is delivered is highlighted. The next column lists the delivery method. Injects can be delivered via telephone, two-way radio, or by means mentioned earlier such as a simulated TV news broadcast. Listed next identifies who the message is "from" and "who" it is directed to. The simulator responsible for the inject may telephone the public relations manager in the EOC, pretending to be a news reporter. The instruction may begin "Reporter to PIO." The instruction follows. The final column could be for any expected action or response to be noted on the form. Some inject lists contain a final column that indicates if the inject is a contingency message.

Contingency messages are used to force participant action and keep the scenario on track. Many of the events and injects are designed to trigger an action so that an objective can be met. Some of the actions may be designed to trigger other actions. However, if the participant does not make the correct response, a contingency inject is designed on the spot to direct the person to satisfy the desired action after waiting an appropriate amount of time to see if it is in fact accomplished. The amount of time to wait varies, but it should be approximately 15–20 min. This type of contingency message is issued only when necessary and at the direction of the controller or exercise director. The message can be given directly, but consider sending it through the Sim Cell so that the controller or exercise director does not need to worry about documenting injects. This also carries the advantage of concentrating all injects in one place for easier inclusion in the AAR.

Contingency messages are also used to keep the exercise moving at the proper pace. Despite a good design team and detailed MSEL, certain participants or groups in the exercise may wind up with nothing to do either because of "poor" design or a group that accomplished their tasks sooner than expected. In this case, and only at the direction of the exercise director or controller (as agreed to and communicated before the start of the exercise), the simulators will craft one or more injects to keep people busy in a manner that is relevant to their function or objectives. These injects must remain realistic, reasonable, and achievable. Injects for this purpose should be developed ahead of time.

Simulators must have an intimate knowledge of the scenario and conditional data used in the exercise. It is a good idea to have at least one or more potential simulators participate on the scenario and exercise design team. They must know how to change the conditional data and under what conditions they could change, but any changes are used with extreme caution and only with the knowledge and agreement with the exercise director. Subject matter experts as necessary may be stationed in the Sim Cell.

The Sim Cell should be located in an out-of-the-way secured location, usually a large conference room with a sufficient number of telephones, workstations if exercise software is used, and comfortable workspace. However, it should be close enough to the exercise operations so the exercise director can easily visit. In some exercises, the Sim Cell became the control center for the exercise. Most exercise staff wear some type of color-coded identification vest with the name of their function clearly displayed on the vest. Because none of the participants need to see the simulation team members, a vest is not required. Not wanting to feel left out, the simulation team for one exercise chose to wear vests with the word "Liar" as their function. The simulation team members are in effect factual liars because they are simulating events and conditions. If possible, vests worn by other functions (controllers, evaluators, observers) should be of a different color and not duplicate the color of vests worn in the EOC (EOC participants often wear a colored vest to identify their membership in the different EOC positions: command, operations, logistics, finance and administration, safety, PIO, etc.).

The Sim Cell, depending on staffing levels and the complexity of the exercise, can get quite busy, especially if injects and return messages occur with little time in between. Simulators should divide the delivery of messages or the receipt of messages so that no one is overwhelmed. Caution is always used to monitor the sequencing of messages so that a message is not injected out of sequence. The need to stop the exercise, explain the mistake, and rewind the exercise detracts from the sense of realism and reduces its effectiveness by revealing what is to come next. It is also incredibly embarrassing for the Sim Cell members.

Simulators must remember to begin and end all messages with, "This is an exercise," especially when using two-way radio communications. The news media and radio hobbyists listen to radio traffic and may assume there is a real (and serious) event taking place.

9.6.8 CONTROLLERS

Controllers ensure exercise continuity by managing exercise play. This is accomplished by monitoring the exercise timeline, increasing or decreasing the insertion of event information and injects, issues exercise material to participants as required, and solving issues that pose risk to the exercise objectives. The number of controllers may increase as the complexity of the exercise increases. In this case there may be a senior controller to supervise other controllers. The exercise director may serve as the senior controller.

Controllers are positioned at control points or locations where they need to provide information or manage their portion of the exercise. These positions must be pre-identified and written into the plan.

Similar to evaluators, controllers should understand the standard practices and terminology the participants will use so that they can properly interact and manage their portions of the exercise. They must also have the ability to recognize any hazards presented by the exercise operations. Controllers also have the responsibility for the safety and security of the participants under their jurisdiction. In other words, controllers should have the following:

- Knowledge: An understanding of the layout of the grounds and facilities, of protocols that will be used by responders, and of the details of the exercise injects used to keep the exercise on pace toward the achievement of the objectives.
- Experience: Controlling a large-scale exercise for the first time involves many decisions and a lot of responsibility. Controllers without experience should be assigned to the lowest risk positions if possible. Controllers should be able to recognize "free play," in which participants are allowed room for innovation and problem-solving that was not anticipated in the design of the exercise. Free play is often encouraged as long as:
  - The safety of the participants, property, and the environment is not jeopardized.
  - Security protocols are maintained.
  - The free play does not radically go outside of the scope of the exercise.
  - It does not significantly put pressure on the timelines.
  - It does not impede the achievement of the exercise objectives.
- Technical expertise: An expert firefighter would not make a good controller for a hot site relocation exercise unless he or she is also a technically proficient IT professional. Controllers must have the ability to recognize situations that may derail the exercise objectives and take action to correct the situations.
- Positive approach: The best conceived plans can quickly unravel or pose major roadblocks that were not anticipated. Participants recognize when things are not going correctly and mistakes can intensify. The controller must maintain an even temperament and guide the exercise back to the proper path.

Controllers must be trained in their duties and responsibilities in general and specifically in the details of the exercise. The purpose, scope, and objectives of the exercise must be completely understood by the controllers. Safety and security concerns, communications, exercise suspension, and termination are key subjects for training. The methods and constraints used by controllers when providing information is ideally practiced so they are proficient in the field and do not detract from the flow of the play. For example, the controller will not inform participants of the radiation level unless or until someone attempts to take a radiological reading with the proper instrument (another reason the controller must be technically competent to be in a position to identify if the wrong instrument is used or it is used improperly. This applies also to Evaluators). Controllers must attend the pre-exercise orientation.

In large-scale exercises, a controller and evaluator (C/E) handbook is produced from the exercise plan. The handbook supplements the exercise plan by presenting detailed information about the exercise scenario, the controller and evaluator's responsibilities, and any special details not included in the exercise plan. The handbook is distributed only to controllers and evaluators. In addition to information from the exercise plan (timeline, MESL, etc.), the handbook usually contains the following sections:

- Detailed scenario information
- Fact sheets specific to the controller's positions and for the simulation team
- Roles and responsibilities for each of the controller and evaluator's positions
- Controller communications plan
- Exercise evaluation guides (EEGs) and forms
- Any special logistics

9.6.9 EVALUATORS

Evaluators perform one of the most important support functions of the exercise. They observe, analyze, and document performance against established criteria in accordance with the EEGs in their designated area of the exercise. The EEGs are typically found in the C/E handbook. Their observations and evaluation of performance provides direct input for continuous improvement by identifying strengths and weaknesses in training, performance, and process. To effectively perform their duties to determine if the exercise met its objectives, the recruitment of evaluators must consider several conditions:

- Evaluators must have experience and the technical expertise in the functional area they are evaluating so that they can judge the adequacy of player or system performance. As we mentioned above, they must understand the terminology and practices, if not best practices for the behaviors, tasks, or specifications they are asked to judge.
- They must understand the exercise process, goals, and objectives. The participants must be evaluated in light of the exercise expectations and goals. The expectation or goal may call for some action that is less than what the evaluator would have personally done if in a live situation, but if it meets the objective of the exercise it must be considered as "meets all requirements."
- They must be fair and unbiased. Evaluators must remain open minded when observing different departments or agencies that they may have had difficulty with in the past. In other words, no personal or political agendas.
- They must be able to understand the intricacies of the scenario. What actions are realistic and effective given the details of the postulated situation is a question the evaluator must keep in mind when analyzing performance.

Each task to be evaluated must have an accompanying performance expectation. The evaluator will decide the following:

- Was the task completed?
- At what level was the task completed? Levels of completion can include (these levels are usually listed on the evaluation form and defined in the exercise plan):
  - Fully completed (or fully demonstrated)
  - Partially completed
  - Not completed (or inadequately completed)
  - Not applicable (there should rarely be a need for this checkbox)
- Was the task or objective completed in an expected or appropriate time frame? Time frames can apply to an individual task or to a group of individuals.

These decisions are applied to

- Task-level analysis: Task-level analyses are applied to individuals or groups.
- Activity-level analysis: Activity-level analysis concentrates on demonstrating a broader capability of the participants. In other words, did the actions of the group as a whole successfully accomplish all activities?
- Capability-level analysis: This looks at the organization's ability as a whole to achieve a higher level objective.

An EEG is prepared for each evaluator position (or positions) to focus attention on only the evaluation points for which the evaluator is responsible. The guide is often combined with the controller guide. The guide contains much of the information described above (i.e., exercise description, scope, purpose, timeline, and MSEL) as well as evaluation assignments, rules, definitions, and forms. The focused evaluation checklists that are tied to each objective the evaluator is to judge are appended to the guide. Information collected in the checklists is used to analyze the results of the exercise and to help produce the AAR. The guide should be in a form that enables the evaluator to complete the checklists in the field in real time. Spiral binding can help keep checklists from becoming victims of the wind and allows easy access to the timeline and other information.

The checklists outline the step-by-step actions that the participants should follow to meet their objectives. Once the actions are listed, the evaluation criteria are added. The checklists should be organized in the time sequence that the events will (hopefully) be observed. If outside agencies or organizations participate in the exercise, then ask them to verify the criteria assuming they were not part of a team that developed the checklist. Figure 9.1 presents an example exercise evaluation checklist.

Many checklists add a column for comments that can be useful to a complete evaluation; that is, evaluators may include notes about "if" and "how" targets were met. Other issues identified in comments may include the following:

- How the objectives were or were not met
- Causes or reasons the objectives were not met
- Significant decisions made or information used to make decisions
- Requests made or how requests were processed
- How effectively were resources used

Evaluators should avoid making recommendations on the checklist—this is better served by discussion in the hot wash or AAR. Findings are not discussed until the hot wash. Evaluators are expected to attend the hot wash and any other after-action meetings such as the controller and evaluator debriefing.

The standard includes an example of a checklist that scores the level of attainment of each item evaluated. The sum of the points indicates the degree of success for the function evaluated. The scoring method used assigns the following values:

- 0 points: "Criterion not met."
- 1 point: "Only basics are covered. The function may not be effective enough."
- 2 points: "The function is partially effective."
- 3 points: "The function is fully effective."

Evaluators must be positioned at the proper location or locations to have the ability to observe the actions or information they are evaluating but not where they can get in the way of operations. The MSEL can provide clues about where to place evaluators with the most technical experience and at what times to move them, if necessary, to a different location. Needless to say, evaluators must arrive at their positions before the arrival of the participants. The evaluators must know what the action is to occur next and see that it was accomplished. Remember that evaluators should have no conversations with players and provide no information to them unless initiated by the evaluator to clarify a player action.

All checklists and summaries of notes should remain as exercise archival documents.

Exercise Evaluation Checklist						
Position:		Emergency Operations Center – EOC Director				
Location:		EOC				
Assigned:		Jane Smith				
ID	**Yes**	**No**	**N/A**	**N/O**	**Action / Objective**	**Notes**
Check the appropriate box: Yes: Successfully demonstrated action No: Did not successfully demonstrate action or did not complete action N/A: Not applicable or already accomplished by another player or group N/O: Did not observe action but there is evidence of its completion						
EOC 010	❑	❑	❑	❑	Did the EOC Director receive initial assessment report from the Incident Commander?	
EOC 011	❑	❑	❑	❑	Did the EOC Director conduct adequate briefing?	
EOC 012	❑	❑	❑	❑	Did the EOC Director activate the Operations Chair?	
EOC 013	❑	❑	❑	❑	Did the EOC Director notify the Corporate Management Team?	
EOC 014	❑	❑	❑	❑	Did the EOC Director Activate the Crisis Management Team?	
Signature and Date:						

FIGURE 9.1

Example of exercise evaluation checklist (notice different evaluation criteria and absence of enabling task).

9.6.10 AFTER-ACTION MEETINGS AND REPORT

The exercise plan and supporting documents (C/E Handbook, EEGs, etc.) are combined with the evaluation checklists to produce the AAR and corrective actions to demonstrate that:

- The plans are valid.
- Resources were available and used efficiently.

- Learning objectives were achieved.
- Exercise objectives were met.
- Root causes of objectives that were not met and how they will be corrected (as we will discuss in the next chapter, the determination of a "root cause" can be a lengthy process).
- Regulatory requirements were satisfied.

AARs typically are produced for full-scale exercises, but all exercises regardless of size should summarize its results and corrective actions. Smaller exercises such as a tabletop exercise can simply add the appropriate number of paragraphs to its exercise minutes.

The process to produce the AARs involves the collection and analysis of data from the evaluation checklists, EOC logs and notes, participant surveys, and information from discussions at the following:

- Hot wash: The hot wash is a meeting held with all participants immediately after the conclusion of the exercise to discuss their observations and suggestions for improvement. This meeting can be used by evaluators to clarify questions about actions in the field and how they arrived at a particular decision. Participants can use this time to complete an exercise questionnaire (participant feedback form) designed to improve the orientation, scenario, or exercise process if the organization chooses to do so (Figure 9.2). The hot wash should be as brief as possible. Water, coffee, fruit, and pastries provided during this meeting are almost always appreciated by the participants.
- C/E meeting: After the hot wash, controllers and evaluators attend a debriefing to discuss their observations and the recommendations they believe will improve the process. Notes they made in the checklists can be expanded or clarified and submitted to the exercise director or to the person responsible for the AAR.
- Draft AAR meeting: This meeting can take several forms. First, if the result of a multiorganization or multijurisdictional exercise, meet with the principals to debrief and/or revise the draft AAR and improvement plan (corrective actions). If no eternal organizations participated in the exercise, hold this meeting with personnel who can refine the draft AAR and improvement plan.
- Presentation of the final AAR: The contents of the final report (i.e., the results and findings of the exercise) along with the improvement plan are presented to the relevant interested parties. In the case of a full-scale exercise, this may include top management. The improvement plan should follow all of the rules for corrective actions that we will discuss in the next chapter.

The AAR should summarize the information from the exercise plan so that each document can stand alone. The AAR will outline the purpose, scope, and exercise scenario. A description of the exercise, participants, activities, and resources used are included in the report. It should describe the objectives of the exercise in some detail and state how effectively they were met. It should list the issues, findings, and concerns identified during the exercise. In other words, why were objectives not met or only partially met. Although not necessarily a one-for-one requirement, each deficiency should be assigned a corresponding corrective action. A summary and conclusion paragraph is usually included. In some organizations, top management is required to approve the report. A summary report should be distributed to participants so that they learn from the report's findings and to reinforce the value they provided by their participation. ISO guidance suggests that exercises that exposed major deficiencies should be repeated after corrective actions are implemented.

PARTICIPANT OBSERVATIONS:	
This information is used by Emergency Management to evaluate and improve the Emergency Management Program. Please print neatly, and feel free to also provide positive comments. Return this at the completion of the critique.	
Name: (Optional)	
Role:	☐ Observer ☐ Player ☐ Controller/Evaluator ☐ Other _____
Date Exercise Conducted:	
Area Exercise Conducted:	
Area(s) Observed:	
Observations and Comments:	
Did you attend the training offered?	☐ Position Specific ☐ Evaluator/Controller ☐ Other _____
Did the training increase your ability to perform your responsibilities for the exercise?	☐ Yes ☐ No ☐ N/A
Observations and Comments:	
What other training would you like to see offered?	

FIGURE 9.2

Participant evaluation form.

9.7 REVIEW

Once plans are developed, a documented program is established to validate the strategies, ensure the availability of resources, and to develop the proficiency of the responsible individuals to perform their tasks under the plans in conditions that will be less than ideal. The middle of a disaster is not the time to discover that the backup infrastructure you put in place does not work. For these and many other reasons, an exercise and testing program is one of the more important elements of the business continuity management system.

Exercises and tests will identify poor or absent assumptions, reveal gaps and missing data in the plans, and will help ensure that the business continuity management system objectives can be achieved.

A documented exercise and testing program helps to demonstrate top management's commitment to the program and the standards require their active participation in the program. This is accomplished by including top management in the exercise of their individual plans, in full-scale exercises, and in the planning and acceptance of AARs and corrective action plans.

All elements of all plans must be tested in a progressive manner that increases in complexity as the program matures. Exercises should start with simple tabletop exercises and graduate to full-scale exercises.

Exercises are a form of training that focuses responsible individuals, including top management, on the objectives of the program, thus reducing spontaneous, independent action by leaders that may become detrimental to meeting the goals of the business continuity management system.

An exercise is an activity that rehearses the plans to ensure they contain the appropriate information and produces the desired result when put into effect. Exercises focus on processes and people. Testing incorporates a pass or fail objective and is used to determine if equipment, systems, and infrastructure will work under disaster conditions to their expected specifications. There can also be a human element to testing.

Exercises are based on scenarios. Plans are executed based on the conditions imposed by the scenario narratives. Exercises can be based on discussions or operations. The types of exercises are described in the ISO guidance document on exercising and testing that outlines the activity to be exercised, but it also defines what most business continuity professionals would recognize as a type of exercise known as "exercise methods." These methods include seminars and workshops, tabletop exercises, games, drills, functional exercises, and full-scale exercises. Other exercises include a desk check, call tree exercise, relocation exercise, offsite storage retrieval, and multifunction tabletop exercises.

Exercises must be scheduled and completed at "planned intervals" and should be referenced in the exercise program document. It is up to the organization to determine what the best schedule is for exercises, but the frequency should be no less than one per year per function. Some governmental organizations are required to annually conduct a full-scale exercise with one that includes outside agencies and jurisdictions every 5 years. Organizations should include outside interested parties in their exercise program. If used by the organization, warning systems should be tested on a more frequent basis. In this case, a test each month seems to be the norm.

Each exercise should have an exercise plan (this in practice applies to larger scale exercises—a series of simple tabletop exercises can be described in the exercise program document) that details important information that includes a description, purpose and scope of the exercise, objectives, confidentiality, and exercise safety. Risk to the exercise is identified and mitigated using the risk assessment and risk treatment methods described in ISO 31000. The conduct of the exercise should never disrupt the normal operations of the organization. Risk to players, property, and the environment is also identified and treated. The exercise plan will list the scenario, timeline, MSEL, and message injects. A separate document for exercise controllers and evaluators is prepared and orientations are held to explain duties and expectations.

At the conclusion of an exercise, several meetings are held depending on the type and size of the exercise to discuss the strengths and weaknesses of the test objectives that were revealed by the exercise. In the case of a tabletop, a review and summary are sufficient, but in a larger full-scale exercise several meetings are held with all players and staff to develop a formal AAR and improvement plan.

BIBLIOGRAPHY

International Standard ISO 22301:2012 Societal Security – Business Continuity Management Systems – Requirements.
ISO/DIS 22398.2 Societal security – Guidelines for exercises and testing.
International Glossary for Resiliency, Maintained by DRI International, www.dirr.org.

CONTINUOUS IMPROVEMENT

10

CHAPTER SUMMARY

The processes that today enable continuous improvement of Business Continuity Management Systems are based less on the maintenance of the Business Continuity Plan than was the focus in the past. Business Continuity Management standards emphasize the continuous improvement of its entire set of its programmatic elements through the trending of performance metrics that monitor critical success factors, key performance indicators, and thorough internal audits that ensure the effectiveness of the management system. The results of trends and management system audits are reported to the top management level of the organization for action. Any nonconformity with the requirements of the standards is investigated to determine their root cause and a corrective action plan is developed to prevent the recurrence of the issue that caused the nonconformity. A Responsibility Assignment Matrix can support the management of the implementation of some corrective actions. Once implemented, the success of the corrective actions is examined through a process of effectiveness reviews to help guarantee they were effective in achieving their goal.

Any number of Root Cause Analysis tools is acceptable for use by the standards and include Failure Mode and Effects Analysis (FMEA), Human Performance Improvement (HPI), and Five-Whys. The Root Cause Analysis will often include an "extent of condition" review to determine if the potential (or the actual existence) for an identified issue or nonconformance to exist in other activities, processes, or programs within the Business Continuity Management System or within the remainder of the organization as a whole.

Updates to the program and the plans are tracked through a Change Management system that can operate on either an Organizational Change Management or Process Change Management level. The Change Management system is documented so that modifications to the Business Continuity Management System are introduced in a controlled and coordinated manner.

This chapter discusses the elements that the Business Continuity Manager must apply to keep his or her program in a mission ready state, or to borrow a term from the Quality Management arena, "fit-for-purpose." It will enable the manager to maintain momentum toward a mature program that will meet the expectations of the standards and achieve a world class Business Continuity Management System.

KEY TERMS

Change management; Continuous improvement; Corrective action plan; Critical success factors; Effectiveness review; Extent of condition; Five whys; Human performance; Internal audit; Key performance indicators; Management review; Nonconformity; Performance metrics; Program maintenance; Root cause analysis.

KEY POINTS

- Plan and Program Maintenance are vital to mission readiness but are often neglected processes
- The Business Continuity Manager must understand Change Management
- Performance metrics and internal audits provide input to the annual Management Report

- Nonconformity is any of the standard's requirements that were not met
- Root Cause Analysis is required to clear any identified nonconformities
- Corrective Actions that result from nonconformities must be documented and addressed in a systematic, graded manner that prevents recurrence
- The Business Continuity Management System must be evaluated and audited at planned intervals
- The engine that drives the standards and the entire Business Continuity Management System is Continuous Improvement

10.1 INTRODUCTION

The next step in the Business Continuity process after testing and exercises used to be called "Plan Maintenance." Directives were written into the Basic Plan or into Business Continuity Policy that required managers and team leaders to "update contact and resource information in team plans on a quarterly basis and review strategies annually or when there is a major change in the organization." And this is the point at which the plans ended.

However, the standards impose a Management System on the Business Continuity Process and good managers know that performance must be measured, analyzed, and reported to upper management to ensure the continued quality of the program. The adage attributed to Peter Drucker that "you can't manage what you don't measure" holds a great deal of truth despite the fact that Drucker never exactly said this. Good managers also know that action based on the results of performance metrics supports the continuous improvement of their programs.

Plan Maintenance is still an important piece of the continuous improvement process and although testing and exercise programs contribute to this effort, their frequency does not allow adequate satisfaction of the requirement to enhance performance. The mechanics of keeping the plan up to date is a small portion of what should be considered *Program* Maintenance.

Mergers, acquisitions, program updates, revised standards, and the installation of new systems can force major changes on the Business Continuity Management System. Change Management is necessary to understand how the introduction of new concepts is best socialized within the organization in a manner that removes the roadblocks to change. Tracking process changes provides a history of program maintenance.

Continuous improvement of the Business Continuity Management System is in part achieved through the tracking and trending of performance metrics, formal internal audit, and the results and actions from the Management Review that is required by the standards. Nonconformities identified by these processes are monitored through a formal corrective action system.

10.2 PROGRAM MAINTENANCE

Team Leaders should be tasked with keeping their plans up to date, and the Business Continuity Manager should be tasked with keeping the Business Continuity Management System up to date. Supporting the Business Continuity Manager in this effort is the Top Management sponsor and the Steering Committee. They can alert the Manager to changes in any strategic direction of the organization or with any structural changes that may not be widely announced (some organizations are constantly reorganizing, forcing the rearrangement of existing plans). The Business Continuity Manager keeps both the plans and the program integrated within context of the organization. Plans that are kept up to date demonstrate a positive Business Continuity culture within the organization.

As part of the Business Continuity awareness training, team members should be instructed to immediately notify the Team Leader of any change in status, address, or other contact information. This will flag the need to update the team plan. Purchasing personnel should also know to forward changes in vendor information to the Team Leader(s). Ideally, the Team Leader should check team member information quarterly but no less than annually. Strategies are reviewed and the team task instructions associated with the strategies are adjusted accordingly. In addition to checking that resource requirements are still fresh, the Team Leader will ensure that interdependencies have not changed. If there are significant changes to the plan, the Team Leader must inform the Team Members, and the Business Continuity Manager must do the same for broader changes in the program.

This Program Maintenance process must be independent of the testing and exercise program, that is, do not depend on testing and exercising as the sole method used to update plans. Another test of Business Continuity culture is Team Leaders who consistently analyze the impact of changes inside and outside the organization to their team and to their plans.

The organization mandates the policy to maintain the program and the plans in a state of mission readiness, managed by the Business Continuity Manager. The policy or procedure should spell out these responsibilities and list its minimum expectations. The manager will define and document a Change Management or change control process, if one is not already present within the organization or within the Information Technology (IT) function. This will help ensure that changes made by a Team Leader will filter up to the Business Continuity Manager. Plan and Program Maintenance is often the most neglected part of the Business Continuity process and a Change Management procedure will help to overcome this neglect. The inclusion of plan maintenance metrics and a heat map that shows who has updated their plans on a regular basis, and who has not should get management's attention when reported as part of the Management Review.

This is when Business Continuity Management software can add value. Some programs will email those who have pending due dates or at least indicate the date of the last update. Team member names and their associated information are often found in multiple locations throughout the plans. These software programs allow the planner to make a single change in the database, and the software will make the adjustments throughout the plans.

As we have mentioned throughout the text, updates to the plans and to the process (i.e., the Business Continuity Management System) should be completed:

- At planned intervals
- As significant changes occur
- Because of the findings from exercise and testing
- As required by contractual and regulatory changes
- As required by internal or external stakeholders
- Because of Root Cause Analysis nonconformance Corrective Actions
- Because of internal or external audit or self-assessment
- Because of post-incident review or lessons learned
- Because of updated Business Impact Analysis (BIA)
- Because of updated Risk Assessment

"Planned intervals," although not defined in the standards, in effect means at least annually because the management review must be submitted annually. Significant changes can include a change in the strategic direction of the organization as mentioned previously, a change in organizational structure, changes in risk or risk appetite, and similar conditions. Contractual demands by customers or other outside interested parties may also dictate the frequency of plan and program updates. The standards also require an evaluation or reevaluation of its effectiveness after significant changes such as those listed above. A documented post-incident review is also required whenever an incident necessitates the activation of the plan.

10.2.1 CHANGE MANAGEMENT

However, what if a Team Leader makes major changes to his or her plan? What happens if the Business Continuity Manager makes a significant change to the program? A written Change Management or Change Control Process must be documented that ensures changes to the Business Continuity Management System are introduced in a controlled and coordinated manner.

Change Management has many definitions but it is generally accepted to mean a process or an approach to transition individuals, teams, or the entire organization to a future state in a manner that controls the impact of the change and that reduces barriers to its implementation. It focuses on the introduction of new initiatives, programs, and changes in policy or strategic direction. This process is often referred to as Organizational Change Management and is contrasted with managing process changes to system hardware and software, infrastructure, procedures, and documentation. Many of the elements of both types of Change Management are similar.

The Information Technology Infrastructure Library, which is a set of practices for IT Service Management, defines the goal of Change Management as a process to ensure that standardized methods and procedures are used for efficient and prompt handling of all changes, to minimize the impact of change-related incidents upon service quality, and consequently improve the day-to-day operations of the organization. ISO/IEC 20000 (previously BS15000), the International Service Management Standard for IT Service Management, describes the objective of Change Management as a process "to ensure all changes are assessed, approved, implemented and reviewed in a controlled manner."

The standards seem to emphasize the process control aspects of Change Management over Organizational Change Management, but the full force of the Organizational Change Management process may be necessary when the Business Continuity Management System is first implemented, especially if no program existed to begin with. Even in the case in which a mature Business Continuity capability exists, the added rigor, documentation, and audit requirements necessary for third-party certification against the standards may represent such a culture shift that Change Management processes are necessary to ensure success.

A formal, structured program is necessary because people generally resist change, even when they understand and acknowledge that the future state will be better or to their advantage. Workers become comfortable in "how the way things are done," especially if they are successful with the present state. Many fear change because it is not clear to them how they will fit into the new way, or if they will have the new skills necessary for a different or higher expectation. This, and the fear of uncertainty by those with a low risk tolerance, combine to set the stage for mediocre support, if not outright rebellion. The Change Management process is designed to overcome these roadblocks and to ensure the path to a future state is achieved.

Imagine the Business Continuity Manager who announces to the organization that on Monday, everyone will need to implement a program in which they will participate in a BIA and a Risk Analysis, document all kinds of plans and processes, take a lot of training, participate in exercises twice each year, and then be subject to internal audit, all in addition to their regular duties. The manager's chances of success in meeting his or her goals for the Business Continuity Management System without using some if not most of the elements of a Change Management program are dismal at best.

Distinct phases in Change Management can be described as follows:

- Preparing for change
- Managing change
- Evaluation of change

These phases can be broken into elements of an Organizational Change Management Program that can include:

- Top Management involvement
- A clear definition of the future state
- Involvement of all Stakeholders
- Mitigate roadblocks
- Implement change
- Maintain momentum
- Audit

Top Management sponsorship and involvement is necessary for initiatives that have an organization-wide impact. Before the initiative or change is rolled out to the employee population, management must ensure that resources that will be devoted are justified and provided throughout the course of the process. Top Management must demonstrate to all of the stakeholders that they are supportive of the change and use their leadership to push engagement to middle management and to the individual worker. This is often not difficult because Top Management will likely have initiated the changes in policy or strategy. Senior staff who have instilled a culture and a capacity to change will find that new ideas and initiatives are more readily accepted. The organization's present change culture must be understood to leverage its support or to develop strategies to overcome resistance. Once the Business Continuity Management System is accepted and functional, Top Management must still support the ongoing Change Management program with their participation, either directly or through the steering committee and/or by devoting the necessary resources for it to function properly.

The future state, that is, what you want to change, and what it is changing to, must be clearly understood by those who are tasked with making the change. Often, a major reason that change is not completely successful is because the end vision was not clearly conceived or described. As is said, you can't get there if you don't know where you are going. It must be stated in terms the responsible parties at all levels can understand. Make a compelling case for the reason to change and show how it will benefit each of those affected by the change. This may require different messages to different groups, both internal and external to the organization. Involve as many of the Stakeholders as practical early in the development of the future state so that misunderstandings can be corrected early and to ensure that correct changes are made. The stakeholders can provide input into the future state that may or not add value. One of the reasons people resist change is that they were not included or did not have the ability to influence the direction of the change. Ensure the people affected understand what processes will be involved to achieve the future state.

A clear vision and statement of the future state will eliminate some of the roadblocks to success. Assess the impact on the individuals affected by the change and on the organization's policies, structure, culture, and customers. How the present processes will be affected and what else will need to change along with them must be identified. Search for unidentified consequences the change may produce and take action to eliminate or to mitigate the consequences. Assess the risk to the achievement of the future state.

Identify and train "Change Agents," who can act as mentors or ambassadors to help those tasked with implementing the change or with transitioning to the future state. Anticipate what modes of communication will be necessary before implementation and organize the delivery of messages and training. This could be part of a formal implementation plan. The plan may include a training needs assessment. Understand that change and people's reaction to change are not linear processes.

Sustain momentum. Leadership must articulate its belief in an improved state and demonstrate its passion for change as the degree of change increases. Others may not recognize the excitement about the vision that the change sponsor has, so the message must often be reinforced. Ensure the implementation plan accounts for any slack in the time line. Delays in implementation or false starts can kill any chance of success. This is especially true of Business Continuity programs. Programmatic inaction will, in computer terms, "time out" the effort causing it to stall, and lose momentum and interest. Managers today have many issues to deal with on a daily basis and, if the Business Continuity effort is not always front and center, it will be pushed to the bottom of the pile of things to do. Maintain the urgency of the project.

Finally, once the change is implemented, ensure that it achieves its intended goals. Worker feedback, performance metrics, and other data can lead to corrective action for continuous improvement. Reinforce the success to help build a Change Management culture. The same can be said for reinforcing the success of Business Continuity exercises and tests.

The scope and rigor of the Change Control structure for process updates can be of a scale that matches the complexity of the organization and of the Business Continuity Management System. This can be as simple as a database or spreadsheet to track the changes (with some degree of review and approval) to, as mentioned above, something that can mirror the system used by the organization's IT department. The Information Technology Change Control System is typically designed to regulate the implementation of all changes made to a device, system, infrastructure, or application. It is in part designed to ensure that the level of system availability, that is, the stability of its data systems is not compromised by the introduction of a change.

Changes are classified as follows:

- Standard Change. A Standard Change is one that is scheduled and receives the full application of the change process including approval for implementation from the Change Advisory Board.
- Emergency Change. An Emergency Change is one that carries a level of urgency that necessitates its implementation prior to approval from the Change Advisory Board. It will generally require higher levels of approval such as the Top Manager from the IT function. Incident response for IT emergencies is typically not considered to fall under the change control umbrella because it should involve the in-kind replacement of existing equipment or applications. However, problems can still be encountered with unexpected incompatibilities or prior configuration changes that were made and not duplicated with the new installation; hence, this is one of the reasons for a

change control process. Incompatibilities will be compounded if making changes in platforms or application versions during an incident.

A rigorous process (IT focus) can include the following steps:

- Formal request for change
- Documented justification for change, usually part of the request
- Risk Assessment
- Peer review
- Coordination for implementation
- Approval by change manager and Change Advisory Board
- Changes communicated to user community
- Changes monitored and issue closed

Information Technology Change Control software exists to assist with the implementation and documentation of these steps, either off the shelf applications, existing applications modified to accommodate the needs of change control, or developed internally.

The formal request for change is submitted on a Change Request Form that forces the requester to populate certain fields such as the type of request (standard or emergency). It is used to initiate the request and to tract its progress throughout the process. The person who requests the change is identified and must provide all requirements and objectives of the change, reason, and justification for the change, including all technical requirements for implementation. The requester should provide an initial assessment of the level of risk. The cost of equipment, time, and other related expenses (such as training costs) is calculated. Once this is completed, it may be handed off to a Change Facilitator who becomes the owner of the change throughout implementation. The Facilitator will:

- Ensure the completeness of the Change Request Form and work with the requester to clarify any missing information
- Coordinate risk analysis
- Coordinate peer review
- Resolve questions or issues relative to the proposed change
- Enter information into the Change Management software or database
- Review necessary changes to documentation
- Coordinate approvals
- Coordinate testing and implementation
- Communicate changes to appropriate users
- Follow up and report effectiveness

The Change Facilitator performs a risk assessment prior to submission for Peer Review. The Risk Assessment should consider the following:

- The probability of impact and the degree of impact to users
- The probability of impact and the degree of impact of the change on system incompatibilities
- The probability of the success or failure of the change
- Impact on Recovery Time Objectives
- Impact of failure

Risk levels can be defined as follows:

- High: Any outage of a mission critical system or application or that causes the inability of multiple users to perform their normal business functions
- Medium: Any outage of a nonmission-critical system or application
- Low: Causes a service interruption with no impact on the user's ability to perform their normal business functions
- No impact

Consider how changes to the IT environment, dependencies, and contractual and regulatory requirements will impact or change the Business Continuity Management Plans or Management System. Once the risk and impact are determined, they are balanced with the need for the change prior to the submittal of the change for approval. Anticipated impacts should be communicated to the end users. If accepted, the Change Request is offered for Peer Review.

The Peer Review can consist of a committee or a single person with technical knowledge of the environment that the change will affect. The review will evaluate if the steps planned to implement the change and the associated risks are correct. This group or person is not responsible for the review of the nontechnical elements of the process. Once the review is completed and the change accepted, the Request for Change form will be signed off by the group or the peer reviewer.

The Change Facilitator will then check to see if the implementation of the proposed change does not conflict with critical events and that all other steps in the preapproval process are completed. The change is then submitted to a manager responsible for Change Management for the first level of approval. If rejected, the requester is notified and an explanation provided. If approved, the request is sent to a Change Advisory Board.

A Change Advisory Board is a group of individuals that represent various IT and user functions. One member should include the Information Security Manager if such a position exists within the organization. In a Business Continuity application, the Steering Committee may substitute for the Change Advisory Board, but not for routine changes such as plan updates. The Board is responsible for the final review, approval, or rejection of a standard request for change. The Board should meet at scheduled intervals dependent on the number of changes they need to review. The person who requested the change, in addition to the Change Facilitator, should attend the Board meetings when they have an action pending so that they can present the change to the Board and respond to any questions the Board may have. The Board members will review each Request for Change and decide if:

- it meets all requirements of the Change Management Program
- the risk is offset by the need for the change

They will notify the requestor of its acceptance or rejection. One important duty of the Board is to check if the preparation of the change included an examination of its impact on Business Continuity. Although the Board will have little choice but to approve any changes required by law, they should still check to see if the change will have any unintended consequences. If accepted, the change is submitted by the Change Facilitator to the proper entity for implementation. Although emergency changes are not approved by the Change Advisory Board, the Board should still be notified when an emergency change is implemented.

Once the change is implemented, communicated, tracked, and documentation updated (which may include an update to Business Continuity Plans), the Change Facilitator must monitor the change to ensure it is effective and has not caused any unintended consequences. If no issues are identified, the

Facilitator will close the issue. If not, Corrective Actions are taken or, in an extreme situation, the changed state will be "rolled back" to the original state. The communication of changes should include the Business Continuity Manager or a business continuity staff member.

Remember that the standard's documentation requirements warn against the use of outdated information. Part of your change control program should refer back to these mandates. Remember also, if major changes are made to plans or to the management system, they may need to be re-tested or exercised.

10.3 PERFORMANCE EVALUATION AND METRICS

Effective managers know that one of their most important tasks is to measure the performance not only of the people who work within their areas of responsibility but of their functions as a whole. They may be on the right path to success but they need to know how far they are along the path, how fast they are heading toward their goals, and if there is a better path to take if one is encountered. They may also need information to decide if the need to blaze a new trail is necessary. Managers also need to know if they have lost their way on the path and are heading in the wrong direction. One of the problems encountered by Business Continuity managers is they don't really know how effective their programs are until their procedures are used in an actual disaster. Exercising and testing provide real clues, but the final test of the system is its successful response to an incident. The use of performance measurements like exercising and testing will help bring the manager closer to a confidence level that the Business Continuity Management System is functioning as it should.

The Business Continuity Management System cannot be in a state of continuous improvement unless it knows where it is and where it still needs to go. It needs to be monitored and measured, and the results reported on a regular basis to those who can take action on the results. This is accomplished through the development of performance metrics. A performance metric is a measure of the organization's activities. Better known in the Business Continuity profession as Key Performance Indicators, they allow the organization to understand how its various parts are meeting their goals, to improve accountability, and to provide for better management by focusing effort where improvement is necessary. They show in near real time any need to readjust the direction of effort before the organization's goals are impacted. Metrics provide a basis for better decision making.

The standards require the development and use of performance metrics, so the Business Continuity manager must use them to both manage the Business Continuity function and satisfy the requirements of the standards in a manner that is auditable. Fortunately, what the manager would do to satisfy the requirements parallel what would be done in their general course of managing the function. The Business Continuity manager must be aware that this must be captured by some sort of documentation.

The standard refers to "deficient performance," but the results and actions from the results of metrics do not always spring from a deficiency. Personnel actions that result from poor performance can sometimes be difficult to document due to their sensitive Human Resources nature.

Metrics should meet the following criteria:

- Appropriate to the organization
- Actionable
- Monitor compliance
- Enable trending

- Simple, uncomplicated
- Show ongoing performance

Metrics must be appropriate to the organization, that is, the Business Continuity function. Metrics are developed from a need to understand the performance of Critical Success Factors or to develop leading indicators of success or failure, not because a pile of data is lying around. A Critical Success Factor is that which is necessary for an organization or function to achieve its goals or mission. Key Performance Indicators are mapped to Critical Success Factors. Several methods are used to identify and develop metrics. Performance models (or "Frameworks") can help the manager identify the best metrics to use. One popular model uses the following:

- Balanced Scorecard
- Strategy Maps
- Stakeholder Model
- Program Logic
- Performance Model
- Cascading Functions

10.3.1 BALANCED SCORECARD

The Balanced Scorecard is a performance measurement framework that is used by most organizations and adds strategic, nonfinancial performance measures to traditional financial metrics giving managers a more "balanced" view of organizational performance. The balanced scorecard collects and analyzes information to develop metrics in relationship to four different views of the organization:

- Learning and Growth
- Business Process
- Customer
- Finance

Learning and Growth refers to both personal and organization continuous improvement as a basis for organizational success. It views the human assets as a major resource to the organization. Its metrics are focused on the results of training, that is, the transfer of knowledge or learning through classes, seminars, or mentors. It also develops metrics that are strategic or forward thinking in nature to foster growth.

Metrics based on internal business processes measure the health of the organization and indicate how well it is meeting its objectives. These metrics measure continuous improvement of quantity and quality of the organization's products or services.

Attributes that customers value in the organization are measured and often combined with leading indicators to understand if they are delivering the best customer service that meets the objectives of the organization. These metrics are leading indicators themselves because poor customer satisfaction may indicate an organization in decline or one that will soon be in decline. Although mostly thought of in terms of external customers, this can also apply to internal customers.

Financial metrics are used in this application to show the financial health and value of the organization to owners, investors, and financial institutions. Although traditionally the most emphasized metric used in organizations when used, by itself it can present an unbalanced depiction of the organization.

Business Continuity, because of its ties to active management support, may have a higher expectation for strategic metric reporting than its actual position within the organization may indicate. Because much of its focus is on meeting the operational parameters defined in the strategic initiatives of the organization, it may find it difficult to develop metrics that fit the Balanced Scorecard. Business Continuity metrics should be used, however, in a strategic fashion. The standards require performance metrics, but metrics that apply to strategic initiatives involving Business Continuity should be developed, trended, and reported.

10.3.2 STRATEGY MAPS

Strategy Maps take the four views of the organization used in the Balanced Scorecard and tell a story of cause and effect for each. Increased learning rolls up to increased efficiency in Business Processes that leads to a lower cycle time that rolls up to Customer, and so on. It demonstrates how the goals of the organization are implemented through the four views.

10.3.3 STAKEHOLDER MODEL

How the organization meets the requirements and expectations of Stakeholders is measured by this model. Stakeholders include internal and external interested parties (employees, customers, suppliers, regulators, and investors). Each group of Stakeholders will have a different set of metrics that are relevant to them and not necessarily to the others. The performance metrics related to each are identified and evaluated. This model can show how some interests may either complement or be in conflict with others. Metrics are not theoretical; they must be practical and applicable to Stakeholder needs. The manager must bear in mind the needs of the audience to whom the metrics are presented. Top Management may be more interested in leading indicators, strategic, and financial measures, whereas operations groups may be more concerned with information on the progress of their team's planning efforts.

10.3.4 PROGRAM LOGIC

The Program Logic model describes measurements for the inputs, outputs, activities, and outcomes of the organization, functions, or programs. The inputs to the program are listed along with a list of the activities of the program. Its outputs are then identified and listed, and the conditions that result from the outputs are described. This forms the starting point for the design of the Program Logic metrics.

10.3.5 PERFORMANCE MODEL

The Performance Model consists of three components that measure and manage performance:

- Effectiveness
- Efficiency
- Improvement

How effectively the purpose of the organization is realized is basic to the measurement of progress toward its goals. Organizations that are not effective in its critical success factors usually are not around for very long. These metrics should question how well the purpose of the organization is met.

Related to Effectiveness is Efficiency in the organization's operations. Efficient operations will add to its bottom line allowing the organization to be competitive. To paraphrase, efficiency cannot be managed if it can't be measured. These metrics will indicate how efficiently the organization is meeting its purpose.

Continuous Improvement streamlines processes, reducing costs and increasing production time, and allows the organization to invest in new ideas to sustain its mission into the future. These forward-looking metrics are designed to show how well the organization is positioned for the future. Examples include milestones for strategic initiatives or the status of competitors.

10.3.6 CASCADING FUNCTIONS

This model works by defining the Critical Success Factors of tiered functions and how they help the next higher level to meet its goals. At the department level, Accounts Receivable, Accounts Payable, Payroll, and Cash Management support the next higher function of Finance. Finance supports the mission of the organization. Staffing, Benefits, Labor Relations would roll up to Human Resources, and so on.

Each function identifies the goals and Critical Success Factors of the next higher level and designs metrics that show how the lower function contributes to the Critical Success Factors. In other words, when examining the goals of the function, it must decide whether it has a role in achieving the higher goals. This process can work in either direction, either flowing down from the top or aligning effort from the bottom up.

10.3.7 DESIGNING METRICS

The models help to define the Critical Success Factors and what metrics we must use to measure them. Deciding what to measure is usually a three-step process. First, based on the models, list the performance topics. Then identify the Critical Success Factors. Finally, define specific performance measures or indicators that will show the progress of the factors. Every Critical Success Factor must be measured, but not everyone needs to see each one every time. Metrics are tracked and trended. All metrics must be actionable, and only a few need to be elevated for a higher level of attention. Action taken should be documented and potentially entered into the Corrective Action System. Ask management what they want to see measured. They may wish to see a set of metrics on a regular basis, and then include those that are trending in a direction that needs review.

Metric design can be a good project for the Steering Committee, either as a whole group or by assigning a person to lead a subcommittee to design the metrics. The subgroup will provide regular reports on their progress (a metric on the metrics?) and develop a due date for completion.

Metrics should be graphical and uncomplicated, showing trends over time in a clear manner that communicates the measurement. They show ongoing performance that is appropriate to the needs of the organization in a quantitative or qualitative manner. Monitor the results and actions of metrics. See if the metrics are measuring the proper things and are balanced in what the metric is trying to achieve.

Don't rely on metrics supplied by vendors; they may contain a spin in their favor. If their metrics are important, develop your own using raw data if possible.

A Metrics dashboard can be included on the organization's business continuity intranet or internet page to demonstrate progress toward goals that the manager wishes to highlight or to show to potential clients or interested third parties that a healthy Business Continuity Management System exists in full force. If this course of action is followed, it is vital that the information remains up to date.

Examples of metrics the organization may use include (see Figures 10.1–10.3):

- Number of scheduled exercises completed on time or the progress of the testing schedule (a heat map may work the best)
- Percentage of exercise and test goals met or number of goals met versus those not met
- Average cost per person for training/orientation, non-Business Continuity staff
- Average cost per person for training/orientation/continuing education for Business Continuity staff
- Progress of Team Plan completion (heat map)
- Satisfaction with a Business Continuity Help Desk
- Number of Business Continuity Help Desk issues resolved
- Unscheduled unavailability of IT systems by type of failure
- Uptime of IT systems
- Progress of critical supplier audits
- Number of critical suppliers with and without business continuity programs/certification
- Issues with critical suppliers, precursors to problems
- Number and type of emergency response incidents
- Number and type of incidents involving reputation issues
- Number of media contacts
- Number and type of incidents involving regulatory noncompliance
- Progress of awareness and training against goals
- Understanding of awareness and training
- Progress or program development
- Number of public warnings
- Time from incident to warning
- Time from incident to notification of regulatory agencies
- On-time data backup
- Downtime of call centers
- Progress of mitigation projects
- Costs and usage of funds for mitigation
- Progress of audit nonconformity correction
- Overdue Corrective Actions
- Budget versus expenditures
- Effectiveness of service level agreements
- Time to detect disruptions
- Cost per terabyte of data replication
- Number of audits and audits completed
- Extent to which business continuity policy, timelines, and objectives are met
- Performance of strategies to protect prioritized activities
- Deficient performance
- Compliance with standards

10.4 EVALUATIONS AND INTERNAL AUDIT

The standards also require the ongoing evaluation of business continuity procedures and capabilities within the framework of plan and program maintenance and separately through periodic reviews, post-incident analysis, performance evaluations, and internal and external audits. The evaluations must include legal and regulatory requirements, business continuity best practices, and the policy and objectives of the Business Continuity Management System. Internal audit is required; external (third party) audit is optional.

Periodic reviews, as we described above, are conducted by Team Leaders who are mindful of internal and external events and changing conditions that could affect their strategies, procedures, and resources necessary to implement the strategies. The Business Continuity Manager, Top Management, and the Steering Committee similarly monitor events and conditions that can impact the program and its objectives. Reviews and evaluations are always documented.

A documented post-incident analysis is required any time the plan is activated (incident response). According to the ISO 22313 guidance document, the analysis may include:

- A characterization of the incident and its root cause
- An evaluation of management's response (the guidance says nothing about an evaluation of other responders)
- How well Recovery Time Objectives (RTOs) were met (assuming the incident involved RTOs). This is often described as a Key Performance Indicator but because, hopefully, it is a rare occurrence, it has little value in trending and reporting except for the annual Management Review
- An assessment of how effective the system prepared employees for the incident
- How effectively did the BIA predict the impact of the incident
- Critique from those who participated in the incident response

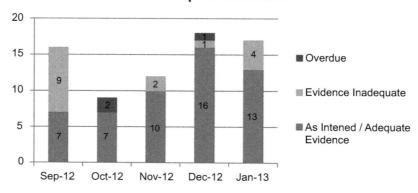

FIGURE 10.1

Example of simple corrective action metric.

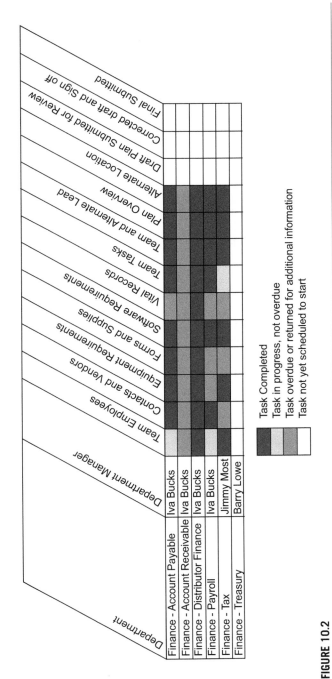

FIGURE 10.2

Example of planning progress heat map metric.

Issue	Risk	CA #	Corrective Action	Responsible	Manager	Due Date	Status	Actions
Team information not updated within specified time.	Med	001-1	The Accounting department will conduct a work load study to determine if additional staffing is justified.	Imbruglio	Buettner	8/1/14	Completed but documentation not provided	8/2/14 requested documentation from manager.
Team information not updated within specified time.	Med	001-2	The Team Leader will attend a time management class.	Weppener	Buettner	8/1/14	Overdue	8/2/14 team leader ill and missed scheduled class. Class rescheduled for 9/25/14.
Team information not updated within specified time.	Med	001-3	The Organization's Business Continuity Manager will devise a program to remind all Team Leaders to update their Team Plans on a regular basis.	Van Leuven	Ugale	8/1/14	Overdue	8/2/14 manager expects completion 8/15/14.

FIGURE 10.3

Example of overdue corrective action metric.

The Performance Evaluation refers to a review of the performance of individuals tasked with business continuity roles and responsibilities. This task should be part of the organization's normal Human Resources Performance Review process. Although it is not clear from the standards if this applies to responsible individuals within the entire organization, it is much simpler to apply to the Business Continuity staff. This requirement comes from the Business Continuity Institute Good Practice Guidelines that seem to suggest that it only applies to the Business Continuity staff. However, it can be written into the job description of responsible individuals that they are responsible for attending all exercises, training, or other pertinent Key Performance Indicators. A portion of their performance review can be based on these requirements. The performance of suppliers is often suggested as a point of evaluation as defined by the obligations created in the purchase contract.

10.4.1 INTERNAL AUDIT

As we mentioned above, exercising and testing do not provide an audit of plans and process. An audit does not have training or testing components. The audit is an impartial examination of both the plan and the management system to assess whether they meet the requirements of the standards and that the management system will function as needed at the time of the disaster. It is an independent and documented process that obtains objective evidence to determine the extent to which criteria of the standards and the Business Continuity Management System are fulfilled. It looks to see that the system is effectively maintained.

The standards require that the organization conduct internal audits at planned intervals. Planned intervals should mean at least annually, to align with the preparation of the Management Review. The entire Business Continuity Management System should be covered by the audit, but a number of limited-scope audits can be used on a graduated schedule. ISO 19011 Guidelines for Auditing Management Systems can be used to satisfy this requirement. The standards also require that the organization establish and maintain an audit program that includes:

- Responsibilities
- Competencies
- Objectivity and impartiality
- Frequency and schedule
- Audit methods
- Planning requirements
- Audit criteria
- Audit scope
- Reporting and document retention

The audit program should be based on the results of previous audits and on the results of risk assessments. Any nonconformities, including their causes, should be corrected "without undue delay." The effectiveness of the Corrective Actions are verified and reported.

The program should assign responsibility for its management that may include the Business Continuity Manager, but, ideally, ownership should reside outside of the Business Continuity function. If the organization has an established internal audit function, the manager or lead auditor would define the parameters of the program, delegate responsibilities to an audit team if the size of the organization justifies the use of a team, and manage the audit components listed in ISO 19011. This also includes the identification of risk to the program, audit objectives, scope, procedures, and methods. They would also establish the resources needed by the auditors. The frequency of the audits and the development of an audit schedule are established by the auditor who considers the requirements of the standard and any obligations imposed by contracts or regulations.

Auditors should understand the ISO 19011 guidelines and possess demonstrated competence in audit principles and audit methods. When auditing to the standards, they should have experience with management systems and the documents referenced by the standards. They must understand the context of the organization they are auditing including its legal and regulatory environment. An understanding of business continuity and incident management principles is helpful. As with any professional, certification and continual improvement through professional development is expected. Competence of the auditor is one of the basic principles of auditing.

One of the primary reasons the Business Continuity Manager is not directly part of the audit process is to ensure objectivity and impartiality. The auditor must be free of bias and any conflict of interest. Internal auditors should not report to the manager or be in the management chain of the functions audited. This may be difficult to accomplish in a small organization. Their conclusions must be based solely on the audit evidence.

An evidence-based audit approach is a method that produces repeatable and verifiable results. Auditors examine documents, interview subject matter experts within the organization's management system, and in some cases observe operations and conditions. The number of documents they need to examine may be overwhelming, but a statistical valid sample of material is acceptable for review. However, certain key documents such as the context of the organization, BIA, and the Risk Analysis should be examined in detail.

The scope of each audit is established that meets the audit objectives. This is developed in part by an examination of the audit criteria. The criteria are what the evidence is compared against. This can include policies, team plans, BIA, and Risk Assessment Reports.

The records related to the audit program and its implementation are maintained in a manner consistent with the standards. The audit report will highlight conformity or nonconformity with the audit criteria and include supporting documentation. Notable good practices may be identified in the report. The auditor should meet with the Business Continuity Manager prior to the publication of the report to ensure that the evidence is accurate and that any nonconformities are understood. Disagreements with the findings should be mentioned in the final report.

10.5 MANAGEMENT REVIEW

Top Management is required to review the Business Continuity Management System to ensure that it is functioning as intended. This review must take place at "planned intervals." The standards do not define what this means, but auditors generally take this to mean annually. Once the review is completed, the expectation is that Top Management will take any necessary action to correct deficiencies and nonconformities.

The ISO 22301 lists a number of elements that must be included in the review, most of which are those normally found in a functional report to management. However, in practice, some readers can interrupt the standard to require input into the report (and primary preparation by) the Business

Continuity Manager and some input by Top Management, perhaps through the management sponsor. Some of the pertinent issues to include in the report are (not all are listed here):

- Action items from previous management reviews (unless large capital projects that involve mitigation initiatives, most action items should be resolved and reported in less than a year's time)
- Internal or external changes that will affect the Business Continuity Management System. This is a requirement that Top Management may need to communicate to the Business Continuity Staff as they are potentially more likely to be aware of external business conditions and strategic plans that could affect the management system. Another example of an external change would be adoption of a new regulatory requirement
- Performance metrics and the results of their trending (a properly managed system will report the results of trending on a more regular basis)
- Audit results both internal to the Business Continuity Management System and to critical suppliers
- Required changes to the Business Continuity Management System, in particular its policies and objectives, and recommended opportunities for improvement. A discussion on the adequacy of the policy if necessary
- Identify any risks or impacts not adequately identified or addressed in the BIA and Risk Assessment or subsequent assessments. This is another issue that, if identified, should not wait for an annual review
- Emerging good practices, techniques, and products that could be used to improve the Business Continuity Management System. Depending on how this requirement is prefaced in the presentation and report, this requirement should be approached with caution. Top Management can ask if and why the Business Continuity Staff is not using emerging good practice (that may or may not be proven effective or advantageous to the mission of the Business Continuity Program). If a product is presented to Top Management, it should be thoroughly vetted against the many other products as the one that the function will need to use. A complete justification for its use should be prepared ahead of time for presentation if requested. Some managers may view this as an effort to justify a purchase through the "back door"

Any actions or changes to the Business Continuity Management Program that result from the Management Review must be documented and processes and procedures revised as appropriate. The results of the management review must also be communicated to relevant parties including those outside the organization if necessary.

Finally, remember that this is a report and presentation to the top executives of the organization. It must be polished, accurate, relevant, and, to the greatest extent possible, brief but complete. Before presentation, it should be reviewed by the Top Management sponsor and potentially by the Steering Committee.

10.6 NONCONFORMITY AND CORRECTIVE ACTION

Nonconformity is any of the standard's requirements that were not met as determined primarily through internal or external audit but can include those identified through exercises and testing. The organization must strive to identify nonconformities and to take Corrective Actions in a timely manner. ISO requires the organization to "deal with the consequences" but it does not define what this means except that the Business Continuity Management System must be changed if root causes of the nonconformity justify such action.

A Root Cause Analysis can pinpoint why the nonconformity occurred, an Extent of Condition Review can determine if similar nonconformities exist, and a Corrective Action Plan (or simply Corrective Actions) that use a graded approach to remedy the issue can help to ensure that nonconformities do not recur.

10.6.1 ROOT CAUSE ANALYSIS

ISO 22301 requires that the organization only determine the causes of a nonconformity identified by exercises, audits, or other drivers of Corrective Actions. It does not require the organization to identify the *Root Cause* of the issue. The identification of the Direct Cause or the Apparent Cause may be sufficient to eliminate or correct the issue and these processes require much less rigor than a Root Cause Analysis. The guidance documents (ISO 22313 and ISO 22398.2 and the Homeland Security Exercise and Evaluation Program) do, however, suggest the performance of a Root Cause Analysis. If the organization wishes to gain third party ISO 22301 certification, the auditor will require a Root Cause Analysis to identify the underlying issues that caused any deficiency noted on the preaudit inspection before the final audit is completed.

Root Cause Analysis is the utilization of any number of techniques (or combination of techniques) designed to get to the underlying condition, action, or lack of action that caused the incident or nonconformity. It looks for the lowest level of causation, not contributing factors in which corrective action is often focused. When the root cause is missed, Corrective Actions may not be as effective in preventing a recurring problem. The virus is the cause of the illness (some would argue that the virus' ability to attach to the human cells is the root cause), not that the person's immune system was compromised, nor that the person did not lead a healthy lifestyle. The Root Cause can be defined as an event or condition that, if corrected, would prevent recurrence of the event of concern and of similar events. The absence of best practices or the failure to apply knowledge that would have prevented the problem (or significantly reduce the likelihood or consequence of the problem) can also define a root cause. Other higher-level causal factors can be defined as:

- Direct Cause: The immediate events or conditions that caused the accident, event, or condition
- Apparent Cause: The most probable/reasonable cause(s) of an incident that management has the power to control and fix through effective Corrective Actions
- Contributing Cause: An event or condition that, collectively with other contributing causes, increased the likelihood of the accident, event, or condition, but did not alone cause the accident, event, or condition
- Causal Factor: Mistakes or failures that, if corrected, could have prevented the incident from occurring or would significantly mitigated its consequences
- Generic Causes: Systemic problem that allows a Root Cause to exist

Root Cause Analysis is a collection of different methodologies that can be classified into five categories:

- Safety (Occupational Safety and Health)
- Production (Quality Control)
- Process (Business Processes)
- Failure (Maintenance and Engineering)
- Systems (Systems Analysis)

Within these classifications, the types of Root Cause Analysis methodologies include:

- Barrier Analysis
- Bayesian Inference
- Causal Factor Tree Analysis
- Change Analysis
- Current Reality Tree
- FMEA
- Fault Tree Analysis
- Five Whys
- HPI
- Ishikawa Diagram (Cause and Effect of Fishbone Diagram)
- Kepner–Tregoe
- Multi-Decision Criteria Analysis (MDCA)
- Pareto Analysis
- RPR Problem Diagnosis
- Cause Mapping
- Apollo Root Cause Analysis
- Why-Because Analysis

FMEA, Five Whys, Fault Tree Analysis, HPI, Ishikawa Diagram, and RPR Problem Diagnosis are the most common methods that can be used for Business Continuity Planning Root Cause Analysis. MDCA is not common but gaining in popularity due to its effectiveness and acceptance in the courts in the event something must be litigated. FMEA, Fault Tree Analysis, and RPR Problem Diagnosis are best for the analysis of system, process, or equipment failures, although Fault Tree Analysis is useful for both. Barrier Analysis and Change Analysis are often used in injury investigations but are also useful for process-type issues. Depending on the situation or incident, one or more of these methods can be used together because each has its strengths and weaknesses. A nonconformance may have elements of a technical system failure (FMEA would be used) and elements of human error (HPI would then be combined with FMEA). Some literature says only one root cause exists; others say more than one can exist. In the case in which multiple root causes are possible, likely one or more are actually direct or apparent causes.

The Business Continuity Manager and/or the Business Continuity staff should become proficient in one or more of these root cause methods (remember that Bayesian Inference or Bayesian Analysis is an effective risk assessment methodology). The manager can solicit the assistance of an inhouse safety professional to assist with the analysis.

The goal of the Root Cause Analysis is to develop Corrective Actions directed at the proper level of causation so that the issue is solved in a manner that ensures it does not happen repeatedly. The analysis is systematic and documented using, in most cases, an investigative process with a team composed of a Root Cause Analysis, Subject Matter Expert, and others as we will mention below.

Many root cause methodologies and investigations share these common requirements and steps:

1. Obtain Top Management support and communicate this support to interested parties so that they understand that their participation in the analysis is mandatory and that managers make documents and employees available when needed.

2. If a team is used, elect a Team Leader. Each person should be tasked with taking notes of interviews, but it is generally the responsibility of the Root Cause Analysis team member to take notes because they are usually the ones tasked with writing the final report.

3. Define the problem or describe the issue factually and completely according to what is known. Describe any nonconformities and the source of the nonconformity (i.e., what should have been accomplished that was not).

4. Decide what Root Cause Analysis method(s) are best suited to the incident or nonconformity.

5. Identify those who have information about the incident and those who should be interviewed. Persons closest to the incident or those who may possess some degree of culpability should be interviewed last. This will allow the team to develop as much information as possible to test validity of the information given by these witnesses. Develop an interview schedule and invite interviewees, informing them of the purpose of the interview. Be sure to allow sufficient time for the interview that is conducted in a private, neutral location (i.e., not in the person's office). Before any witnesses are interviewed, the investigative team should meet to discuss and list what questions they should ask of each interviewee.

6. Gather and review data, relevant documents and other related evidence. Make this information available to team members and review these documents prior to any interviews.

7. During the interview, inform the person of the intent of the analysis and explain that the purpose of the interview is fact-finding and not to assign blame. Being interviewed by a team of investigators can be quite intimidating. Begin by asking what information the person has about the incident and let them speak uninterrupted until finished. The team will then, one by one, ask their prescripted questions or followup questions. Questions should be simple, that is, not compound questions and in most cases designed to produce a narrative or qualitative answer. In the end, thank them for their participation.

8. Some Root Cause Analysis methods list the sequence of events and conditions present during the events on a white board or software program that dissects the incident or nonconformance along a linear timeline; others branch the events according to logical "and" "or" gates (Fault Tree Analysis). This allows the analysis to visualize relationships and to pinpoint the root cause. The timeline includes the events leading up to the incident, the incident itself, and the events after the incident. The conditions associated with the events are listed underneath the time line. Conditions can include night/day, sunshine/rain, and so on. Some methods will then list what should have occurred when it differed from what was actually done (Change Analysis).

9. Identify the causes associated with each step in the sequence toward the defined problem or event.

10. Complete a detailed Root Cause Analysis report. The report can list recommended Corrective Actions under each root or apparent cause. The report should contain at least the following information:

  a. Title page with signature approvals
  b. Table of Contents
  c. Executive Summary that describes the incident or nonconformity, the types of analysis used, the root or apparent causes, and the recommended Corrective Actions
  d. Background/description of the issue or nonconformity and why the issue is nonconforming
  e. Types of Analysis used
  f. Findings of the investigative team

g. Root Causes with associated recommended Corrective Actions
h. Appendices that include the list of personnel interviewed, documents reviewed, and any supporting information that should be achieved with the report

Remember to include all document control requirements imposed by the standards.

10.6.2 EXTENT OF CONDITION

An Extent of Condition review is a process to discover if the potential (or the actual existence) for an identified issue or nonconformance to exist in other activities, processes, or programs within the Business Continuity Management System. Generally included as a subset of the Root Cause Analysis investigation for high-risk issues, an Extent of Condition review is required by the standards for all nonconformities. Using the Root Cause Analysis team for this purpose makes sense because they should be intimately familiar with the nonconformance and its causes and can better recognize other manifestations of the causes of the issue. In addition, questions relating to extent of condition can be asked during and Root Cause interviews.

The causes of the nonconformance are compared with past incidents, previous audit results, other Corrective Actions, repair and maintenance reports, exercise and testing reports, and other documents to determine if similar problems can be identified. If similar situations are found, an Effectiveness Review may be necessary or additional Corrective Actions suggested preventing recurrence.

The results of the review can become part of the Root Cause Analysis report or included in a separate formal report. If included in a separate report, it should follow all document control protocols and roughly mirror the outline for the Root Cause report. Include a description of any sample size and the basis for determining the sample size, lines of inquiry (i.e., the questions asked, if any), and results of the review. Quantify in some manner the breadth of any problems identified.

10.6.3 FIVE WHYS ANALYSIS

Five Whys, also known as a "Why Tree Analysis" is a simple approach to Root Cause Analysis. It is associated with quality control, lean manufacturing, Six Sigma, and is closely related to the Cause and Effect Diagram (Fishbone). Developed in Japan for Toyota Motor Company, Five Whys asks a "Why" question to get to the root cause of a problem. The iteration of questions stops at five because it is believed this is sufficient depth to get to the root cause and asking additional questions will cloud the issue or become meaningless. Others, however, suggest asking as many "Why" questions as necessary until the root cause is established or further questions yield no additional benefit.

This method of Root Cause Analysis comes with a number of advantages and disadvantages:

- Advantages include:
  - Simplicity—it is straightforward and easy to apply, but its simplicity can become a disadvantage unless used properly
  - Can quickly determine the root cause
  - Can be used in conjunction with other Root Cause Analysis methodologies

- Leads to thinking more deeply or creatively about a nonconformity, problem, or issue
- Excellent for simple operational issues
- Disadvantages include:
  - The tendency of the analyst or analysis team to stop questioning at higher-level causes and not reach the root cause
  - Reliance on the analyst's ability to ask the right questions, especially if the issue is of a technical nature outside the analyst's knowledge
  - Results are not repeatable. Different questions may result in a different conclusion between two different groups analyzing the same issue (for this reason, Five Whys may work better as a team effort)
  - May not be of sufficient rigor for complex investigations
  - Not useful (generally) to determine culpability for an incident
  - Why questions can have multiple answers. Answers must have some evidence to support the triggers to the questions, that is, there must be confirming evidence

The Five Whys process begins with a Problem Statement. The Problem Statement is a critical element to the accuracy of the analysis. If not correct, the analysis will not be correct. Multiple Problem Statements are possible to cover a single incident. The Problem Statement describes the "who" and "what" of the nonconformance, incident, or problem. It must answer the following questions:

- Who did what?
- What is the weakness or vulnerability?
- What requirement is not being met?

Problem Statements must be based on factual conditions but should not

- Describe the solution (i.e., "The Business Continuity Training Program is too complex and should be streamlined")
- Propose the expected cause (i.e., "Project Management is poor because management oversight is inadequate")
- Combine multiple problems (i.e., "The Business Continuity Management System did not establish and maintain the training program")
- Vaguely describe the problem. It must be clear and concise (i.e., "The training program failed")
- Speculate
- Assign blame or fault

Once the Problem Statement is clearly defined, ask the first "Why" question in response to the Problem Statement. Ask what may be a rational reason the Problem Statement exists. Seek the most plausible answer. Next, test the validity of the answer—is there evidence to support it? Continue this process on multiple answers if necessary. If the problem or circumstance to be corrected was addressed in whole or in part, a valid first "Why" may have been identified (there can be multiple first "Whys"). If not, continue the analysis for the first "Why."

The same sequence of steps are used to determine the second "Why" using the first "Why" as the basis for the question. Each "Why" statement is a rational explanation of the preceding statement. The final "Why" is reached when no more plausible answers arise and/or further questions do not provide additional useful information.

If the Problem Statement is "I am suffering from the influenza virus," the question chain leading to a root cause could be:

1. Why?—I had contact with an infected person.
2. Why?—I went to the clinic to get a flu vaccination.
3. Why?—My poor lifestyle reduced my resistance to influenza.
4. Why?—I did not yet get my influenza vaccination.
5. Why?—The influenza virus attacked my cells causing the illness (root cause).

Another simple example found in many sources describes the problem that "My car won't start":

1. Why?—The battery is dead.
2. Why?—The alternator is not functioning.
3. Why?—The alternator belt is broken.
4. Why?—The alternator belt was well beyond its useful service life and has never been replaced.
5. Why?—I have not been maintaining my car according to the recommended service schedule (root cause).

10.6.4 CORRECTIVE ACTION PLAN

We have used the term "recommended corrective action" in reference to the root cause team findings. Some organizations rely on the analysis to only identify the root or apparent causes and leave it to Senior or Top Management to craft Corrective Actions. The rationale here is that senior personnel are in a better position to craft more impactful solutions without the reluctance or worry of political consequences. A Corrective Action Plan can take the "recommended" Corrective Actions proposed by the casual analysis team and either adopt them, change them, or combine them into higher-level action that better resolves the root causes identified by the team.

10.6.5 CORRECTIVE ACTION DATABASE MANAGEMENT

Corrective Actions that result from nonconformities or those designed for continuous improvement must be captured, managed, and documented in a systematic manner. Corrective action software can be designed in-house, or off-the-shelf database programs can be adapted for this purpose. Ideally, they are web based so they can be seen and used by all interested parties throughout the organization.

The management of Corrective Actions can benefit the entire organization beyond the Business Continuity Management System. It can include recommended improvements to operations, facilities maintenance, or to any other function. It manages the identification of an issue and follows it through to its resolution. The history of the issue is documented and archived for future reference. It can be used to pinpoint problem areas or to predict future problem areas.

When designing Corrective Actions and the corrective action database (assuming the organization does not already have one in place), consider the following:

- Assign a unique number. A unique sequential number should be assigned to an issue and to any Corrective Actions associated with the issue. A single issue may produce a number of Corrective Actions. An issue can be defined as the cause of the incident or the nonconformance. For example, if the Team Leader did not update his team plan information within the period specified by policy or procedure, and the root cause was too much pressure from other duties, the issue could be listed as "Team information not updated within specified time." Associated Corrective Actions could include:

- The (function's name) department will conduct a work load study to determine if additional staffing is justified
- The Team Leader will attend a time management class
- The Organization's Business Continuity Manager will devise a program to remind all Team Leaders to update their Team Plans on a regular basis

The organization can choose to assign a sequential number to all three Corrective Actions (001, 002, and 003, for example) and list the issue with each one. This can become tedious if many Corrective Actions are associated with a single issue; especially if conducting an Extent of Condition or Effectiveness Review (see below). To simplify the process, other organizations will list all Corrective Actions under the issue in their database, describing the issue only once and attaching subnumbers to the Corrective Actions. In this case, the example may appear as follows:

Issue #001	Team information not updated within specified time	
	CA#001-01	The (function's name) department will conduct a work load study to determine if additional staffing is justified
	CA#001-02	The Team Leader will attend a time management class
	CA#001-03	The Organization's Business Continuity Manager will devise a program to remind all Team Leaders to update their Team Plans on a regular basis

CA stands for "Corrective Action."

- Identify the issue. As described above, the issue is listed to frame the reasons for the Corrective Actions. The issue may also reference how the issue was identified. Internal or external audit, findings from exercises, or Management Reviews often serve as sources of issue and corrective action identification. Listing the issue also gives the organization the opportunity to assign issue categories and trend their occurrence for the identification of systemic causes that demand further analysis and treatment. Examples of trends that can be listed include:
  - Policies/Procedures/Instructions not used (was a policy, procedure, or other written instruction or document that existed, but was not used, not adhered to, not followed, or intentionally followed incorrectly)
  - Policies/Procedures/Instructions used incorrectly (a mistake was made in following a policy, procedure, or instruction or was the intent of the same not understood)
  - Policies/Procedures/Instructions deficient or not in existence (a policy, procedure, written instruction, or document lacked sufficient information or contained confusing or conflicting information)
  - Communication issue (applies to a lack of verbal communication or if verbal communication was misunderstood or misinterpreted. The failure to communicate important information within the Management System or response structure)
  - Equipment deficiency or incompatibility (equipment was not according to specification or did not operate according to expectations. This can include failed restorations or infrastructure inadequate)

- Maintenance less than adequate (this can apply to the lack of maintenance of physical equipment or to the failure to maintain the plans or programs, although a separate category for the former is appropriate according to the wishes of the organization)
- Training and awareness not adequate (training should have been provided but was not, or it was inadequate to provide the necessary knowledge and skills needed to successfully complete a task or requirement)
- Technical proficiency not adequate (personnel or team selection was determined to be incorrect or inadequate)
- Regulatory or contractual requirement not met (a regulatory or contractual requirement was missed or not adequately addressed)
- Resources inadequate or not available (resources were not adequate to meet the objectives of the program or to support the implementation of strategies)

The organization should expand upon these examples to include metrics it wishes to track and trend.

- Risk/Severity. Risk or severity levels can be assigned to the Corrective Actions to flag a higher level of attention in the rigor and management of its resolution. The organization can define, dependent on its risk appetite, what would qualify as a High, Medium, or Low risk. The risk definitions should also consider environmental, safety, financial, reputational, operational, and compliance (regulatory) factors
- Corrective Action description. Briefly but completely describe the corrective action. It must clearly state the expected action in a manner that is understood by anybody connected to its resolution. When crafting the wording for a corrective action, be very careful of the words used as an auditor may (and usually will) interrupt them very literally. As mentioned before, the word "all" means 100%, not most. For example, the corrective action "The Business Continuity Department will retrain the responsible individuals within organization on the use of the XYZ Corporation Business Continuity Software update module" means that this retraining will need to be repeated to cover those out on sick leave, vacation, disability, and so on. The use of the word "program" can mean something bigger than what the corrective action designer intended.

Corrective actions must be "SMART." SMART is a acronym for Specific, Measurable, Accountable, Reasonable, and Timely:

- Specific: The corrective action must specifically detail what will be implemented to fix the problem or address the root cause of an issue. Be certain that the intent of the corrective action is reflected in its wording. Although an individual will later be assigned as the person responsible for the corrective action, it should in general terms specify who will be responsible for its implementation. "The Business Continuity Manager will ...," for example
- Measurable: The completion of the corrective action should be documented and verifiable. It should indicate what criteria will satisfy its requirements and what evidence will be acceptable to verify that the corrective action or issue was completed as intended. Corrective actions that are vague are often difficult to demonstrate or to verify completion. Be as specific as possible: "a statistically valid sampling," "the entire function," "all of the offsite storage boxes will audited"

- Accountable: Responsibility for implementing the corrective action should be assigned to an individual who has the authority and appropriate resources to implement the action. The person assigned responsibility for the corrective action's implementation should be consulted before it becomes official, that is, entered into a database or other corrective action tracking system. Verify that the person is in fact the proper person for implementation, the time frame for completion is reasonable, and that funding can be obtained for its correction
- Reasonable: The corrective action should be feasible (see Accountable) and will effectively prevent the recurrence of the issue. Corrective actions should be hard hitting and address the underlying issues that caused the problem. Far too often, politics, budgets, and the avoidance of complexity prevent the implementation of long-term effective measures. Corrective actions that begin with "Re-train," "Review," or "Assess" are typically not very effective
- Timely: The corrective action should be completed in a realistic time frame to fix the issue and prevent recurrence. Some Corrective Actions can be immediately corrected and some can take a number of years to complete. Generally, a three-month period is sufficient. Anything longer can cause the responsible person to delay action until it is too late to complete the requirements in the allotted time

- Date entered. Record the date the corrective action was entered into the system and who entered it
- Responsible person. Identify who will be responsible for the completion of the corrective action. See above for information on agreement and notification
- Due date. The due date (see Timely above) is established and entered into the corrective active system. The due date should be monitored by the Business Continuity function or by the person responsible for the corrective action system. Some software that can be used to manage Corrective Actions have the capability to notify the responsible parties and their immediate supervisor of the due date, and send reminders at 30, 15, and 10 days before the date. This is important because extensions of the due dates should be granted only after stringent predefined conditions are met. The inability of a third party supplier to deliver materials if the order was placed in a timely manner may be one condition. The point is to not allow extensions because the responsible person did not manage their time properly. All extensions should only be granted by a member of upper management. Corrective actions that have gone into overdue status (i.e., past their due dates) should not be extended. This will allow (see below) management to focus resources on their timely completion
- Date completed. The date the corrective action was completed as intended is listed along with the name of the person who entered the completion date, that is, who is it that closed the corrective action. Some organizations do not allow the responsible person to close a corrective action and require that the evidence of closure is forwarded to a single person charged with the responsibility to compare the evidence against the wording of the corrective action. This independent review can prevent the premature closure of Corrective Actions without evidence or with insufficient evidence. The evidence used for closure should in some way be electronically attached to the corrective action for future audit and documentation

10.6.6 RESPONSIBILITY ASSIGNMENT MATRIX

An Responsibility Assignment Matrix (RACI) chart may be used to manage the timely and effective completion of a high risk corrective action or a complex set of Corrective Actions. A Responsibility Assignment Matrix, also known as an RACI matrix, describes the participation by people in various roles to complete tasks or deliverables for a project or business process. It is especially useful in clarifying roles and responsibilities in cross-functional/departmental projects and processes. RACI is an acronym derived from the four key responsibilities most typically used: Responsible, Accountable, Consulted, and Informed. It is a form of process mapping that provides a clear understanding of the roles and responsibilities surrounding a work process and avoids misunderstanding of responsibility and authority between departments or different functions. The standards do not call for the use of an RACI process, but it can be useful to ensure high risk or complex Corrective Actions are implemented in an effective, sustainable manner.

The RACI elements are assigned to the Corrective Actions by the name of the appropriate individual (see Figure 10.4):

- Responsible—The Responsible individual is the person, team, or function who is tasked with completing the work
- Accountable (also approver or final approving authority)—Is the person or position that is ultimately answerable for the completion of the task. This could be the next level of management or senior management. There must not be more that one "accountable" assignment per task
- Consulted—These are others such as a subject matter expert, stakeholder, or customer whose input is useful to produce a deliverable
- Informed—Those who are updated on the achievement of milestones or performance metrics

Weekly meetings can be held with the RACI individuals to track progress and discuss any roadblocks that may be encountered.

Corrective Action	Responsible	Accountable	Consulted	Informed	Due	CA#
The Accounting Department will conduct a work load study to determine if additional staffing is justified.	Imbruglio	Buettner	Miller	Gawron	8/1/14	001-01
The Accounting Team Leader will attend a time management class.	Weppener	Buettner	Tucker	Gawron	8/1/14	001-02
The Organization's Business Continuity Manager will devise a program to remind all Team Leaders to update their Team Plans on a regular basis.	Van Leuven	Ugale	Tucker	Bailey	8/1/14	001-03

FIGURE 10.4

RACI Matrix Example.

10.6.7 EFFECTIVENESS REVIEW

The standards require that all Corrective Actions are reviewed to determine if they were effective in achieving their goal and that the organization retains documented evidence of the corrective action results. For low-risk issues the Business Continuity Manager should examine and document the associated Corrective Actions to determine if their implementation meets the criteria listed below.

An Effectiveness Review is a form of management review to determine if the suite of high-risk Corrective Actions associated with a significant incident were successful in attaining their goals. Management selects a team composed of a representative from the function involved or who "owns" the original issue, an independent person from a different organizational function who had no relationship to the original incident, a subject matter expert who helps the team evaluate the information collected, and sometimes an independent observer. This team will conduct an indepth formal investigation to determine:

- Does the corrective action(s) address the root cause?
- Does the corrective action(s) prevent recurrence of similar conditions due to similar causes?
- Has the corrective action(s) been implemented as intended?
- Does the corrective action(s) demonstrate endurance and sustainability?
- Has the corrective action(s) introduced negative unintended consequences?
- Has the corrective action(s) improved the program/process performance?

The team will interview personnel who were responsible for the corrective action's implementation and those who will have knowledge (or a sampling of those who will have knowledge) of the answers to the above questions. The team or team leader, in conjunction with the subject matter expert, will craft a suite of questions to ask any interviewees that focus on the particular details of the inquiry. The team will review relevant documents that support effectiveness, or that show the Corrective Actions were not effective or only partially effective. The team will look for similar subsequent issues or comparable subsequent Corrective Actions (i.e., are the issues recurrent) to help justify their conclusions. The team may wish to examine each correction in the review separately, as a whole or by Corrective Actions grouped together in a logical manner.

Because the review can be time-consuming, management may wish to "charter" the team so they are not under pressure to conclude the investigation prematurely. The first meeting of the review team should be attended by a member of upper management to stress the importance of their efforts and that the intent is not to find fault with any individuals but to engage in an effort of continuous improvement.

At the conclusion of the review, the team will issue a report that documents their findings whether the Corrective Actions or groups of Corrective Actions were effective, not effective, or only partially effective. The report should contain an overview of the justifications for their conclusions and can (and should) recommend additional Corrective Actions to close any gaps identified in the review.

10.7 REVIEW

Plan and Program Maintenance is vital to the mission readiness of the Business Continuity Management System, but it is often a neglected process. Business Continuity Managers often fight the perception by team leaders that once the plan is completed it can be reprioritized as they move on to other pressing tasks. Team Leaders should be tasked with keeping their plans up to date and the Business Continuity Manager should be tasked with keeping the Business Continuity Management System up to date. The responsibilities should be mandated by organizational policy.

Plans are updated on a regular basis and when changes to personnel information, resources, or strategies need revision. The program is updated when significant changes such as adjustments to the strategic direction of the organization, a change in organizational structure, changes in risk or risk appetite, and similar conditions occur. Contractual demands by customers or other outside interested parties may also dictate the frequency of plan and program updates. A documented post-incident review is required whenever an incident necessitates the activation of the plan and lessons learned incorporated into the plans and program as appropriate.

A Change Management or Change Control Process must be documented so that changes to the Business Continuity Management System are introduced in a controlled and coordinated manner. Change Management is generally accepted to mean a process or an approach to transition individuals, teams, or the entire organization to a future state in a manner that controls the impact of the change and that reduces barriers to its implementation. Organizational Change Management is a process designed to overcome the natural resistance to change and to ensure the path to a future state is achieved. Although Organizational Change Management is important to the Business Continuity Professional, the standards seem to emphasize Process Control Change Management in which the emphasis is "to ensure all changes are assessed, approved, implemented, and reviewed in a controlled manner."

Performance measures that are appropriate to the needs of the organization monitor the effectiveness of the organization's strategies and help to tell us if objectives are met. They identify the potential for nonconformities and trigger action to prevent the consequences of negative trends. They reveal the effectiveness of the Business Continuity Management System and pinpoint areas that need attention by management. Metrics support continuous improvement.

Performance metrics, also known as Key Performance Indicators, allow the organization to understand how its various parts are meeting their goals and improve accountability, and allows for better management by focusing effort where improvement is necessary. A Critical Success Factor is that which is necessary for an organization or function to achieve its goals or mission. Key Performance Indicators are mapped to Critical Success Factors.

Performance metrics are required by the standards. They should be graphical and uncomplicated, showing trends over time in a clear manner that communicates the measurement. All metrics must be actionable and when the measurement shows an unacceptable trend, action must be taken to correct the trend.

The standards also require the ongoing evaluation of business continuity procedures and capabilities within the framework of plan and program maintenance and separately through periodic reviews, post-incident analysis, performance evaluations, and internal audits. The evaluations must include legal and regulatory requirements, business continuity best practices, and the policy and objectives of the Business Continuity Management System.

Performance metrics measure the health of the business continuity systems and help to predict future success or inefficiencies. Metrics must be appropriate to the organization, actionable, monitor compliance, and enable trending. They must be simple, uncomplicated, and show ongoing performance. In part, metrics measure Critical Success Factors and Key Performance Indicators. Performance models or "Frameworks" can help the manager identify the best metrics to use.

The ongoing evaluation of business continuity plans, procedures, and capabilities are required by the standards. These evaluations must include legal and regulatory requirements, business continuity best practices, and the policy and objectives of the Business Continuity Management System. In addition to periodic reviews, post-incident analysis, and performance evaluations, impartial internal audits are required.

The standards also require that the organization establish and maintain an audit program. ISO 19011 Guidelines for Auditing Management Systems can be used to satisfy this requirement. Internal audits are scheduled at planned intervals. Planned Intervals mean that the audit should be completed at least annually to align with the preparation of the Management Review. Audits are evidence based. Auditors examine documents (or a valid statistical sampling of documents), interview responsible individuals, and in some cases observe operations and conditions. The audit report will highlight conformity or nonconformity with the audit criteria and include supporting documentation.

The Business Continuity Management System is reviewed by Top Management to ensure that it is functioning as intended. This review must also take place at planned intervals. Once the review is completed, Top Management will take any necessary action to correct deficiencies and nonconformities. Any actions or changes to the Business Continuity Management Program that result from the Management Review must be documented and processes and procedures revised as appropriate. The results of the management review must also be communicated to relevant parties including those outside the organization as necessary.

A Nonconformity is any of the standard's requirements that were not satisfied. The organization must identify nonconformities and to take Corrective Actions in a timely manner. When nonconformity is identified, many of the guidance standards require the organization to perform a Root Cause Analysis to determine why the deficiency occurred. Root Cause Analysis is the utilization of any number of techniques (or combination of techniques) designed to get to the underlying condition, action, or lack of action that caused the incident of nonconformity.

An Extent of Condition review is a process to discover if the potential (or the actual existence) for an identified issue or nonconformance to exist in other activities, processes, or programs within the Business Continuity Management System. This is often combined with the root cause investigation and may be included in the Root Cause Analysis report. The result of the Root Cause Analysis, as with exercising and testing and other processes is the creation of Corrective Actions.

Corrective Actions that result from nonconformities or those designed for continuous improvement, must be captured, managed, and documented in a systematic manner. A Corrective Action Plan manages the identification of an issue and follows it through to its resolution. The history of the issue is documented and archived for future reference.

Corrective actions must be SMART. An RACI Chart may be used to manage the timely and effective completion of high-risk Corrective Actions or of a complex set of corrective actions. It describes the participation by various individuals in completing tasks or deliverables for a project or business process. RACI is an acronym derived from the four key responsibilities most typically used: Responsible, Accountable, Consulted, and Informed.

The standards require that all Corrective Actions are reviewed to determine if they were effective in achieving their goal and that the organization retains documented evidence of the corrective action results. This is accomplished by an Effectiveness Review. At the conclusion of the review, a report is issued that documents whether the Corrective Actions or groups of Corrective Actions were effective, not effective, or only partially effective. The report should recommend additional Corrective Actions to close any gaps identified in the review.

Program maintenance, the trending of metrics, Change Management, internal audit, management review, and a corrective action plan are all about continuous improvement of the Business Continuity Management System. Because of the potential complexity of the business continuity program, a complete and mature system cannot be devised from its first iteration.

This chapter discussed the elements that the Business Continuity Manager must apply to keep his or her program in a mission ready state, or to borrow a term from the Quality Management arena, "fit-for-purpose." It will enable the manager to maintain momentum toward a mature program that will meet the expectations of the standards and achieve a world class Business Continuity Management System.

BIBLIOGRAPHY

Good Practice Guidelines 2013 Global Edition; A Guide to Global Good Practices in Business Continuity, Business Continuity Institute. www.thebci.com.

Appendix A: Sample Competencies Suggested for Business Continuity Manager

See Chapter 3

The following job posting for a Business Continuity Manager suggests the competencies expected for the leader of a Business Continuity Management System. It is designed for a managing consultant but is representative of what would be required for the manager of a Business Continuity Management System:

An experienced top consultant and project manager who will take a leadership role in strategically delivering complex business continuity-related services to satisfy advanced requirements. This position will involve project management, delivery, client/staff mentoring, and participation in business development activities.

Mandatory Skills and Experience:

- Bachelor's Degree or higher
- Certified Business Continuity Professional (CBCP), Master Business Continuity Professional (MBCP), Member of the Business Continuity Institute (MBCI), or Fellow of the Business Continuity Institute (FBCI)
- Minimum of 8 to 10 years performing business continuity consulting services (business-oriented, not exclusively technology-oriented)
- Outstanding writing skills
- Experience managing and executing complex projects on time and on budget
- Familiar with designing or performing all aspects of the business continuity lifecycle (program design, Business Impact Analysis (BIA), risk assessment, strategy development, plan documentation, exercise facilitation, training and awareness, and assessment)
- Advanced familiarity with leading standards (i.e., ISO 22301, NFPA 1600) and regulatory requirements (e.g., FFIEC)
- Experience delivering thought leadership to individual companies (C-level executives) or via conference presentations/journal articles
- Ability to coach and mentor junior business continuity professionals and client personnel
- Experience and ability to deliver outstanding, second-to-none client service
- Flexibility and creativity with applying industry practices to solve complex problems

Desired Skills and Experience:

- Familiarity with enterprise risk management concepts and practices
- Familiarity with Six Sigma practices
- Familiarity implementing and manipulating leading software packages
- Project Management Professional (PMP) certification
- Experience growing existing projects/client relationships, or participating in business development activities (including proposal development and client presentations)

The above courtesy of Alicia Stevens at the Business Continuity Search Firm of BC Management, Inc. 2014, http://www.bcmanagement.com.

Appendix B: Required Documents under ISO 22301

See Chapter 3

Listed here are the minimum documents required under ISO 22301. Depending on the complexity of the Business Continuity Management System, a single document can include one or more required documented processes.

- The context of the organization
- Process for the identification and compliance with legal, regulatory, and contractual requirements. List the requirements and provide evidence of compliance. These can be separate documents as necessary
- Business Continuity Policy, Scope with any exclusions, and Objectives. These can be separate documents as necessary
- Competence development program that includes assessments and training
- Business Impact Analysis (BIA) and process. The process is a required document but the analysis is in some cases considered optional, but practically the manager or consultant will produce both of these documents (and rely on them heavily)
- Risk assessment and process. Again, the process is the required document.
- Business continuity strategies and those that were considered but rejected
- Incident response plan and recovery procedures
- Exercise program and after-action reports
- Performance monitoring
- Internal audits
- Top management review
- Corrective action plan and tracking

The following documents may also be required to demonstrate the effectiveness of the management system. Many of these can also be combined with the documentation of similar processes described above:

- Customer contracts and service level agreements
- Contractor and supplier notification and response procedures. These would normally be included in the individual team plans
- Determination and selection of business continuity strategies (can be discussed in response to recommendations in the Business Impact and Risk Assessment)
- Overview of incident response. This should be normally included in the incident response plan
- Business Continuity Awareness Program
- Exercise schedules. These would be specific schedules in which the required document above could refer to a general schedule requirement
- Postincident reports including near-hits, recommendations or lessons learned, and how they were communicated
- Steering Committee and Top Management meeting minutes.

Appendix C: Emergency Plan Table of Contents

Appendix D: Sample Business Impact Analysis Questions

See Chapter 5

Business impact analysis (BIA) questions are divided into two parts: questions that apply to most all functions of the organization within the scope of the analysis and those that are specific to the function itself. Since many managers combine the BIA process with the collection of resource needs that support the implementation of the function's recovery, strategy questions related to resource documentation and information that supports the continuity plan are distributed near the end of the interview (or as part of the BIA tool kit sent out prior to the interviews).

The following is not necessarily intended to be a complete list of questions that can or should be asked from each functional leader; the environment of each different organization may necessitate additional questions or the elimination of others. It is important that the manager understands the intent of the question so that they are in a position to ask clarifying questions or additional questions that allow the manager (and often the process owner or functional leader) to better understand the impact of the risks to their products and services.

GENERAL QUESTIONS (ASKED OF ALL FUNCTIONAL LEADERS)

If part of a paper or electronic tool kit, be sure that a field identifies the name of the recipient and the function(s) they represent.

1. Describe your business unit and what it does (include business functions and processes).
   a. How does it contribute to the goals of the organization?
   b. What are your responsibilities?
   c. Does it produce income to the organization?
   The intent of this question is to begin the conversation, contribute to the "understanding of the organization," and to help the business continuity manager decide if the function or business unit requires more than one continuity team in the plan.
2. Which of these functions described above would need to be recovered first?
   Although the emphasis on assigning criticality or recovery sequence should be based on the financial and operational loss data, the answer to this question and the next question can help to verify the data, but the functional leader may reveal insights not necessarily derived from objective data.
3. Why did you choose the above ranking(s)?
   Some of the questions we recommend the analyst to ask are intended to be used to verify the responses to others. See the explanation for question #2 above.
4. If not answered above, what would be the impact of the loss of these functions (i.e., how would the company be affected if the previously identified critical functions were unavailable (negative publicity, loss of business, regulatory or liability issues, etc.))?
   This question contributes to the understanding of risk, clues the analyst to risks that may need additional exploration, and verifies other data.

231

5. If your department or function generates revenue for the organization, what are the sources of this income? Sources of income can include:
   a. Product sales (list by product lines)
   b. Services rendered to outside clients
   c. Discounts or commissions
   d. Interest from investments or floats
   e. Incentives for on-time or ahead-of-schedule completion dates or milestones
   f. Tax base, if a government agency
   g. License and use fees
   h. Maintenance fees
   i. Other: _____

   This question also contributes to the understanding of risk and clues the analyst to risks that may need additional exploration. It may help to identify interdependencies between functions.

6. In addition to the loss of revenue, what other types of financial impact are realized if your department or function is lost? These may include:
   a. Canceled orders due to late delivery
   b. Penalties for late payments
   c. Regulatory requirements, late filings, and fines
   d. Contractual obligations delayed or not met
   e. Interest on borrowed funds
   f. Wages paid to idle staff
   g. Other _____

   Helps to identify risk.

7. In how many days would this impact become (1) damaging and (2) critical to the operation of the company, i.e., please estimate the amount of time your critical function(s) can be unavailable without adversely affecting the overall business objectives (your outage tolerance)?

   This question asks for the process owner's subjective estimate of the value of their operations to that of the organization.

8. Are there any periods during the business cycle (week, month, or year) when processing or operations are especially critical?

   In other words, when can an outage hurt you the most? This information is useful to the management team making strategic "corrections" or modifications to the recovery plan made necessary by the timing of the disaster. It can illustrate changing priorities and allow decision makers to redirect resources to where and when they are needed most. Critical times are typically the end of each quarter or year, or some significant product-related event. A toy manufacturer may list the months of September, October, and November as its most critical time, preceding the Christmas season. When using a questionnaire, allow respondents to provide free-form answers. Some questionnaires and BIA software programs only allow for the selection of individual months. Although this monthly period may be sufficient for the analysis, it may not be significantly focused for recovery purposes. Later, this information is included in a matrix within the continuity plan.

9. Where could your group(s) go to operate if access to the corporate campus (or normal facilities) is denied, damaged, or destroyed?
   a. Are similar functions performed at other company locations upon whose resources you could depend on an interim basis? Please state the unit and office location(s).

    b. Does your function need to relocate with any other function, i.e., does it need to be in close proximity with another function to operate properly?

    Not related directly to business impact, this question asks about alternate work sites. Is there a location at another company site, can a person work at home, or one of the other options we will discuss in the chapter on strategies?

10. How many employees are in each of your critical functions and how many would be needed in the first hours, days, and weeks after a disaster?

    The answer to this question tells the manager how many seats are need at an alternate location. This allows the manager to plan for the number of supporting resources such as furniture, workstations, phones, and the like.

11. What resources or special accommodations are necessary to operate from the above location?

    Same as the above, only from a more technological, manufacturing, or other operational need.

12. Do your functions utilize any third-party suppliers?

    a. If so, where are they located, and do they have continuity plans?

    Related to supply chain risk.

13. Do you use any sole source suppliers?

    a. Do they have continuity plans? (Request copies for review if not certified under one of the standards.)

    Also related to supply chain risk.

14. What are the lead times for the replacement of critical equipment, materials, or supplies?

    Related to risk. If the lead time(s) for the replacement of equipment or the reestablishment of the equipment's environment is longer than the Recovery Time Objective (RTO), then adjustments in strategies or mitigation must be made.

15. How would the organization obtain resources minimally necessary to continue to provide an acceptable level of service (i.e., services, hardware, software, documents, forms, supplies, etc.)?

    a. Have any arrangements or agreements been made with your vendors for emergency delivery of critical resources?

    After a regional disaster, resources are likely to be in short supply and difficult to obtain. As the reader can likely tell from the questions, the question is used to identify any gaps in preagreements with suppliers for the prioritized delivery of services to the organization and therefore gaps in preparedness. Although in practice the organization that hands out the most cash will receive whatever services are available, many enter into written agreements with suppliers such as diesel or debris box providers to deliver these services.

16. Does your function maintain its own data systems?

    a. Is there a significant amount of data within your department that is not stored on network drives and therefore not included in a normal backup routine?

    Related to RPO and backup strategies. Occasionally a department or function will maintain data systems or has equipment that is not part of the IT network. If this is the case, backup and off-site storage strategies must be explored.

17. What vital records are maintained by the department?

    a. Are they duplicated and stored off-site in a commercial facility that specializes in records storage?

    b. Is work in progress stored in fire-resistant containers?

    c. How quickly, if at all, can these documents be reconstructed?

    d. Are there locations outside of the organization such as a law firm where duplicate copies can be obtained?

This question explores risk to vital records. These are documents that must be available to send to regulators or that are necessary to conduct normal operations. The loss of vital records, especially for a small- to medium-sized organization, is one of the primary reasons organizations fail after a disaster such as a fire or flood. Many of the regulations focus on the protection of vital records, in particular financial records.

18. Are there any additional risks to your organization and to your unit's functions?
    a. How can you minimize the risk or effect of a loss of your functions?
    Some may argue that this should be one of the first questions asked, in the form of "What are the risks to your organization and function?" But others would argue that many middle managers do not think in terms of risk to their operations, and the preceding questions may help to start the mental process of thinking in terms of risk.

19. Are there other consequences or concerns that you can express if your functions are lost or delayed?
    In other words, what have we missed or failed to ask relative to the consequences of the risk to the organization or to their functions?

20. What strategies would you use to recover your functions if they were lost or access to them was denied for any reason?
    This question could be restated earlier in the interview with, "Do you currently have any plans in place for the continuity or recovery of your function's operations?" If a software tool kit is used, one of the questions or fields to complete will ask for the first 30 things the functional leader (later translating into a continuity team leader) would need to do to continue or restart their operations. This question is designed to give the analyst and functional leader an idea of initial strategies to explore.

21. Are there any other functions upon which you are dependent for data, information, products, or services before your function can perform its tasks?
    a. Who is dependent upon your function's output/product?
    This question is asking for the function's interdependencies. Similar to IT processes, if a critical function cannot operate without the input from a function that is not deemed by itself critical, its status may need to be elevated to support the critical function. The answers to this question can also be used to craft continuity or recovery tasks to support dependencies.

22. How many separate instances are you aware of where the ability to function ceased or was severely impaired, and how long did the interruption last?
    a. How did you resolve this problem?
    This question leverages the experience from the reaction to past service outages or disasters and provides lessons learned, potentially highlights process or support inefficiencies, verifies the ability to meet recovery time objectives, and can begin the process of identifying strategies that worked (or did not work) in the past.

23. What software programs and processes are used by your function, and how long can you afford to be without these applications?
    Good information that helps map IT processes to criticality. It also will identify any software not supported by IT that the function may need to replace on its own. Commercial BIA software or tool kits will ask for a list of these programs, the number of licenses required, and registration numbers and the like so they can be reinstalled and run at an alternate location. When the commercial BIA software is used, or a tool kit distributed that asks for a list of software programs, some analysts may skip this question in the interview.

24. What would be the impact to third parties (interested party) outside of the organization if your function failed to provide its service or product?
    a. What strategies are currently employed to minimize or eliminate the impact of an outage?
    b. Is there a strategy or procedure to communicate disruptions to interested parties?
    Is your organization a sole-source supplier for another organization? Would the failure of your function to deliver products or services cause a loss of good will to a customer or their customers?
25. What contractual or legal obligations (including regulatory requirements) apply to your functions?
    a. List these obligations.
    b. Are there any written agreements or memorandums of understanding that pertain to business continuity between your function and outside parties (provide copy)?
    c. Do you have a written procedure to identify and assess these requirements? If yes, please describe and provide a copy of the procedure.
    d. What strategies are currently employed to avoid, minimize, or eliminate the impact of a failure to meet legal or regulatory requirements caused by an outage?
    e. How are these obligations or requirements communicated to affected employees or other interested parties when they change or when new obligations or requirements are introduced?

The standards emphasize that the organization's contractual and legal obligations are taken into account when establishing, implementing, and maintaining the Business Continuity Management System. They also require the assessment of the regulatory requirements and the establishment of a procedure to identify, assess, make available, and maintain compliance relative to continuity operations. While this task is usually found under the responsibilities of the legal and purchasing functions, other functions such as sales or facilities may have entered into agreements or have some type of regulatory requirement. Remember that this pertains to business continuity management.

FINANCIAL AND OPERATIONAL IMPACT QUESTIONS

The financial impact of the loss of the various functions within the organization over time is important to understanding recovery priorities and cost justifications for selected recovery strategies. Managers should be asked to complete the table below for each business function that they own. Indicate the loss anticipated if the outage occurred during "normal" noncritical times (these figures go in the "Minimum" columns of the table) and what the estimated loss would be under the worst-case business cycle scenario ("Maximum" column) for each source (type) of loss, i.e., is the loss caused by canceled orders, fines/penalties, litigation, etc. The analyst would adjust the time periods to report based on what is most meaningful to the organization. These questions are typically not asked during the interview (but can be reviewed and discussed since they are usually distributed ahead of time as part of a software program or tool kit). Include an estimate of how the figures may be affected during a serious pandemic situation where key personnel may not be available (or working from home), supply chains interrupted, and the delivery of products and services disrupted. Most managers will have difficulty understanding the impacts of a pandemic and will therefore need to work closely with the business continuity manager to arrive at these figures (Table 1).

Because it is sometimes difficult to quantify the loss of some functions in financial terms, a separate chart of operational impacts is included for each business unit/function. Functional owners are asked to estimate the impact using a scale of 1–5, with 1 equal to little impact and 5 equal to a severe impact to the goals of the organization (Table 2).

Table 1   Financial Impact Spreadsheet

Exposure	Day 1		Day 2		Day 3		Day 4		Day 5		Week 2		Week 3		Week 4	
	Min	Max	Min	Max	Min	Max	Min	Max	Min	Max	Min	Max	Min	Max	Min	Max
Lost sales																
Canceled orders																
Lost trade discounts																
Penalties–late payments																
Loss of future business																
Contractual penalties																
Fines																
Availability of funds																
Pandemic flu situation																
Other:																
Other:																
Total:																

Table 2 Operational Impacts

Impact	Severity (1–5)
Cash flow	
Competitive advantages	
Customer service	
Financial control	
Financial reporting	
Increase in liability	
Industry image	
Legal/contractual obligations	
Public image	
Regulatory	
Shareholder confidence	
Vendor relations	
Other interested parties	
Safety	
Environmental damage	
Other:	

FUNCTIONAL SPECIFIC QUESTIONS

The functional specific questions combine to further the understanding of the organization, to further identify gaps in preparedness, and to form the basis for recommendations to close any identified gaps. We have not listed all functions that may be found within an organization nor all of the questions that may be asked, but these should give the manager an idea of the types of questions posed to functional leaders. These questions are asked in addition to the general questions as applicable. Some of the questions may also apply to multiple functions but are not necessarily repeated in those paragraphs.

CUSTOMER SERVICE/TECHNICAL SUPPORT (SEE TELECOMMUNICATIONS)

Organizations with a customer service or technical support unit are obviously highly dependent on telecommunications. The analyst would concentrate internally (if this function is not provided by an external third party) on the digital phone switch that is essentially a computer server, its connections to the outside world, the path to the phone company's central station, and the specialized software that supports the switch. A central station is the telephone company's switching station where the area telephone lines converge into their equipment and can serve as a single point of failure. While these systems are increasingly fault tolerant, the analysis will look at all parts of the communication system for risk. Data and specialized software backup, staffing issues, and access to technical documentation are some issues to explore.

1. Is customer service or the call center in house or contracted to a third party?
2. If a third party, do they have tested business continuity plans in place (obtain a copy for review)?
3. What are the hours of the call center?
4. What geographical areas does the call center serve?
5. If more than one third party is used, can the other call centers handle all product lines?
6. Are there any recovery strategies in place now? What strategies are in place or contemplated? Are there any arrangements with a call center hot site?
7. Can manual methods be utilized during a systems failure?
8. Do other call centers exist within the organization? What types of calls and products do they handle?
9. What forms of alternate communications exist between centers?
10. Is there direct and diverse routing between centers?
11. How can "lost calls" or calls in transit be tracked?
12. Can employees and technicians work from alternate locations?
13. What will employees and technicians need to work from an alternate location?
14. Are current technical documents, forms, and stored manuals located at alternate locations or call centers?
15. What types of calls are received in the call center (i.e., sales, technical, service, etc.)?
16. What is the volume of each type of call?
17. What is the revenue generated by each type of call (total)?
18. How many personnel are assigned to each type of call?
19. How are these calls routed?

20. What servers, switches, and applications control each type of call?
21. Is payment information collected (i.e., credit card, etc.)?
22. Which servers support payment processes?
23. Have you studied the effects of call delay (i.e., how long will a caller wait before going to a competitor, deciding not to purchase, or changing products in the future)?
24. What is the estimated loss of business if each type of call is down for 30 min at peak times, 60 min, 90 min, 120 min, …?
25. What percentage of the above do you expect to later recover by callbacks?
26. Do sales or other types of orders arrive via fax? If so, what is the percentage, number of lines, and how are they entered into the system as orders?
27. Do sales or other types of orders arrive via Web or e-mail? If so, what percentage, what is the dollar loss per half hour increments, servers and applications used including interface to order entry, distribution, etc.?
28. What products does the call center handle?
29. At what capacity are all call centers operating?
30. Are there any contractual obligations that could be affected by a delay in call center operations?
31. Can customers incur financial loss from a delay or outage? Estimate the losses.
32. What service level agreements are negotiated for emergency repair, replacement, or drop shipping to other locations?
33. What redundancy is built into the system?
34. How will infrastructure be set up or connected at the alternate site?
35. What data is backed up, where is it stored, and how often is it taken off-site?
36. Is there a list of circuits and descriptions, circuit numbers, carriers, etc. for each call type?
37. Is there a systems topography map?
38. Is any diagnostic software utilized? Why not?
39. Is the facility dual entry? i.e., do phone lines enter the building from divergent directions?
40. If plans are in place to roll over calls to another company location, will data/telecommunications switch over automatically?
41. Will it be necessary to send representatives to major customer sites during an outage?

EMERGENCY PREPAREDNESS AND RESPONSE

Emergency preparedness and response, if not under the purview of the business continuity manager, is often found under safety and security, facilities, or human resources. Emergency preparedness and response do not directly contribute to the RTO or MAO, but bear in mind that preparedness and a good response (stabilization) to an emergency will position the organization to recover their operations in a timely manner.

1. Is there a written emergency plan?
   a. Does it address all foreseeable emergencies (hazards)?
   b. How have these hazards been mitigated?
   c. Does the plan list all of the appropriate people and agencies responsible, along with primary and alternate phone numbers?

    d. Does the plan contain all of the necessary components?

    e. Are the plan owners knowledgeable in the characteristics of the hazards?

    f. Does the plan contain emergency evacuation procedures, assembly locations, and actions to ensure that everyone has evacuated?

    g. How often are drills conducted?

    h. How is this plan communicated to employees and guests?

    i. Do emergency procedures accommodate the handicapped?

    j. Are assembly points posted?

    k. Are floor wardens used?

    l. Are employees trained in evacuation signals, i.e., how are affected individuals notified of an emergency?

    m. Is the plan constructed in a manner such that information is easy to find?

2. Is an emergency response team utilized, or how does the company respond to emergencies?

    a. How are responders trained?

    b. Do responders use the incident command system?

    c. What equipment is available for response and rescue?

    d. Is the team trained in blood-borne pathogen safety?

    e. Is safety equipment for in-house emergency response personnel like safety glasses, gloves, handheld toxic gas detectors available?

3. What first aid supplies and training are available?

    a. Are first aid/CPR training offered for a response team and the employee population?

    b. Does the organization keep track of employees qualified in first aid and other disaster-related skills such as licensed amateur radio operators?

    c. Are disaster first aid supplies maintained? After a regional disaster, first aid supplies beyond Band-Aids may be necessary. These supplies can include larger compresses (6×6 in.), pressure bandages, air splints, antiseptics, and the like.

    d. How often are first aid kits inspected and replenished?

4. Does the company stockpile emergency food, water, sanitary supplies, and other provisions?

    a. Are "go bags" issued to employees?

5. Is there a mass casualty plan?

    a. Is a supply of body bags maintained?

    b. Is cold storage available?

6. What warning systems exist to detect an imminent emergency?

    a. How is the information processed and communicated to affected employees and potentially to other interested parties?

7. What public–private partnerships are established?

    a. Are there any written agreements or memorandums of understanding that pertain to business continuity or emergency preparedness and response between the function and outside parties (provide copy)?

    b. Is there a relationship with or does the organization work with the local government office of emergency services?

    c. What partnerships need to be established?

8. Are digital cameras available for damage assessment and documentation (the use of smartphone and tablet cameras should be discouraged after a disaster, especially if electrical power is not available). The phone battery should be saved for data or voice communication unless there is a need to transmit the picture.

9. What training is provided to prepare workers at home and in the organization for emergencies and disasters?
   a. Is there a business continuity management intranet Web page that contains links to preparedness information?
   b. How does the organization incentivize preparedness?
10. Is there any risk of environmental damage due to foreseeable incidents?
   a. Would any environmental damage result in fines to the organization?
   b. Would any foreseeable environmental damage require reporting to an outside agency?

FACILITIES

The facilities department, sometimes referred to as plant maintenance, is often composed of many different functions that include maintenance of the building, grounds and infrastructure, real estate, space planning, custodial, capitol projects, mail services, civil and structural engineering, and the like. In the business impact analysis, you can treat the cost of the loss of an asset, i.e., the loss of a building (assuming the organization owns the building) or the replacement cost of the same in the business impact analysis. In addition, the cost of temporary relocation can be considered. It is also important to characterize the performance of the structure and its ability to support critical functions after a disaster so that corrective actions (recommendations) are in place to mitigate the risk. Facilities will likely become one of the largest support teams in the recovery from a disaster.

1. Structural. (Repeat for additional buildings. List the location of additional buildings and the operations they house.)
   a. Building age:
   b. Type of construction (wood frame, concrete tilt up, unreinforced masonry, etc.):
   c. Are seismic studies completed for the building?
   d. Is the building designed to be rigid or flexible in an earthquake?
   e. Is base isolation built into the design?
   f. Is roof drainage good and well maintained?
   g. Is the building owned or leased?
2. Is the site located in an unincorporated or incorporated jurisdiction?
3. Describe the stability of the power grid and any redundancies.
4. Is the public address system included on battery or backup power circuits?
5. Are there redundant feeds for electrical (is there a need)?
6. Are there redundant feeds for natural gas and other utilities (is there a need)?
7. Is incoming power monitored?
8. Are there backup power generator(s)?
   a. Quick-fit connections in transfer switch?
   b. Run time?
   c. Minimum/maximum load?
   d. What does it feed?
   e. Type of fuel?
   f. Fuel on hand and what arrangements for refueling?

  g. Testing schedule?
  h. Tested under load conditions?
  i. Tested in conjunction with uninterruptible power systems (UPS)?
9. Utilities:
  a. Internal protection?
    - Are critical utilities located on the outside or core of the building?
    - Do utilities enter through slip vaults in seismically active areas?
    - Are hazardous utilities and process gasses equipped with seismic shutoff valves? At what acceleration level are they set?
  b. External protection and risks?
    - Stability of utilities (frequency grid failure)?
10. Are the following protected from seismic motion?
  a. Tall objects (bookcases, file cabinets, storage racks)?
  b. Large equipment?
  c. Water heaters?
  d. Process gasses?
  e. Lights and ceiling tiles?
  f. Sway bracing for sprinklers (riser and distribution pipes)?
  g. Flex connectors for natural gas and boiler pipes?
  h. Outside structural elements (parapets, etc.)?
  i. Outside nonstructural elements?
  j. Equipment on roof (braced, weight issues)?
  k. Sensitive equipment on seismic damping mats?
  l. Public address system?
11. Are disaster-related tools and materials available (plywood, glass cleanup brooms and shovels, etc.)?
12. Is a restoration service company that specializes in the drying of facilities and documents identified?
  a. Has the organization preregistered with this company?
  b. Will they deliver debris boxes?
  c. Where can/should the debris box be located?
  d. Has a salvage area been designated?
13. Are contractors for drywall, cosmetic repairs identified?
14. Are temporary fencing contractors identified?
15. Have facilities staff received training in rapid building damage assessment?
16. Are there structural or civil engineers on staff?
  a. If not, are there engineers on call with preagreements for prioritized response?
  b. Does the local jurisdiction allow for internal or contract engineers to evaluate structures according to ATC 20 (Applied Technology Council) and green/yellow/red tag the structure in place of the jurisdiction's engineers?
17. Is there a damage assessment checklist that includes inspection of critical utilities, HVAC, and life safety systems?
18. Communications
  a. Does the Facilities Department utilize two-way radios? If so, describe the technology (simplex, repeater, trunked)?

b. Do other functions that have a response/recovery need have access to these radios or to the frequency?

c. Is anyone trained in the use of amateur radios and is equipment located on-site?

19. Vital records

a. Are CAD, tenant improvements, as-built drawings and space plans copied and stored off-site?

b. Are real estate agreements backed up and copies stored off-site?

c. Same for other important documents?

20. Does Facilities have access to vehicles and trucks (i.e., what transportation vehicles are available)?

21. Have moving companies been prequalified and agreements made for prioritized treatment if needed after a regional disaster?

22. Are there any agreements with real estate firms for emergency or low cost (guaranteed) floor space or replacement facilities to be used if the current workspace is damaged or destroyed?

23. What remote facilities within the organization are available for relocation? What must be accomplished to accommodate relocating workers and processes at this/these locations? How quickly would they be available?

24. Mail room questions

a. What alternate locations are available if the mail room is damaged or destroyed?

b. How can mail and package delivery be rerouted if alternate locations are used?

c. Can this group help to check in relocating employees at an alternate location (if a hotel or hot site is used, this service is usually provided)?

d. Are there plans to notify the Post Office to forward mail and packages?

25. Is critical equipment marked for quick removal? (Some fire departments will remove or allow the removal of critical equipment for a brief period of time after a fire or other damage to the building. Marking the equipment or material in some manner will expedite its removal.)

26. What fire prevention and control systems, including alarm systems and after-hours monitoring are installed?

a. Do the fire systems meet code, and are they adequate to protect the facilities, processes, and occupants?

27. Is there any risk of environmental damage as the result of the loss of organizational function?

TREASURY AND OTHER FINANCE QUESTIONS

Work with the chief financial officer (CFO) to refine pertinent questions and expand as appropriate to include cash management, accounts payable, and accounts receivable, etc.

1. How are fixed assets tracked?

2. Are ledger accounts for recovery-related expenses established ahead of time?

3. What initial steps will the finance and treasury functions need to take to prevent financial damage to the company? Long-term steps?

4. What financial obligations may the company miss because of a disaster, and what are the consequences?

5. How will the company post cash and cover any floats subsequent to a disaster? What impact will this have if delayed?

6. Are critical payroll, accounting, and financial records duplicated and stored off-site? Are important on-site records stored in fire-resistant containers?
7. Where and how can finance and treasury functions and employees operate if access to the building is not possible?
8. Are force majeure clauses included in royalty and other contracts or agreements?
9. Is there a policy to pay employees furloughed by the outage? If so, for how long? Include details about this policy.
10. How will employees be paid if the payroll department cannot function (i.e., would you request your payroll processing service to duplicate the previous run and make adjustments at a later date)?
11. How will payroll checks and funds be distributed?
12. Who do you use as the payroll processing service, and do they have a tested business continuity plan in place? Obtain a copy for review.
13. Are petty cash reserves sufficient to cover anticipated emergencies in a cash-and-carry environment?
14. Are recovery team leaders authorized to receive petty cash, or are signature levels at a level consistent with their recovery duties?
15. How are receivables tracked, and can manual methods be used?
16. How can receivables and work in process be recreated?
17. How will receivables and blank checks, etc. be protected?
18. What payables must be met, and how can they be identified and satisfied after a disaster? What payables can be delayed?
19. What is the impact of the delay in the above?
20. How can finance and treasury keep track of the changing financial position of the company after a disaster and provide reports to senior management?
21. How will financial controls be maintained throughout the incident?
22. Are credit card accounts established for recovery team members who may be required to travel or to purchase supplies and equipment?
23. How are the financial records of the organization protected against loss or damage? This question is repeated for the legal function.

HUMAN RESOURCES

Depending on one's perspective, many business continuity managers concentrate on the technological aspects of continuity, but as disaster after disaster have shown, the real emphasis must be on the people that use the technology to accomplish the organization's goals. Many managers argue that without the people resources, the technology is meaningless. The human resources (HR) function plays an important part in business continuity management by supporting the workers before, potentially during, and after a disaster. Human resources may be the watchdog to detect the onset of a pandemic that affects the organization through the monitoring of spikes in absenteeism and sick leave.

1. Does HR (or any other department within the organization) have a current pandemic plan?
   a. Are employees informed of the contents and their responsibilities under the plan?
   b. Does the HR department or any other function within the organization monitor developing pandemics around the world?
   c. Does the HR department track and compare absenteeism on a timescale significant to identify trends that may indicate the need to implement a pandemic plan?

    d. Does the plan incorporate "trigger points" and thresholds for implementing different levels of response activities as described by the World Health Organization and the United States Centers for Disease Control and Prevention?

    e. Is there a policy and procedure to restrict travel (such as video conferencing or delayed travel) to areas of the country or world where communicable disease outbreaks are active?

    f. Are employees cross-trained to fill in for absent key workers?

    g. Can retired workers be recalled to fill in for absent workers?

    h. Have arrangements been made with temporary personnel firms to supply individuals to fill in for absent workers?

    i. Does the organization encourage or provide annual influenza vaccinations for employees?

    j. Have policies been established for employee compensation and sick-leave absences unique to a pandemic, including policies on when a previously ill person is no longer infectious and can return to work after illness? This may include extensions of family leave, vacation time, and employee assistance programs.

    k. Is telecommuting allowed and enabled by the IT function?

    l. Are flexible work hours allowed and possible?

    m. Are there clear policies concerning the restriction of workers who exhibit the signs of an illness (influenza), i.e., immediate mandatory sick leave?

    n. Are employees trained in the recognition, prevention, and steps to minimize the spread of a pandemic such as influenza?

    o. Are prevention and hygiene supplies such as alcohol-based hand sanitizers, tissues, and closed receptacles for their disposal available at convenient locations?

    p. Does the organization stockpile gloves and N-95 face masks (training and medical certification may be required for the use of the masks in the workplace)?

    q. Has the organization discussed the stockpiling and use of antiviral medications?

    r. What other pandemic preparedness measures have been established?

    s. How could the organization adapt its operations if social isolation is necessary?

2. Can the operations of the organization adversely affect the public?

    a. What plans does the organization have to warn and protect the public?

3. How does the company intend to communicate with employees after a disaster (common options include preestablished toll-free hotline or voice mailboxes located out of state, direct phone contact with each employee, phone trees, personal contact, e-mail, Web page, or even a note on the front door)?

4. Does the plan to communicate with employees include agreements with local radio stations to broadcast messages regarding the status of the organization, where to report for work, and other relevant messages?

5. How does the company intend to pay employees furloughed or temporarily out of work due to the disaster (pay all normal wages for the duration, use vacation time, no work–no pay)?

6. To what extent will the company compensate the temporary relocation of family members at an alternate location (i.e., if a worker has children or is the caretaker of an older adult, will the company pay to house and feed children or the adult at the alternate location)?

    a. What would be the financial impact of these decisions?

7. Do the employee assistance program providers maintain posttraumatic stress counselors or does the department maintain these counselors on call? Are there plans to increase the allowable or subsidized visits after a disaster? Are there plans to bring counselors on-site after a disaster or traumatic event?

8. Are there plans to establish on-site employee day care centers after a disaster or to change policy and allow children in the workplace?
9. Are there any plans to provide low interest loans or grants to employees affected by the disaster?
10. Does the HR team wish to contact or account for each employee after a disaster? How can this be accomplished, and what is needed to carry out this task? This is required under NFPA 1600:2013.
11. Does the HR department plan to maintain and publish a list of employees who need assistance and encourage furloughed employees to volunteer their assistance?
12. Does HR wish to maintain a list of prequalified home repair contractors to provide to employees? Have arrangements been made to offer discounts to company employees?
13. Has the department prequalified real estate agents and is it prepared to distribute this list to employees?
14. Is there a management succession plan, and, if so, where is it maintained?
15. Is there a mass casualty plan? During a serious regional disaster, the coroner's office may become overwhelmed and unable to pick up bodies in a timely manner. The organization may need to properly deal with the bodies of fellow employees.
16. What resources does the organization want to provide to the next of kin after a fatal injury (maximum amount of money to cover funeral or other expenses (specify))?
17. Are emergency supplies of food, water, and sanitary supplies maintained for employees who are required to remain at the facility or for employees who may be delayed getting home? Describe.
18. Is there a policy or decision process to close facilities when emergency conditions are imminent? Who has the authority?
19. What records or portions of employee files are considered vital or need to be copied and sorted off-site? How is this currently achieved? Are unachieved records stored in fire-resistant cabinets?
20. Is the HR database included on a network drive that is routinely backed up? Can this database be replicated to employee laptop computer systems?
21. Are there any agreements with temporary employment agencies to provide first choice of temporary staff if needed subsequent to a disaster?
22. Will the benefits function need to do anything different or special to serve the needs of employees after a disaster locally, regionally, or in another part of the world?
23. Have employees received training and resources on disaster preparedness in the home and office?
24. Are disaster kits (go-kits) encouraged or provided in the workplace?
25. What other services are now in place or contemplated for postdisaster services to employees?
26. What are the names, addresses, and phone numbers of the hospitals and medical clinics used? Include map and directions.
27. What taxi company or means of transportation is used to send injured employees to the hospital or clinic?
28. Does the organization have a strategy to provide temporary and long-term housing, feeding, and care of employees displaced by an incident as required by NFPA 1600:2013? This would apply only if planning under NFPA standards.

INFORMATION TECHNOLOGY

Most IT managers have a good command of the business continuity process and can provide a description of risks and mitigations designed into their systems and processes. Often the information the analyst needs is already established. Absent this information, the following questions are designed to establish an overview of data center risk. Depending on the size and complexity of the organization's needs, data centers typically involve hardware platforms (mainframe and server banks, and desktop systems), networking and infrastructure, support, and often telecommunications.

1. Does the IT department have a current disaster recovery plan in place?
2. Are agreements established with a hot site vendor?
3. If no hot site vendor, what strategies are implemented, planned, or desired to continue critical processes?
4. Describe systems and platforms:
5. What redundancies are built into the systems and the data center?
   a. Redundancies built into equipment such as dual power supplies?
   b. What are the RAID levels?
   c. Fail-over servers (same location or separate)?
6. Are there any other redundancies?
7. Are there other company locations that have data centers capable of accepting some or the entire load or have sufficient space and infrastructure to build out replacement servers? Describe.
8. Describe data center protections not included above. Consider:
   a. Are racks secured both on top and bottom?
   b. Are subfloors on seismically resistive pedestals?
   c. Is the HVAC system separate from the rest of the facility?
   d. Are critical systems connected to UPS?
   e. What types of power backups exist?
9. Describe data backup routines and policies:
   a. Daily incremental?
   b. Archived – monthly, quarterly, yearly?
   c. What technology used?
   d. What is the off-site storage schedule?
   e. Are operating systems also backed up and stored off-site?
   f. What user training and policies exist (i.e., are users encouraged to store C: information on the network drives)?
   g. Who is responsible for tracking inventory of off-site storage containers?
   h. What is the name and location of the off-site storage facility?
   i. What are their delivery capabilities and agreements?
   j. Are critical manuals and documents stored in the containers?
   k. What capacity exists for storage of documents?
10. Is equipment standardized?
11. Do any other departments maintain their own systems/servers? Describe.
12. What service level agreements exist?
13. Are there any quick ship agreements in place?

14. What data links are established to third parties, customers, and vendors, and how will these be recovered in a disaster?
15. Provide network diagram(s).
16. Are Web pages maintained internally?
17. Are RTOs established?
18. Are RPO's established?
19. Is the recovery of systems and processes prioritized?
20. How will access and security be addressed if required to connect remotely or to rebuild systems?
21. What security is built into cloud computing?

INSURANCE/RISK MANAGEMENT

The risk manager, who may be a member of the finance department, is an important partner to the business continuity manager. Often the business continuity function reports directly to risk management. This is an appropriate organizational placement since business continuity, like safety and security, is a subset of risk management.

1. Is the organization self-insured?
2. What is the organization's appetite for risk? What is its philosophy on risk?
3. What are the top three (or more) risks to the goals of the organization?
    a. How are these risks treated?
4. Are insurance policies written for actual cash value or replacement cost?
5. If not for replacement cost, what would be the approximate difference in current value versus replacement cost?
6. What gaps or exclusions in policies exist that could be significant to a claim to a hazard related to a disaster?
7. Have carriers provided instructions on claims requirements?
8. Who has the authority to negotiate and settle claims?
9. Are digital cameras available to document damage?
10. Is additional staffing required to consolidate claims and activity logs after the recovery period?
11. Are policies in place for business interruption and contingent business interruption?
    a. What do these policies cover and exclude?
12. What is the value of building contents for each location?
13. How are the organization's assets tracked and maintained?

INVESTOR RELATIONS

Also known as financial communications, investor relations is a function that communicates with the financial community and other interested parties and is responsible for maximizing the value of the organization's stock value. It also fields inquiries from shareholders and investors, as well as others who might be interested in the organization's stock or financial stability. Investor relations may be a subset of the finance department reporting to the CFO or treasurer and occasionally reporting to the public relations function.

1. How will investor relations communicate with the investment community to advise them of changes in the health of the organization after a disaster?
2. How will investor relations communicate with investors after a disaster if access to the main facilities is not available?

3. What is the regulatory impact if deadlines and filings are missed due to the disaster? How can this be mitigated?
4. What predictions can be made concerning the impact of a disaster on the value of the company?
5. How will the company post SEC information?

LEGAL

The legal department will usually oversee all legal and external affairs including litigation, investigations (independently or in conjunction with security), compliance, mergers and acquisitions, contracts, and international trade issues. The standards emphasize an understanding of the legal and regulatory obligations of the organization relative to business continuity, so this is a function that the manger must work with closely.

1. What contractual obligations legally bind the organization that could be affected by the effects of a disaster?
    a. What is the impact to the organization if these obligations are breached?
    b. What steps should the organization take to mitigate a breach of the obligations caused by a disaster?
2. What regulatory obligations affect the organization that could be impacted by a disaster (such as the inability to deliver services, loss of records, reduced quality, etc.)?
    a. Would any foreseeable environmental damage require reporting to an outside agency?
3. Are corporate records stored in fire resistant cabinets or copied at off-site locations (that can be easily reconstructed)?
4. Are force majeure clauses included in contracts and purchase orders or agreements to perform a service or deliver a product that could be delayed by a disaster?
5. Is litigation conducted in house or by outside firms? If outside, do they have continuity plans?
6. Is legal responsible for financial filings, and if so, how will they be affected if the site is destroyed or access denied?
7. How would a disaster affect legal's critical functions?
8. If relocating to alternate locations, what permits would need to be reestablished or modified?
9. How would cases in progress be handled if the facility was lost?
10. How are financial and other corporate records of the organization protected against loss or damage? This question is repeated for the finance functions.

MANUFACTURING

Lead times for the re-creation of a manufacturing capability can be extensive due to the need to replace facilities, equipment, and the re-creation of any unique environment necessary for the equipment to operate. In these cases, the prevention of damage to the facility and equipment is emphasized.

1. Describe the manufacturing process:
2. Describe the supply chain:
    a. How would an outage affect raw material inventories?
3. What sole source suppliers exist?
4. What other single point of failure exists?
5. Can out-of-area contract manufacturing be used?

6. Are any reciprocal agreements with competitors for space or produce executed?
7. How can critical process or production equipment be duplicated at an alternate site or another production line?
8. What are the lead times for the replacement of critical equipment, including the re-creation and any validation of its environment?
9. Can virtual manufacturing be used?
10. Where are inventories and raw materials located, and how are they protected?
11. What are the values of these inventories?
12. What percentage of capacity at other locations could be used?
13. Can shifts be expanded to make up backlog?
14. Does an inventory list of equipment exist?
15. How are manufacturing drawings and other documents protected?
16. Are there work-arounds if the link to order processing and production control is lost?
    a. Does this include prioritized orders or customers?
    b. How is inventory usage tracked if reverting to a manual system?
17. Are alternate shipping and distribution channels established?
18. What typically is the value of work in progress?
19. Can a competitor's product be temporarily rebranded until production is back in service?
20. What are the lead times to replace manufacturing equipment?
21. What are the lead times required to re-create the environment necessary for replaced manufacturing equipment?
22. Is manufacturing and support equipment inspected and secured against seismic or other damage from foreseeable risk?
23. Are fire prevention inspections conducted on a regular basis?
24. Will any permits or other regulatory compliance be necessary in a recovery or continuity situation?

PUBLIC RELATIONS

The public relations function is often part of the management or crisis management team.
1. What type of crisis situations could the company face? Examples include the loss or serious illness of a key employee, company fraud, labor dispute, product liability, etc.
2. Can the operations of the organization adversely affect the public? What plans does the organization have to warn and protect the public?
3. What are the indicators of an impending crisis if not obvious?
4. What items are available or already prepared to use in a media kit (company brochure and description, biographies, favorable news articles, awards, civil recognition, contributions, etc.)?
5. Are public statements prepared in advance?
    a. Are these also statements in HTML format for rapid publication?
6. Is a list of media and other crisis contacts prepared?
7. Has a spokesperson been chosen, and has this person received on-camera training?
8. Are employees instructed to not speak to the media? What sanctions exist if this instruction is not followed?

9. Is background footage about the company (b-roll) prepared and available for the media?
10. Is there a predetermined location designated and equipped for meeting with the media?
11. Is there a predetermined location designated for meeting with families of victims that is separate from the media?
12. Who is the public relations firm and what duties have been assigned to them (clipping services, etc.).
13. Is there a plan to tape-record any news conferences?
14. Is there a plan to set up additional switchboard capacity and staffing if an increase in communications traffic is anticipated?
15. Who is responsible (public relations, sales and marketing, or investor relations) for keeping stakeholders and customers informed about the progress of the organization's recovery? What avenues will be/can be used to accomplish this task?
16. Are copies of contact information and databases kept off-site?

PURCHASING/PROCUREMENT

The purchasing or procurement department buys all necessary materials needed for production or for the daily operation of the organization that might include raw materials, tools, machinery, and office supplies as needed. Purchasing also sources and oversees the vendors that supply the organization with the items it needs to operate properly. A purchasing department also is charged with continuously evaluating whether it is receiving these materials at the best possible price in order to maximize profitability. Purchasing processes the paperwork involved with ordering and delivery of supplies and materials and ensures the timely delivery of these materials. It tracks purchase orders and works in conjunction with the receiving and the accounts payable departments to ensure that deliveries are received in full and are paid for on time.

Before making a purchase, the purchasing department will ensure budget approval is obtained and purchasing policy is followed. Purchasing is another source of contractual obligations that may affect business continuity.

Recent emphasis has been given to the resilience of the supply chain due to the increasing dependence on worldwide trade and recent disruptions due to natural disasters and terrorist events. Purchasing may be the function, in conjunction with the business continuity manager, to monitor and manage these risks, but the manager must determine where supply chain management resides within the organization. Is it a separate designated entity, does it belong to procurement, or is it monitored and managed through operations or manufacturing?

Understand the concepts of supply chain risk management (SCRM) and the requirements of ISO PD 25222:2011 Guidance on supply chain continuity and the ANSI/ASIS SCRM.1-2014 Supply Chain Risk Management: A Compilation of Best Practices. Explore the need to directly interview sole source suppliers or suppliers who are perceived to possess exceptional risk to their ability to deliver supplies, services, or products.

1. What contractual obligations legally bind the organization that could be affected by the effects of a disaster?
   a. What is the impact to the organization if these obligations are breached?
   b. What steps should the organization take to mitigate a breach of the obligations caused by a disaster?

2. To what extent have critical suppliers and their supply chains, sole source suppliers, suppliers of just-in-time materials, been identified?
    a. Are supply chains mapped, including each tiered supplier, their location, and hazards associated with each one?
    b. What steps have they taken to ensure resilience?
    c. Are their business continuity management programs certified under ISO 22301, ASIS, NFPA, or a regional standard?
    Note: When auditing the continuity plans of suppliers and their downstream supply chains, include in the audit an evaluation of their ability to satisfy your organization's needs and objectives (your recovery time objectives), not simply their ability to recover their operations. Check that their management system addresses the elements of emergency management, has demonstrated management support, focuses on continuity and less on recovery as appropriate, is a mature program, and is appropriately tested.
    d. Has the organization physically audited the operations of critical suppliers and their supply chains?
       - What risks have they not identified or resolved?
       - Do they or their downstream suppliers use practices that are not in line with the ethical values of the organization that pose a public relations risk? Examples include the use of nonsustainable products, sweat shops, child labor, and high injury rates.
    e. Sole source suppliers?
    f. What is the level of prioritized service provided to your organization?
    g. What is the physical proximity of the supplier to your production location, i.e., will a regional disaster disrupt both your operations and those of the supplier?
    h. How easily can the supplier divert shipment to an alternate location?
    i. What redundancies do they employ in their ability to deliver their products?
    j. What is your inventory tolerance, i.e., how long will inventory last before the next shipment arrives?
    k. What is the turnaround time to qualify alternate suppliers?
       - Will they need any regulatory approval such as from the Federal Drug Administration?
       - Is product testing required?
    l. What systems are in place to monitor the health of the suppliers and the supply chain?
    m. To what extent is direct communication maintained with suppliers?
3. Are the requirements of the organization's business continuity needs written into purchase agreements and contracts?
4. Are force majeure clauses included in supply contracts?
5. Does purchasing maintain service-level agreements with major suppliers?
6. Are credit cards or accounts established for selected business continuity leaders for the emergency purchase of goods and services after the disaster?
    a. What are the limits?
    b. Is a use policy established and communicated?
7. Does purchasing or accounting maintain sufficient petty cash to make necessary purchases after a disaster?
8. Have arrangements been made with out-of-the-region services such as building maintenance and repair (construction) if local services are not available after a regional disaster?

9. What methods should be used to request the purchase of equipment, materials, and supplies if data systems are not available?

10. Are there any special needs for purchasing to function from an alternate location?

SALES AND MARKETING

Sales and marketing is a key source for financial impact information. Marketing brings in the customer; the sales staff closes the deal and manages the account. Depending on the size of the organization, these functions may be combined or separate and may be responsible for the organization's brand identification, often considered to be the most valuable asset the organization may own. Customers and interested parties, especially if they depend upon the organization's services, may make decisions detrimental to the organization if not kept informed about the health of the organization after a disaster. Many continuity plans call for the sales force to contact their customers directly after a disaster and indirectly through media information, Web page updates, or voice mail messages. Even if not directly affected by a disaster, it may be good advice to initiate this process because, for example, after a large earthquake in the Los Angeles area of California, customers believed a firm in San Francisco was affected by the earthquake. Due to California's geology, San Francisco, 525 miles north of Los Angeles, would not be directly impacted by such an event.

1. How many customers do you currently have for your products or services?
2. Are there other sources for your products or services?
3. How many of these customers would seek an alternate source for your products or services?
4. What would be the average length of time your customers would wait before seeking an alternate source?
5. How many of the customers going to an alternate source would return to your products and services after you are back in business?
6. In a disaster situation, would your function have the responsibility to notify customers directly of the status of the company and their orders?
   a. How would customers be prioritized for notification?
   b. Is there an out-of-the-area sales office that could make these notifications?
7. How are orders received?
8. What data systems and processes (applications) receive new orders from sales? Are there any manual work-arounds?
9. Is there a possibility that orders could be lost if the facilities or data systems are destroyed? How can these be re-created?
10. Does the department maintain written sales agreements or contracts, and what is the impact of their loss?
    a. Can they be reliably created?
    b. Are they stored on-site in fire-resistant cabinets?
    c. If critical, are they duplicated and stored off-site?
11. List sales volume and income for each product:
12. What would you need to spend in advertising to repair company reputation if an outage or failure to deliver services occurred? If diminished due to a public relations disaster?

SECURITY

Security or protective services are typically found in larger organizations staffed with a professional security manager or director who may also be responsible for safety, emergency response, and business continuity management. Smaller organizations may utilize the services of a contracted security force, often without the presence of a security professional. Where a security department is not part of the organizational structure, any access control devices or other security hardware and equipment may be the responsibility of the facilities of IT departments. Where necessary, the services of a security consultant may be to the organization's advantage.

1. Has the security function completed an analysis of the supply chain that identifies criminal and physical risk that could affect the organization's service levels?
   a. If security has completed an analysis of the supply chain, have they offered recommendations to treat the risk?
2. Are databases and operating systems for access control systems backed up and stored off-site?
3. Are agreements in place with security equipment vendors to provide 24-hour replacement of equipment?
4. Are agreements in place with contract security guard firms to provide additional staffing?
5. Do they have the capability to provide emergency staffing?
6. Is equipment available on-site to provide emergency lighting during a sustained power failure?
7. Are critical systems included on any backup power generators?
8. Are critical systems connected to uninterruptible power supplies?
9. Is there an on-site 24/7 security central control station, and what information can the station provide to assist with site damage assessment, salvage, and information about the nature of the disaster?
10. Is there a plan or need to prioritize security coverage for on-site and local off-site facilities?
11. Are security communications systems and radios capable of utilizing off-the-shelf nonrechargeable batteries?
12. Do security stations maintain first aid kits that contain supplies more appropriate for postdisaster injuries?
13. Is security responsible for emergency response, and, if so, are the teams and security staff trained and organized under the incident command system?

TELECOMMUNICATIONS

Virtually every organization is dependent on voice and data communications. The business continuity manager will look at the risk to these systems and the impact of their loss.

1. Describe the telecommunications system and phone switch.
2. What redundancies are built into the switch?
3. What is the backup schedule?
   a. Are backups stored off-site?
   b. Are system configurations included in the backup?
   c. Is the operating system included in the backup?
4. Are there any service-level agreements? Describe.
5. Describe the system topography and routing.

6. Is there a dual entrance into the building? i.e., do phone lines enter the building from divergent sides?
7. Is there a "power fail" bypass to the switch, and are there analog phones available?
8. What toll-free numbers exist, and are there plans to transfer these numbers to other locations?
9. What environmental controls are required/in place for the switch?
10. Where is the main distribution frame (MDF) located?
11. Is the MDF located in a secured, limited access room?
12. Is the switch connected to backup power?
13. What circuit protection is provided?
14. What analog lines are available?
15. What diversity or redundancy is built into communication routes?
16. What forms of communication are available for information processing and telecommunication (video feeds, news media, monitoring of governmental communications, satellite phones, redundant cellular carriers, amateur radio, social media, etc.)?

Appendix E: Sample Continuity Team Resource Tool Kit

See Chapter 5

Often included in the Business Impact Analysis (BIA) tool kit/questionnaire are instructions to the functional managers to begin the process of scripting continuity instructions for their teams that are designed to implement their continuity strategies. Included in this process is the collection of resource information necessary to implement the strategies. Resource information includes people (team member and vendor contact information), the equipment the team will need at an alternate location (or to be replaced) to be productive, software that supports the operations of the function, forms and supplies they will need to use, and vital records that the function needs to operate or to maintain for regulatory compliance. This information is later included in the Business Continuity Team Plan.

Although this information does not need to be part of the BIA, many managers include it as part of the analysis because information useful for the development of the continuity plans has value to the BIA. An understanding of the number of team members required in the initial days after the disaster will tell the manager what level of staffing at a hot site or other alternate work site is necessary so they may predict the costs and make contractual agreements for sufficient space and workstations. It also allows them to estimate the costs to house and support relocated personal and potentially members of their families.

The BIA and the collection of resource information can be accomplished with business continuity software or Excel spreadsheets that can be distributed as the tool kit mentioned above. Although many different ways are available to collect the information using a spreadsheet, placing the resource categories in separate workbooks with the corresponding instructions (see below) included in each cell as a "note" provides a simple and effective way to collect resource information. At a minimum, include the following:

INSTRUCTIONS

The first (opening) workbook should contain instructions to the user on how to navigate from one workbook to another, explain the purpose of the tool kit, and what is expected by its completion. A simple instruction may include:

Use this Excel spreadsheet with its associated workbooks to enter data that we will use to craft your team's business continuity plan. These workbooks contain cells to record your mission and goals; list very detailed instructions to your team members to implement your goals and recovery strategies and to enter resource requirements that you may need to carry out your team's goals and strategies.

TEAM INFORMATION

This table asks for basic information about your team, its leaders, and what you see as its mission and objectives.

Question:	Answer:
Team name:	Note: Expand the size of this column to accommodate answers.
Team leader:	
1st Alternate team leader:	
2nd Alternate team leader:	
Describe the purpose (objectives) of your team:	
If your main (current) facility is damaged, where can your team meet to continue its operations and/or support the other teams?	
Are there any other comments or information that you wish to include as an introduction to your team plan? please list:	

INSTRUCTIONS

Team Name: Please list the name of your team, "Disaster Assessment Team," or "Human Resources Team," for example.

Team Leader: Who is the team leader? Be sure to also list this person in the Team Employees list. If your team has a number of subteams, please include these leaders also, that is, Team #1 leader: Gene Tucker; Team #2 leader: Suzie Noble; and so on.

1st and 2nd Alternate Team Leader: Who is the alternate or backup team leader? Remember to list the Team Employees.

Describe the purpose (objectives) of your team: What is your team supposed to do during a recovery or pandemic situation? A brief example may be: The purpose of the Stores Team is to quickly recovery its operations to a level sufficient to support material and supplies needs of the other recovery teams while transitioning to full internal recovery either at the present location or at an alternate location.

Alternate location: Where should your team meet to begin recovery operations? If the building you normally occupy is 'red tagged,' where will your base of operations (temporary or permanent) be? Other comments to include as an introduction to the team plan? There are four major parts to your team plan:

1. An introduction/overview that briefly discusses the purpose and objectives of your team's duties and outlines from a high level your recovery strategies, alternate operating locations, and who is the team leader and alternate;
2. Team member list and contact information;
3. Detailed instructions to your team (Team Task Instructions) that they will use to implement the strategies and carry out the purpose and objectives.
4. Resource requirements.

   You may place in this section any additional information you wish to convey in the introduction/overview.

TEAM EMPLOYEES

This table asks you to list your team members with as much contact information as you can obtain. Home address and home phone numbers are important.

Employee Number	First Name	Last Name	Title or Position	Address #1	Address #2	City	State	Zip Code	Home Telephone	Work Telephone	Cellular Telephone	Alternate Telephone	Company email	Home email	Priority	Called By:

Team Employees

The individual columns in the spreadsheet's workbook for Team Employees should be labeled as:

- First Name
- Last Name
- Title or Position
- Address #1
- Address #2
- City
- State
- Zip Code
- Home Phone
- Work Phone
- Cellular Phone
- Alternate Phone
- Company email
- Home email
- Priority
- Called by

INSTRUCTIONS

First Name: List the first names of employees assigned to your team. Avoid capitalization of the entire name, that is, we prefer "Joe Q. Employee", not "JOE Q. EMPLOYEE." List only the First Name in this column, not the entire name so that the list can be better sorted if necessary.

Last Name: List the last names of employees assigned to your team. Avoid capitalization of the entire name, that is, we prefer "Joe Q. Employee", not "JOE Q. EMPLOYEE." List only the Last Name in this column, not the entire name.

Title or Position: Indicate the team member's title or duties within the team. For example: Team Leader, Alternate Team Leader, Carpenter, Support, and so on, are acceptable. The title may be different from the team member's normal working title.

Address #1: List the team member's home address or the address of where they normally stay. The addresses may be used in a variety of ways such as direct contact post disaster to see if they are OK, Zip Code sorts to pinpoint workers who may be most impacted by the disaster (and then to give team leaders an idea of when they can or cannot be expected if communications are impossible) . This information, as with the telephone numbers, is confidential. Only individual team members or team leaders are provided with this information. Although you may feel like you live at work, don't enter the organization's address.

Address #2: List clarifiers or other pertinent address information, if applicable. This information, as with the telephone numbers, is confidential.

City: Indicate the city where the address is located.

State: If the person resides outside of the State, reconsider their need to be on the team.

Zip Code: Enter five digit Zip Code.

Home Phone: List the team member's home (or where they are usually found) phone number. Use the format: 510-555-1212.

Work Phone: List the team member's desktop phone number using the format: 510-555-1212.

Cellular Phone: List the team member's cellular phone number using the format: 510-555-1212.

Alternate Phone: List any additional phone numbers in the format: 510-555-1212. Leave blank if none.

Company email: List your work email address.

Home email: List the team member's home email address or the address where they usually stay.

Priority: Identify at what point during the recovery process the individual is required according to the following (generally, not all staff are necessary during the initial recovery phase; space and resources may be limited): 1=Required within the first 24 hours, that is, an essential person or continuity; 2=required 24–72 hours; 3=required 3–5 days; 4=remain on standby until advised. You may also reference the "Response, Stabilization, Initial Recovery, Partial Normalization, or Full Recovery" Phases.

Called by: If you are setting up call trees, indicate who calls the team member. Use Last Name only. A call tree is an arrangement where one person will call a small group of team members with a message, and then those persons will contact other team members and pass on the message, until finally all relevant members of the team have been notified.

VENDOR/SUPPLIER CONTACT LIST

This workbook asks you to list your outside contacts (and can include internal contacts) such as vendors and suppliers that you will need to support your recovery operations.

Vendor Number	Vendor Name	Address #1	Address #2	City	State	Zip Code	Telephone	Corporate Telephone	Fax Number	email	Name of Representative	Representative Telephone	Describe Product or Service	Account or PO Number	Passwords or other Information

Vendor

The individual columns in the spreadsheet workbook for the Vendor/Supplier Contact List should be labeled as:

- Vendor Name
- Address #1
- Address #2
- City
- State
- Zip Code
- Telephone
- Corporate Phone
- Fax Number
- Email
- Name of Representative

- Representative Phone
- Describe Services or Product
- Account or Purchase Order (PO) Number
- Passwords or Other Information

INSTRUCTIONS

Vendor Name: What is the company name of the vendor? If this is an internal contact, list the name of the person or the person's department.

Address #1: What is the street address of the local vendor? Use the corporate address if not local.

Address #2: Enter additional address as appropriate.

City: City where the address/business is located.

State: Enter the two letter State designation, "CA" for example.

Zip Code: Five digit Zip Code.

Telephone: Contact's local phone number in format: 510-555-1212.

Corporate Phone: If there is an alternate or out-of-state phone number such as for their corporate offices, include here in the format 800-555-1212.

Fax Number: (Do people still use fax machines?) Same thing: 800-555-1212.

Email: Enter either local, corporate, or home email of the vendor or contact.

Name of Representative: Or the name of the contact. Who is it that you normally deal with from this organization, service, or department?

Representative Phone: List this person's local, home, or cellular phone number.

Describe Services or Product: One- or two-word description of what service or product this person or company provides.

Account or PO Number: List any account or Purchase Order numbers associated with this vendor. Remember that this information may have been destroyed during the incident so it will be useful to list the numbers in the plan.

Passwords or Other Information: List any necessary passwords or other account identification information. Again, this information may be destroyed during the event. Also, remember that the distribution of this team plan is restricted to only your team members and Business Continuity Management Staff.

EQUIPMENT REQUIREMENTS

This section will ask you to list equipment that you will need in both the short term (less than five days) and long term (greater than five days) after a disaster for your team to use to accomplish their recovery strategies. In this case, it is not used to list all equipment that must be replaced to bring the function back to full service (we may ask this later).

Description of Equipment	Type or Model #	Quantity < 5 days	Quantity > 5 days	Equipment Source

Equipment

The individual columns in the spreadsheet workbook for Equipment Requirements should be labeled as:

- Description of Equipment
- Type or Model #
- Quantity <5 days
- Quantity >5 days
- Equipment Source

INSTRUCTIONS

Description of Equipment: Please, as briefly as possible, list each piece of equipment in this column (you will have the opportunity to specify quantities in other columns). This may include, but not be limited to: Personal computers (PCs) (if possible state configuration or hardware requirements), printers, fax machines, calculators, phones, modems, chain saws, jacks, monitoring equipment, and so on.

Type or Model #: You may further define the piece of equipment.

Quantity <5 days: How many of these do you need in the first 1–5 days following the event? In general, this equipment is purchased ahead of time and stored in a secure, survivable location for immediate use.

Quantity >5 days: How many of these do you need after the 5 days following the event? In general, this equipment is purchased after the event. Be sure lead times are appropriate.

Equipment Source: Where is this equipment stored (short term) or where can it be purchased (contact information included in Vendor section)?

FORMS AND SUPPLIES

List Forms and Supplies your team will need to implement its recovery strategies. Do not include items like paper and pencils. Copies or templates of special forms may be attached and included as an appendix to your plan.

Supply Description	Quantity < 5 days	Quantity > 5 days	Supply Source

Supply

The individual columns in the spreadsheet workbook for Forms and Supplies should be labeled as:

- Supply Description
- Quantity <5 days
- Quantity >5 days
- Supply Source

INSTRUCTIONS

Supply Description: List the forms and the supplies required.

Quantity <5 days: How many of these do you need in the first 1–5 days following the event? In general, this equipment is purchased ahead of time and stored in a secure, survivable location for immediate use.

Quantity >5 days: How many of these do you need after the 5 days following the event? In general, this equipment is purchased after the event. Be sure lead times are appropriate.

Supply Source: Where is this equipment stored (short term) or where can it be purchased (contact information included in Vendor section)?

SOFTWARE REQUIREMENTS

Software Requirements: List any software that may be needed to implement your recovery strategies.

Software Requirements	Platform or Device	Licenses	Location	Passwords

Software

The individual columns in the spreadsheet workbook for Software Requirements should be labeled as:

- Software Requirements
- Platform or Device
- Licenses
- Location
- Passwords

INSTRUCTIONS

Software Requirements: List the name of the software that must be reinstalled, that is, the software or data processes you will require at an alternate site, new location, or re-built location.

Platform or Device: What equipment is this to be loaded on? Be sure to include this in the equipment section.

Licenses: How many licenses or "seats" (users) are required?

Location: Where are backup or downloadable copies of the install sets found?

Passwords: List user IDs and passwords.

VITAL RECORDS

List in this section the vital records your team will need to implement its strategies. Vital records should always be backed up and stored at an offsite location, but electronic copies may be stored in a manner for immediate retrieval. Examples of vital records may include inventories, as-built drawings, damage assessment forms, and so on.

Vital Records	Internal Storage	External Storage	Additional Information

The individual columns in the spreadsheet workbook for Vital Records should be labeled as:
- Vital Records
- Internal Storage
- External Storage
- Additional Information

INSTRUCTIONS

Vital Records: List the records the team will need or will need to protect.
Internal Storage: Where are these records normally found within the organization?
External Storage: Where are copies (backup) or these records stored or found off site?
Additional Information: Include any additional information about the record such as an archival record number, and so on.

TEAM TASK INSTRUCTIONS

List the detailed instructions to your team members to carry out the recovery strategies, responsibilities, and duties. Begin with "action" words. The instructions should be detailed, but brief. Don't include the entire text of an operation manual, but include enough that someone loosely familiar with your operation can execute the tasks. The instructions should be sequential in time, but you may group sub-instructions together, that is, Stabilization Phase, Initial Recovery Phase, Pandemic, and so on, or by task and subtask. To the greatest extent possible, make as many decisions ahead of time as possible, keeping in mind that the team leaders may modify these instructions at the time of the disaster. This is an important part of the planning process so give it a good deal of thought. Also remember that at the time of a disaster, routine tasks are often forgotten and decisions difficult to make.

In the spreadsheet, this can simple be a column number and then a task column.

Task#	Instruction
1	
2	
3	
...	
30	

Appendix F: Websites That Contain Hazard Information

See Chapter 6

The following Web pages serve as examples of where the manager can find hazard information specific to their organization's location. Many states have a Department of Geology whose Web pages contain information about the location of active faults, recurrence rates, and expected maximum magnitudes or shaking intensity of earthquakes. The National Weather Service, the Federal Emergency Management Agency (FEMA), as well as state and local emergency management agencies are also good sources of searchable hazard information. This list is by no means exhaustive.

EARTHQUAKE AND LIQUEFACTION HAZARDS

- Advanced National Seismic System (ANSS): http://earthquake.usgs.gov/monitoring/anss/
- Association of Bay Area Governments (San Francisco Bay Area): http://quake.abag.ca.gov/earthquakes/
- California Department of Conservation: http://www.consrv.ca.gov/CGS/rghm/psha/Pages/Index.aspx
- Central United States Earthquake Consortium: http://www.cusec.org/
- Earthquake Hazard Mapping of Greater Victoria: http://www.empr.gov.bc.ca/Mining/Geoscience/SurficialGeologyandHazards/VictoriaEarthquakeMaps/Pages/default.aspx.
- FEMA Earthquake Hazard Mapping: http://www.fema.gov/earthquake/earthquake-hazard-maps
- Idaho Department of Geology: http://www.idahogeology.org/webmap/
- California localized hazard maps for earthquake, flood, fire, and tsunami in California: http://myhazards.calema.ca.gov/ and http://myplan.calema.ca.gov/
- Missouri Department of Natural Resources: http://www.dnr.mo.gov/geology/geosrv/geores/eqmaps.htm
- Natural Resources Canada: http://www.earthquakescanada.nrcan.gc.ca/hazard/index-eng.php
- NEHRP – National Earthquake Hazards Reduction Program: http://www.nehrp.gov/
- Oregon Department of Geology and Mineral Industries: http://www.oregongeology.org/sub/earthquakes/EQs.htm and http://www.oregon.gov/dogami/pages/earthquakes/eqs.aspx
- Pacific Northwest Seismic Network. Includes hazard mapping for urban seismic hazards, landslides, tsunami, volcano hazards, flood plain, and liquefaction hazards: http://www.pnsn.org/outreach/earthquakehazards
- Ready.gov: http://www.ready.gov/
- Southern California Earthquake Center (SCEC): http://www.scec.org/
- United States Geological Survey: http://earthquake.usgs.gov/

FLOODING AND DAM INUNDATION

- Federal Emergency Management Agency flood hazard mapping site: http://www.fema.gov/national-flood-insurance-program-flood-hazard-mapping
- Interactive flood and dam inundation mapping for the San Francisco Bay Area with links to California flood mapping: http://quake.abag.ca.gov/floods/

- Localized hazard maps for earthquake, flood, fire, and tsunami in California: http://myhazards. calema.ca.gov/ and http://myplan.calema.ca.gov/
- Sea level rise and coastal flooding impacts in San Francisco Bay Area: http://quake.abag.ca.gov/ climate_change/

LANDSLIDES

- Association of Bay Area Governments Landslide Hazard Mapping (San Francisco Bay Area): http://quake.abag.ca.gov/landslides/
- Pacific Northwest Seismic Network: http://www.pnsn.org/outreach/earthquakehazards/eq-hazard-maps/landslide-hml
- USGS landslide hazard map: http://landslides.usgs.gov/hazards/nationalmap/

SEVERE WEATHER

- County-level lightning hazard data for the United States, for 1995–2000 and 2001–2009: http://maps.google.com/gallery/details?id=z4f-ZuCLmiKg.k5QgnA8lQKYM&hl=en
- Current Weather Hazards United States: www.wrh.noaa.gov
- Localized hazard maps for earthquake, flood, fire, and tsunami in California: http://myhazards.calema.ca.gov/and http://myplan.calema.ca.gov/
- Space Weather Prediction Center (Geomagnetic Storms): www.swpc.noaa.gov/NOAAscales
- The Tornado Project (lists locations of past tornados in the United States and worldwide): www.tornadoproject.com
- United States Weather Service Storm Prediction Center: www.spc.noaa.gov

TSUNAMI

- National tsunami hazard exposure mapping: http://nws.weather.gov/nthmp/NTHMP_Web_Resources.html
- Pacific Northwest Seismic Network Tsunami maps: http://www.dnr.wa.gov/Publications/ger_tsunami_inundation_maps.pdf
- Tsunami Risk San Francisco Bay Area: http://quake.abag.ca.gov/tsunamis/

WILDFIRE

- California Fire Hazard Severity Zone Map Update Project: http://www.fire.ca.gov/fire_prevention/fhsz_maps_contracosta.php
- Localized hazard maps for earthquake, flood, fire, and tsunami in California: http://myhazards.calema.ca.gov/ and http://myplan.calema.ca.gov/
- Wildland–Urban Interface Fire Threat maps in the San Francisco Bay Area: http://quake.abag.ca.gov/wildfires/
- Wildland Fire Assessment System: http://www.wfas.net/
- National Significant Wildland Fire Potential Outlook: http://www.predictiveservices.nifc.gov/outlooks/outlooks.htm

Appendix G: Examples of Natural, Technological, and Man-made Hazards

See Chapter 6

NATURAL HAZARDS

Animal Attacks
Avalanche
Blizzard
Dam Inundation
Drought
Earthquake
Flash Flood
Flood, Regional
Geomagnetic storm (solar flare)
Ground Burst
Hailstorm
Heat Wave
Hurricane/Typhoon
Ice Jams
Ice Storm
Insect Swarms
Landslide/Mudslide
Liquefaction
Limnic Eruption (rare)
Mold Growth
Pandemic
Rockfalls
Sandstorm
Severe Lightning
Sinkholes
Snowstorm
Storm Surge
Subsidence
Temperature Extremes
Tornado
Tsunami
Volcanic Eruption
Wildfire
Windstorm

TECHNOLOGICAL HAZARDS

Building/Structure Collapse
Carrier Cable Cuts
Equipment Failures
Explosion
Fire
Flood, Internal
Fuel Shortage
Generator Failure
Hazardous Waste Sites
Hazmat Exposure, Internal
Hazmat release from surrounding area (industry, transportation)
HVAC Failure
Information Systems Failure
Internal Electrical Problem
LAN/WAN Communication Failure
Loss of Electrical Utilities
Loss of Vital Records
Natural Gas Failure
Nonstructural Damage
Other Facilities Exposures
Radiological
Raw Material Shortage
Sewage Intrusion
Structural Damage
Supply Shortage
Transportation Accident
Transportation Disruption
Water Delivery Failure/Contamination

HUMAN CAUSED HAZARDS

Absenteeism Due to Disaster or Pandemic
Arson and Criminal Actions
Bomb Threat
Communications Failure
Community Action Groups
Death of Key Employee
Denial of Service Attack
Denied Access to Facilities
Economic Instability
Electromagnetic Pulse (EMP)

Embezzlement/Theft
Executive Kidnapping
Flood Water Contamination
Food-borne Illnesses
Hazardous Materials
Hostage Situation
Human Error/Procedural Problems
Human Stampedes
Labor Action
Legal and Regulatory Issues
Loss of Proprietary Information
Pandemic/Epidemic
Pipeline Failure
Political Instability
Product Liability
Riots/Civil Disturbance
Sabotage/Vandalism
Terrorism
Uncontained Biological Research
War/Insurrection
Workplace Violence

Appendix H: Excerpt from Risk Assessment Report—Hazards

See Chapter 6

The following is an excerpt from the hazards section of a risk assessment report for a new company location that gives the reader an example of how the risks may be described in the report. This is not the only format the analyst may use. The recommendations to treat the identified risks were included in a separate section of this sample report.

TORRANCE, CALIFORNIA, LOCATION

Three types of natural hazards can directly affect the Torrance site to the extent that a Federal emergency could be declared. Earthquakes are recognized as the greatest hazard in the immediate area, but although a 100-year storm could cause significant flooding and related damage, the rupture of the Walteria and Ben Haggott Reservoirs could cause significant property loss and fatalities if they should break. Hazardous materials releases from the nearby refinery have affected the site in the past and have the potential to affect operations and the safety of workers and guests in the future.

FLOODING

Rainfall in the area averages 14.8 in per year with a large percentage of this amount produced during sporadic and often heavy storms. There are no major rivers or streams in the immediate area. The Dominguez Channel, a storm control viaduct, is located about one-half mile to the northeast of the site, and portions pass through soil subject to liquefaction during a significant earthquake. The site is not located in a flood zone but is located just outside the flood inundation area described above.

HAZARDOUS MATERIALS

Many fuel and oil pipelines crisscross the city and border the facility that could rupture during an earthquake. This includes hydrogen gas and petroleum pipelines that are buried at the exterior of the site along 130th Avenue.

A major company oil refinery is located at Van Ness and 190th, approximately 1.4 miles to the west. In the past, the facility has been affected by releases of material from the refinery. Risks have included the instantaneous release of 700,000 pounds of liquefied petroleum gas (LPG) from a storage sphere and 50,000 pounds LPG within 10 min from a railcar explosion. The facility also uses chlorine gas that could potentially cause a toxic plume for 1.3 miles within 5 min by their estimate if the entire 2000-pound supply is released. Larger quantities of modified hydrogen fluoride can be released over a 3.2 mile radius within 10 min. Other toxic chemicals that could affect the Torrance facility include:

Butane	1.8-mile modeled plume
Hydrogen sulfide	0.9-mile modeled plume
Anhydrous ammonia	0.9-mile modeled plume

The city of Torrance alerts the public in close proximity to the major company refinery of a chemical release and the need to shelter in place through warning signs, a Community Alert Network (CAN— an out-of-state telephone system with the capability to alert citizens of an emergency), Radio Alert Network (a city-activated radio system within certain public and private facilities), and through its CitiSOUNDS AM 1620 radio system. The Torrance Amateur Radio Association maintains communication links to the Torrance Emergency Operations Center.

A number of rail lines pass near the site, and the facility is located near the intersection of Interstates 405 and 110 that carry hazardous materials. Based on the hazardous materials miles and historical information, the risk from an accident is low to moderate. This level of risk is sufficient enough to warrant emergency planning that considers these events.

LANDSLIDES

Landslides have occurred in the western portion of the city but should not directly affect the proposed company facility (indirect effects such as reduced access to the site from the west, and damage to infrastructure or the release of toxic materials could affect the wider area).

SEISMIC RISK

The 1988 Uniform Building Code shows this area of Los Angeles County in seismic risk zone 4, on a scale of 0–4, with 4 as the highest risk. Accelerations (velocity) from earthquakes in the area near the site are estimated between 40% and 50% gravity but could be greater with large events and differences in local soil conditions (see appendix of report). Soil composition in this area (Dublin clay and Ramona loam) tends to transmit or amplify seismic forces more easily than surrounding areas, especially near unstable bay and river areas where sand and silt can cause liquefaction or soil failure (see appendix of report). The site is located outside, but very close to, an historic liquefaction zone.

A number of major strike-slip and blind thrust faults are located in the area that can cause catastrophic damage. Identified faults include the San Andreas, Newport–Inglewood, Palos Verdes, Whittier, and Santa Monica.

The largest recent recorded earthquakes occurred in 1857 at Fort Tejon (magnitude 7.9), 1872 in Owens Valley (magnitude 7.6), Kern County in 1952 (magnitude 7.3), and Landers in 1992 (magnitude 7.3). Earthquakes of lesser magnitude (1971 San Fernando, 1992 Big Bear, 1994 Northridge, and 1999 Hector Mine) have also occurred in more recent times, causing widespread severe damage and loss of life. In 1945, a 4.8 Richter magnitude earthquake struck approximately 5 miles from the site causing damage in the city that included the surrounding refineries. The closest earthquake occurred in 1990 two miles to the northeast and measured a magnitude of 3.3.

The probability of a major earthquake in the region within the next 30 years is 85%.

Fault System	Distance	Expected Magnitude	CRI*
San Andreas	100 miles	7.4	220 years
Newport–Inglewood	5 miles	6.9–7.4	651 years
Palos Verdes	3 miles	6.0–7.1	650 years

Characteristic return interval.

Most public buildings and critical infrastructure including roadways and bridges in the immediate area are subject to significant damage from a major earthquake. Although most state-owned overpasses have been strengthened, many county-owned overpasses and bridges have not.

The company has contracted with an earthquake engineering firm to study the seismic performance of the facility under various seismic forces. Their report was not yet available for inclusion in this report.

TSUNAMI

The danger from a tsunami is minimal, due to its inland location and the 50- to 100-ft-high natural cliffs along the shoreline.

WILDLAND FIRES

The facility is located in an urban area and is not subject to the risk of wildland fire.

WINDSTORMS

There has been no major windstorm damage in the area since 1970, and building codes in effect during the construction of the facility are stringent enough to mitigate potential windstorm damage. The site is located about 100 miles west of the mountains that generate "Santa Ana"-type winds that diminish when approaching the coastal waters. There is no indication of significant windstorm or wind damage in the official or historical records except for anecdotal stories from the 1970s. The south coastal region of California, including the Los Angeles Basin, has the greatest incidence of tornadoes in the state. The cause of many, if not most, of the Los Angeles Basin tornadoes seems to be linked to the terrain layout of the basin, specifically the natural curvature of the shoreline and the location of the coastal mountains. Tornadoes in the Los Angeles Basin are typically less severe than those in other parts of the country. Since 1950, there have been 32 tornados in Los Angeles, ranging in intensity from F0 to F2 (Fujita scale) that mostly occurred in the months of November–March (atypical of the rest of the country).

OTHER

The greatest risk from a volcanic eruption is from the Mono–Inyo Craters on the eastern side of the Sierra-Nevada range. Volcanoes in this area erupt once every 200 years. Due to the expected advanced warning and average favorable wind conditions, the risk from such an eruption is low. The next closest volcano (the Long Valley Caldera, south of Mono Lake) erupts only once every 10,000 years.

The cities of Torrance and Los Angeles are equipped to respond to multiple high-technology and natural disasters and have had extensive training and experience in dealing with these issues. As mandated by law, the cities utilize the Incident Command System, the National Incident Management System, and participate in the Emergency Management Mutual Aid agreement.

Appendix I: Full Scale Exercise Example

SunRise Corporation
Annual Full Scale Exercise 2014
Exercise Plan
"Bad Day"

Prepared by:
_____   _____
Suzie Que, Exercise Director   Date

Reviewed by:
_____   _____
John Smity, BCMS Manager   Date

Approved by:
_____   _____
John Do, Chief Executive Officer   Date

Revision Summary		
Issue	**Section**	**Change**
01	All	Initial plan
02	Some	Draft plan
03	All	Final plan

TABLE OF CONTENTS

INTRODUCTION

The Sunrise Corporation (Sunrise) annual exercise is conducted by the Business Continuity Department. This exercise plan (ExPlan) was produced with input, advice, and assistance from the exercise planning team, as well as subject matter experts. The team followed the guidance set forth in the Federal Emergency Management Agency (FEMA), Homeland Security Exercise and Evaluation Program (HSEEP) guides.

The ExPlan gives officials, observers, media personnel, and players from participating organizations the information necessary to observe or participate in an exercise focusing on emergency response plans, policies, and procedures for emergency response. The information in this document is current as of the publication date, July 4, 2014, and is subject to change as dictated by the exercise planning team.

The Annual Full-scale Exercise is an *unclassified exercise*. The control of information is based on public sensitivity regarding the nature of the exercise. Some exercise material is intended for the exclusive use of exercise planners, controllers, and evaluators, but players may view other materials deemed necessary for performance. All exercise participants may view the ExPlan, *but the Controller and Evaluator (C/E) Handbook is a restricted document intended for controllers and evaluators only.*

All exercise participants should ensure the proper control of information within their areas of expertise and protect this material in accordance with current directives. Public release of exercise materials to third parties is at the discretion of the exercise planning team.

PURPOSE

The purpose of the exercise is to test or validate the effectiveness of Sunrise's Emergency Response Organization in accordance with the site's emergency plan, the Standardized Emergency Management System (SEMS), and National Incident Management System (NIMS).

SCOPE

Sunrise is conducting an exercise at its main site in Los Angeles, California, on Tuesday, August 2, 2014. This will be a full-scale exercise and will demonstrate the ability of the Emergency Response Organization to gather and disseminate information and coordinate the response to an incident requiring both on-site and off-site resources.

The scope of this full-scale exercise is the evaluation of the Emergency Response Organization in their performance of roles and responsibilities during a response to an incident involving a security event.

FOCUS AREAS—PROGRAM ELEMENTS

1. Communications and Notifications
2. Emergency Facilities and Equipment
3. Emergency Medical Support

4. Emergency Public Information
5. Emergency Response Organization
6. Interoperable Communications
7. Off-site Response Interfaces

PARTICIPANTS

The following organizations will participate in the exercise. Their level of participation is indicated in the table below, which is organized in alphabetical order.

Participant	Location	Level of Participation
Los Angeles County Office of Homeland Security and Emergency Services/Emergency Operations Center (LACO OHSES/EOC)	Off-site	Simulated
Local Medical Center (LMC)	Off-site	Full
Los Angeles Emergency Medical Services (EMS)	Off-site	Simulated
Los Angeles Office of Emergency Services/Emergency operations Center (LA OES/EOC)	Off-site	Limited—Notification of activation and termination of event.
California Governor's Office of Emergency Services (CAL-OES)	Off-site	Limited—Notification only of activation and termination of event.
Los Angeles County Fire Department (LACFD)	On-site	Full
Federal Bureau of Investigation (FBI)	Off-site	Full
Sunrise Emergency Response Team (Sunrise ERT)	On-site	Simulated
Sunrise Operations Center (Sunrise EOC)	On-site	Full
Sunrise Emergency Response Organization	On-site	Full
Sunrise Environmental Health and Safety (Sunrise EHS)	On-site	Full
Local Fire Department (Sunrise SFD)	Off-site/On-Site	Full
Sunrise Health Services (Sunrise HS)	On-site	Full
Sunrise Public Relations (Sunrise media)	On-site	Full
Sunrise Security/Police Department (SPD)	Off-site/On-Site	Full

CONDUCT FOR PLAYERS

- Players will follow all safety and security procedures, practices, rules, and laws, which apply to Sunrise.
- Players will immediately notify a controller of safety concerns.
- Players will begin and end all transmittable communications with the announcement, "This is an Exercise."
- Players may ask a controller to clarify a certain operation or role if it is unclear.
- Players will not simulate any actions that have not been identified or approved by a controller.
- Players will speak when they take an action. This procedure will ensure that evaluators are aware of critical actions as they occur.

- Players will avoid conversations with observers or evaluators.
- Players will play out the scenario as if it were real and minimize simulation.
- Players will abide by the player directory for all of their communication activity.

SAFETY AND SECURITY

Safety takes precedence over all exercise requirements and activities.
- Any Sunrise employee who deems the situation unsafe will implement their "stop work" authority.
- To prevent injuries or security infractions, real situations (outside of the exercise) demanding immediate attention may be mitigated by players, controllers, evaluators, or observers. Notify controller of any actions taken.
  NOTE:
  - In the event that the exercise is temporarily suspended ("paused"), controllers at all play locations will ensure that all exercise activities including exercise-related conversations are stopped. The lead controller will coordinate with the controller organization prior to the restart of exercise play.
  - An exercise may be temporarily suspended or terminated by the lead controller if conditions warrant.
  - Security protocols, rules, or regulations shall not be relaxed or suspended for exercise purposes.

SECURITY

Security will not be relaxed during the exercise. No additional security will be required.

SAFETY

General Safety
- Exercise participants are responsible for their personal safety and will monitor their physical condition for signs of overexertion. Participants must be aware of heat stress when exposed to the elements. Any time that a participant feels that his or her safety or the safety of others is in or is about to be in jeopardy, the participant will stop the activity about to occur and report to the lead controller.
- Weather conditions may present an unsafe condition. If weather conditions threaten an individual's safety and/or health, that individual will notify the lead controller.
- In the event of a real emergency or injury during the exercise, the exercise activity will be stopped and the emergency or injury immediately reported to the lead controller. A determination will be made if play should continue or the exercise terminated. Play will remain halted until the command "Resume Exercise" is given by the exercise director/lead controller.
- All participants must be aware of both vehicular and pedestrian traffic during the exercise.
- In the event of a real emergency, all pedestrian and vehicular traffic will provide egress to first-responder vehicles.

Safety References
- Emergency Response Plan
- Sunrise Worker Safety and Health Program Manual

Identification of Controllers/Evaluators and Observers

- Controllers and/or evaluators will wear black vests labeled "Controller and/or Evaluator."
- Observers will wear a brown vest with "Observer" written on it.

EXERCISE NARRATIVE

It is Tuesday, August 2, 2014, and Sunrise is operating under normal conditions. The exercise will use real-time weather. A researcher arrives at work and finds a box on the hallway floor outside of his office in Building 8. The researcher takes the box inside his office and opens it on his desk. The researcher finds that the product has been improperly packaged and is damaged. Inside the box, the researcher sees a broken bottle and that there is some type of powder on the box's bottom and also parts of a label. The label resembles that used for radioactive materials. While trying to clear away packing material to get a better look at the label, the researcher cuts his right hand on a piece of broken glass.

Emergency Response Actions: The researcher makes a call to Environmental Health and Safety (EH&S) to request spill response. EH&S interviews and surveys the researcher for exposure. EH&S calls 911 because the researcher cut his right hand. EH&S continues to survey the area and prepares the researcher for decontamination and subsequent transport to medical services. Sunrise Security/Police Department (SPD) is dispatched to Building 8. The Emergency Response Organization hears of the incident via two-way radio, and the emergency manager activates the emergency operations center (EOC) to stand by as a precautionary measure. SPD dispatches Los Angeles County Fire Department (LACFD).

LACFD arrives on the scene. EH&S detects contamination on the floor in the hallway where the box was and ensures the affected area(s) and item(s) in Building 8 (B8) are secured, properly posted, and controlled. EH&S thinks about where the box had been and how it was delivered here, leading to the discovery that B28 (mail room) personnel delivered it that morning. LACFD establishes an incident command post outside of the radiological hazard perimeter. LACFD establishes a unified command structure as required.

LACFD obtains preliminary radiological hazard assessment from EH&S. LACFD orders evacuation of B8 as a precautionary measure. SPD conducts traffic control and facilitates area containment. EH&S/ LACFD decontaminate the exposed researcher as required. LACFD establishes and maintains a radiological hazard perimeter. The researcher declines transport to hospital and requests to go to Sunrise's Health Services (Building 2). LACFD is released from the incident and the scene is turned over to EH&S/Sunrise. EH&S transports the researcher to Health Services for evaluation.

The researcher arrives at Health Services. While at Health Services, the researcher's cell phone rings. It is answered by either EH&S or the Health Services staff. The caller says, "This is payback, how does it feel to be a guinea pig?" and hangs up. This is now more than an accidental spill; it is a malicious attack aimed at the researcher. Whoever answers the researcher's cell phone (EH&S or Health Services) calls 911 to report the threat to SPD. The Emergency Response Organization hears about the information over the radio and decides to escalate the incident/malicious attack. The emergency manager becomes the EOC manager, activates the EOC to full operation, and recalls Emergency Management Team (EMT) personnel to the EOC. SPD notifies the FBI of the incident.

The Security Control Center informs the security manager of various calls they have received from Sunrise personnel asking what is going on. The public relations team is activated to support the event. Medical personnel treat the cut on the researcher's hand. EH&S personnel work with medical personnel and continue to provide contamination controls. SPD cordons off B28 areas to prevent any further contamination of staff. EH&S personnel control and survey the vehicle (van) that transported the researcher for contamination. The public information officer (PIO) in the EOC develops information for internal publication (the media center could also develop some of these items, per PIO request). The FBI arrives on scene. The researcher becomes anxious and wants to be sent to local medical center (LMC) for evaluation. Health Services calls 911. SPD dispatches LACFD. LACFD arrives on scene and calls LA EMS for patient transport and LAMC to notify them of incoming patient.

The FBI consults with EH&S; and since EH&S's resources are limited, the FBI requests radiological assistance program (RAP)'s support to help package the product for further lab surveying and provide assistance with off-site researcher/patient transport. RAP arrives and splits into two teams; one team helps package the product on-site and the other assists with the research/patient transport. FBI Hazardous Evidence Response Team arrives. EH&S interviews Building 28 personnel, surveys potentially affected staff, spaces, and vehicle(s). Personnel (3) in B28 begin to worry that they have been exposed and are requesting medical attention. The FBI is processing the crime scene.

Personnel (3) request transport to hospital for evaluation. LACFD is dispatched and arrives at B28 if they are not already on scene. LACFD conducts assessment of personnel. LACFD advises that no hospital transport is needed and sends personnel to the Sunrise Health Services for additional assistance. LACFD briefs SPD on the status of incident, transfers command to SPD, and begins planning for demobilization. The FBI finishes their crime scene processing. The FBI and RAP package product for transport to approved lab. Exercise End.

Termination Conditions: The exercise director terminates the exercise when all exercise objectives have been demonstrated.

SCENARIO/SEQUENCE OF EVENTS

ETA	Bldg.	Activity
08:30	B28	Package delivered via Shipping and Receiving B8.
10:30	B8	**Exercise Start**: Researcher arrives at work and finds a box on the floor, in the hallway, outside his office, in B8.
10:31	B8	Researcher takes the box inside his office. He opens the box on his desk.
10:32	B8	Researcher soon finds that the product has been improperly packaged and is damaged. When he looks inside the box, he sees a broken bottle and some type of powder on the box's bottom and also parts of a label. The label resembles that used for radioactive materials.
10:33	B8	Researcher makes a call to EH&S to provide spill response.
10:40	B8	While trying to clear debris to get a better look at the label, the researcher cuts his right hand on a piece of broken glass.
10:50	B8	EH&S arrives and cordons off the area.
10:55	B8	EH&S begins to interview and survey the researcher for exposure and identify if product has radiation characteristics. While conducting survey, EH&S discovers that researcher has cut his right hand on a piece of broken glass between the time that he initially contacted them and when they arrived on scene. *(Controller Earned Information Inject—~10,000 dpm of an alpha emitter was detected on the researcher's right hand at the cut area, ~8,000 dpm on the left hand).*

ETA	Bldg.	Activity
10:57	B8	EH&S makes 911 call. EH&S continues to survey and prepare the Researcher for decontamination as required, and subsequent transport to Medical. *(Controller Earned Information Inject—~5,000 dpm of alpha radiation is detected on the right pants pocket)*
11:00	B8	SPD is dispatched to B8.
11:00	B48	SPD hears of incident via SCRBS (radio) and the emergency manager activates the EOC to standby mode as a precautionary measure. *(Controller Contingency Inject—Advise emergency manager of SPD SCRBS radio call, in regard to a researcher in B8 exposed to radiation, having a cut on their right hand requiring attention)*
11:00	B8	SPD dispatches LACFD. LACFD arrives on scene.
11:00	B8	EH&S detects contamination on floor in the hallway where the box was and ensures the affected area(s) and item(s) in B8 are secured, properly posted, and controlled. *(At this time, someone, hopefully, thinks about where the box had been and how it got delivered here. This leads to discovery that B28 personnel delivered it this morning.)* *(Controller Earned Information Inject—~5000 dpm alpha)*
11:01	B8	LACFD establishes an ICP outside of radiological hazard perimeter.
11:04	B8	LACFD establishes a unified command structure as required.
11:05	B8	LACFD obtains preliminary radiological hazard assessment from EH&S.
11:15	B8	LACFD orders evacuation of B8. *(Controller—note request and advise LACFD that this will be simulated and to carry on)*
11:15	B8	SPD conducts traffic control and facilitates area containment. *(Controller—note that this will be simulated by SPD.)*
11:15	B8	EH&S/LACFD decontaminates exposed researcher as required.
11:25	B8	LACFD establishes and maintains radiological hazard perimeter.
11:25	B8	Researcher declines transport to hospital and requests to go to Sunrise's Health Services (Building 2).
11:30	B8	LACFD is released from incident and scene is turned over to EH&S/SUNRISE.
11:30	B8	EH&S transports researcher to Health Services for evaluation.
11:33	B2	Researcher arrives at Health Services.
11:35	B2	Researcher's cell phone rings. EH&S or Health Services staff answers it. The caller says, "This is payback, how does it feel to be a guinea pig?" and hangs up.
11:36	B2	This is now more than an accidental spill; it is a malicious attack aimed at researcher.
11:37	B2	Whoever answers the researcher's cell phone (EH&S or Health Services) calls 911 to report threat to SPD.
11:38	B48	SPD hears about escalated incident/malicious attack over SCRBS (radio), emergency manager becomes the EOC manager, activates the EOC to full operation, and recalls EMT personnel to alternate emergency operations center (AEOC). *(Controller Contingency Inject—Advise emergency manager of SPD SCRBS radio call, reporting that situation involving researcher in B8 with rad contamination has escalated to a malicious attack, after researcher receives a threating call to his personal cell phone).*
11:38	B8	SPD notifies FBI of incident.
11:38	B48	Front gate contacts security manager of various calls that they have received from Sunrise personnel asking what is going on. *(Inject by SIM cell)*
11:38	B65	Media Center is stood up to support event. *(Controller Inject—EOC Manager/PIO requesting Media Center activation to support incident.)*

—Cont'd

ETA	Bldg.	Activity
11:40	B2	Medical personnel treat the cut on the researcher's hand.
11:40	B2	EH&S personnel work with medical personnel and continue to provide contamination controls.
11:50	B28	SPD cordoned off B28 areas to prevent any further contamination of staff. *(Controller—note that this will be simulated by SPD.)*
11:50	B2	EH&S personnel control and survey the vehicle (van) that transported the researcher for contamination. *(Controller Earned Information Inject—No contamination found)*
11:55	B76	PIO in EOC develops SPD information for 1–800 number and Web site for employees. *(Controller: PIO can have Media Center assist with this and the actual posting on Web site or voice mail can read "this is an exercise")*
12:00	B8	FBI arrives on scene.
12:00	B2 LMC	Researcher becomes anxious and wants to be sent to LMC for evaluation. 12:00 LMC Health Services calls 911. SPD dispatches LACFD and LACFD arrives on scene. LACFD calls Berkeley EMS for patient transport and LMC to notify them of incoming patient. *(Controller: Call to Berkeley EMS will be simulated)*
12:05	B8	FBI consults with EH&S; since EH&S's resources are limited, the FBI requests RAP's support to help package the product and provide assistance with off-site researcher/patient transport.
12:25	B8	RAP arrives on scene and splits into two teams, one to help package the product on-site and the other to assist with the off-site research/patient transport.
12:30	B8	The FBI Hazardous Evidence Response Team arrives.
12:40	B28	EH&S begins interviews with B28 personnel, surveys potentially affected staff, spaces and vehicle(s). *(Controller Earned Information Inject—No contamination found)*
13:00	B28	Personnel (3) in B28 begin to worry that they have been exposed and are requesting medical attention. (Actor volunteers walk up to first responders)
13:15	B8	FBI is processing crime scene.
13:25	B28	Personnel (3) request transport to hospital for evaluation.
13:30	B28	LACFD is dispatched and arrives at B28 as they are not already on scene.
13:35	B28	LACFD conducts assessment of personnel. *(Controller Earned Information Inject—No contamination found and other than being worried, nothing physically wrong with personnel)*
13:55	B28	LACFD advises that no hospital transport is needed and sends personnel to Sunrise Health Services for additional assistance.
14:00	B28	LACFD briefs SPD on the status of incident, transfers command to SPD, and begins planning for demobilization.
15:30	B8	FBI finishes crime scene processing.
15:30	B8	FBI and RAP package product for transport to approved lab.
15:30	All areas	Exercise end

EH&S, Environmental Health and Safety; LACFD, Los Angeles County Fire Department; RAP, radiological assistance program; FBI, Federal Bureau of Investigation; EMS, Emergency Medical Services; LMC, Local Medical Center; AEOC, alternate emergency operations center; SPD, Sunrise Security/Police Department.

OBJECTIVES

Local Medical Center	
Obj. Id.	**Objective Statement**
LMC.1	Given emergency operations, the LMC Hospital/Medical Facility, response equipment, communications, and/or materials are operational and readily available for use in accordance with the LMC Hospital/Medical Center emergency plan and procedures.
LMC.2	Given event information, activate LMC Hospital/Medical Facility resources in preparation for receipt of patients in accordance with the LMC Hospital/Medical Facility emergency plan.
LMC.3	Given notification of a contaminated-casualty event, the LMC Hospital/Medical Facility emergency room staff prepare for the arrival of potentially contaminated patients in accordance with the LMC Hospital/Medical Facility emergency plan.
LMC.4	Given notification of a contaminated-casualty event, implements traffic control and security measures in accordance with the LMC Hospital/Medical Facility emergency plan.
LMC.5	Given radiologically contaminated patients, LMC Hospital/Medical Facility staff maintain contamination control measures during and after treatment of individuals in accordance with the LMC Hospital/Medical Facility emergency plan.
LMC.6	Given contaminated patients, conduct medical triage of contaminated patients in accordance with the LMC Hospital/Medical Facility emergency plan.

Federal Bureau of Investigation (FBI)	
Obj. Id.	**Objective Statement**
FBI.1	Given activation of FBI assets, vehicles, communications equipment, weapons systems, and resources are available, operable, and maintained in accordance with plans and/or procedures.
FBI.2	Given activation of FBI assets, deploy the FBI Hazardous Evidence Response Team to process the radiological crime scene in accordance with plans and/or procedures.

Sunrise Emergency Operations Center	
Obj. Id.	**Objective Statement**
Sunrise EOC.1	Given declaration of an operational emergency, facility, equipment, and resources are available, operable, and maintained in accordance with emergency plan.
Sunrise EOC.2	Given an event, recall the EMT and activate the EOC in accordance with emergency plan.
Sunrise EOC.3	Given an event, maintain and process event information reflecting site conditions, personnel safety, hazard conditions, mitigation, significant events, action items, and other event information in accordance with emergency plan.
Sunrise EOC.4	Given an operational EOC, make notifications using EM-Emergency Response Organization-001.
Sunrise EOC.5	Given the potential or actual release of hazardous materials, develop a monitoring plan in accordance with emergency plan.
Sunrise EOC.6	Retrieve essential records necessary to perform emergency response and ensure those essential records are available at the LAEOC.

Sunrise Environmental Health and Safety	
Obj. Id.	**Objective Statement**
Sunrise EHS.1	Given activation of EH&S assets, vehicles, communications equipment, and resources are available, operable, and maintained in accordance with internal procedures.
Sunrise EHS.2	Given activation of the on-site field monitoring teams, respond to the designated location and obtain required equipment in accordance with internal procedures.
Sunrise EHS.3	When sufficient field monitoring team members are present and equipment is operationally checked, declare the on-site field monitoring teams operational in accordance with internal procedures.
Sunrise EHS.4	Given operational on-site field monitoring teams and sampling plan, brief the teams on safety measures then deploy the on-site field monitoring teams in accordance with internal procedures.
Sunrise EHS.5	Given deployed on-site field monitoring teams, conduct measurement operations and report the measurements to EHS in accordance with internal procedures.

Los Angeles County Fire Department (Incident Commander for Event)	
Obj. Id.	**Objective Statement**
LACFD.1	Given a fire department response, the vehicles, firefighting and rescue equipment, communications, and supplies are operational and readily available for use in accordance with LACFD plans and/or procedures.
LACFD.2	Given an emergency, the fire department responds to event scene in accordance with LACFD plans and/or procedures.
LACFD.3	Given the arrival of response assets at the staging area from off-site locations, integrate these assets into the emergency response in accordance with LACFD plans and/or procedures.
LACFD.4	Given identification of the hot, warm, and cold zones, establish decontamination line and conduct decontamination operations in accordance with LACFD plans and/or procedures.
LACFD.5	Given receipt of a request for support, provide fire, rescue, and/or HAZMAT support in accordance with LACFD plans and/or procedures.
LACFD.6	Given an emergency call or alarm, safely respond to the event scene in accordance with LACFD plans and/or procedures.
LACFD.7	Upon arrival at the event scene, establish and maintain communications in accordance with LACFD plans and/or procedures.
LACFD.8	Given an emergency event, implement the incident command system (ICS) in accordance with National Incident Management Systems (NIMS) and/or LACFD plans and/or procedures.
LACFD.9	Upon arrival at the event scene, establish an incident command post (ICP) in accordance with LACFD plans and/or procedures.
LACFD.10	Upon arrival at the event scene, assess the event situation in accordance with LACFD plans and/or procedures.
LACFD.11	Given an established ICS, assess the response element capability, and request assistance in accordance with LACFD plans and/or procedures.
LACFD.12	Upon arrival at the event scene, a safety officer manages responder safety throughout the response in accordance with LACFD plans and/or procedures.
LACFD.13	Upon implementation of the ICS, establish, coordinate, and operate a staging area in accordance with LACFD plans and/or procedures.
LACFD.14	Upon activation, technical safety and health support staff (e.g., Radiological Control Team (RADCON), industrial hygiene, and environmental specialists) will provide support to the incident commander in accordance with LACFD plans and/or procedures.

—Cont'd

Los Angeles County Fire Department (Incident Commander for Event)

Obj. Id.	Objective Statement
LACFD.15	Upon implementation of the ICS, develop and implement an incident action plan in accordance with LACFD plans and/or procedures.
LACFD.16	Given that the incident commander (IC) establishes a unified command structure, members operating under the unified command system operate in accordance with LACFD plans and/or procedures.
LACFD.17	Given an established ICS, transfer command as required in accordance with LACFD plans and/or procedures.
LACFD.18	Given the mitigation of the event, conduct the postevent critique in accordance with LACFD plans and/or procedures.
LACFD.19	Given the mitigation of the event, support reentry and recovery operations in accordance with LACFD plans and/or procedures.

Sunrise Health Services

Obj. Id.	Objective Statement
Sunrise HS.1	Given contaminated patients, Sunrise Health Services staff activate and operate the Sunrise decontamination facility in accordance with the Sunrise Health Services emergency plan.
Sunrise HS.2	Given contaminated patients, Sunrise Health Services staff activate and operate the Sunrise decontamination facility in accordance with the Sunrise Health Services emergency plan.
Sunrise HS.3	Given radiologically contaminated patients, Sunrise Health Services staff maintain contamination control measures during and after treatment of individuals in accordance with the Sunrise Health Services emergency plan.
Sunrise HS.4	Given potential radiologically contaminated victims, Sunrise Health Services staff determine the level of contamination of arriving patients in accordance with the Sunrise Health Services emergency plan.
Sunrise HS.5	Given event information, activate Sunrise Health Services resources in preparation for receipt of patients in accordance with the Sunrise Health Services emergency plan.
Sunrise HS.6	Given event notification, Sunrise Health Services staff record event information and provide notification to LMC management in accordance with the Sunrise Health Services emergency plan.
Sunrise HS.7	Given emergency operations, the Sunrise Health Services, response equipment, communications, and/or materials are operational and readily available for use in accordance with the Sunrise Health Services emergency plan and procedures.

Sunrise Media Center/Public Relations

Obj. Id.	Objective Statement
Sunrise media Center.1	Given activation of the Sunrise Media Center, facility, equipment, and resources are available, operable, and maintained in accordance with Sunrise Public Affairs emergency communications plan.
Sunrise media Center.2	Given activation of the Sunrise Media Center, staff make operational the Sunrise Public Affairs emergency communications plan.
Sunrise media Center.3	Given an operational Sunrise Media Center, conduct rumor control operations in accordance with Sunrise Public Affairs emergency communications plan.
Sunrise media Center.4	Given an operational media center and event termination, transfer operations to the Sunrise Public Affairs organization to provide information in accordance with Sunrise Public Affairs emergency

Sunrise Media Center/Public Relations	
Obj. Id.	**Objective Statement**
	Communications plan.

Sunrise PD	
Obj. Id.	**Objective Statement**
Sunrise PD.1	Given activation of protective force assets, vehicles, communications equipment, weapons systems, and resources are available, operable, and maintained in accordance with SPD plans and/or procedures.
Sunrise PD.2	Given dispatch of protective force assets, the assets safely respond to event scene or assigned positions in accordance with SPD plans and/or procedures.
Sunrise PD.3	Given deployed protective force assets, support the IC in the initial event assessment in accordance with SPD plans and/or procedures.
Sunrise PD.4	Given an established incident command system (ICS, the lead protective force officer or designee provides on-scene direction for the protective force assets in accordance with SPD plans and/or procedures.
Sunrise PD.5	Given deployed protective force assets, cordon the event scene in accordance with SPD plans and/or procedures.
Sunrise PD.6	Given an event, develop and implement a security response plan in accordance with SPD plans and/or procedures.
Sunrise PD.7	Given a security event and arrival of the FBI, transfer command of security forces in accordance with SPD plans and/or procedures.
Sunrise PD.8	Given a security event and transfer of command to the FBI, support the FBI operations in accordance with SPD plans and/or procedures.

GUIDELINES

The following are the Design and Development Guidelines that will be used during this exercise.

1. An ExPlan will be developed at 90, 60, and 30 days for approval.
2. An After Action Report (AAR) will be developed 30 working days after the exercise, which will include the evaluation of Sunrise's emergency response capabilities.
3. A corrective action plan will be developed within 30 days of approval for the AAR.
4. All EMERGENCY RESPONSE ORGANIZATION personnel will activate from their places of duty. Prestaging will not be allowed, with the exception of the LAEOC and off-site responders.
5. Emergency sirens are not authorized on-site or off-site, and all traffic laws will be obeyed. For safety, emergency lights are allowed.
6. All response actions should be in accordance with the agencies' current policies and procedures.
7. All simulations will be considered true.

SIMULATIONS AND DATA REQUIREMENTS

The following are the preapproved simulations and scenario data that will be used during this exercise:

Simulation	Simulation Method
Substance for contamination	Powdered sugar
Package	Package with delivery label
Bottle	Broken bottle
Readings	Provided by EH&S
B8 and B28 area of play	Provided by building manager
Injured employee	Moulage and provided by EH&S
Worried personnel (3) of contamination readings	Provided by LACFD
LAEOC	Will be set up prior to the exercise

CONTROLLER/EVALUATOR DIRECTORY

Assignments/Communications Information				
Location	**Radio Channel**	**Controller**	**Name**	**Contact#**
All areas	EOC Ops	Exercise director		555-555-5555
B9	EOC Ops	Lead controller		555-555-5555
B9	EOC Ops	Controller		555-555-5555
B2	EOC Ops	Controller		555-555-5555
B8	EOC Ops	Controller		555-555-5555
B65	EOC Ops	Controller		555-555-5555
B28	EOC Ops	Controller		555-555-5555
B7	EOC Ops	Controller		555-555-5555
LMC	EOC Ops	Controller		555-555-5555

Assignments/Communications Information				
Location	**Radio Channel**	**Evaluator**	**Name**	**Contact#**
LMC	EOC Ops	LMC		555-555-5555
B8, B28	EOC Ops	LACFD		555-555-5555
B8, B28	EOC Ops	FBI		555-555-5555
B8, B28, LMC	EOC Ops	RAP		555-555-5555
B8, B28	EOC Ops	RPG		555-555-5555
B8, B28, LMC	EOC Ops	RPG		555-555-5555
SPD	EOC Ops	SPD Comm. Center		555-555-5555
SPD, B8 and B28	EOC Ops	SPD field		555-555-5555
B2	EOC Ops	Health services		555-555-5555

SIMULATION CELL DIRECTORY

Simulation Cell (In-Coming)				
Location	**Radio Channel**	**Simulator**	**Name**	**Contact Number**
Bld. 1 room 112	EOC Ops	Sim lead controller		555-555-5555
Bld. 1 room 112	Bld. manager	SCRIC*, misc.		555-555-5555
Bld. 1 room 112	Bld. manager	emergency team, Sunrise employees		555-555-5555
Bld. 1 room 112	None	Misc.		555-555-5555

Southern California Regional Intelligence Center

PLAYER DIRECTORY

Organization Name	Name	Contact Number
LMC	Local medical center	555-555-5555
LACFD	Los Angeles County Fire Department	Actual
LAEOC	LAEOC	Actual
ERT	Emergency response team	Radio: Actual
EOC	EOC	Actual
FBI	FBI	555-555-5555
Health services	Sunrise Health Services	555-555-5555
Sunrise departments	Sunrise departments	555-555-5555
SCRIC	SCRIC	555-555-5555
RAP	RAP	
EH&S	EH&S	Actual
SPD	Sunrise security/Police	Actual

APPENDIX B—PARTICIPANT OBSERVATIONS FORM

PARTICIPANT OBSERVATIONS:
This information is used by Emergency Management to evaluate and improve the Emergency Management Program. Please print neatly, and feel free to also provide positive comments. Return this at the completion of the critique.

Name: (Optional)	
Role:	☐ Observer ☐ Player ☐ Controller/Evaluator ☐ Other _____
Date Exercise Conducted:	
Area Exercise Conducted:	
Area(s) Observed:	

Observations and Comments:

Did you attend the training offered?	☐Position Specific ☐Evaluator/Controller ☐ Other _____
Did the training increase your ability to perform your responsibilities for the exercise?	☐Yes ☐No ☐N/A

Observations and Comments:

What other training would you like to see offered?

APPENDIX C—GLOSSARY

LMC	Local Medical Center
AEOC	Alternate Emergency Operations Center
BET	Building Emergency Team
SFD	Sunrise Fire Department
BM	Building Manager
CP	Command Post
SCRBS	Southern California Regional Communications System
EMS	Emergency Medical Services
EMT	Emergency Management Team
EOC	Emergency Operations Center
EXD	Exercise Director
IC	Incident Commander
ICP	Incident Command Post
ICS	Incident Command System
JIC	Joint Information Center
SCRIC	Southern California Regional Intelligence Center
PIO	Public Information Officer
SPD	Protective Services
RAP	Radiological Assistance Program
EH&S	Environmental Health and Safety
SIM Cell	Simulation/Controller Cell
UC	Unified Command
SPD	Sunrise Security/Police Department

APPENDIX D—MAPS OF EXERCISE BUILDINGS AND AREAS

Not Pictured.

Index

Note: Page numbers followed by "f" and "t" indicate figures and tables respectively